PEOPLE OF THE RAINFOREST

JOHN HEMMING

People of the Rainforest

*The Villas Boas Brothers, Explorers
and Humanitarians of the Amazon*

HURST & COMPANY, LONDON

First published in the United Kingdom in 2019 by
C. Hurst & Co. (Publishers) Ltd.,
41 Great Russell Street, London, WC1B 3PL
© John Hemming, 2019
All rights reserved.
Printed in Great Britain by Bell and Bain Ltd, Glasgow

Distributed in the United States, Canada and Latin America by
Oxford University Press, 198 Madison Avenue, New York, NY 10016,
United States of America.

The right of John Hemming to be identified as the author of
this publication is asserted by him in accordance with the
Copyright, Designs and Patents Act, 1988.

A Cataloguing-in-Publication data record for this book
is available from the British Library.

ISBN: 9781787381957

This book is printed using paper from registered sustainable
and managed sources.

www.hurstpublishers.com

Picture credits

Brigadier Raymundo Aboim, 9.

Rubens Belfort, Arquivo USMA/UNIFESP, 61, 63, 64, 66.

Adrian Cowell Archive, Universidade Pontifícia de Goiás, Goiânia (via Vicente Rios), 11 (Pilly Cowell), 50, 58.

John Hemming, 8, 10, 12, 16, 17, 18, 19, 20, 21, 22, 23, 24, 25, 27, 28, 29, 30, 31, 32, 33, 34, 35, 36, 37, 38, 39, 4, 42, 43, 44, 45, 48, 49, 51, 56, 57, 65, 67, 68.

Orlando Villas Bôas Family Archive, 2, 3, 4, 5, 6, 7, 15, 61, 1 (Jean Manzon); 59 and 62 (Agência Estado); 60 (Pedro Martinelli); 52, 53, 54, 55 (King Leopold III of Belgium).

Mark Plotkin, Amazon Conservation Team, 40.

Noel Villas Bôas, 26.

Murillo Villela, 13, 14, 46.

Map artwork by Sebastian Ballard.

CONTENTS

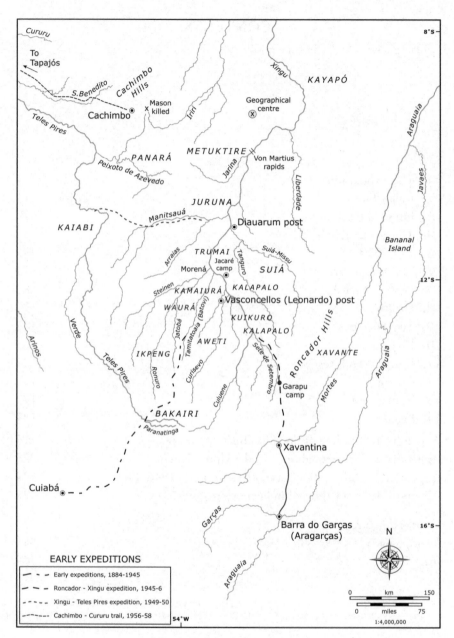

Map 1: Early expedition routes

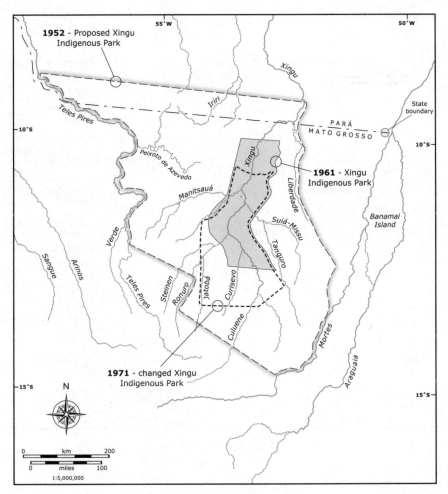

Map 2: Changes to the Xingu Park

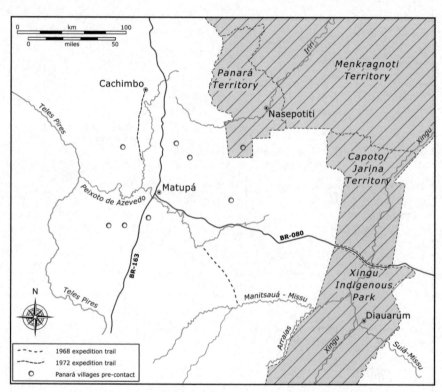

Map 3: Panará contacts

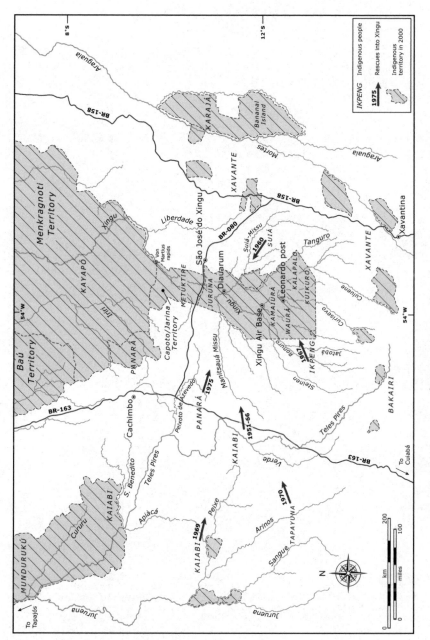

Map 4: Migrations into the Xingu, 1951–75. Indigenous territories in 2000

1

THE EXPEDITION

Late in 1943, in the hot and dusty wilds of central Brazil, a line of leathery bearded woodsmen shuffles forward to enlist on an expedition. Each illiterate man gives his name and puts a cross on the register. A young man, slightly smarter-looking than the others, is offered a pen so that he can sign his name; but he ignores this and enters a cross like the others. He was called Claudio Villas Boas, from the distant city of São Paulo. He and his brothers desperately wanted to join the expedition, but they knew that it was hiring only tough, illiterate backwoodsmen rather than educated city boys. The pen was a trap, to see whether he would make the mistake of writing his name. Had he done so, he would have been rejected—and the story in this book would never have happened.

Brazil occupies half the continent of South America. Its Atlantic seaboard and southern plains have been settled by Europeans for four centuries. But the northern half of this nation is covered by the world's greatest expanse of tropical rainforests, watered by its largest river system, the Amazon. For four centuries Portuguese colonists had explored and plied the immeasurably vast network of Amazonian rivers. They caused fearful destruction of riverbank indigenous peoples from imported diseases, which also wiped out those brought downriver into slavery. But they never seriously penetrated the forests between those waterways. In a sense Brazil was where the United States had been a century earlier, with an equally vast interior of unexplored and dangerous Indian* country.

* Until recently, indigenous peoples of the Americas were always called Indians. This misnomer started because Columbus followed Ptolemy in thinking that the globe of planet Earth was far smaller than it is. So Columbus was unaware of the Pacific Ocean, and was convinced that he had reached Marco Polo's India and

So in 1943 the dynamic but near-dictatorial president of Brazil, Getúlio Vargas, proclaimed a 'March to the West' to penetrate the forested heart of his nation. This was the first such national venture, launched with propaganda fanfare claiming that it would open the wilderness to settlement with farms and towns. The spearhead of this would be called the Roncador–Xingu Expedition, an exploration to cut a trail north-west from a river that marked the edge of 'civilized' settlement, across hostile Indian country, around the low and unknown Roncador hills, and beyond them to the headwaters of the Xingu river. The Xingu (pronounced 'shing-goo') is one of five great rivers that flow north towards the main Amazon, which itself flows from the Andes eastwards across South America to the Atlantic Ocean. Each of these tributaries ranks as one of the world's great rivers: the Xingu is 1,640 kilometres (1,020 miles), which is far longer than the Rhine. Later that year President Vargas created the Central Brazil Foundation (FBC), a federal bureau to supervise the expedition and any settlements it might create. The president appointed the commander of his personal guard, Colonel Flaviano Vanique, to lead the Roncador–Xingu Expedition, answering to the minister of war-time economic mobilization, João-Alberto Lins de Barros. (Brazil had joined the war on the Allied side, and sent a force to fight in Italy.)

This expedition was the venture that the young man who pretended to be illiterate wanted to join. The three older Villas Boas brothers, Orlando, Claudio and Leonardo, were aged between twenty-five and twenty-nine in

---

China when he 'discovered' the Americas after 1492. Nowadays, the correct word for these natives is 'indigenous people'; and their nations, groups, and villages should be called 'peoples'. But I may often use the old terms 'Indians' and 'tribes', for three reasons: because those were the words current in the mid-twentieth century when the Villas Boas were active; because they are less cumbersome; and particularly because they were and are still used, with pride, by many indigenous peoples themselves. Another problem is a generic name for non-Indians. Modern Brazilians are descended from Portuguese colonists, their African slaves, inter-marriage of both races with indigenous peoples, and recent immigration by other Europeans and Asians. In the mid-twentieth century these neo-Brazilians were always called '*civilizados*'; but this term is now unacceptable because in many ways Indians are more civilized than tough frontiersmen. One anthropologist coined the word 'whiteman' but many say simply 'whites'. I will also use this word on occasion, although it has nothing to do with actual skin colour. Indians themselves have beautiful pale-tan skins, whereas other Brazilians range from pink and grey through many shades of dark to pure black.

1943. They loved poring over maps and reading books by or about the great Brazilian explorers. So they were excited when they saw the pioneering expedition announced in newspapers on 4 June 1943. Here was the romance of pure exploration, a patriotic pioneering drive into the unknown interior of their country. The three brothers decided to leave uninspiring jobs in São Paulo and enlist in the challenging new venture.

The Villas Boas had grown up in prosperous coffee plantations in the interior of São Paulo state, in south-eastern Brazil—a world away from the Amazon. Their father Agnello was a pillar of the rural community and a senior Masonic officer. But his farming business went badly, as did his health. So in 1924, when Orlando was ten, Claudio eight, and Leonardo six, the family—including their younger brother and three sisters—moved to São Paulo city. All were sent to excellent schools, and they lived in a large house. But in 1940 Agnello Villas Boas was struck with hemiplegia paralysis: he died in the following year, aged only fifty-five; and five months later his wife Arlinda also died unexpectedly. The seven orphaned children sold the house and furniture and moved into a pension. The older sons got jobs: Orlando with Standard Oil (later Esso), Claudio with the municipal telephone company, and Leonardo with an electrical goods importer called Franchini. But all three decided to quit these desk jobs in order to become real explorers—for minimal pay and in rugged conditions. There was just enough money, and other relatives, to look after the four younger siblings, so that these did not feel abandoned: the family remained close throughout their lives.

There was a burst of patriotic fervour about the president's March to the West. Individuals and companies in São Paulo donated supplies for the Roncador–Xingu Expedition. The Air Force contributed a plane and some dynamic officers; a women's institute embroidered a banner; and Colonel Vanique invited two doctors and some military comrades to join its administration. But, surprisingly, the Villas Boas brothers were the only educated young Brazilians to want to join it. The Colonel and Minister Lins de Barros were established in a hotel in São Paulo, to raise funds, publicize the venture, and start to plan it. But when the three brothers tried to enlist they were turned down—for the curious reason that they were literate. Colonel Vanique was from the open grasslands of Brazil's deep south and had never experienced tropical rainforests, and he was terrified of them. So he had decided to engage only illiterate woodsmen, declaring: 'You cannot imagine the region we are going to penetrate. It is the centre of the country, full of wild Indians, jaguars and so forth.' It would be too much for dainty city boys.

3

The great expedition's stores lumbered inland in three large wagons (one of which caught fire) for months of travel on dirt roads and tracks towards a base on the upper Araguaia river. (The Araguaia is another mighty southern tributary of the Amazon, east of the Xingu.) Nothing daunted by their rejection in São Paulo, the Villas Boas brothers took another remarkably bold decision. Having resigned from their jobs, they had to make a 1,500-kilometre (950-mile) journey inland to the Araguaia by train, bumpy trucks, and carts—all in the slim hope that they could enlist there by pretending to be tough illiterates. Claudio and Leonardo were the first to go; Orlando could not immediately join them because wartime restrictions meant that it took him longer to resign from the American company Standard Oil. At the expedition's first camp, on 1 January 1944, Claudio and Leonardo managed to join the FBC as humble 'expeditionaries' on a monthly contract.

In March–April the ponderous expedition moved on, over even rougher tracks, 300 kilometres (190 miles) north to its final camp on the south bank of the Rio das Mortes ('River of the Dead'), a large western tributary of the Araguaia. The river's dramatic name was because of the many men killed by Xavante (pronounced 'shav-ante') indigenous warriors who dominated the plains to its north. The Mortes river was the boundary between the thinly settled backlands of central Brazil and hostile Indian country.

Luckily, Claudio and Leonardo met Dr Horace Laing, an English engineer and friend of their parents, who was helping with the expedition's logistics. Ling asked what they were doing there; they explained that they wanted to join the expedition but had been turned down; and a few days later the engineer had found places for them. So in May they transferred from the FBC to the Roncador–Xingu Expedition, with Claudio as a supervisor of personnel and Leonardo working in the office with Dr Ling. They sent a telegram to Orlando with the good news. He used his final pay packet to buy what he imagined was forest explorer's kit—a revolver on a holster belt, machetes, pith helmet, and jungle boots—all of which later proved useless. He was as innocent and ignorant of tropical forests as Colonel Vanique; but far younger, bolder, and less opinionated.

There followed another year of preparations, slowly gathering stores for every contingency. One difficulty was finding donkeys, mules, and oxen: there were few in that remote part of central Brazil, and farmers were reluctant to sell them. Recruiting scores of tough woodsmen was easier—for many it was their first salaried job. Colonel Vanique's colleagues from the Presidential Guard were as alarmed by the jungle as he was. They swaggered about the camps for a while with their guns and broad hats; but all then returned to the comfort of military service in coastal cities. The backwoodsmen were different. These were proud eccentrics, often recruited from wildcat mining camps or on the run from murder raps, but at home in what Vanique always referred to as 'the unknown'.

When Minister Lins de Barros visited the camp it was his custom to take an early-morning walk. He had noticed that the three Villas Boas brothers were different to the colourful mining prospectors, cowboys, and woodsmen. So he called them over one morning, said that he could see that they were Paulistas (from São Paulo) who liked adventure, and that he had important work for them. They were to lead the expedition's vanguard all the way to the Xingu. Colonel Vanique protested; but the minister placated him by saying that he would remain in charge of the base, a more important task—which it was not.

President Vargas himself came to the camp on the Rio das Mortes for the expedition's send-off in May 1945. There were flowery speeches about the magnitude and patriotism of the endeavour. Seventy donkeys were lined up with their loaded harness frames. But when the celebration climaxed in a firework display, the animals panicked, broke the ropes that secured them, and bolted into the surrounding bush, where many shed their packs, and supplies disappeared. Other equipment and food was lost when an overloaded barge sank. But on 12 June 1945 the Roncador–Xingu Expedition finally crossed the Mortes river into dangerous Xavante country, and the Villas Boas brothers started their careers as explorers. A photograph at that time showed them lean and rugged, of medium height, with black beards, and with Claudio already wearing what became his trademark dark glasses.

The plains beyond the Rio das Mortes are what Brazilians call *campo*— savannah of sparse grass or bushland. This is a unique ecosystem. Its gnarled trees have shiny leaves that can withstand months of heat and drought, and it looks superficially like a long-abandoned orchard. The plain is studded by hard termite mounds of red earth. The few watercourses have swathes of forest along their banks. At times the dry, thorny vegetation is denser and pricklier: this is *cerrado* (closed) *campo*. But there were rarely enough trees to sling hammocks (beloved of everyone in the Brazilian interior), so that men had to sleep on the ground. Animals were sparse—just anteaters, occasional small deer, armadillos, bats, and rodents—but bird life was abundant. Insects were tiresome: biting blackflies, hornets, stingless sweat-bees that lap up body liquids in men's eyes, grasshoppers, termites, and masses of ants everywhere. Ticks deposited a 'powder' cluster of their young on a leaf; anyone brushing against this suddenly found his entire body itching with hundreds of minute biting ticks, which took days to locate and remove.

Claudio and Leonardo were in a trail-cutting troop of eighteen men; Orlando was in charge of pack animals to bring up staples of rice, black beans, manioc, and salt. Crossing this plain was hard work, searingly hot during the day and cold at night. On more open *campo* country they could advance about 5 kilometres (3 miles) a day. The men were often thirsty during the hours of cutting, because it could be too cumbersome to carry water during the continuous hacking, so they hoped to encounter a stream. But food was a greater problem. At times they suffered hunger. The brothers became convinced that the vindictive Colonel Vanique was keeping them near-starving by sending trivial quantities of food, either in air drops—a low-flying plane just throwing down sacks—or telling Orlando that there was not enough for his supply convoys.

For all these privations, I know from experience that cutting trails (known as *picadas* in Brazil) can be surprisingly satisfying. It is just man against nature, with no human complications; and the steady progress of the path is a tangible measure of achievement. The technique has never changed. It is simply hacking with a machete, since a chainsaw would be too heavy—and unnecessary because trees in *campo* are easily bypassed. Explorers try to keep their trail straight, on a fixed bearing: for the Roncador–Xingu Expedition this was north–north-west. The lead man throws his machete aside (to prevent its deflecting his compass), takes a bearing on a bush or tree, and hacks and pushes towards it, while other men widen the *picada* behind. For this expedition, the trail had to be wide enough for pack mules. Hacking for hour after hour in the searing heat, muscles ache and the blade gets blunter, so that lianas or saplings that were sliced with a ping in the morning need several swipes as the day wears on. It is important to pause occasionally to sharpen machetes with files.

The characters of the three Villas Boas brothers emerged during these months. Orlando was the extrovert, a natural leader, with an outgoing sense of humour. Claudio was quietly steadfast, cerebral, and doggedly patient— the sort of man to pick for any expedition. Leonardo was slightly more dashing. All three were mentally tough and physically fit, but in no sense gung-ho 'explorers' even though they were pushing deep into untrodden and potentially dangerous country. This was their first experience of an expedition.

They got on well with their workmen, a colourful group of frontiersmen, with a wealth of homespun anecdotes and superstitions and, as Orlando recalled, 'proud of their manly bearing. In their ballads, to guitar music around the camp fire, they expressed their inner feelings, sometimes as rampant conquistadores, sometimes humiliated by some adventure that went wrong. They inherited from their distant indigenous ancestry their pride and also the stubborn endurance that helped them overcome hardships that surround them.' They looked like bearded, weather-beaten extras from a Western movie, often with scars or lopsided dentistry.

These men's view of Indians was a serious problem. They feared native peoples, and their instinct was to shoot first. The brothers had difficulty persuading them that this was both wrong and dangerous. This frontier attitude was not helped by Colonel Vanique wanting to send a squad of soldiers, each armed with a gun and fifty rounds of ammunition, to protect the cutting party. It took intervention by Brazil's Indian Protection Service to stop this guard being sent.

The expeditioners knew that they were being watched, but saw no one. Then, on 28 July, over six weeks after crossing the Rio das Mortes, there was suddenly shouting from the woods to the right of the path. The men shouted back, and they were understandably fearful. Luckily, there was a metre-high termite mound beside the *picada*, and Claudio scrambled onto this. Standing on the top, he could see that the shouting was a decoy: a larger contingent of perhaps forty Xavante were running silently from the opposite direction. He shouted to his men to fire their guns, but *into the air* as they had been told they must always do. 'It was like water on fire. The shouting ceased as if by magic, and those approaching in the surprise attack turned tail.' From them on, the Indians merely kept the expedition under observation, sometimes rummaging through its baggage at night, or firing warning arrows. The explorers frequently saw smoke from distant fires, for this people used burning grassland to round up animals for them to kill. But the Xavante were content for the intruders to move through a corner of their nation's rolling territory without conflict, and they knew the power of guns. So there was no face-to-face contact.

* * *

The Roncador–Xingu Expedition's initial objective was to open the centre of Brazil for eventual settlement, and—in areas that could not be reached by river—the best way to start this was by air. So in August and September 1945, after cutting some 80 kilometres (50 miles) of trail, the Villas Boas and their men built their first airstrip. This was done without machinery, but it was fairly straightforward in that flat and open savannah. The men cleared vegetation with their saws and machetes, and levelled the ground with hoes and shovels. The worst obstacles were concrete-hard termite hills. Their reward was an improved supply of food—when Colonel Vanique chose to release some and a plane to carry it.

Nearby they came across an abandoned Xavante hunting camp of rough shelters. These surprisingly still contained many bows, arrows, and other artefacts, possibly because their owners had left in a hurry. The explorers removed nothing, but left a few presents. They then resumed their trail blazing because their mission was to press on towards distant Amazon forests, not to make contact with the feared Xavante.

The Villas Boas brothers were named in a Brazilian newspaper, the *Correio da Manhã* (Morning Post) in Rio de Janeiro, for the first time on 7 September 1945. Later that year, a school friend got Orlando invited to send occasional reports about the expedition to the São Paulo evening paper *A Gazeta*. This was the start of a lifelong romance between the glamorous explorers and the media.

The expedition's trail crossed the south-western edge of the Roncador ('Snoring') hills, which form a low watershed between two great southern tributaries of the Amazon: the Araguaia and the Xingu. This was far tougher terrain—rocks, defiles, and dense thorny vegetation. The exhausted and famished men spent weeks hacking through these tangles, clambering up and down crumbling hills. Beyond, it became easier again because they were entering the basin of the upper Xingu river. The flat plateau was now covered in low dry woods, amid wide lagoons and swamplands, and the rivers were flanked by belts of tropical forest.

The headwaters of the Xingu form a gigantic inverted delta, with a dozen rivers converging after hundreds of kilometres to form the main Xingu. In December 1945 the men finally reached one of these headwaters. They thought that this might be the Tanguro, the easternmost of the fan of rivers, so gave this name to another camp and rudimentary airstrip. A troop of pack animals finally reached the weary and hungry men, and a plane also dropped some sacks of food. But by the middle of the month they were starving again, and were saved only by shooting four peccary—pig-related foragers that roam through the forest in bands. It was now well into the rainy season, with relentless downpours hammering their palm-frond shelters. Some men became seriously ill, vomiting blood, prostrated by malaria or dysentery, and so weak that they had to be carried from their hammocks to defecate in the woods. One man went mad: Claudio had difficulty in stopping the others from simply shooting him, and the patient had to be carried back along the long trail. Finally, on 1 January 1946, after seven months opening 250 kilometres (150 miles) of trail, the expedition moved from savannah and *cerrado* into tropical rainforests. One final burst of cutting took the team far down alongside the headwater of what later proved to be the Sete de Setembro river, named after Brazil's national day. It was hardly surprising that they confused these rivers, for this region was unexplored, scarcely mapped, and devoid of aerial photography.

They now paused to build a big camp called Garapú, the name for a shy deer they managed to shoot; 1,600 *buriti*-palm fronds were gathered to roof the camp's huts. February and March 1946 were spent opening its airstrip, some 600 metres long and 25 wide (660 by 30 yards). This was punishing work, by men armed only with six sickles and five axes. They were now at the edge of the Amazonian rainforests, so there were tall trees, lianas, and denser undergrowth than in the open *campo cerrado* bush; and this was the annual rainy season, with depressing downpours, black clouds, and constant lightning. Worse, planes had great difficulty skidding down this short runway in torrential rain. So when the weather cleared for the dry season, April, May and June were spent improving the airstrip, eventually to 1,000 metres long by 45 wide.

The expedition also spent these months accumulating supplies for the push down the headwater towards the main Xingu. Quantities of food, medical supplies, radios, outboard motors, petrol, and other equipment were transported by air and by pack trains along the trail. The planes also brought brief visits by important people, including the Minister Lins de Barros, the secretary-general of the FBC, their leader Lieutenant Colonel Vanique, the great botanist/garden designer Burle Marx, the French academician André Siegfried, and journalists and film-makers eager to cover the great pioneering venture. Dr Helmut Sick, a German ornithologist who had luckily been in Brazil when the war started, had persuaded the authorities to let him be the expedition's only permanent scientist. In a book published a decade later, he wrote lyrically about the beauty of the forest around Garapú camp, with nights spent silently observing its teeming wildlife.

The Villas Boas asked for expert boat builders, and these were flown in from the Araguaia. They started work at the end of May, at the river 4 kilometres from the camp and airstrip—so they had to be guarded against Indian attack. There they cut trees and made planks to build two large boats, each of 2,000 kilograms (4,400 pounds) capacity. The first was launched on 23 June 1946 (named *Carmen Miranda* because it was frisky in the water) and the second in mid-August. They also made an indigenous bark canoe. Finally, at the end of September the two boats and canoe set off down the unexplored Sete de Setembro. The beautiful river meandered gently between walls of luxuriant forest, totally devoid of people but full of wildlife. The water was low at the end of the dry season, so they occasionally had to jump out to push; but otherwise their small outboards and paddles carried them swiftly downstream. It took only five days to descend over 100 kilometres (60 miles).

On 4 October 1946 the trees suddenly opened to deep blue sky. They had debouched onto the larger and turbulent Culuene river, which had been explored twice during the previous decades, as we shall see. With an aerial in a tree, Orlando Villas Boas radioed the good news, and was congratulated on 'the complete success of our mission', the great national Roncador–Xingu Expedition that they had led. In sixteen months they had cut hundreds of kilometres of trail over totally unexplored country, to advance from the Mortes river past the Roncador hills to the Xingu river. They had opened three camps and airstrips, and crossed the lands of the warlike Xavante without any conflict. The brothers had proved that literate city boys could be tough woodsmen. Years later, Orlando wrote to this author: 'We started as lads, and ended as grownups.'

2

KALAPALO

In October 1946, a couple of days after the Villas Boas' boats emerged onto the Culuene river, they met their first indigenous people. (They had been aware of the Xavante during the previous fifteen months, but had never actually seen any.) They heard a shout from the bank, saw a canoe among the trees, and paddled over to investigate. A few people disappeared into the forest, leaving only a lad—quite agitated, but talking a lot and often saying 'Kalapalo'. Orlando would have known, from reports by earlier expeditions, that the Kalapalo were one of the dozen tribes living among the Xingu's fan of headwater rivers, and that they were friendly. So he approached the young man, put a hand on his shoulder, repeated 'Kalapalo' and also said *caraiba*, which he knew was the local word for non-indigenous white men. The young Indian was now at ease and accompanied them to visit their riverbank campsite with a few companions, including his beautiful young wife.

At their next halt, some kilometres down the river, more Kalapalo came to visit them. At first they arrived five or ten at a time, and then there was a large throng of men, women, and children—a thrilling sight. This crowd was headed by a powerfully built middle-aged man: their chief, Izarari. 'Intelligent and energetic, he beckoned us to approach with a sweeping gesture. We went, and became friends.' Orlando and Izarari established an immediate rapport, with the explorer admiring the chief's 'personality, authority and goodwill' as well as the gentle dignity, magnificent physiques, and naked beauty of the Indians. These were the first Indians with whom the Villas Boas or any of their expeditionary companions had mingled. Indeed, very few of Brazil's roughly 35 million people at that time had seen any of its indigenous people in this pristine state.

Their new friend Chief Izarari invited the brothers to his village, which was close to the Culuene river, opposite the mouth of the smaller Sete de

11

Setembro that the expedition had descended. All upper Xingu villages are identical. Each has five or six huge communal huts, known as *malocas*, circling a clean central plaza. These great huts are oblong, curved at each end, and looking like the upturned hulls of wooden sailing ships, without keels. Their gleaming thatch of smooth *sapé* (satintail grass) curves down to the ground on all sides. These were the finest buildings in the backlands of central Brazil.

A hut is home to about a dozen families—forty or fifty people. For the expeditioners, sleeping in one of these *malocas* was a magical experience. The interior is lit only by two small doors in the middle of each long wall. Each hut is the size of an early Christian church. It takes a moment to discern the lines of tall trees supporting the roof beams far above, to create a central nave space and a chapel-like bay for each family—with a cooking fire, and hammocks slung between a pier and the outer wall. The ecclesiastical impression is heightened by serene quiet. No one raises their voice, not even children, and there is no sound from bare feet on the sandy floor, nor from any metal or instrument. The interior is weatherproof even in torrential rain, insulated by layer after layer of thatch. It is agreeably cool during midday sun, and warmer than the surroundings at night.

The Kalapalo themselves were as handsome and dignified as their surroundings. Both sexes were totally naked, but without being in any way erotic—although, as we shall see, they have a robust attitude to sex. There is no body or facial hair—the few strands that grow are plucked. But head hair is luxuriantly shining black, in round crowns for the men but hanging far down the backs of the women, and always neatly combed. All but the aged have perfect natural figures, with the men powerfully muscular from their favourite sport of wrestling.

The Villas Boas were lucky to see some ceremonial during their brief visit. For this, both sexes adorn themselves in a blaze of feather headdresses and body paint in geometric patterns. The Kalapalo were staging a welcome for two visiting tribes: the Kuikuro people under Chief Afukaká, who came from their village some 15 kilometres (9 miles) down the Culuene opposite its Tanguro tributary, and the less numerous Nahukwá of Chief Kamalive. The beauty, harmony, and social order of these Indians were a life-changing revelation to the expeditioners. Back in São Paulo they had read and been inspired by the lectures of the famous explorer and champion of the Indians, General Cândido Rondon, now in his eighties. But Rondon had been mostly with indigenous peoples of south-western Brazil. There was no popular writing in Portuguese at that time about the tribes of the upper Xingu.

Both the peoples who visited the Kalapalo spoke the same Carib language as their hosts. The dozen tribes of the upper Xingu are identical in everything but language: they speak either Carib or Aruak (both tongues found throughout Caribbean islands and northern South America) or Tupi (a language used from the plains of Paraguay, all along the Atlantic Ocean littoral, and far up the Amazon and its tributaries). Further down the Xingu and on the plateau of central Brazil, peoples (including the Xavante) speak Je.

The original mission of the Central Brazil Foundation in 1943 had been *Desbravamento, exploração, aproveitamento*: 'Taming the wilderness, exploration, utilization'. But the difficulties of the expedition's first two years showed that President Vargas's vision of settlers pouring into this remote region was unrealistic. It became apparent that this heart of Brazil could be opened more easily by aircraft than by laborious trail-cutting and trains of pack animals (which found no grazing once they entered tropical forests). So the foundation's objective changed, from trying to create settlements to opening a chain of airstrips. These would serve three purposes: as emergency landing places for propeller-driven aircraft flying between São Paulo or Rio de Janeiro and Miami; as weather and telegraph stations; and to give the government a presence away from the rivers in the forested half of their country.

The Villas Boas therefore saw it as their duty to clear another airstrip, which they did in a patch of *campo cerrado* near the Culuene river. The months they had spent enlarging the Garapú runway showed how laborious this was in more forested terrain. Great trees had to be felled, and their tangle of roots also had to be removed. It was hard work, with only hand tools, in intense heat, and plagued by mosquitoes at night and blackfly by day. Luckily for them, Chief Izarari decided to help. The indigenous people do not work for pay or reward, they do not obey orders, and they never directly serve another person. But they value generosity, and if they feel like doing some communal work they apply themselves cheerfully and vigorously. So the Kalapalo pitched in—for a while, until they saw some charcoal from a burned tree and went to paint their bodies with this. The small new airstrip was ready by the end of October.

After the Villas Boas's visit to the Kalapalo village, a crowd of Indians and expeditioners walked back to the new Culuene airstrip. On 10 November 1946 they were thrilled to watch the first plane land on it. Word spreads rapidly in the upper Xingu. So the visitors' camp soon also hosted some Aruak-speaking Mehinaku and another Carib group, both with their chiefs. Then, on 17 November, a larger Northwind plane arrived from São Paulo, and its air force pilot decided to offer a short flight to the five chiefs. To everyone's surprise they accepted with alacrity. 'They were all highly contented by the flight. There was no sign of unease or fright. They boarded and alighted from the plane with equal tranquillity.' When the pilot swooped low, one chief even tapped his shoulder and signalled that he should fly higher. It was as though they were seasoned travellers, not hunter-gatherers entering a metal machine, hearing the roar of motors, and then rising into the sky for the first time in their lives.

One plane also brought the Indian Protection Service's (SPI's) official photographer, Nilo Veloso, who was able to film these colourful scenes for showing in cinemas. Meanwhile, the expedition's ordeals and successes were now regularly reported by Brazil's most influential radio programme, 'Esso Reporter'. So the young brothers from São Paulo were becoming increasingly celebrated as explorers.

The Villas Boas themselves were learning about the region they had entered and its remarkable peoples. The Xingu's dozen headwaters form a vast triangle, measuring 350 kilometres (220 miles) from east to west, and they converge like an inverted fan or delta to form the main river. Each of the many headwater rivers has its own name, but the largest are the Ronuro, Batovi, Curisevo and Culuene, each comparable in size to most European rivers. They become the Xingu only after they converge. The villages of some twelve tribes are dotted among the rivers, woods, and lakes of this low plateau. These dwellings are connected by a network of trails and by the rivers themselves—with no draught or domestic animals, travel is solely by walking or paddling canoes.

The upper-Xingu peoples had miraculously survived in isolation while countless other tribes were depleted or extinguished. The half of the South American continent now occupied by Brazil had several million inhabitants when the first Portuguese arrived, in 1500. During the four-and-a-half centuries since then this population had been destroyed, sinking by over 95 per cent to a mere 150,000 by the mid-twentieth century. This was caused by alien diseases spread unwittingly by settlers, slavers, missionaries, miners, and rubber-tappers, and to a lesser extent by their guns and brutality. The most lethal epidemics against which super-healthy Indians had no inherited immunity were smallpox, measles, influenza, and tuberculosis, and, later, malaria and yellow fever.

The Europeans moved inland to settle the more open southern and eastern half of the country, and also up the network of tributaries of the world's largest river system, the Amazon. Their depredations denuded the main Amazon river and the navigable lower stretches of all its great tributaries—including the northern two-thirds of the Xingu river. By the nineteenth century, enslavement of Indians had theoretically ceased—by law, and because almost all accessible people had been captured or destroyed. Outside the forested Amazon basin, most tribes in the more open southern and eastern half of Brazil were depopulated, demoralized, robbed of their cultural identity, half-converted to Christianity, and often crowded into reserves that had once been missions. These were administered by officials of the government's SPI, founded by the then Colonel Rondon in 1910. The Amazonian northern half of Brazil was very thinly inhabited by non-Indians until the 1860s.

Then, to the west towards the Andes, rivers were ransacked by rubber-tappers during the flamboyant rubber boom of the late nineteenth and early twentieth centuries. For a few decades, rubber barons in the upper Amazon grew obscenely rich from their monopoly of the 'black gold', but their rubber-tappers lived in poverty of debt-bondage.

Of the Amazon's mighty tributaries, the upper Xingu was the exception. It owed its isolation to three factors. Unlike other southern tributaries, the Xingu rises deep in tropical rainforests or in the swampy low forests of its fan of headwaters. Thus, adventurers, traders, and settlers could not easily sail *down* the Xingu, as they had for centuries been plying the Tocantins and Araguaia rivers to the east, and the Tapajós and Madeira to the west. Second, a barrier of stupendous rapids and waterfalls, 1,400 kilometres (880 miles) from the Xingu's junction with the main Amazon, stopped Europeans from paddling or sailing to the upper third of the great river. This prevented their reaching its headwater plateau, the area now entered by the Villas Boas. Indigenous peoples slip through forests and migrate constantly, so they had been settled in the upper Xingu for centuries, or even millennia. But outsiders were helpless at penetrating 'jungles', and could travel only along rivers. So the cataract barrier excluded them but not Indians. Third, the Xingu gained its tranquillity by appearing to have no commercial attractions: no minerals, rubber, or potential farmland.

The blessedly isolated peoples of the upper Xingu were first contacted only in 1884, by a team led by the German Karl von den Steinen. He entered the river system by a long march overland from the south-west (an easier and less dangerous route than that of the Roncador–Xingu Expedition from the south-east). Steinen's German–Brazilian team and its ox carts went from Cuiabá, a small town that was capital of Mato Grosso state, north-east of an SPI reserve of Bakairi Indians. This people had split, with half of them semi-acculturated in the SPI post and the northern half still uncontacted in the upper Xingu. But the two parts of the tribe kept in touch with one another. Thus the Bakairi could guide Steinen (and all subsequent outsiders) over the 250 kilometres (160 miles) between their two villages. It took two weeks to walk from the SPI's Bakairi post to the Batovi headwater of the Xingu, more weeks to build eight bark canoes, and then seventeen days to glide down the beautiful empty river. By contrast, the Roncador–Xingu Expedition was the first to approach from a different direction, because its mission was not to contact or study Indians but to push from eastern Brazil into the forested heart of the nation and found settlements—or later, when its objective changed, to open a chain of airstrips.

Von den Steinen was not a trained anthropologist—a discipline in its infancy in his day. But from his first visit in 1884, and another three years later, he gave a wonderfully sympathetic and vivid picture of the lives of those hunter-gatherer fishermen and their simple agriculture. He was the first observer to depict Indians as real people, with individual characters, qualities, and foibles. After his first visit to the enchanted world of the upper Xingu, Steinen's team descended the entire length of that river. Indians guided them down the thundering falls that protect the upper river, and Steinen named these the Von Martius rapids after a compatriot Carl von Martius, who had been a pioneer in studying Brazilian Indians sixty years before him. This name survives.

Steinen went on to be a revered professor of anthropology in Berlin, and he inspired colleagues and pupils to make brief visits the Xingu: Paul Ehrenreich with himself in 1887, Hermann Meyer in 1896 and 1898, Max Schmidt in 1900, 1910 and 1927, and Fritz Krause in 1934. A young American anthropologist, Buell Quain, spent some months there in 1938. The SPI sent teams to map the main headwaters and record their villages, in 1920 and 1924–5. During those six decades since the first encounter, there were also more nefarious visitors—searching for imaginary gold mines, or rubber trees, and in 1925 Lieutenant Colonel Percy Fawcett hoping to find a lost city of a 'superior race', followed in 1928 by an expedition, and in 1934 a journalist looking for the missing British colonel. These various intruders all entered by the Bakairi trail from the south-west, none remained for long, and all (apart from Fawcett) brought plenty of presents. So the upper-Xingu Indians had a generally good opinion of outsiders, as friendly bringers of metal blades and other coveted goods. And Brazilians had learned a little about those indigenous peoples.

* * *

The Roncador–Xingu Expedition's first glimpse of apparently idyllic indigenous life concealed two very serious problems: hunger and disease. The upper-Xingu Indians are hunter-gatherers with limited agriculture. Their main food is fish, which during the dry months is plentiful in the rivers and lagoons of the Xingu headwaters. But during the rains—which were now arriving, in November 1946—fishing becomes more difficult because the fish swim off into the swollen mass of waters. Although these peoples are consummate hunters, they have a curious taboo against most forest game species, other than some types of monkey. Their agricultural staple is the root-crop manioc, which grows easily in forest clearings. Indian women spend most of their lives planting, harvesting, processing, and cooking manioc. But manioc is the only major plant food in the world that is highly poisonous. This means that its tubers have to be grated, pulped, and leached to remove every trace of lethal cyanide (prussic acid) before it can be roasted and eaten.

The horde of Indian men, women, and children who crowded into the expedition's camp were clamouring for food. Bands of foraging peccary (akin to small wild boar) had dug up much of their mature manioc, and it was too soon to process the roots of younger bushes. (Curiously, peccary do not suffer from cyanide immediately after they forage manioc roots.) Thus many of these people were hungry. They were reduced to eating grasshoppers, which were plentiful. (The Villas Boas were agreeably surprised to find that, when stripped of heads and wings, and grilled, these cicadas were as tasty as shrimps.) The explorers were already learning that indigenous society is generous and unmaterialistic. In that spirit they were expected to hand out their meagre stores, which they did: four sacks of manioc *farinha* flour, and a little rice. They radioed for more food to be flown in.

Disease was a far more serious threat than the seasonal shortage of food. During the previous sixty years, when the Xingu peoples had welcomed the few gift-bearing visitors, they did not appreciate that these people could be bringing diseases against which they themselves had no genetic immunity. Despite their isolation, they were struck by the same scourges that had devastated Brazil's original indigenous population—particularly by influenza and measles. Indigenous peoples are superbly healthy, with excellent organic diets, plenty of exercise, and none of the tobacco, alcohol, sugars, salts, saturated fats, chemicals, and pollutants that afflict modern urban societies. These magnificent people can, however, die in a few days from diseases that are relatively trivial for Westerners who have some inherited immunity against them.

When Karl von den Steinen first entered the upper Xingu in the 1880s, he recorded some three thousand people living in thirty-nine villages. Most of these were on the headwaters plain, but he also including the wilder Je-speaking Suiá tribe whom he contacted further down the main Xingu river. Everyone Steinen saw was very healthy, but the few anthropologists who visited during the following decades reported devastating epidemics introduced unwittingly by the intruders. Some tribes were completely extinguished, others lost communal huts, or entire villages. This area's population had fallen by 80 per cent to just 652 people living in ten villages, by the time of the Villas Boas's arrival in 1946.

Tragically, another epidemic struck—brought either by the expedition's own men or by visitors to its new airstrip. By December 1946 both Brazilian workmen and Indians were coughing with congested lungs; but this flu was of course far more serious for the indigenous peoples. Urgent calls came from their villages, to say that people were dying daily. One early victim was Chief Izarari's wife, Quevezo, who was desperately ill. The brothers had almost exhausted the camp's stock of the recently discovered antibiotic penicillin, so they begged Minister Lins de Barros (who had visited the Culuene airstrip) for more. But, as Orlando recalled, 'We got the disconcerting reply: "How can we supply medicines for the Indians when we do not have enough for people in our *favelas* [shanty towns]?" So we were forced to buy the medicines ourselves. After the third injection Quevezo, who was already painted and ready for burial, recovered from her illness. Izarari could scarcely contain his delight—and we our disgust that so little could be expected from the authorities.'

The chief's joy was tragically short-lived; for he too fell ill. Claudio hurried to the Kalapalo village and witnessed a desolate scene, with nine fresh burials in the plaza. As he noted: 'Izarari, the paramount chief, was almost dead. Desolation and hunger pervaded the village. We tried to cure Izarari with the penicillin we had bought. Our medicines were too few to treat the innumerable cases we encountered ... so we helped those who seemed to us to be most critical.' Then Chief Afukaká of the Kuikuro came to say that his people were also afflicted. Orlando and Leonardo made a gruelling march across miles of savannah and swampy marsh to the Kuikuro village, where they arrived to see eight new open graves. They treated the most serious cases, and returned on the following afternoon and night, stumbling through heavy rain and darkness. Twenty-five people died during these epidemics—a serious loss for such tiny communities.

Chief Izarari died on 1 January 1947, less than three months after his first meeting with the expeditioners. The Villas Boas noted that 'although strong and corpulent, he died rapidly. His shaman's smoke incantations and our own remedies were not enough to save him.' His people were inconsolable. 'From the moment of his death, the village lost its tranquil air. Some wept, others gesticulated, giving vent to their grief at this irreparable loss.' Two days later Izarari had a chief's traditional burial, a simple and moving ceremony, which took place amid deafening crying. He was interred with all his personal possessions—a basket full of sumptuous feather ornaments and a prized jaguar-claw necklace, but also trinkets given by the visitors: a machete, a tin box, and a model aeroplane. His grave consisted of two deep holes, 1.5 metres (5 feet) apart, linked below ground by a tunnel, and with an upright post in each hole. The chief's body was wrapped in a Brazilian flag that the brothers had given him. He was lowered into the tunnel, lying in his hammock suspended between the poles. This was so that all his people could ceremonially throw earth into the grave holes without covering his face in the tunnel.

One man did not join the lamentations. The tribal shaman, Maiuri, remained indifferent, knowing that he would be killed because his incantations had failed. He was duly summoned from his hut, at night, by six close relatives of the dead chief. They hurried him to the centre of the village; he did not hesitate or resist; he was immediately felled by a violent blow from a club; he died without a groan or defensive gesture; and he was buried in a simple grave. The Kalapalo laughed when they described this to the Villas Boas brothers. It was lucky for the white visitors that the Indians did not blame *them* for bringing the disease that had killed their chief, nor for the failure of Western medicines to cure him.

The Villas Boas were in despair that their expedition had brought these lethal epidemics. They urgently asked for medical assistance, and during the ensuing months three Brazilian doctors did arrive. The diseases had abated, so the doctors made a medical survey of some tribes. They examined people's eyelids, tongues, pulses, spleens, and hearts. The Kuikuro and others were impressed and delighted by the rituals surrounding this new medicine. One of the arrivals was Dr Noel Nutels, an ebullient man of great charm and good humour, loved by both Indians and outsiders. Of Ukrainian Jewish descent, Nutels was already famous for creating a flying tuberculosis service that X-rayed and treated thousands of people all over central Brazil. He was also an expert on malaria, and he and the other doctors were alarmed to find that many of these isolated and healthy indigenous people had enlarged spleens—a sign that they had once suffered malaria. They must have caught it from infected earlier visitors, because the anopheles mosquito that transmits the malaria plasmodium from one human being to another has a range of only a couple of kilometres.

* * *

By March 1947 the epidemics had apparently ceased and, mindful of their mission to create a chain of airstrips, the Villas Boas moved their boats and men down the meandering Culuene to find a location for a new one. After a few days another large and beautiful headwater river, the Curisevo, entered from the west; and after a further 20 kilometres (12 miles) they paused to open a riverbank bivouac. From here, the three brothers were invited to walk westwards for a day to visit a third large village, that of the Tupi-speaking Kamaiurá. It was on the bank of an idyllic lake called Ipavu. Among the many Kamaiurá whom they met was Chief Karatsipá, the oldest man in the upper Xingu, venerated for his age and shamanic prowess. It is not known how the brothers communicated on these visits. They may have picked up a few words of Tupi, Carib, or Aruak, although they were never good linguists; otherwise someone on their team might have known these; or a few Indians could have learned a smattering of Portuguese from earlier visitors. Also, sign language was always an easy bond.

A younger Kamaiurá called Maricá decided to join the expedition. A week later, by now some 120 kilometres (75 miles) of river journey below the Kalapalo airstrip, Maricá showed them what they were seeking—a site for another camp and landing ground. He steered them through a labyrinth of flooded forest to the almost-deserted village of a people called Trumai. When Steinen had seen this tribe sixty years previously it commanded a flotilla of war canoes; but now only one of its three communal huts was thinly occupied. The Trumai village, Jacaré (the Tupi word for an alligator-like caiman), was a perfect location for the Villas Boas's next camp. The Indians had planted pequi, mangaba, and other favourite fruit trees, and nearby was the essential patch of flat savannah for an airstrip. Trumai and other Indians decided to help with clearing the ground, and by the end of April 1947 Jacaré camp and landing strip were ready.

The ornithologist Helmut Sick, who was still with the expedition, recalled how they built many thatched huts for the Jacaré camp, with the largest for their team's leader, Orlando. It was a lovely place. 'Swinging lazily in our hammocks, we used to chat all day long, and the Indians were perpetually coming and going.' These were understandably curious about the white visitors, and they knew that they were always welcome and would probably get presents. So people came from many tribes and villages. Jacaré was to be the brothers' main base for the next few years. They created a relaxed open-door way of life that contrasted with the colonialist atmosphere on indigenous posts and missions in other parts of Brazil.

The expedition survived the depressing downpours of the 1946–7 rainy season. In the Xingu, temperatures are similar throughout the year—hot by day and very cold at night. But the wet and dry seasons are sharply defined. Indians sleep in thin fibre hammocks, naked and without blankets, but they do keep small fires burning through the night. Having endured the discomfort of their second rainy season, the Villas Boas must have welcomed a spring awakening in April when the natural world bursts back into life under dark-blue skies. They spent the dry months of 1947 getting to know the extraordinary people whose world they had penetrated.

The formidable director of Brazil's National Museum in Rio de Janeiro, Dr Heloisa Torres, took a keen interest in the expedition—partly as a possible source of ethnographic treasures for her collections. She sent two young anthropologists: Eduardo Galvão (the first Brazilian to gain a doctorate in anthropology, studying under the Amazonian scholar Charles Wagley at the University of Florida); and Pedro Lima. They arrived by plane in 1947, and their anthropological training and linguistic skills helped the brothers learn about the indigenous peoples. Every visitor to the upper Xingu is struck by the way in which its dozen tribes have become identical in every aspect of their lives, apart from language. This phenomenon is found almost nowhere else. Eduardo Galvão listed some thirty elements in this cultural uniformity. Villages are always close to a lagoon or river, because all these tribes are primarily fish-eating, they need fresh drinking water, and everyone loves to bathe and swim throughout the day. Each village has a circle of great communal *malocas* enclosing a clean sandy plaza—identical to those seen by the Villas Boas when they visited the Kalapalo. In the middle of the village plaza is a men's house which women may not enter. The tribal elders meet outside this every evening to smoke and discuss hunting, possibly gossip and sex, and other communal business. There is also a conical cage of upright logs containing an untameably fierce harpy eagle (*Thrasyaetus harpyia*). This unruly mascot is seen as a link between the village chief and the spirit world: it is not worshipped, but it is kept, fed, and from time to time its feathers are plucked for use in headdresses.

Galvão's list of similarities covered every aspect of kinship, personal relations, life cycles, shamanism, and mythology—the grist of any anthropological study. Artefacts at that time were identical for each people: bows and arrows, a few pottery cooking utensils, baskets, hammocks (of cotton or palm fibre), canoes, and animal-shaped stools which were the only solid furniture. Everyone caught fish either in trellis traps across rivers at rapids, or by shooting with bow and arrow, or (at the end of the dry season when streams are low) temporarily stunning fish with rotenone in juice from *timbó* lianas (*Lonchocarpus utilis*). Manioc is everyone's basic food crop. As we have seen, each day Xingu women leach prussic acid or cyanide from its tubers by grating, pounding, and washing them repeatedly through a coarse fabric of *buriti*-palm petioles. (Most other Amazonian peoples squeeze the poison out of manioc pulp using long basketry tubes called *tipitis*.)

Men and women look alike in all these Xingu peoples, identical to those the brothers had seen in the Kalapalo and Kuikuro villages. At normal times people went unadorned. But for major ceremonies, festivals, sporting matches, or personal celebrations the men and women love a riot of decoration. Their skins are canvasses for brilliant body painting. People of the same age and gender paint one another, sometimes in abstract fantasy, but more often geometrically according to careful rules. The basic colours are red and black, both derived from berries of bushes abundant throughout Amazonia: red from annatto (*urucum* in Tupi, *Bixa orellana* botanically), black from genipap (*Genipa americana*) or from charcoal. Skin artists could also use a palette of chalky white, greys, and yellows derived from clays and rocks. This body paint is topped by equally elegant featherwork: crowns on basketry circlets; fluffy armbands, and earlobe pins like bursting flowers. The hunters knew exactly which birds they wanted for their coloured feathers: white from egrets, long red and blue from macaws, black from curassows or cotingas, yellow from some toucans, tanagers, or flycatchers, green from parakeets, tawny from eagles and owls, and so forth amid the hundreds of species in their forests and skies. They used blunt arrows that stunned but did not wound the birds, so that their blood would not stain the feathers.

Men and women wore necklaces of *urapei*, white freshwater mollusc shells; and, for the most important men, of jaguar or anteater claws. A woman who had passed puberty rites wore only one garment or ornament: the *uluri*. This is a tiny triangle of barkcloth, attached to a string girdle between her legs, and tucked out of sight in the lips of her vagina. Women take great pride in their *uluris*, look after them carefully, and feel undressed without them. They gave women control over when to have sexual relations, for no man would ever touch an *uluri*. No other women in the world wear such a *cache-sexe*. So Galvão coined the term '*uluri* culture' for these identical tribes. They are now more commonly called Xinguanos.

There were about a dozen tribes—it is difficult to be precise because these peoples often fragment or amalgamate, and some were near-extinction or had disappeared altogether. Several had more than one village, but the total of these communities was far less than the thirty-nine recorded by Von den

Steinen. The Villas Boas visited eleven villages, widely scattered on the vast triangle of headwaters. But the land was flat and crossed by trails, so that all could be reached from their new base at Jacaré in a day or two of hard walking or river journey. This was no problem for the three brothers, in their late twenties or early thirties and extremely fit after their two-year expedition. The brothers also met more peoples when they went half-a-day downriver to Morená, the apex of the triangle of headwater rivers where these converge to form the main Xingu. This beautiful stretch of river is sacred for all Xinguanos, because they believe that Morená was the place where their mythological ancestor Mavutsinin created mankind. People of the upper river rarely ventured below Morená, and they feared the more warlike tribes who lived in the forests down the Xingu to the north.

During these months the three Villas Boas saw the idyllic side of native life—it was only as they became more expert in later years that they learned about flaws, tensions, and hardships. They found the Xinguanos 'gentle and hospitable, doing everything possible to be agreeable. At times we tactfully rejected some of their food; but they, out of politeness, never refused what we offered them. Their children are docile and affectionate. We never witnessed an argument or saw a brusque gesture that betrayed ill-will. They live an enviable social life.'

The brothers were privileged to watch some of the ceremonial gatherings that brought the upper-Xingu peoples together. Inter-tribal rituals were a bond, a lingua franca between these villages speaking different languages. The Indians imagined their diverse festivals in a tripartite structure, with 'the mythical cosmology as its portal, and with body painting, dance, and ornamentation as its end. But music is the pivot between these two points.' This music is from horns and flutes, with rhythm struck by maracás—gourd or nut rattles either attached to ankles or hand-held—and occasional singing. It is simple and melodious.

The most important of these ceremonies was the kuarup festival to honour important dead men or women. Before this happens, the chosen host village spends weeks catching and drying mountains of fish and storing basketsful of manioc, to feed the visitors. (A kuarup is always held at the end of the dry season, when fishing is easiest.) The ceremony lasts for two days and a night. Every detail is as full of spiritual significance as the liturgy of a funeral in any other religion. On the first day, people of the host village are summoned from each hut by a pair of warriors blowing long trumpets, each with a young girl holding his shoulder and tripping behind. Every visiting group then performs dances, processions, and mock charges around the dead man's closest relatives. Meanwhile, the dead chief is represented by the *kuarup*, a tall log of *mavunhá* wood associated with the heroic creator Mavutsinin. This post is erected in the middle of the village. During that first day, shamans decorate it with feather ornaments and geometric patterns of paint, and then consecrate it—all according to precise traditions. People gaze at the post, often weeping, and remember the dead man. Throughout much of the night, which is illuminated by a full moon and a heaven of stars, a small fire is lit below the *kuarup* post. Pairs of shamans, men and women, stand behind it with their bodies bent forward, each leaning on a bow in their left hand as a cane, and quietly singing lamentations. Orlando recalled that at one ceremony in the Kamaiurá village, 'old Karatsipá was one of the singers in this kuarup. It was impressive to see an old man of almost ninety, with almost no voice, weeping throughout the early morning while beating time with his maracá rattle, a magical instrument made from a gourd.'

On the second day there is a tournament of *huka-huka* wrestling, the region's favourite sport. The rituals all end with the *kuarup* log being carried down to the river and floated away, perhaps to travel down the entire length of the Xingu, then a thousand kilometres of the lower Amazon, and out into the Atlantic Ocean—although the Xinguanos were of course unaware of the geography of this funerary voyage.

These gentle warriors have almost no possessions, so they are unmaterialistic. One of their most honoured virtues is generosity. Indians could not understand why outside visitors were possessive about their belongings and did not share everything with them. There is of course no form of money in their society; but there is rudimentary exchange between tribes and villages. The brothers witnessed another ceremony that impressed them: the *moitará*, a market gathering for ritual barter.

Although the Xinguanos had become so culturally similar, there were still specialities associated with individual tribes. Thus, the Carib-speaking Kalapalo and Kuikuro were masters of making necklaces: *uruca* from shells (worn as necklaces by both sexes and as girdle-belts by men) and *urapeí* from mollusc mother-of-pearl (worn by boys and young men). All these necklaces were highly valued because they take many months to make. The Tupi-speaking Kamaiurá and Aweti specialized in making bows from black hardwood *ipé* (*Caesalpinia* and *Bignonia*). Others were master builders of bark canoes. With the Aruak peoples, the Waurá and Mehinaku, it was the women who had a monopoly of pottery-making, particularly the cartwheel-sized *camalupe* pans essential for roasting manioc. Because of this skill, Waurá women were in demand as wives. These various specialities were exchanged by their makers at every *moitará* ceremony—but always without haggling or bargaining.

At one *moitará* watched by the Villas Boas, the chief of the Trumai explained that his people were perilously short of food. He was therefore able to offer only a symbolic lump of paste made from the pequi fruit (a favourite of all Xinguanos). The Kamaiurá chief and his senior men and women tasted tiny pieces of this paste, and accepted it as a suitable token. In exchange they laid out huge baskets containing hundreds of kilos of manioc loaves. The brothers were delighted by this beautiful demonstration of solidarity and generosity—all the more impressive because the Trumai and Kamaiurá had for years been bitter enemies.

Indians often travelled to visit Jacaré camp, wandering in and out as they pleased, singly or in groups. One contingent was of Waurá, who lived far to the west. They were 'tranquil and orderly, disturbing nothing', thanks to the presence of their dignified chief, Patacu. At another time the Villas Boas cheerfully reported that there were scores of Indians on their patch:

> Noise, shouting, chatting and laughter all day long. Children running, babies crying and men shouting. No movement by us is unobserved by them. There are never fewer than three leaning against the wattle wall of our hut, spying on us inside. The door may be bolted but they prefer to watch through the cracks, spending hours in that position. Their attentions double and their eyes shine if someone inside opens a suitcase.

Jacaré's most distinguished visitor was Chief Karatsipá of the Kamaiurá, respected by all as the oldest man in the upper Xingu. He came as the personal guest of the Villas Boas and slung his hammock in their hut. They were flattered that he 'called us his sons and favoured us very much. He would wake us up late at night, to tell us stories about the Xingu.' Karatsipá was so old that he remembered the first visit by Karl von den Steinen sixty years earlier, and then those by Hermann Meyer in 1896 and 1898.

The influenza that had devastated the Kalapalo and Kuikuro upriver had not ceased. It now reappeared ferociously among the Kamaiurá. The ornithologist Helmut Sick recalled that at Jacaré:

> Every day new patients were brought to us to be cured. Their confidence in our medicines was unbounded. … The coughing, sneezing and groaning that emerged from the huts defies description. The Indians, who are normally such very clean people, became dirty and bedraggled. Hollow-eyed and weak, brown figures staggered about the camp. All their usual light-heartedness had gone. The expression on their faces had become inscrutable. They coughed and

spat unrestrainedly. The walls of the huts were befouled with mucus. Gaunt and yellow, shivering with fever, they lay apathetically in their hammocks.

When an Indian at Jacaré realized that their end had come, they would be carried down to a canoe and paddled towards their village; but many died en route. The elderly were particularly vulnerable. Old Karatsipá was one of the first to go. Orlando recalled seeing him singing and dancing by himself during a fierce rainstorm. He had told the chief's son that the old man would suffer from such exposure; but the son's reply was fatalistic: 'Leave him alone, he wants to die.'

The influenza germs also struck young people, including one beautiful Kamaiurá woman called Arawiku. When she died, her body was washed, her little *uluri* was changed, her forehead and legs were painted with red *urucum* as for a festival, and she was adorned with her necklace. She lay in her hammock, with her face and body covered by a *tuavi* mat:

> Her husband Takaruai sat on the ground at her head and, with many sobs, pronounced the customary words. His ear decorations of toucan feathers lay on the ground in front of him. Finally he rose, removed the tuavi mat and placed his hand on Arawiku's breast-bone, hoping against hope to detect some flutter of life in her stilled heart. Then he placed his poor bunch of bright feathers on her right breast and covered her up again.

She was buried that evening in front of the hut, in the middle of the camp. The sad monotone groans of the Indians sounded throughout the night.

The Villas Boas worked tirelessly to treat the sick, administering a vast number of penicillin injections. But when their supply was exhausted, the Central Brazil Foundation (FBC) refused to send any more, as it was going through one of its frequent financial crises and penicillin was in short supply. So the brothers again had to send to buy the antibiotic, initially at their own expense, and then try to get reimbursed by the SPI.

In March 1948 the FBC formally ended the Roncador–Xingu Expedition, which had fulfilled its mission by reaching the Xingu river. The Foundation then launched its successor, the Xingu–Tapajós Expedition. This was to push the trail-cutting and airstrip-building far to the west, towards the next great southern tributary of the Amazon, the Tapajós (called Teles Pires and Juruena in its higher reaches). In the following year Colonel Vanique was removed from the FBC and returned to the army, and Orlando Villas Boas was named leader of the new expedition.

Orlando was more pleased also to be appointed, in mid-1948, as the representative of the SPI in the upper Xingu, by its eighty-three-year-old founder

Cândido Rondon, now promoted to marshal. The Villas Boas venerated Rondon, Brazil's greatest explorer, who had done so much to change his nation's attitudes to its indigenous peoples. Rondon was an officer of the army engineers who spent the final decades of the nineteenth century leading a team of dedicated officers in exploration of a vast swathe of south-western Brazil—a region now named after him as the state of Rondônia. This was true exploration because, as well as penetrating and mapping countless new plains, forests, and rivers, the team published over a hundred volumes of scientific findings. In the course of these expeditions, Rondon and his men often encountered Indians, admired them, were helped by them, and wanted to protect them. On his rare visits to the capital, Rio de Janeiro, Rondon gave lectures that filled the opera house with the nation's elite, from the president down. He always extolled indigenous people.

In 1910 a group of humanitarians had decided that Brazil needed a professional and non-missionary SPI, with Rondon as its head. A sympathetic minister got the approval of state governors in the interior—by implying that Indians would be 'civilized' to become much-needed agricultural workers. So the SPI legislation was rammed through in a matter of weeks. Only then did the Church realize that indigenous affairs had been removed from its remit. For a while the SPI was a world leader, but it then had a chequered history. The frustrated Church persuaded the war minister to remove Rondon from his new SPI and recall him to the army. The SPI was often starved of funds or run by mediocre directors. During the 1930s Rondon fell out of favour with Brazil's strongman president, Getúlio Vargas, for political reasons; but they eventually became reconciled; and by the late 1940s Rondon was promoted to marshal, the highest rank in the army, and became the grand figurehead of a rejuvenated SPI. This was the period when the Villas Boas reached the Xingu. But after Rondon's death in 1958 his SPI sadly lapsed again into incompetence and corruption.

The young Villas Boas brothers were thrilled when Rondon wrote a series of short letters to them, the first of which reached them in their camp on the Culuene in 1947. Dr Noel Nutels had told Marshal Rondon about the tragic death of Chief Izarari and the epidemics among the Kalapalo and Kuikuro, so Rondon praised 'the noble sacrifice that you made of your own food to lessen the sufferings of these Indians'. Other letters commended their patriotism and devotion to the Indians, and ended with 'an affectionate embrace from your aged admirer'. The brothers were even more delighted when (as explained by the anthropologist Carmen Junqueira) 'Rondon had the humility to admit that his policy of *civilizing* Indians had been mistaken. He appreciated that in their work the Villas Boas would not allow whites to impose their values on indigenous peoples; and this had resulted in a modern indigenist policy that has had worldwide relevance.' Instead of being forced to conform to frontier society, Indians should be entitled to continue in their admirable way of life. Orlando felt that Rondon's change of heart 'gave us freedom to evolve a new indigenist system. That was the moment when we realised that we must remain with the tribes—which is what we did.'

3

ONWARD EXPLORATION

In August 1947, a few months after inaugurating the airstrip at Jacaré, Orlando and Claudio Villas Boas left their younger brother Leonardo in charge of this camp and made an exploratory excursion down onto the main Xingu. They went beyond the sacred site Morená, where the big headwater rivers—Ronuro, Batovi, and Culuene/Curisevo—converge to become the Xingu itself. Surprisingly, they were the first serious investigators to do this since Karl von den Steinen when he contacted the Suiá on the main river in 1884, as later anthropologists had all concentrated on studying the Xinguanos of the headwater plateau. The Villas Boas' excursion was delightful but uneventful—along a gently flowing river with no rapids, full of fish and with vibrant bird life on its luxuriantly forested banks. This was the first time that the silence of the Xingu had been disturbed by the noise of an outboard motor—in this case a small long-shafted 5-horsepower Swedish Penta, which was the favourite at that time.

It was only after they had descended about 130 kilometres (80 miles) to the mouth of the Manitsauá, a large tributary entering from the west, that they suddenly saw their first people. These were unknown, uncontacted, and potentially dangerous. What they saw was a canoe full of Indians; but these landed and disappeared into the forest. Half an hour further downriver there was a cluster of palm-thatched huts on a lovely beach. But as the explorers' boat approached, the inhabitants of these huts leapt into eight canoes and paddled away as fast as they could. The brothers bravely landed, and were impressed by this attractive place, with macaws and other domesticated birds running about between the huts, fires still lit, and hammocks and bows on the beach about to have been loaded. These unknown people could have been watching, hidden in the forest, and might have returned in force to attack the trespassers. Three days later, farther down the Xingu, the expedition saw a large thatched *maloca* on the shore. They approached cautiously; but once again the mysterious Indians had fled into the forest, leaving fires lit and hammocks slung. The intruders collected a selection of artefacts, for identification purposes; but they carefully left a present in the place of each thing they took—machetes, axes, bead necklaces, small knives—as well as more of these on the beach as they left. Leaving presents had been the invariable tactic for contacts ever since the first Europeans landed in Brazil, because sharp metal blades were irresistible to people living in a world of trees and vegetation and because gifts were an obvious sign of peaceful intentions. Back at Jacaré a week later, various Xinguanos had different theories about which tribe had made the objects collected in the hut. But old Karatsipá (who was still alive in mid-1947) had no doubt: he declared that they were made by a people called Juruna.

A year elapsed before the Villas Boas ventured down onto the main Xingu again, to try to contact this unknown people. During the intervening months, the brothers had learned more about warfare between Xingu peoples. Fighting was not about territory: forests and rivers were limitless and no one owned them, any more than they did the air or water. Nor was it about material possessions: Indians had very few of these, and everyone preferred to make their own. Women and children were another matter. If a tribe was short of people, perhaps from disease, or had a gender imbalance, its men might raid to capture desirable human commodities. This was not slavery, because the newcomers became part of the capturing tribe's society. However, a more sinister *casus belli* was hostility sparked by imagined evil sorcery, or by ancient feuds, vendettas, and hatreds. As we have seen, the dozen peoples of the upper river, the '*uluri* people' or 'Xinguanos', were generally at peace with one another, with identical customs and regular festivals and gatherings. Their animosity and fear were therefore directed against tribes further down the Xingu, people who were thought to be more barbaric and dangerously warlike.

Orlando and Claudio Villas Boas led the 1948 expedition, again leaving their younger brother Leonardo in charge at Jacaré. Their three boats held fifteen woodsmen and three Indians: one Kamaiurá, one Waurá, and, surprisingly, a Juruna called Tamacu—possibly from the people they were trying to contact. Tamacu's story illustrated the warfare that was a regular aspect of life on the river. He knew that he had been seized from his Juruna parents as a child by the fierce Suiá, then taken from them by the Trumai, and from them by the Kamaiurá, among whom he was now a respected figure.

Moving down the Xingu river, the expedition passed a beautiful place that they had noticed in the previous year. This was an abandoned village called Diauarum (meaning 'Black Jaguar'). Tamacu told them the gruesome history of this site. This was where Steinen had in 1884 made a perilous contact with a crowd of shouting, gesticulating, bow-waving Suiá. Half a century later, in 1939, the Tupi-speaking Juruna (Tamacu's original people) attacked the Suiá with guns obtained from a rubber baron from the lower Xingu called Constantino Viana. They hoped to capture some young people, but instead were repulsed by the Suiá. This may have been when the child Tamacu was captured from his Juruna parents. For a while the warlike Suiá continued to dominate this part of the Xingu. They annihilated small nearby tribes and became hostile to all strangers, including whites.*

Then, on one fateful day in the early 1940s, black-painted warriors suddenly emerged from the forest around Diauarum. Tamacu told how 'the [Suiá] women and children wept at the surprise. The men, seeing the attackers' superiority, retreated into the huts.' One old Suiá, Cocoró, remained in the centre of the village, dancing and chanting defiance; but the enemy ran forward and felled him with a blow from a club. 'This was the signal for the attack. Wave after wave of Indians came out of the woods screaming. They invaded the village, storming the huts and attacking the people inside.' 'A battle took place. The Suiá admitted the superiority of the enemy: many [abandoned their bows and clubs and] ran for their canoes to cross the river. From the far bank, they witnessed throughout the night the macabre dance of their enemies around their slaughtered brothers.' Having no weapons, they could not fight back. For three days

> the invaders stayed in the destroyed village, spending most of their time playing their flutes and dancing among the corpses. When the strangers finally departed, the Suiá crossed the river to see the carnage. Nobody was left alive in what had once been their village. In the clearing, now encircled by ashes, the corpses were laid out in a row. The women, whom they thought would have been spared, lay face up, their lifeless bodies in an advanced state of putrefaction, their legs spread apart by wooden struts forced between the knees.

* Both indigenous peoples in this conflict decided, towards the end of the twentieth century, to change their names. The Juruna now prefer to be called Yudjá, and the Suiá are now Kisêdje. The Kaiabi, about whom we will hear much, now also like to be called Kawaiweté.

From then onwards Diauarum was abandoned. The defeated Suiá fled up an eastern tributary (later named after them as the Suiá-Missu) and built a new village far from its mouth.

The Villas Boas learned about the dangerous Suiá, and also conjectured about the fearsome warriors who had destroyed their village at Diauarum. These were probably a sub-tribe of a warlike nation known as Kayapó, who dominated the forests and plains of central Brazil. If so, they would have spoken Je (as did their enemies the Suiá, and also the Xavante—the savannah dwellers whose lands had been traversed by the Roncador–Xingu Expedition; Je was one of the four main indigenous language trunks of Brazil, alongside Tupi, Carib, and Aruak).

It took the 1948 expedition only a few hours to descend from their camp at Diauarum to the mouth of the Manitsauá tributary. They saw the huts of the previous year's village, but there were now so many canoes plying the river that they feared a contact would be too dangerous. Then they saw a group of eight Indians across the river on a high bank. Frightened that these might be fierce Suiá or the Kayapó who had massacred them, the brothers nonetheless bravely dropped their guns and waded ashore. Six of the group ran off into the forest, leaving only two men, one old and the other young and vigorous. 'Their shouts seemed to be warning us not to approach further.' But the Villas Boas continued to wade towards them through waist-high water. There was an immediate volley of arrows—but fired above their heads, not at them. 'We were advancing with great caution. One man on the bank was still suspicious, holding a clutch of arrows in his right hand, and signalling that we should not advance another step.' Then Tamacu, who had been born a Juruna, realized that the Indians were shouting in that people's Tupi-based language. So he called out his birth name, 'Xatuná', which was almost the only word of their language that he could remember. This had a dramatic effect, because the older of the two men on the bank remembered the kidnapping of the child Xatuná:

> We took advantage of his moment of amazement, climbed the bank and remained three metres [10 feet] from the stupendous younger Juruna. Broad-shouldered, strong, with a waving mass of hair descending to the middle of his back, rigid as a statue, clutching an enormous bunch of arrows, this Indian gave us a hard look. We, quaking with cold, each holding two machetes, stopped for a moment in silence before that extraordinary person who had been keeping us at a distance with his bow.

Orlando went towards him, offering a necklace; and the Indian responded by removing his feather headdress and holding it out towards them, as well as arrows with their points towards himself. It was later learned that the older of the two men was Chief Jubé, and the powerful young one was his son Pauaide. The Villas Boas later took a posed picture of this naked 'Tarzan', legs akimbo, that caused a sensation in the Brazilian media (albeit with his genitals blurred).

It is rare to have a contact described by an Indian. But years later a Juruna boy called Carandine remembered those traumatic moments. He explained that everyone had fled into the forest from fear that the strangers were Kamaiurá enemies from upriver:

> Then I heard the noise of a motor, and people said: 'No, these are not Indians, they are whites.' Claudio and Orlando brought a Kamaiurá who spoke Juruna. [The kidnapped Xatuná was now the adopted Kamaiurá called Tamacu.] He called to us: 'Come here!' But we could not understand his language. 'Come here for the whites do not want to fight you. They just want to pacify you and give presents.' But no-one believed this, and all fled into the forest, leaving their hut and hammocks. The boat remained there, and they went on calling to us; but out of fear we did not want to go.

Three days later, the whites entered a village from which everyone had fled. 'They did not touch anything, not even things for a festival. Orlando would not let them interfere with anything, not hammocks, or anything else. They just left machetes, sickles and shirts hanging.' When the Juruna returned, they were impressed. 'We thought: "Perhaps the white men are friendly. Perhaps whites do not want to kill us? So let us go and talk to them".' As always, it was the presents on that return visit that made the greatest impression—particularly 'a box with two hens to be raised'. Orlando 'embraced us and gave machetes and mirrors. We decided that "This is the father of the Indians. He does not want to kill us, no."'

It was later learned that this had been the first contact with a group of Juruna, most of whom had never seen whites. This Juruna nation had undergone a remarkable history. Their first contact with Europeans had been at the Xingu's mouth into the main Amazon, in the seventeenth century. During the three centuries since then they had gradually migrated over a thousand kilometres up the Xingu, always fleeing from white slavers, settlers, or missionaries. In the rubber boom of the early twentieth century, some Juruna had been controlled and forced to tap rubber by the *seringueiro* (rubber boss) Constantino Viana. They had finally escaped from him and moved above the raging Von Martius rapids. Thus, the older Juruna had known Brazilians far down the Xingu and regarded them as enemies; but this group had become isolated again. The young Carandine recalled that the Villas Boas visit 'was where I [first] saw white men and what they are like. None of us [young] knew whites. Those who had previously known whites would have killed them all.' All the Juruna were now terrified of the ferocious Kayapó, the warriors who had massacred the Suiá at Diauarum. They constantly feared an attack by these forest nomads, which was another reason why they had initially been so suspicious of the Villas Boas.

This was the brothers' first contact with unknown Indians. They instinctively felt that it was best to keep this visit short, so withdrew after two days. They returned three months later, in December 1948, for another rapid visit. To their surprise they received a cool reception—children cried when they saw the strangers, and their parents were mollified only when presents of tools and necklaces were distributed. One elderly man called Mibina was resolutely hostile. He glowered, turned his back, and 'maintained an attitude of reserve, suspicion and caution'.

The next move was on 8 January 1949: a flight low over the village, with Xatuná in the plane calling out his name. On the very next day, a group of Juruna appeared at Diauarum, where the Villas Boas now had a camp, and were pleased to see Xatuná there. They came in a huge dugout canoe, 10 metres (33 feet) long and cut from a single tree, with a capacity of a metric ton; making such dugouts was a Juruna speciality, beyond the capability of upper-Xingu people who could build only bark canoes. They were of course given as warm a welcome as the new camp at Diauarum could provide.

Contact with the Juruna was confirmed later in 1949 with another visit to their village. This time the entire village was on the riverbank to welcome the Brazilians—apart from two old men who remembered how evil whites could be. One was Mibina, slightly less frosty than before. Orlando went to embrace him in his hammock and 'more relaxed, without being expansive, the old Indian received us without a smile but decidedly more amiably'. The other suspicious man was Mibina's brother Kaiá, who had gone into the forest to avoid contact. The Villas Boas sent someone to fetch him. These aged brothers were particularly important because they were sons of the Jurunas' most influential figure, an octogenarian matriarch called Jacui. 'Fat, almost 140 kilos (300 pounds), with some white hairs in her dark hair, she is the village's counsellor ... and without doubt its greatest attraction.' The brothers were delighted that Jacui immediately called them her sons. She had had a more remarkable life than anyone in the Xingu. Born far down on the middle river, her group of Juruna had been persecuted by rubber-tappers, and had steadily moved upstream to escape. They eventually fled above the Von Martius rapids, but although this protected them from whites, they were at war with the terrible Metuktire tribe of Kayapó, and also with this people's enemy, the Suiá. After some years of conflict, another adversary appeared: the Kamaiurá from the upper Xingu (whom the Villas Boas liked so much). In one battle, the Kamaiurá had captured Jacui and her son Mibina, then an infant. The doughty woman lived for some years as the wife of a Kamaiurá in their lovely village on Lake Ipavu. (By chance, both the Juruna and Kamaiurá spoke Tupi.) But although life seemed good, she was still a proud Juruna. So one day when bathing in the lake she took a canoe and fled downriver with her son. The Kamaiurá pursued and tried to recapture Jacui, but she eluded them, sometimes by sinking her canoe and hiding herself in the forest. It took her a month to rejoin her people.

The Villas Boas were pleased to have made their first contact with a potentially unfriendly tribe. The Juruna differed from the upper-Xingu peoples in several ways. The men had their hair long, parted in the middle and hanging down their backs, and they did not bother to pluck their sparse body and facial hairs. They were naked like all Indians, but Juruna men held their penises with tiny sheaths. Both sexes painted their skins with vivid scarlet *urucum* dye, and the name Juruna meant 'the red people'. Fine hunters, they ate every form of forest game in addition to fish, which was almost the only animal food of upper Xinguanos. They also differed from these, and indeed from all the Je-speaking tribes, by brewing a mild alcohol: *caxiri*, from manioc and sometimes maize with its fermentation started by women's saliva. From their many years on the lower river and with rubber-tappers, the Juruna had also acquired skills such as making pottery and magnificent dugout canoes. When a canoe ceased to be seaworthy, it was plugged and used as a vat for brewing *caxiri*.

Having managed this easy contact, the brothers then attempted something more ambitious: to broker peace between the Juruna and some of their enemies. Their first move was to organize trading, persuading some Trumai to paddle down to Diauarum to barter with the Juruna. The Villas Boas then arranged for the respected Juruna chief Jubé—the older man who had confronted them on the riverbank—to be taken up to their Jacaré base to meet Kamaiurá elders. This audacious move to connect two warring peoples was surprisingly successful. The Kamaiurá made lengthy speeches in Jubé's honour, for both tribes spoke a variant of Tupi, and they loaded him with presents when he left.

* * *

The brothers were still employees of the Central Brazil Foundation (FBC), which, as we have seen, in March 1948 formally ended the Roncador–Xingu Expedition and launched its successor the Xingu–Tapajós Expedition, with Orlando as its leader. This new phase was to push westward to the next great southern tributary of the Amazon: the Tapajós, whose upper reaches were the Teles Pires and Juruena rivers. (At 1,930 kilometres (1,200 miles), the Tapajós was even longer than the Xingu.) The first move was to spend the final two months of 1948 clearing an airstrip at Diauarum, the delightful abandoned village that was destined to become their permanent northern base. They then spent months gathering the necessary equipment, food, petrol, and men for the new Xingu–Tapajós Expedition.

The push towards the Teles Pires river (the upper Tapajós) finally set off on 12 June 1949. The route was down the Xingu to the Juruna village, then up the empty Manitsauá tributary. This was pure exploration. The brothers described the river journey as uneventful, with

> no clearings, no beaches. The same forest along the banks, the same curves, the same dark water flowing rapidly. ... Nothing beyond the sensation of navigating up a totally unknown river. At times, on a sharp bend, we surprised bands of curious monkeys who came to watch us from the bank and then disappeared into the forest chattering and whistling. ... The river continued to have an average width of a hundred meters [330 feet]. The riverbank vegetation now changed slightly with an abundance of wild banana trees, which give the forest a more sombre appearance. There were high crowns of gigantic kapoks on the banks. Here and there we could see most beautiful and luxuriant mimosas, shading lesser trees. The austerity of the Manitsauá is obvious: there are no signs—recent or ancient—of Indians in these parts.

Orlando pondered the morality of such exploration. He felt that this virgin river did not welcome intruders, and that it had every right to preserve 'its millennial tranquillity. It prefers to live roughly, as wild as when it was born. Let those with machines go and descend other valleys; not here. Here its own noises are sufficient: the rustling of trees blown by the wind and the rush of waters splashing over rocks.'

After eight days the expedition moored its boats, but there was nowhere suitable for clearing an airstrip. So they started to cut a trail westwards. Opening this *picada* was weary work, far harder than crossing the more open *campo* of Xavante lands had been. There was plenty of game in this virgin forest; but there were also plagues of mosquitoes, blackflies, sweat-bees, and aggressive hornets. When the cutting party saw a hornet nest hanging from a branch, they motioned to the others to proceed gently and silently in order not to disturb the dreaded insects, and their trail made a detour around them. There were some poisonous snakes: men knew never to step *across* a fallen log, but to climb *onto* it and glance below to ensure that there was not a viper among the carpet of fallen leaves on the far side. When cutting, swinging a machete for hour after hour, it is easier not to carry a heavy water-bottle, so the team would hope to come across a stream; but on some days there was none, and they would be reduced to slaking their thirst by finding water-bearing *bauhinia* lianas—swiftly cut, a meter-long piece of one of these will yield a cupful of pure water. The terrain was not level, with hills and ravines to cross. There was often a fallen tree that bridged a gully: Indians, with perfect balance, walked across these easily, but outsiders (like this author on similar ravines) could be reduced to crawling ignominiously along the tree on all fours. Some men developed feverish colds, others became depressed by many weeks without seeing open sunshine. They advanced on average 6 kilometres (almost 4 miles) a day—throughout July, then August, then September. Food had to be carried forward, and bivouacs (just a circle of hammocks around a fire) were advanced roughly every week. Finally, after cutting about 150 kilometres (93 miles) of *picada*, the forest opened to reveal the great Teles Pires river (which changes its name to Tapajós before joining the main Amazon). The men joyfully plunged in to celebrate.

The expedition then had to bring up tools and equipment to build a more permanent camp and airstrip. The brothers joined their men in a hard six-day walk back along their trail, each man with his hammock, blanket, and some food for night camps. Then came the tough task of carrying loads forward, a punishing 25–30 kilograms (55–66 pounds) per man. If a weary porter found somewhere to sit with such a heavy pack, he could topple onto his back like a beetle; and his seat might prove to be a rotten log infested with ants or termites. Walking along a freshly cut trail, every step has to be watched. There is a constant tangle of slippery roots, with holes to twist an ankle, and stepping onto—never right over—a fallen tree to be sure that there is not a snake on its far side. Lianas can catch one's head, and it is best to wear a hat against the shower of insects that can tumble out of a creeper. If a man stumbles, he must avoid grabbing the nearest vegetation because it may be covered in spines or thorns.

The expedition's supply chain was helped by having two donkeys that could each carry 80 kilograms (180 pounds); but these required a slightly wider trail, and there was nothing for them to graze in a tropical forest. These donkeys had been flown into the Xingu, where they were a revelation to the Indians. These consummate hunters thought that they knew every creature in existence. No animal native to Amazonia can be domesticated; yet here was a docile beast that was not immediately hunted and eaten, but which stood still and placidly carried loads. As the ornithologist Dr Sick wrote: 'The delight they took in this new animal and the admiration they felt for it knew no bounds.' However, the donkeys on the expedition did not survive: one was killed by a jaguar and the other ran off.

The Teles Pires was home to the Kaiabi, 'restless and unpredictable Indians' who had once had a warlike reputation. The explorers were on guard in their hammock camp. 'This vigilance was because, on the previous night ... we heard jaguar growling, monkey howls, bird calls, even the grunting of pec- cary.' Such a diversity of noises, from animals that did not normally coexist, and some of which were diurnal, meant that these were Indians calling to one another. Knowing that the Kaiabi speak Tupi, the brothers shouted out some words in that language. 'The imitations ceased, as if by magic.' Instead, there were answering cries from the forest across the broad river. 'We clearly heard "Aiôt" ("Come here").' So the Villas Boas embarked in a small canoe and even- tually met two Kaiabi on the far bank:

> They were nervous and agitated, moving from side to side, but they did not flee on our arrival. Looking intently at us, they beat their chests and said in a perturbed manner: 'Kaiabi! Kaiabi! Kaiabi!' We slowly climbed the bank and each held out a machete, deliberately saying, in the Tupi of the Kamaiurá, 'Icatu ié' ('We are friends'). With the most expressive gestures that occurred to us, and using some Kamaiurá phrases, we managed to instil confidence in the two Indians, eventually convincing them to accompany us to our camp on the far side of the river.

The Indians were sent home with more presents. Soon, large groups of Kaiabi visited the Villas Boas' camp, always bringing very welcome presents of food—fish, game, and palm hearts.

The Kaiabi proved almost pathetically eager to befriend these well-inten- tioned whites. This tribe had suffered terribly. Although their forests along the Teles Pires river were remote from developed parts of Brazil, they lay at the eastern edge of the natural habitat of *Hevea brasiliensis* rubber trees. There had been a small revival of Amazonian rubber-tapping during the war, because the Japanese had captured the Malayan and Sumatran plantations and this commodity was essential to the Allied war effort. *Seringueiros*, as rubber- tappers were called, reopened rubber stations in much of Brazil, including on the Teles Pires. Some Kaiabi worked as cheap labour for a rubber com- pany called Erion during the 1940s. Then, at the war's end in 1945, there was a tragic measles epidemic. During a terrible two weeks 198 people died, leaving only 40 survivors in one part of the tribe. As one Kaiabi, Aturi, later remembered: 'Everyone caught this disease, measles. At that time there was no doctor nor health monitor, nothing. That epidemic finished off four Kaiabi villages. Everyone died. How could they save themselves? From that disease I lost my mother, my brother.' (A vaccine against measles was not developed until the late 1960s.) A further threat came from a land-colonization company called Conamali that was bringing settlers from southern Brazil, claiming indigenous land as *devoluta* (unoccupied), and aggressively deforesting the region. There was conflict not only between Indians and rubber men or land speculators, but also with a wretchedly ill-equipped Indian Protection Service (SPI) post. What the Villas Boas did not know was that some of the nervous Indians they met on the Teles Pires were on the run from an SPI post on the Teles Pires river. (One rumour was that one of them had killed this post's oppressive administrator.) The Kaiabis' only help came from a Jesuit mission, run for many years by the German Father João Evangelista Dornstauder, whom many of them loved. But this was far to the west on another headwater of the Tapajós.

Now that the Villas Boas had accomplished the FBC's mission of moving overland from the Xingu to the Tapajós/Teles Pires, their priority was to open another airstrip there. This was a formidable task, in tall tropical rainforests. The Kaiabi were by now convinced of the expedition's good intentions, so started visiting its camp in large groups. They never came empty-handed, but always brought food. They then decided to help with the airstrip, which had been started by the expedition's woodsmen. The Villas Boas described them as 'brave, valiant and tireless, lacking ambition and uninterested in barter'. They worked with a clamour of shouting, laughter, and goodwill. Unlike the few Xinguanos on the expedition, the Kaiabi slept on the ground rather than in hammocks, and they always wore some ragged clothing—a legacy from their years of contact with frontier society. A rough landing ground was finished by the end of 1950. But pilots were reluctant to fly there from the Xingu because it was a short strip, and a long way for some of their aged single-engine two-seaters that had been 'patched up time and time again'.

Nevertheless, using this rudimentary airstrip and with better light planes, the brothers explored the forests to the north-east, heading towards a range of low hills called Cachimbo ('Pipe'). This part of Brazil was totally unexplored and unmapped, without even aerial photography. All three brothers were on one of these reconnaissance flights, in a single-engined Stinson piloted by a friend, Air Force Major Leal Neto. But after half an hour the plane started to cough, which the pilot thought was due to ice on its carburettor. Worse, he had difficulty gaining altitude, and his plane was short of fuel. He managed to fly across six rocky outcrops, and suddenly

a seventh outcrop loomed in front of us, higher than the others and with an enormous object on top—either a tree-trunk or a large rock. The pilot shouted a warning: 'Hold tight! Hold tight! It isn't going to work; we are going to hit! … I'll try to make a crash landing.'

The plane skimmed the outcrop; the pilot pulled the joystick so that the aircraft's nose lifted; but this lowered its tail, which hit the tree trunk on top of the rock, hurling the plane to the ground. Luckily the little Stinson had its wings above the cockpit, so that these were not damaged. There was then a miracle. Amazingly, the ground beyond the outcrop proved to be a small stretch of treeless sunlit savannah, a natural clearing in the midst of forests to the horizon in every direction. The pilot managed to crash-land. Orlando and Claudio climbed out without a scratch, as did Leonardo after he was released from tumbled boxes and freight. The plane was only slightly damaged; the pilot radioed for aviation spirit; and he was able to take off again a few days later from that bumpy patch of *campo cerrado*.

The Brazilian air force immediately asked the FBC to develop this providential clearing into a full-length airstrip. Cachimbo was exactly where they needed a base: it was on the São Paulo–Manaus–Miami route; it was the right distance beyond Jacaré in the Xingu (which later became an air force base); and it was in the middle of an unexplored, unmapped, and uninhabited region. So the Foundation ordered its Villas Boas explorers to build yet another landing ground, which they did during the dry season of 1951.

For some unknown reason, Cachimbo was plagued by insects: mosquitoes at night, ticks in the long grass, but above all swarms of blackfly (*pium* or *borrachudo* in Portuguese; *Simuliidae* to entomologists) during daylight hours. These bloodsuckers leave an itchy red sore where they have bitten. Even the tough brothers complained that they were driven crazy by 'the greatest concentration of pium on the planet'. They improvised protective sacks of coarse cotton oakum with two eye holes, that made them look like Ku Klux Klansmen. So vicious were the *pium* that they could do the heavy work of breaking stone outcrops only before dawn or after dusk or on a moonlit night—to escape both the blackfly and scorching daytime heat. Another curious pest was woodworms, which appeared from nowhere but smothered hammocks and crawled all over anyone trying to sleep in them. For a while there were only five people at Cachimbo: the three brothers, a Juruna called

Coá, and a Kaiabi boy, Pionim. Other workers then arrived, and it took three months of hard labour to clear a 600-metre (660-yard) runway. The air force then completed its base with three small stone buildings. President Getúlio Vargas (who had been re-elected) came to inaugurate Cachimbo air force base. A phalanx of military brass welcomed the president. But, to the brothers' delight, Vargas learned that it was they who had done the hard work, so he insisted that they be brought forward from behind the uniforms and medals, and congratulated them.

4

THE MEDIA JUNGLE

Back in 1947, when the Villas Boas first reached the upper Xingu, they were reminded that this was the area in which Lieutenant Colonel Percy Fawcett, his son Jack, and Jack's friend Raleigh Rimmel had disappeared twenty-two years earlier. Orlando's media contacts begged him to try to discover exactly what had become of the British colonel. He was told that everyone knew that it had been their friends the Kalapalo who had killed the three intruders.

Fawcett had served for twenty years in the Royal Artillery, mostly in Ceylon, and rising only to the rank of captain. Back in London in 1905 the army let him take the Royal Geographical Society's (RGS's) course in field surveying. This was the height of the giddy Amazon rubber boom, and the finest wild rubber trees grew in south-west Brazil and north-western Bolivia. For geographical and financial reasons Bolivia had just sold its rubber-rich territory of Acre to Brazil, and it needed its new northern frontier mapped. So the Bolivian government approached the RGS for a surveyor to try; the RGS's secretary asked Fawcett whether he wanted to do this; and he accepted. During fourteen months after July 1907 the captain and his Bolivian team surveyed the new frontier along the Acre and Abunã rivers. This expedition was quite tame because the surveyors steamed from one rubber station to the next. The Bolivians were pleased with the quality of Fawcett's survey and asked him to do another on the Verde river in the remote north-eastern corner of their country. His first, three-week, attempt to do this in 1908 was an ill-planned disaster on which five of his six 'peons' died; but he returned in 1909 and succeeded, with an experienced Brazilian–Bolivian team. Fawcett surveyed other Bolivian rivers in 1910 and again in 1911. During the First World War he rejoined the artillery and served with distinction, rising to lieutenant colonel.

Fawcett had for many years been a spiritualist, a devotee of the charlatan Madame Helena Blavatsky. This interest in the occult steadily developed into a conviction that there might once have been an advanced civilization in the heart of Brazil. He hoped to find 'amazing ruins of ancient cities—ruins incomparably older than those of ancient Egypt' in the Amazonian forests. After the war he returned to South America to search for this chimera. In 1920 Fawcett tried to walk into the Xingu, because this was the easiest place to see little-contacted but peaceful indigenous peoples in the heart of tropical forests. He approached from Cuiabá by the usual Bakairi trail, but his pack-ox died and he turned back. Fawcett then spent a year seeking the mysterious city—curiously on the rail-head inland from Salvador da Bahia on Brazil's Atlantic coast. His obsession developed into delirious writings that the place he was seeking was 'a mystical Atlantean kingdom, which resembled the Garden of Eden ... "the cradle of all civilizations" ... where a group of higher spiritual beings helped to direct the fate of the universe'. So in 1925 Fawcett again tried to walk into the upper Xingu, this time with his young son Jack and Raleigh Rimmel. The great General Rondon helped them get pack animals and drovers in Cuiabá, but after some weeks Fawcett decided to send these back and for the trio to continue alone. They were guided by Bakairi Indians along the same route as all expeditions during the previous forty years. However, unlike the earlier visitors, the three Englishmen were never seen again.

Fawcett had no experience of cutting into or moving through virgin tropical rainforests—on his Bolivian surveys he had been on rivers or existing trails. But he expounded the suicidal theory that 'Where the real wilds start ... it is a matter of cutting equipment to the absolute minimum, carrying it all oneself, and trusting that one will be able to make friends with the various tribes one meets.' The three Englishmen could not conceivably have done this without porters or guides, trying to cut trails while carrying their guns and ammunition, machetes, hammocks, food, cooking pot, and even a bag of presents for the 'higher spiritual beings' they hoped to find. The only expedition into uncharted territory that Fawcett had led, on the Verde river in 1908, with a team of local men, had almost starved to death in three weeks.

The disappearance of a British colonel, searching for a 'lost city', in dense Brazilian jungles, amid naked Indians, caused a media sensation. There were fanciful 'sightings' of the missing adventurer by publicity seekers in several parts of central Brazil. But only one search expedition actually entered the upper Xingu. This was in 1928, led by a British–American naval aviator called Commander George Dyott and under the auspices of the RGS. Entering by the conventional route and down the Curisevo river, Dyott's team spent a week with two Xinguano peoples, before descending the entire Xingu river in a panic to escape the Indians' importunate demands for presents. Dyott did find various belongings of the missing adventurers among the Indians he visited. He reckoned that a small tribe called Nahukwá (Carib speakers like the nearby Kalapalo and Kuikuro) had killed the Englishmen; although the Nahukwá said that they had escorted them to the Kalapalo, who were responsible; and the latter blamed the warlike Suiá further down the Xingu for the murders.

In 1943 a Brazilian writer, Edmar Morel, and the distinguished film-maker Nilo Veloso went to the Xingu. There they met the Kalapalo chief Izarari, who admitted that his people had killed the trio of intruders, and Morel published this sensational news. When the Roncador–Xingu Expedition arrived three years later, Orlando said that 'all the tribes in the Xingu knew that the Kalapalo had killed the three Englishmen'. (The same was written by an Indian Protection Service (SPI) operative, Ayres Cunha, who had been on the first visit to the Kalapalo village in October 1946 and who admired Fawcett's dotty quest for a 'lost city'.) When the brothers became friends of the same Chief Izarari he offered to show them the graves after the rainy season had ended; but, as we saw, Izarari tragically died of influenza in January 1947 before he could do so. His successor, Yacumã, was too frightened to talk. But after he too died, the next chief, Comatsi, was in 1951 willing to explain it. Orlando gave a very full account of what happened, to various people including the distinguished author Antonio Callado (who was later elected an Academician) and the young British writer and film-maker Adrian Cowell, who spent 1957 in the Xingu and became a very close friend of both Orlando and Claudio. Callado published this account in an article in 1953 and Cowell in his excellent book *The Heart of the Forest* in 1960.

Orlando said that Chief Comatsi took all his Kalapalo people to a bluff overlooking a small lake and talked about Fawcett for three hours, with his tribe sitting in a semi-circle around him. Orlando was present. The chief recalled that, back in 1925,

> the three caraíba [white men] were one old and two young men. They carried things on their backs, had guns, and one was lame. They came from the west with Chief Aloique of the Nahukwá, and his son, who escorted them from their village on the Curisevo river. At that time, all the Kalapalo were in their fishing village to the east beyond the Culuene, apart from [a man called] Cavuquiri and his son who were in the main village [which at that time was far up the Culuene]. These two agreed to guide the Englishmen to the fishing settlement, so that they could pass beyond it into the country to the east.

The two Nahukwá were also with them, making a party of seven.

After walking for a day and a half, Fawcett shot a duck. Cavuquiri ran to pick it up, and was examining the bird when Fawcett snatched it from him as though he had been about to steal it; the English colonel cut the bird up that evening, and brusquely pushed aside an Indian boy when he played with his knife; Fawcett also insisted that only his trio eat the duck. These seem trivial offences. But striking an Indian in anger is a deep insult. All indigenous peoples are also infuriated by aggression against a child, since they are deeply affection-ate parents and *never* reprimand their young. And native hunters invariably share out their game, being the last to eat any themselves. Cavuquiri had heard the rattle of beads in the Englishmen's packs and thought that he would be rewarded; but when the village gathered to say goodbye to the strangers, no presents were given. Fawcett clearly planned to take his trade goods on towards his 'lost city' rather than distribute them among his current hosts. During his Bolivian expeditions, Fawcett had briefly stayed with two amiable tribes who had kindly fed him. This gave him the dangerous notion that Indians would look after him for nothing, unaware that Xinguanos valued generosity in any man and expected visitors to bring them presents—as every previous expedition had done. They had no other way of obtaining essential and coveted metal blades (machetes, knives, and axes) or manufactured beads.

As Chief Comatsi told it, according to Orlando: Cavuquiri decided to kill the disagreeable visitors, and obtained the agreement of his then chief, Caiabi, on condition that it be done beyond a small lake called Verde ('Green') so that the Nahukwá should not see. So Cavuquiri and Kululi went ahead and hid in ambush, and a boy named Tuendi ferried the Englishmen across the lake. On the far bank was a small but steep bluff, which Fawcett climbed first, leaving his companions to bring up their baggage.

> As he got to his feet, he turned to look down at the young men below. Cavuquiri emerged from behind his tree with a club he had cut from a sapling. He struck his blow on the back of the neck. The old one cried out, wheeled, clutched a tree, and started to fall swivelling round it. Cavuquiri hit again on the right shoulder and the body collapsed, doubled up on the ground. At the cry, the young Englishmen dropped their baggage and started to climb the cliff. Immediately the two Kalapalo [Araco and Kululi] hidden in the bushes at the bottom leapt out and struck upwards at their necks and heads. Their bodies toppled back into the water.

Orlando Villas Boas later slightly changed this account. In 1977 he wrote in an article:

Chief Caiabi was taken by surprise ... and was very angry with Cululi, Araco and Cavuquiri. ... The chief said: 'Now the civilizados will come here to punish and kill us. The Bakairi will tell that these men had been here. We will be given no respite. So go now and hide their remains. Bury the one on the bank and make sure that the other two, who must be floating on the lake, are secured on its bed.'

All this was done. Adrian Cowell recorded many more details that he had heard about the burials of the three unfortunate explorers.

Captain Vicente Vasconcellos, who had mapped the upper Xingu for the SPI in the previous year, 1924, lamented that 'Colonel Fawcett ... was deaf to all advice. He went ahead, accompanied by the young men, one of whom was his son, without reaching an understanding with the SPI, which at that time could fully have guaranteed [their safety] with all the tribes of the sources of the Xingu.' (Captain, later Colonel, Vasconcellos became an effective director of the SPI.) The Villas Boas commented that 'Fawcett was the victim, as anyone else would have been, of the harshness and lack of tact that all recognised in him'.

In 1951 Comatsi showed Orlando a mound that he said was the colonel's grave. This seemed too small, but Comatsi explained that the corpse had been doubled up. So they dug there, and found two parts of a skull and a number of bones, as well as an old machete. The Villas Boas said that they got forty Kalapalo to dive into Lake Verde to search for the skeletons of the two younger men in the mud of its bed; but nothing was found.

The pieces of skull and bones of Colonel Fawcett were a sensational journalistic story, and the Brazilian ambassador to London at that time happened to be South America's most powerful media magnate, Assis de Chateaubriand. One of Chateaubriand's hundred periodicals was the influential pictorial weekly *O Cruzeiro*, which had always reported the Villas Boas' explorations and the attractive Xingu Indians. So the bones were soon on their way to London in the diplomatic bag. The flamboyant publisher–diplomat fully appreciated the publicity value of Fawcett's bones. He hosted a lavish reception at Claridge's Hotel, with the relics theatrically displayed on a salver flanked by candelabra on a black-draped table. But this party was spoiled when the explorer's surviving son, Brian Fawcett, refused to accept that the skull and bones belonged to his father.

The remains were therefore sent to the Royal Anthropological Institute in London for expert examination. This was done by a professor of anatomy, a museum curator of human osteology, and a Cambridge University lecturer in anthropology. These experts found that the relics were those of a middle-aged

47

man. The damaged teeth did not appear to belong to an indigenous person (who would have had fine teeth), and the dental work done to them seemed English. However,

> the upper jaw provides the clearest possible evidence that these human remains were not those of Colonel Fawcett, whose spare upper denture [false teeth] is fortunately available for comparison. ... Neither in size nor in the number of teeth missing does the denture correspond with the portion of upper jaw examined.

Also, the leg bones appeared to belong to a man shorter than Fawcett's 6 feet 1½ inches (1.86 metres). The controversial relics were returned to Brazil to a storeroom of the Museu Nacional. Fawcett's son Brian was then brought to Brazil by Chateaubriand and taken to the Xingu, but he continued to deny that the bones were his father's.

Contradicting Orlando, the American anthropologist Ellen Basso, who studied the Kalapalo seventeen years later in 1968, wrote that these people 'emphatically deny any knowledge of this incident and judge it to be the slander of other Indians who wished to provide overanxious information-seekers with anything deemed worthy of payment'. Thirty years later, in 1998, Vajuvi, the headman of the Kalapalo village Tanguro, repeated this version to the British adventurer Benedict Allen, claiming that Fawcett had spent only one night with his ancestors before moving off to the east, that Orlando had fabricated the entire story of the killing, and that to please him the Kalapalo had exhumed the bones of Vajuvi's tall grandfather and reburied these for Orlando to find.

As we shall see, Orlando was becoming an exuberant raconteur who loved a good story, and was capable of having embroidered this one. Talking to a journalist in 1979 he radically changed it, saying that most of the Kalapalo tribe had watched the murders, not just the three killers, while most of their people were away fishing. But there is much in favour of Orlando's report of Comatsi's speech. First, Edmar Morel and Nilo Veloso had written that Chief Izarari told them that his Kalapalo did the killing—in 1943, three years *before* the Villas Boas reached the Xingu and met Izarari. Second, Basso was wrong to say that the Kalapalo might have been paid to invent this: she knew that there were no payments in the Xingu, least of all for fake news stories. And all Indians would have regarded it as normal to kill odious strangers, so the Kalapalo would not have expected a reward for falsely admitting having done this, nor would 'other Indians' for pinning it on them. Third, it is unthinkable that the Kalapalo would have exhumed the bones of a recently dead chief from a grave in his village and reburied him in order to please Orlando. Even if they had committed this sacrilege, the reburied bones would not have had poor un-Indian teeth as found by the experts in London. Almost no whites were recorded as having been killed there in the previous decades. Fourth, Orlando gave this account and sent the bones to Chateaubriand immediately, in 1951. He would never have risked making a fool of the most powerful press mogul in Brazil, had he not believed it. He also told the story to the future academician Antonio Callado, who published it in 1953 as an article about 'the skeleton in the Green Lagoon'. In 1957 Orlando repeated it in great detail to Adrian Cowell—who could easily have asked the Kalapalo to confirm or deny it.

Partial corroboration came from a lowly SPI worker called Ayres Cunha who was with the Villas Boas on their first visit to Izarari's Kalapalo village in October 1946. As we shall see, Cunha visited the Kalapalo often during 1952 and 1953, then lived in their village and became a good friend of Chief Comatsi. Cunha published a layman's account of this tribe's society. In this book, he described Colonel Fawcett as 'fearless', and believed his fantasies about finding a dazzling 'eleven-thousand-year-old' lost civilization. He wrote that the colonel and his young companions were taken by the Kuikuro to the Kalapalo, who then guided them eastwards towards Xavante country. 'But near the Tanguro, Fawcett was killed by the Kalapalo together with [his son] Jack and Rimell [sic]. The Englishmen were killed because they abused the Indians, so that these did not want to accompany them [eastwards] towards the north bank of the Rio das Mortes.' Ayres Cunha thought that the dead explorers' bodies were not buried but had either been left where they were killed or were thrown into a river, and would therefore never be found. Very curiously, he did not mention his friend Chief Comatsi's talk about it to his assembled people in 1951. The idea that the three Englishmen might have walked eastwards towards Xavante country but run out of food and died of starvation was advanced by the German anthropologist Max Schmidt, who was with the southern Bakairi in 1927, and by two American missionaries, Leonard Legters and Thomas Young, who were also far south of the Xingu at that time. However, no skeletons or packs have ever been found by Xinguano or Xavante Indians in almost a century since the disappearance.

Orlando later told me that he remained convinced that the bones were those of the English explorer, for various reasons. The burial in a shallow grave under a tree was different to that of an Indian, who would have been buried in or near his *maloca*. And a police pathologist had told him that, using a different method of analysis, the thigh bone could have belonged to a man of Fawcett's height. Orlando said that the jaw bone had a crack; and when he met Brian Fawcett he learned that the colonel had suffered a broken jaw when playing football as a young man. Orlando wrote in 1977 that he 'went to the Museu Nacional and "stole" the box of bones. It is under my little desk here in São Paulo.' The mystery could have been solved by DNA profiling. But this technique was discovered only in 1984, by which time Colonel Fawcett's son Brian was dead and his surviving daughter Joan (married to a Swiss engineer called Montet) was in her seventies and never asked to give a DNA sample.

* * *

The Villas Boas also learned the fate of a lone searcher for the missing colonel. Albert de Winton Jones was born in Wales, moved to California, and was naturalized as an American, then acted in two minor Hollywood movies under the stage name Albert de Winton. In 1934, aged fifty-five, he made his way alone into the upper Xingu, hoping to learn something about Fawcett. He followed the standard route taken by the Englishmen nine years previously and by Commander Dyott's expedition in 1928. Guided by the Bakairi, Winton descended the Curisevo headwater, visited the Nahukwá, and was taken by them to the other Carib-speaking Kalapalo—just as Fawcett (probably) and Dyott had been. The Kalapalo decided to eliminate the solitary bearded stranger—either because they disliked him, or wanted his possessions, or, if they were indeed Fawcett's killers, to prevent his learning this. So they gave Winton water laced with arsenic leached from manioc. They put him into a canoe and towed this down the Culuene until he was out of their waters, when they set him adrift to continue his search—and perish. Surprisingly, Winton did not die. After two days, near the Morená start of the Xingu river, the badly weakened, ill, and starving adventurer met a canoe with two Kamaiurá men, Maricá and Avaé—who told all this to the Villas Boas thirteen years later. Winton could hardly speak, but indicated that he would give a 0.44 carbine to anyone who would take him to 'a civilized port'. Maricá pretended that they would guide him down the entire Xingu—an impossibly long and difficult journey. After some hours they paused for a rest, dragged the weakened man out of his canoe onto the bank, and, while eating fish, killed him with a club blow from behind. They threw his chests and body into the river. (This was about 150 kilometres (over 90 miles) downriver of the Kalapalo, so Winton's bones cannot have been the ones exhumed and sent to London.) Later, perhaps fearing punishment, Maricá traded the gun with a Waurá chief for a manioc-roasting pan. The chief still had the gun in 1954, and the two elderly Kamaiurá were still alive then.

* * *

In 1952, a year after his presentation of the bones in London, the press baron Assis de Chateaubriand was involved in another controversial story involving the Kalapalo. This time it was about the SPI official Ayres Cunha. Cunha had been on the Roncador–Xingu Expedition from its start in 1945, and was at the first meeting with the Kalapalo on the Culuene in October 1946. When Chief Izarari invited the Villas Boas to visit his village, Cunha was one of the five men who went. After a five-hour walk along a trail, they reached the handsome Kalapalo village of eight great communal thatched huts. One of these *malocas* had a partitioned section; Cunha tried to enter this, but was restrained, because inside was a young girl in seclusion as part of her puberty initiation. But Izarari allowed him to enter because he was a stranger and not an Indian. So the thirty-year-old Ayres Cunha violated the secluded area and discovered a beautiful thirteen-year-old inside it. He touched her and asked her name: Diacuí.

During the following six years, Cunha visited the Kalapalo village several times and wooed the teenage girl. In 1952 he asked permission to marry Diacuí. The tribal elders agreed, but on condition that he lived with her in the village as an Indian husband. Cunha then flew to Rio de Janeiro to seek permission from the SPI to marry the indigenous girl, something that Rondon had always forbidden. The SPI director José Maria da Gama Malcher and the anthropologists Darcy Ribeiro and Eduardo Galvão all tried to dissuade him—they had received a denunciation of his dubious behaviour from Orlando. But Ayres went above them to the minister of agriculture, then the SPI's parent ministry, who sent him and a team (including journalists) to the Xingu to confirm that Diacuí and her people really wanted the marriage. They said that they did. So on 14 November 1952 Cunha, now thirty-six, and the twenty-year-old Diacuí flew to Rio, with the Kalapalo chief Comatsi and two of his men. There Diacuí was lodged in a hotel, given a dress, taken to a beauty salon, and was calm and smiling—despite being clothed and in a city for the first time. They were taken to meet Assis de Chateaubriand, who of course saw another terrific news story. The Council of the SPI continued to do all it could to prevent the marriage: they were concerned that if such unions became widespread it would destroy tribal society, and 'because of the immense cultural gap between the races'. But a media frenzy resulted, with public opinion finding it romantic; and the presence of Chief Comatsi together with support from politicians and tycoons carried the day. It was argued that any two Brazilians had the right to marry one another. So, later that month, the couple had a civil ceremony and then a religious wedding in the Candelaria church. The bride was driven there in Chateaubriand's Cadillac and the media baron himself gave her away—in a blaze of flash-bulbs and a sea of rose petals, in a church jam-packed with journalists and well-wishers.

According to Ayres Cunha, who wrote a book about his marriage, the couple spent nine happy months of 1953 in the Kalapalo village while Diacuí was pregnant. She was always calm and dignified, and Cunha claimed that he 'hunted, fished and did other tasks expected of an Indian husband.' But detractors said that he became bored, and was increasingly absent. When she gave birth, attended as was customary by older women, Cunha was far away in Aragarças (the town where the Villas Boas had tried to join the Roncador–Xingu Expedition ten years earlier). Diacuí saw her baby girl. But she then suddenly deteriorated, haemorrhaged, and died. Cunha flew back, and the Kalapalo wanted him and the baby to stay with them. He called her Diacuí after her mother. But he left the Xingu and the SPI for good, and returned to his family in southern Brazil with their daughter. The girl was brought up by his family, attended a convent school, and lived as an ordinary Brazilian woman.

* * *

Orlando and Claudio Villas Boas now faced a similar awkward situation involving their younger brother, Leonardo. Colleagues described Leonardo as tough and macho, but rather introverted and not as amiable as his brothers. Unlike Orlando and Claudio, who remained in their posts and visited tribes only when invited, Leonardo 'seemed happiest when squatting among the [Indian] men in the village plaza, or lying in a buriti [palm-fibre] hammock in the house of the Kamaiurá chief rather than on the wooden beds of other caraíbas [whites].'

This led in 1950 to the thirty-four-year-old Leonardo having a liaison with a beautiful Kamaiurá called Mavirá, a relative of Chief Tamapu. We do not know whether their sexual relationship started in her village. But that autumn Mavirá feared that she was going to be punished by her people (for seeing a ceremony forbidden to women), so she fled to Leonardo's hut in Jacaré post, and stayed with him for several weeks. Various Central Brazil Foundation (FBC) workers at Jacaré confirmed this. One said that the Kamaiurá surrounded the hut there in order to kill Leonardo and Mavirá, but they escaped through a hole in its back wall, at night, and left in a boat with an outboard motor. They moved upriver to the new Culuene post—further from her village. Orlando arrived soon after and learned of his brother's behaviour. He told the workmen to keep quiet about it because he was going to find a solution. All three brothers then left for Cachimbo, where they were starting the hard work of clearing an airstrip. Three weeks later, Leonardo unexpectedly returned in an air force plane and asked the men to help him pack all his belongings to take to Cachimbo.

Early in 1951 Mavirá gave birth to a daughter and called her Mayalu. In the following year Leonardo's treatment of his Indian love was being unfavourably compared to Ayres Cunha's marriage to Diacuí. So the anthropologists Eduardo Galvão and Darcy Ribeiro rallied to their friend. Darcy sympathized because 'he must have been feeling the weight of torture imposed by his isolation. So the lapse took place ... Nine months later the Indian woman [Mavirá] had a daughter.' Another FBC workman testified that on 1 May 1951 an air force turboprop plane piloted by Major Leal Neto suddenly arrived, bringing Leonardo. Next day, Leonardo begged Mavirá to 'let him take the baby girl'; he offered her clothes and a necklace; but she 'always refused to hand over the girl'. So the radio operator Dorival grabbed Mayalu from her mother and handed her to Leonardo, who ran to the plane which was on the airstrip with its engine running. Many decades later, Mavirá recalled that she was weeping when the baby was snatched from her. Surprisingly, she blamed Orlando rather than her lover Leonardo for the kidnap.

Leonardo had asked the SPI for permission to marry Mavirá, but this was refused because it would create a precedent that could be exploited by disreputable elements of Brazilian society. Orlando and Claudio were displeased by their brother's behaviour. They got Leonardo to leave the Xingu, first to work for the SPI on Bananal island in the Araguaia where a hospital for Indians was being built. He was then sent to try to pacify the northernmost group of Kayapó, the fierce Xikrin of the Itacaiunas river far down the Araguaia. Leonardo did achieve a first contact with a group of Xikrin in 1952; and other elements of this people were brought into SPI tutelage in subsequent years.

The journalist Jorge Ferreira, a great supporter of the Villas Boas, heard his colleagues in O Cruzeiro's editorial office discussing the two liaisons, of Ayres Cunha and of Leonardo. He suspected a plot by opponents of a proposed Xingu Park, the governor of Mato Grosso and the head of the FBC. They might try to discredit and destroy the Villas Boas by contrasting Ayres Cunha's church wedding to his indigenous lady with Leonardo's failure to do so with his. So Ferreira got Chateaubriand to send a plane to take him to see Leonardo, who was with the Xikrin Kayapó, to persuade him to bring his daughter to São Paulo, and to explain everything. Leonardo agreed, but said to his friend Ferreira: 'If this is a trap, I'll kill you!' He was able to confirm that he had tried to marry Mavirá but that the SPI had refused to let him. He then asked his sister Lourdes to be a foster mother to the baby Mayalu in São Paulo.

Leonardo Villas Boas never returned to the Xingu, but he did other assignments for the SPI. He contracted 'infectious rheumatism' during the Xikrin contact, which may have contributed to his tragic death in 1961, aged only forty-three, during a failed cardiac operation in São Paulo. His older brothers immediately renamed a new post in the upper Xingu Posto Leonardo in his honour—it had originally been called Vasconcellos after the 1924 Xingu explorer who had gone on to become director of the SPI.

5

THE 1950s

The 1950s proved to be a seminal decade for the Villas Boas brothers. It was when they changed from being young adventure-seeking explorers for the Central Brazil Foundation to humanitarians devoting their lives to the Xingu's indigenous peoples. During those years they achieved an inward migration, two dangerous and important contacts, suffered tragic epidemics, and made two punishing but futile expeditions.

The migration was of successive waves of Kaiabi people entering the Xingu. When the Villas Boas' arduous trail reached the Teles Pires river in 1949 they made friends with a group of Kaiabi. As we saw, these brought food to the hungry expeditioners, and then cheerfully helped them open an air-strip. So when the expedition left (by air, to build Cachimbo) three Kaiabi in 1950 agreed to a suggestion to follow the long trail eastwards to the Xingu.

One of the three was a remarkable leader called Iperuri, later known as Prepori in the Xingu, where he became an important figure. The son of a Kaiabi woman and a non-Indian rubber-tapper who had long since disappeared, Prepori had been brought up for twenty years at the Indian Protection Service (SPI) José Bezerra post. He was baptized, learned Portuguese, and helped as a handyman. He also visited the state capital Cuiabá and worked in an SPI inspectorate there. He married and had children, of whom only one boy survived. One rumour (which Prepori denied to the anthropologist Suzanne Oakdale) was that in 1949, when in his late twenties, he had killed an SPI manager but had succeeded in fleeing down the Teles Pires with his wife and son, hoping to reach another group of Kaiabi. This was how he met the Villas Boas, who had no idea that he might have been on the run. He said that Claudio had urged him not to go to the other Kaiabi, where whites would probably force him to tap rubber or gather Brazil nuts. Instead, it would be far better for him to accompany Claudio to the sanctuary of the Xingu.

The overland trek from the Teles Pires to the Xingu took three months, because the trail was already becoming overgrown and a month was spent making a canoe and descending the Manitsauá river. When the three Kaiabi finally reached the Xingu, in 1951, they were housed in a Juruna village. Prepori recalled that 'the Juruna were nervous, and my people were frightened, but I was not.' It helped that both tribes spoke Tupi, and that a Juruna had been on the Teles Pires expedition. Also, the Juruna brewed mildly alcoholic *caxiri*, and they drank plenty of that with their new friends. After a while the visitors were taken to Diauarum; and from there Claudio arranged for them to go up to Jacaré, where they got to know the Kamaiurá, who were also Tupi speakers. Prepori approved of what he saw of the Xingu, so he returned to the Teles Pires to fetch his wife and son and a few other families. This group settled on the Arraias tributary of the Xingu, where they rapidly made clearings and grew food—the Kaiabi were always industrious.

Prepori then returned to the Teles Pires, where he persuaded the important chief Ewafuá to emigrate to the Xingu with some of his people. As this chief's young son, Mairawé, later recalled, 'my father's group was large and the distance to be travelled long and exhausting, since they had to carry their children and belongings, including food, seeds and saplings. When their food ran out, they progressed by eating what they could gather, hunt or fish.' This group also settled on the Arraias, helped by the Juruna. Prepori was convinced that his Kaiabi people were better off in the Xingu. So he returned a third time and persuaded Chief Ewafuá's brother to come with fifteen more people.

Claudio Villas Boas was as keen as Prepori to attract the Kaiabi, partly to rescue them from oppression by rubber-tappers who had the Indians working as virtual slave labour. They did this by the time-honoured trick of 'giving' them tools and other goods, and later claiming that these had been sold on credit (at hugely inflated prices), thus keeping the Kaiabi in perpetual debt bondage. So in 1955 Claudio sent Prepori back yet again to his former SPI post on the Teles Pires, to try to persuade its chief, Sabino, to migrate. This took time, because Sabino was fairly happy working with the *seringueiro* (rubber men) and *mateiro* (loggers), some of whom he regarded as friends. But Prepori was charismatic and persistent, and he visited each family to warn them of the dangers of staying there. Not surprisingly, the Brazilian bosses did not want to lose their workforce, so they threatened Prepori and tried to stop him recruiting. But he finally succeeded: Sabino came, with a further sixty-eight people. Once again, this was a difficult journey, with many children and old people. As they travelled they dared not leave signs such as fires or smoke that would alert gunmen sent by the *seringueiros* to recapture them. Arriving at the Manitsauá river after two months, they were welcomed and taken to settle near their relatives.

Prepori was by now becoming an important figure in the Villas Boas' world of the Xingu. With his mixed parentage, he looked unlike other Indians. His hair was slightly curly rather than straight and shining black, and he always wore clothing. When he had visited the Kamaiurá he was impressed by their chief, Takuman, because he was a notable shaman. Prepori was fascinated by the spirit world and so, as time went by, he himself trained to be a shaman. He then adopted 'Biblical ringlets and a prophetic face, and liked to think of himself as the Moses of his people.'

Later in 1955 a dedicated Jesuit missionary, Father João Evangelista Dornstauder, flew to the Xingu to meet the brothers and see how the Kaiabi were settling in there. There was little animosity or rivalry between the Jesuit and the Villas Boas, because all were primarily concerned with the well-being of the indigenous people. With Chief Sabino's arrival, there were now about a hundred Kaiabi in the Xingu Park. Dornstauder still had 108 Kaiabi people in his mission, called Anchieta, in their original spiritual heartland on the Peixes ('Fish') river (some 200 kilometres (124 miles) west of the Teles Pires and 400 kilometres (248 miles) west of Diauarum). And a further 130 Kaiabi were scattered in villages and in another SPI post along the Teles Pires river. This once-proud people had been devastated by disease during the previous decades, dropping from some 2,000 to the 338 now divided between these three locations.

Sabino's group soon moved down to the main Xingu and built villages near Diauarum. Characteristically they planted forest gardens and introduced crops such as large peanuts to the Xingu. It was they who supplied Diauarum with food over the ensuing years—bananas, peanuts, manioc flour, and corn—without which the administrators there would sometimes have starved.

* * *

The major contact during the 1950s was of the Metuktire group of Kayapó.* We saw how, when the Villas Boas had first ventured down onto the main

---

* The Juruna's pejorative name for the Metuktire people was Txukahamãe, meaning 'men without bows', and they were known thus for some years. They were a sub-tribe of the northern Kayapó nation that dominated the plateau of central Brazil between the Araguaia and Xingu river basins. Most Kayapó live in fairly open *campo* and *cerrado*, but two groups had penetrated high forests to the west and south of

Xingu in 1947 and 1948, they kept hearing about very fierce people living in the forests to the north. These were the warriors who had slaughtered the Suiá at Diauarum in the early 1940s; and in about 1945 they had even raided into the upper Xingu, killing a Kamaiurá chief during a brief battle. After the Juruna were contacted, they kept telling how frightened they were of those aggressors, who 'were greatly superior [to the Juruna] in numbers and in fighting tactics, with their ambushes and surprise attacks'. So in 1952, after the brothers had cut the trail to the Teles Pires, met and moved some Kaiabi, and built the Cachimbo airstrip, they had to tackle the daunting challenge of contacting the warlike Metuktire Kayapó. These Indians were very dangerous.

* * *

The Villas Boas had caught fleeting sightings of people who were almost certainly the fierce strangers. In 1949 they saw a group of Indians on a sandbank near the Auaiá-Missu (a tributary downriver from Diauarum), but they disappeared into the forest when approached. The brothers left presents. Then, in a remarkably bold tactic, they persuaded the Juruna also to leave some of their ornaments and arrows for their enemies as a sign of good will. These presents were removed a few days later—a good omen in any contact operation. But in the following year, 1950, the Juruna were alarmed to see smoke from campfires and a newly built trail ominously near their village.

For almost two years there were no further sightings of the forest warriors. But the Villas Boas kept trying a novel tactic of asking the Juruna to act as their intermediaries, despite the previous hostility between the two tribes. They left trade goods with the Juruna for them to give to the forest nomads, with an indication that these came from the whites. This had the desired effect. The warriors apparently realized that they could be *given* machetes and other blades, for which they used to raid settlers' homesteads (killing their inhabitants) over a wide swathe of central Brazil. In 1952 some Metuktire suddenly appeared at a Juruna village, calling and beckoning insistently. They

---

these savannahs. The forest peoples were the Mekragnoti and Metuktire, and it was the latter who spent most time in the Xingu. There are, as always, many ways to spell these various indigenous names. Even 'Kayapó' is a settler word meaning 'lip-disc wearers', but it has stuck and is accepted by the indigenous peoples themselves—although their auto-denomination is, if anything, Mebengokre.

brought large bundles of arrows and feather headdresses as offerings, and by sign language 'asked for machetes and axes. The Juruna made sure that the [Metuktire] should understand that the machetes and axes they were receiving came from caraíba [white men] who lived very far away. The dangerous visitors then withdrew, but indicated that they would return at a later date.' A young Metuktire later recalled this exchange: 'We gave arrows and the Juruna gave us knives, beads for our ears, and water from their canoe.' This 'water' was the manioc alcohol *caxiri*, which the Juruna ferment in old dugout canoes. It proved too strong for the teetotal Metuktire, who were 'sick for many days' from it.

When the Villas Boas heard about this unexpected contact, they hurried to the Juruna village, hoping that the warriors would return. Investigating further, the Villas Boas followed a trail and could see that it had been opened by hand, breaking branches without cutting tools. They entered a hunting camp that had just been vacated, of a dozen rough shelters containing banana-leaf mattresses for some eighty people. They left more presents. This was a brave move, because the large group, which had just left its camp, was almost certainly watching, hidden in the surrounding forest, and could easily have destroyed the intruders.

These warlike Metuktire Kayapó had never had a peaceful encounter with whites. For decades there had been open hostility across a swathe of central Brazil, with fast-moving bands of Kayapó surprising isolated rubber-tappers or pioneer farming families in order to steal their guns and knives. The black-painted raiders often killed their victims or were shot at by those colonists. It was reminiscent of the American Wild West of the previous century.

The next signs of these elusive people came in early 1954 at Piá—a former Juruna village down near the Von Martius rapids that had been totally destroyed. The explorers shouted, and were pleased when their calls were answered. They retreated to their boats and called again. A group of Indians then emerged from the trees, all painted in black genipap dye—a sign that they were ready for battle. The Villas Boas brothers paddled slowly towards them. It was a very tense moment. Before Claudio stepped out of the canoe, he unbuckled his belt so that his revolver dropped and he was seen to be unarmed. In his journal, he wrote: 'They appeared very agitated, confused, making sweeping gestures and talking ceaselessly. ... There were over forty there, most of them young men.' Orlando recalled:

> They asked, with gestures, for machetes, axes and other things. ... Rather anxious, and immediately seeking to hide in the forest, the Indians gathered up the presents that were offered to them. We saw no women or children, doubt-

less because this was a hunting party. This direct contact with the [Metuktire] proved to us that they were definitely Je-speaking Indians, with the same characteristics as the other hordes generally called Kayapó. Almost all had their lower lips exaggeratedly deformed with enormous wooden discs, their heads shaven above their foreheads, and their ears pierced.

The lip-discs were enlarged as a man grew and his pierced lower lip expanded, until they were the size of large jar lids. They were intended to make a warrior look fearsome—which they certainly did. But they had drawbacks: they flapped up and down when the man spoke, food had to be pushed in behind them by hand, and they could leak saliva. The black-painted Metuktire were lean, muscular, and totally naked.

The warlike Metuktire were clearly being seduced by metal blades and beads—the presents that had been the basis of every contact in recent Brazilian history. They were shrewd enough to appreciate that it was far better to be given these by the new strangers than to capture them by raiding and killing isolated colonists.

Returning in August of that year, 1954, the Villas Boas had a friendlier encounter with another large group on the Jarina river (a western tributary 160 kilometres (100 miles) downriver from Diauarum and not far upstream of the great rapids). Although they carried too few presents for so many Indians, these seemed content.

The brothers met the important Metuktire chief Krumare and, in a breathtakingly unorthodox move, persuaded him and six of his men to accompany them for a ten-day voyage to their base on the upper Xingu. The arrival of these seven feared 'Txukahamae' ('Men without Bows') caused a sensation among the Xinguanos, who 'were terrified, confused and nervous when confronted with what they had regarded as impossible'. But, to their credit, they guardedly welcomed the awesome strangers. Another surprise was that the fine Jesuit missionary João Evangelista Dornstauder happened to be visiting the Xingu at that moment in November 1954—he had come to see that all was well with the Kaiabi who had chosen to move there. In his notes Dornstauder recorded that he baptized Chief Krumare and his wife as well as the Juruna chief who had accompanied them upriver. Later, when the Xingu became a protected area, missionaries were totally excluded. So these three Christian baptisms were the only ones ever performed in the upper Xingu; and the three baptized Indians may not have understood the significance of the ceremony.

All that remained, to complete the contact, was for the Villas Boas brothers to be invited to enter a Metuktire village. So they obtained a large stock of presents from the SPI and returned to the Von Martius rapids in November

1954—with Chief Krumare. He summoned his people, and groups gradually appeared, so that there were eventually over three hundred at the expedition's riverbank camp. These included Kretire, a chief whom Krumare described as the most aggressive leader of war-parties raiding settlers' outposts:

> Painted black, highly agitated, they beat their chests as they spoke and did not stay in one place for a second. They seemed to be walking on a hot plate. ... Next day, in the best order possible, we distributed the presents. We were pleased to see that they were highly satisfied and, to demonstrate this, they sang almost all that night and the following day.

The brothers' reward was an invitation to visit Krumare's village, making them the first whites ever to do so. The contact group comprised Orlando and Claudio, Jorge Ferreira (their favourite journalist, from *O Cruzeiro*) and four Juruna—including Pauaide, the Tarzan-like warrior whom they had met on their first encounter four years earlier. These seven were taken along a forest trail for a punishing ten-hour trek, walking rapidly westwards up and down hills towards the Indians' village, Roikore, far up the Jarina river. The visitors were understandably apprehensive, in the midst of a long file of hundreds of excitable warriors. During the journey, they noticed some Indians scooping up handfuls of earth from termite hills to devour the protein-rich insects—this confirmed a report that these people ate earth. Although the chiefs had told the village of their approach, 'our arrival caused confusion. Men beat their chests and said that they were our brothers; women hastily hid behind trees or buried themselves in the forest; boys and girls ran about. Infants cried.' The tough Chief Kretire (Krumare's brother and co-leader) gradually restored calm.

During two days in the village, the Villas Boas noted that these Metuktire Kayapó had very few utensils—none of the pottery, manioc-graters, stools, or hammocks of the upper-Xingu peoples. They were, however, starting to grow some manioc, maize, and yams, a first sign of their transition from being totally nomadic hunter-gatherers. Bananas, their favourite food, they ate at all times. But they were omnivores who consumed every form of meat and fish they could catch, including stingrays, jaguars, and hawks; and 'from their big game nothing was wasted, not even tripe'. The Metuktire were clearly at a transition point, learning agriculture, the use of bows and arrows in addition to their favourite clubs, and other practices from years of contact and warfare with more sophisticated people such as the Juruna. They had had no boats, which was why the Suiá at Diauarum and later the Juruna had escaped them by crossing rivers; but they were soon to acquire canoeing skills.

After the two-day visit, the black-painted warriors escorted the explorers back to their camp on an island in the Xingu. More Indians appeared there during the following days, and were given more presents. One night, twenty warriors swam across to the expedition's camp with their clubs tied to their backs, and urgently demanded that the Villas Boas immediately accompany them. They explained that their women were angry that there had been no presents for them. So the brothers went, this time accompanied only by Pauaide and one other Juruna. It was a stormy night, and they marched to the light of burning-grass torches. In a rainforest, with the canopy far above, it is gloomy at all times; but at night the darkness is total. Each of the four men had warriors tightly holding both his arms as they rushed through the pitch darkness—which must have been terrifying. At the forest camp, they were greeted by some four hundred agitated warriors, painted in black genipap dye. The Metuktire women, as tough as their men, remained hidden in the surrounding forest. One man called out, in Je: 'Kill! Kill! The white men are worthless,' and there were more calls for their deaths. An aggressive warrior advanced and kicked out the campfire, plunging the camp into darkness. Claudio had to restrain the big Juruna Pauaide from trying to grab a club and fight his way out.

Then the Villas Boas saw a woman's face appear from the darkness as she approached the embers of the fire:

> She was an aged woman who was chewing something, which she deposited in her hand and rubbed onto our faces. We gently led her close to the fire and asked her to summon the other women. She understood and did so. Soon after, over two hundred women emerged from the forest, dozens of them with children on their backs and carrying enormous loads of food. They were angry and did not speak to the men, but merely demanded pacova (banana leaves). A dozen men went into the forest and soon returned loaded with banana leaves. A platform was made with the leaves, on which the women deposited the reserves of food

which they had been keeping out of the rain. The brothers were baffled by the women's next move. Although their own men were hungry, 'the women gave *us* some beijus [manioc pancakes]; but what was left over they put on the ground and trod on it, giving not a scrap to their men'. When the brothers promised that they would bring many presents for the women on their next visit, the hostility evaporated. The visitors were allowed to return to the river, accompanied by two young women as guarantors that they would keep their promise.

Orlando commented that 'this reminded us of the importance of women, particularly old women, in [Metuktire] communities.' He and Claudio wrote that these women are

> generally tall, enjoy excellent health and are strong. It is they who carry almost all the loads during marches. A married woman is rarely without a baby suspended in a shoulder band. They paint themselves with [black] genipap, in broad stripes and highly varied designs. They are completely naked and do not pluck body hair, but they pierce their ears and cut their hair in the same way as men—namely in a wide crescent above their foreheads

and hanging loose behind.

On subsequent visits, including a two-month stay in a village, the Villas Boas won the friendship of the Metuktire and related Mekragnoti Kayapó. It was later learned that this was a turbulent period in these Kayapó peoples' history. The Belgian anthropologist Gustaaf Verswijver later brilliantly pieced together the feuds, ruptures, migrations, and diseases they suffered during these years. Epidemics of influenza struck various villages, including one on the main Xingu above the Von Martius rapids. So in 1956, two years after the Villas Boas' visit to the village, Chiefs Kretire and Krumare, together with Chief Bebgogoti of the Mekragnoti, decided that the Xingu was bewitched and that they must leave. They and their families migrated through the forests for some 250 kilometres (160 miles) north-west to Piydiam village on a tributary of the Iriri river (a major tributary of the Xingu, which joins it far to the north, close to its mouth on the main Amazon). For a few years Piydiam became the largest of all forest Kayapó villages, with four hundred inhabitants. Its people were contacted again in 1958 by Francisco Meirelles, one of the SPI's top professionals (who was famous for having made the first peaceful contact with a group of Xavante, in 1946, soon after the Roncador–Xingu Expedition crossed another part of their territory).

These forest Kayapó moved partly in order to find better medical help. They realized that the new diseases ravaging them came from outsiders, and reasoned that these could best be treated by Western medicines. But ironically and tragically, those who went to the Iriri were worse hit by epidemics than a few who remained on the Xingu. The migrants suffered about a hundred deaths from imported disease during the decade after their move in 1956.

When Orlando took Chief Krumare back to his people at the end of 1954, two of his sons, Bebcuche and his half-brother Rauni, chose to stay at Jacaré camp among the Xinguanos of the upper river. These teenagers then helped Orlando build a new post south of Jacaré. They did odd jobs, served in the kitchen, and learned some Portuguese—all totally new experiences for these wild forest warriors. In 1957 these two young Metuktire formed a close, playful bond with a young Englishman called Adrian Cowell, who had just arrived in the Xingu. Cowell was recently down from Cambridge, had been on an expedition to northern Brazil, and then found his way to the Xingu, where he gradually became Orlando and Claudio's dearest foreign friend. He was later a brilliant writer and prize-winning television film-maker.

Cowell noticed how the two Metuktire brothers differed from one another:

> Rauni was the younger, about eighteen, with broad shoulders and standing some 5 ft. 9 ins. [1.75 metres] in height. His long tresses hung back over his shoulders, bead necklaces dangled from his earlobes, and ever since childhood his lower lip had been extended by bigger and bigger pieces of wood [lip-discs]. He was quick to learn, jovial, keen to talk once some friendship had been established, and very much a back-slapping sort of person. He was, however, basically unreliable, selfish and shameless as he used his charm to extract presents from visiting pilots and air-crews. Bebcuche, on the other hand, was seven or eight years older and the reverse of almost every trait to be found in his half-brother. Where Rauni's face was smooth and comparatively handsome, his seemed beaten, anthropoid and rather menacing in its structure. Bebcuche spoke only a few guttural words of Portuguese, was slow to learn, and had none of the jovial inquisitiveness that made Rauni such an amusing companion. He stood aloof; he looked ugly and sombre; he seldom talked to anyone who was not already a friend. But ... he was loyal, unselfish, gentle by nature, and thoughtful in the interests of the Villas Boas. ... He was neither a clever nor an amusing man, but an Indian of immense dignity.

The next contact with the few Metuktire who had chosen to remain on the Xingu came in 1958. Young Bebcuche guided the Villas Boas to the village of a group who had moved to the lower Liberdade river (which joins the Xingu from the east, below the Von Martius rapids). Adrian Cowell was invited to join this expedition. He recalled a dramatic night-time march from the river to this village, again by the light of flaming grass torches. When they finally arrived, the campfires were made to flare up to welcome the strangers:

> These fires cast a red and roaring light over a scene that, in its confusion, can only be compared to a dervish dance in a foundry blast furnace. Tribes-people shouted and whirled about. A score of dogs lunged yapping at our legs. Women and children pawed at our clothes. There was a wailing generated by some emotion beyond all [non-indigenous] understanding. Primitive faces rattling lip-discs peered into mine, and then whirled away. We had leapt, quite sud-

denly, from the peaceful night into the noise and glare of one of the most primitive societies on earth. That society had gone berserk at our coming.

The village proved to have only a dozen small huts and some fifty people. The welcoming dance soon gave way to a song by three attractive girls, while a gourd of wild honey was passed around by an old woman. Each man of the village then came forward to greet the Villas Boas. The brothers were the only strangers accepted as guests by a people who had previously had friendly relations with no one. This peaceful contact was another notable triumph.

Adrian Cowell observed the subtle manner in which the Villas Boas introduced the Metuktire to useful new products. The tribe proved eager to learn, but the brothers were already realizing that the process of acculturation must be gradual. Some Metuktire already knew how to build and paddle dugout canoes 'which the Juruna under the protection of the Villas Boas had shown them how to make; a small patch of rice was growing at one of the abandoned villages; Bebcuche owned two pigs; tomorrow, pots, knives, hooks and bullets would be handed out at the boat'.

Chatting to his friends, Cowell learned how warlike these Indians had been—and how little killing worried them. The otherwise gentle Bebcuche told Cowell how a group had once raided towards the Curuá river far to the west. 'We kill all seringueiros [rubber-tappers] in hut. Then we take clothes and rifle and knife. ... We slaughter everyone, man and woman too.' When Cowell asked why they had not kept the settlers' women, Bebcuche explained that '[Metuktire] only keep children. Much time before, we have three girls from over there. They all finished now, but axe and gun and line for fish still good.' Just before their contact, they had also plundered the colonial frontier in the opposite direction, as far east as the Araguaia. 'Rauni go and bring back rifle, machete, knife and clothes. He go with Mengire and Krumare, who already kill two. Mengire long ago go to the green forest and see women working clothes in water near man with carbine. Man runs and has much fear. Krumare comes near man. ...' Bebcuche imitated a terror-stricken settler, crouching and making croaking noises, with his arms sheltering his head. 'Krumare beat man with war-club. Dead. Mengire slaughter women. They carry [back] carbine, knife, machete and much clothes.' On their return the raiding party had met a group of six Xavante women with their children. Bebcuche killed a woman and dashed out the brains of two children. Cowell asked him: 'Did you take many guns or clothes from them?' 'No, only one knife.' 'Then why did you kill?' 'We don't know them. First time we see.'

* * *

The imported diseases that had killed so many upper-Xingu people in the late 1940s, and the Kayapó in later years, were influenza, colds, possibly tuberculosis, and other pulmonary infections. Then, in 1954, a new scourge appeared: measles. This disease (often confused with smallpox in the past) had been a lethal killer of South American indigenous peoples during the preceding centuries. One SPI doctor, João Leão da Mota, described how, during that dry season, the upper Xingu 'was ravaged by a tremendous epidemic of measles. Its inhabitants paid the high tribute of 114 lives in a short interval of time.' That loss represented almost a *fifth* of the area's meagre population. Dr Mota believed that the disease had been introduced by the son of the Kamaiurá chief Tamapu, who was taken for medical treatment to the town of Xavantina and caught measles there. Others felt that the measles had come from a worker on the new 'Xingu' air force base. Whatever the source, the contagion spread rapidly from the Kamaiurá and Trumai to the Aweti, then to the Yawalapiti and to the Kalapalo. A serious problem was that the doctors had only penicillin and sulpha drugs, neither of which cured measles. But they felt that as many deaths were caused by complications (dysentery or gastroenteritis and pneumonia) as by the measles itself, and that these afflictions were exacerbated by poor nutrition. In all, 393 Indians were treated, and there would have been more deaths but for the SPI's medical help. Dr Mota praised the work of Orlando and particularly of Claudio, who had 'an undoubted medical vocation and a polymorphic talent, and who showed extreme dedication to the natives, in exhausting and monotonous tasks, from the first patient to the last, both at the Post and in their villages'.

With so many deaths, the brothers were in despair, as were the indigenous peoples themselves. Claudio lamented: 'The Tsuva tribe has already vanished from the Xingu. The Nahuquá and Matipuhy are almost gone. The Aweti have one hut, no dances, no chief. The Trumai and Yawalapiti are down to twenty. The Kamaiurá had twelve huts when I first came; now they have five.' In later years Aritana Yawalapiti recalled the terrible impact of the measles, when he was a boy:

> At the Kalapalo village now called Jakui there were many dead but no-one to bury them. A white man was there and he buried the dead, but not in [the traditional] grave in a round hole: he made a long burial pit and threw the Indians into it. The ugliest [epidemic] was in the Kalapalo village. ... Then it passed from there to the Kuikuro, the Kamaiurá where it killed more Indians ... then more strongly to the Mehinaku. ... I cannot forget it, to this day. It was horrible.

When the anthropologist Ellen Basso was with the Kalapalo in 1968, she was shown the graves of those who had died fourteen years earlier. The measles had produced many orphans, a constant reminder of 'the life which they led in the old villages, a subject of frequent reminiscences'. Half the Waurá (the furthest west of all the Xinguano peoples) were destroyed by measles in 1954:

> Suddenly in every household people were sick and dying. Our mothers and fathers, our children and our wives were all dying in their hammocks, and there was nothing we could do. We tried to bury them with dignity, but we were too weak ourselves and could only dig shallow pits and push them in. ... People became frantic with fear. ... People died in their hammocks and their corpses began to rot in the same house where others lay dying. Infants lay against the bodies of their dead mothers, crying with hunger. ...

Even thirty years later, the Waurá could not tell the anthropologist Emilienne Ireland about that tragedy without weeping. Measles remained a terrible killer until the discovery of a vaccine against it in the 1970s.

Influenza was another constant threat, but one that was at least treatable with antibiotics. In 1958 Adrian Cowell was with Claudio at Diauarum when some Kaiabi who had migrated in with Prepori were struck by a serious epidemic of influenza. 'The Kaiabi lay in filthy hammocks in filthy clothes, sick and showing that they knew they were sick; all the animal vitality that usually made them such noble beings had utterly gone. Bows, firewood, pans, odd bits of food were scattered amongst the dirt on the floor.' Although the Indians appreciated that the white men were trying to help them, they also understandably blamed them for the disease. So 'all of us could feel the resentment creeping across the hut's filthy floor, licking over boxes, sliding round hammocks, and curling about our part of the building'. Claudio worked hard and saved the most lives. But he said that Indians could be bad patients: 'Without supervision the sick took no rest, ate no food and spat out medicine as soon as the doctor's back was turned. Only injections—painful and involving a fussy process of sterilization and manipulation—were appreciated, as a magic that was both interesting and powerful.' Claudio's ministrations saved many Kaiabi; but it was a hollow victory. Cowell recalled this admirable man, 'so plump and dirty, with clothes hanging about him, so unimpressive in the squalor, hopeless, knowing in despair if he saved a life now it would probably, in a few years' time, be lost for some [other] reason. ... For the Indian it was different. Previously he had been proud as the king of his forest; now he owed his life to a stranger. It was a bitter thing to swallow.'

* * *

Cachimbo air force base, which the Villas Boas had built in a natural clearing in the forests, was as isolated as an island in the midst of an ocean. Its communications were only by air. Someone in the Central Brazil Foundation (FBC) thought that it would be good to have a land link, and therefore ordered a trail cut from Cachimbo westwards towards the Cururu tributary of the Teles Pires/Tapajós river. Perhaps this trail might one day be converted into a road. Claudio Villas Boas was put in charge of this operation, which started in October 1956 and occupied the following year and much of 1958. It proved to be 'unquestionably the toughest' of all the expeditions. It was through 600 kilometres (375 miles) of rugged terrain in the Cachimbo hills, a wild region full of unexpected ravines, with streams gushing from caverns that became impassable, and incessant rainfall during the wet months. All the trail had to be hacked through dense, humid, and totally unexplored forest. Claudio set out from Cachimbo with sixteen men and twenty mules; but the pack animals could not continue for long without fodder. After many months, one good workman 'succumbed to fever and delirium' while others were so demoralized that they begged to return to Cachimbo. There was a delay of several weeks at one camp along the trail, for more men and supplies to arrive. By July 1957 Orlando reported that Claudio's expedition had lost nine pack mules, from hunger or eaten by jaguars. It was by then taking twelve long days to walk from Cachimbo to the trail-head: days during which a man had to carry his hammock and food. They eventually reached the Cururu tributary of the Tapajós and started to open an airstrip—the usual backbreaking work of felling and uprooting trees, clearing undergrowth, removing rocks, and levelling the ground, all by hand. Claudio returned to Cachimbo and then Rio de Janeiro to get the air force to parachute food to the men clearing the landing ground.

Claudio later recalled the hardship of hacking into those virgin forests, day after day while carrying a pack. There was always a liana to tangle or tear your clothing and flesh, branches to bang one's head on, holes hidden under the ever-present carpet of dead leaves, roots to trap feet, and when you stumbled you risked grabbing a tree covered in spines. Claudio advised patience. 'You must not get angry and yank violently at lianas. If the creeper is thin it may break, but there are always others ahead of it and in this struggle they invariably win. Its companions are there to grab you by the neck, or body, clothing or pack.' This author can sympathize, having spent months cutting a trail into unexplored forest in those same Cachimbo hills. We did not carry cumbersome water-bottles, hoping to find a stream—but on some days none was encountered and we returned to camp with a raging thirst. In the morning one's machete severed creepers easily, but as the day wore on cutting arms grew tired and machetes blunter—despite pauses to sharpen them with a file. Camps were just a ring of hammocks around a fire and beside a stream. They were moved forward every week or so, and then cooking utensils and supplies had to be carried on to the next bivouac.

This trail was the final stage of the Roncador–Xingu and its successor the Xingu–Tapajós Expedition. The ordeal cost many months of hardship and the lives of one man and thirty mules. But both the air force and the FBC lost interest and finally cancelled it. When Claudio went to report his great achievement to the head of the FBC, Arquimedes Lima, he was treated with contempt. Unusually for such a mild man, Claudio Villas Boas lost his cool. He accused the director of conniving with the governor of Mato Grosso to sell indigenous lands in the Xingu, and 'I called him an imbecile and a crook. He was a swindler, and I was ashamed to work for him.' The director was, however, right about one thing: the trail west from Cachimbo did prove to be entirely unnecessary. It should never have been ordered. The air force did not need it for access to the base, and it could never conceivably have been widened into a road. Rapidly abandoned, it was consumed by the forest.

* * *

Soon after Claudio completed the Cachimbo–Cururu trail, the brothers were sent off on another futile adventure. Someone had drawn lines on a map joining the compass extremities of Brazil, and these crossed at a point near the Xingu river, north or downriver of the Von Martius rapids. It was thought that it would be a propaganda coup if a president of Brazil could land there and place a marker at this hypothetical 'heart of the nation'. So Brazil's most seasoned explorers, the Villas Boas brothers, were asked to reach this ridiculous place. When old Marshal Rondon endorsed the request, the brothers felt that they could not refuse.

Orlando spent months in 1958 accumulating food, fuel, and equipment for this Geographical Centre Expedition. It finally set off in a large dugout canoe and two small metal boats, each powered by a 4½-horsepower Penta outboard motor that was the favourite at that time. The leaders were Orlando and Claudio—who joined immediately after completing his two-year trail west from Cachimbo. There was a government surveyor, four woodsmen and boat mechanics, Adrian Cowell and two other friends, and five Indians including Pioni Kaiabi and the young Metuktire warriors Rauni and Bebcuche. Down near the roaring Von Martius rapids, some Juruna joined because they alone could steer boats through its rocks, eddies, and waterfalls. Camp was made 60 kilometres (37 miles) below the rapids. The team then had weeks of very tough cutting and carrying for 18 kilometres (11 miles) into the forests. There they proudly erected a hardwood marker inscribed 'Geographical Centre of Brazil'. The trees were too mighty and the vegetation too dense to clear an airstrip near the sign-board, so one was made in savannah well to the north. President Juscelino Kubitschek was due to inaugurate this centre-point; but he never came, and nor did any later president. So the forest devoured the marker, and the arduous exercise proved as futile as the Cachimbo–Cururu trail had been.

* * *

The only positive outcome of the Geographical Centre Expedition was contact with the Suiá people. These were the Je-speaking warriors who had had a tense meeting with von den Steinen in 1884, but had thereafter reverted to being dangerously hostile. They had later kidnapped from the wretched Trumai 'all their women who were more or less young ... leaving only a small group of old witches of mythological ugliness'. Then, after spending some peaceful decades at Diauarum, the Suiá had themselves been massacred by the Metuktire Kayapó. The few young men who escaped were desperate to replace their murdered women. They captured some wives from the Waurá, and then disappeared up a river that joined the Xingu from the east at Diauarum. (This was later called the Suiá-Missu after them). But in the early 1940s these kid-nappings of women 'were avenged by an expedition in which Waurá, Mehinaku, Trumai and Kamaiurá participated, constituting a flotilla of over twenty canoes. The Suiá village was attacked by surprise and burned. The Kamaiurá said that the Waurá grabbed Suiá infants, abandoned by their parents, to throw them into the burning huts.' The tribes who perpetrated this atrocity were then in constant fear of Suiá reprisals. The Villas Boas were also apprehen-sive. They were aware of Indians (almost certainly Suiá) prowling near Diauarum and even entering its clearing to gather their beloved pequi fruit from trees they had planted there. So contact with these dangerous Suiá was a priority. It would be another milestone in bringing peace to the region.

In 1959, as the Geographical Centre Expedition was starting down the Xingu, it met three canoes full of Juruna who, surprisingly, said that they were returning from a visit to the feared Suiá. They had gone far up the Suiá-Missu river and had a friendly meeting, partly by enlisting them as allies against their common enemy, the Metuktire Kayapó. The man in charge of one of these canoes later recalled that 'Claudio and Orlando told us Juruna to help pacify the Suiá, so that we would no longer fight them'. They might be helped in achieving this, because the returning Juruna brought with them an important Suiá called Tamiçoti, a brother of that tribe's chief, and because three Juruna spoke some of the Suiá dialect of Je (learned from mothers who had been captured from that people). Orlando therefore halted the Geographical Centre Expedition for a few days, so that he himself could learn some words of Suiá. He might need this vocabulary during a future contact.

When Orlando was returning from the Geographical Centre escapade, he got the Suiá chief's brother Tamiçoti to guide him far up his people's Suiá-Missu river. Murillo Villela (a young doctor who became a close friend of the Villas Boas) recalled how, as they moved up a side stream, Tamiçoti 'became tense and very concentrated, trying to hear or see signs of his people. After half an hour he started to call in a loud voice, and signalled that we should advance rapidly.' After a period of great tension, there were replies from the forest, then a loud and rapid dialogue with people hidden from view. Suddenly there were emotional cries from Tamiçoti, when he greeted the appearance of several canoes. 'Each of these was manned by four, six or eight Indians, all men heavily armed with bows, arrows and clubs that they brandished above their heads as they talked ceaselessly.' These surrounded the expedition's canoes and motioned them to follow. After some 500 metres there was a high bank on which stood another group of armed Suiá. Dr Villela recalled that they beached their canoes and climbed the bank. 'When we reached the top there was a disturbance among the Indians—provoked by the presence of Orlando's German shepherd [Alsatian] dog who was with the expedition, because the Suiá had never seen dogs.'[†] Villela recalled Tamiçoti making a speech, which they took to be explaining why he had come with these strangers. There was then 'about an hour of mutual observation, tempered with a degree of mistrust'.

The Villas Boas decided that this was the moment to give presents—the crucial factor in every contact. They wrote that the Suiá

> were gesticulating violently that we should go away. We pretended to be unconcerned and started to converse, pretending to ignore their presence. They had no alternative but to lower their bows and continue to stare at us. As naturally as possible, we brought a box of presents out of the boat—mirrors,

[†] The Suiá would not remember, but at their first fleeting encounter with von den Steinen's expedition, seventy-five years before, in 1884, they had been equally alarmed by a big dog barking in the prow of his canoe.

necklaces, knives, machetes and axes—and placed them at the foot of the bank. We gestured that they should come and gather these. They were perplexed, immobile. One of them, bolder than the rest, descended the bank and approached the box. ... We gave him a knife, a machete and an axe. We called to the others. They came. We asked them to bring their women.

The Suiá went to their houses and reappeared,

each bringing his wife, or rather dragging her. [The poor women may have thought that they were to be kidnapped or sacrificed.] We went there and each of us took care of one woman, removing her from her husband's hands and decorating her with an attractive necklace. The mirrors were also a success with them. Some shouts, and more women appeared. They were suspicious, but curious about the mirrors and necklaces. The fraternisation was complete. They laughed—but both men and women avoided looking at the two Juruna [their former enemies] who had remained seated in the boat.

The Villas Boas then withdrew, having learned that it was best to make a contact gradual.

The anthropologist Harald Schultz said that in the following year, 1960, the Suiá appeared at Diauarum 'making unequivocal signs of their peaceful intentions'. He then went to visit them, in a 'hunting village' of temporary shelters, as opposed to the finely thatched communal *malocas* of their main village. This was called Soconi ('Heron'), a few hours from Diauarum up the Suiá-Missu and a narrow side stream. There he found that the once-mighty people were in a wretched state. Peccary had destroyed most of their manioc plantations and they were barely existing on a diet of *inajá*-nut meal, fish, wild honey, and occasional monkeys, curassow, or other game. The Villas Boas then persuaded the Suiá to move permanently to that hunting village, so that they would be close to Diauarum with its metal tools, food, and medical assistance. The brothers were justifiably proud that they had consolidated the harmony of the region by bringing peace between the Suiá and the Juruna, just as they had done between the Juruna and the 'Men without Bows' (the Metuktire Kayapó). They were achieving what came to be known as the Pax Xinguana, a precious gift to peoples once in the thrall of murderous vendettas.

6

THE XINGU PARK

During the 1950s, when the Villas Boas were so active in exploring, learning about the peoples of the Xingu, bravely contacting new tribes, and surviving media sensations, they also found themselves venturing into the murkier worlds of politics and property speculation.

Back in 1948 the new airstrips at Culuene and Jacaré had opened the upper Xingu to science. During the previous six decades, researchers had been able to reach this region only by a long trek from Cuiabá, overland on the Bakairi trail and down headwater rivers. So the only academics to visit had been anthropologists, and none could stay for long. Now, planes could bring scientists, doctors, politicians, and journalists—with their equipment and the supplies to sustain them—in a matter of hours. Dr Heloísa Torres,[*] director of the National Museum in Rio de Janeiro, took a keen interest in the expedition and sent not only the anthropologists Eduardo Galvão, Pedro Lima, and Mário Simões, but also a team of natural scientists. The latter included a zoologist, José Candido Carvalho, who was thrilled that the Xingu's 'flora and fauna preserve their primitive splendour, because civilized man has not yet modified their biological balance'. One of the journalists who covered the Roncador–Xingu Expedition was Manoel Rodrigues Ferreira, and he credited

---

[*] Dr Heloisa Alberto Torres (1895–1977) was both an anthropologist/archaeologist and a geologist. She had done notable fieldwork—particularly excavating ancient ceramics from Marajó island in the mouth of the Amazon. She was director of the National Museum in Rio de Janeiro for twenty years from 1935 to 1955, the first Brazilian woman to run a major institution, and she vastly increased its holdings. The treasures of Xingu art collected by Dr Torres and later anthropologists were lost in a tragic fire that in 2018 destroyed the National Museum, housed in the elegant—but wooden—old imperial palace of São Cristóvão in the Quinta da Boa Vista in Rio de Janeiro.

73

Carvalho with a brilliant idea. At Jacaré camp one evening the Villas Boas brothers and a group of their friends were discussing the future of the Xingu's unique environment and indigenous peoples. Carvalho suggested that they should try to get the entire region protected as a vast 'park', closed to all but its native inhabitants and a few invited researchers. All agreed, and Manoel Ferreira offered to publicize this exciting proposal. He did this through articles in the São Paulo daily *A Gazeta*, as well as a picture book of scenes of indigenous life, and a successful film, *Aspetos do Alto Xingu*, which was shown in art-house cinemas in Brazil and Europe.

By coincidence, this idea of catering for both human and natural scientists was timely. There were two popular views about tropical rainforests at that time. One—which is still valid—is that only indigenous people can move through or live within this dense vegetation, so that they are the custodians of this critically important ecosystem. They alone regard forests as their home, and have the skills to subsist by hunting, fishing, and gathering, with some farming in *roça* (clearings). Outsiders from more temperate regions see the rainforest as an enemy that has to be demolished to yield open land for farming, ranching, and towns. The other view was the great misconception that luxuriant vegetation equates with fertile soil. Everyone—including Alexander von Humboldt, Alfred Russel Wallace, and ex-president Teddy Roosevelt—imagined that 'hard-working' farmers from northern countries could turn Amazonia into an agricultural cornucopia. There had been several tragic failed attempts to do this. Unknown to the group around the campfire at Jacaré, this great error had just been demolished by Betty Meggers of the Smithsonian Institution in her seminal book *Amazonia ... Counterfeit Paradise* (1947). She showed that tropical rainforests are totally different to temperate forests, because they are evergreen, five times as dense, and constantly growing at five times the speed. There is no winter during which the system slows and humus accumulates. All the millions of trees are desperate to grow straight up into the sun and rain of the canopy far overhead. Each therefore has horizontal roots to capture every falling scrap of nutrient before it enters the soil. The result is that the topsoil is often little more than impoverished acidic sand. If the forest and the root-and-litter mat are removed, this weak soil is washed away by heavy rain, or baked by the sun into what one scientist vividly called a 'pink parking lot'. Add to this the fact that the most diverse ecosystem on earth has countless insects, blights, and parasites to attack every plant, so that most agricultural crops or pastures are doomed. These were the underlying reasons why the Central Brazil Foundation (FBC) was forced to change the mission of the Roncador–Xingu Expedition from creating settlements to opening airstrips.

Flights into the Xingu also brought a series of dignitaries and luminaries. These included two rising politicians, João Café Filho and Jânio Quadros, both of whom would in time become president of Brazil. Both men were highly impressed by every aspect of the expedition. Café Filho was a federal deputy who visited the upper Xingu with a congressional delegation in 1948. President Getúlio Vargas, who had launched the Roncador–Xingu Expedition and created the FBC, was forced to step down as president in 1945, but was democratically re-elected in 1950—with Café Filho as his vice-president. So, when Vargas tragically committed suicide in 1954, Café Filho succeeded as president for over a year, the remainder of the presidential term.

The other sympathetic politician, Jânio Quadros, was three years younger than Orlando and a personal friend of the Villas Boas family. Quadros was lean, moustachioed, and bursting with energy and charm. He became a dynamic mayor of São Paulo in 1953, aged thirty-six. In the following year, 1954, his city celebrated its 400th anniversary, and the mayor decided to include Indians in this great parade. The aged Marshal Rondon participated, and Orlando Villas Boas brought ten chiefs from the Xingu to march in this flamboyant ceremony—a controversial move that must have been a great cultural shock for them. Jânio Quadros became governor of São Paulo state in 1955. He visited the Xingu and was of course thrilled by what he saw. Then in 1960 he was elected president of Brazil in a landslide victory.

Another influential visitor was the air force brigadier Raymundo Vasconcellos Aboim. Brazil's first trained aeronautical engineer, Aboim had been supervisor of plane manufacture during the war, and then became Brazil's director of civil aviation. Energetic, important, and popular, he took a keen interest in the Roncador–Xingu Expedition, particularly when its objective became the creation of a string of emergency airstrips. As with all visitors, he was captivated by the Indians and the beauty of their river and forests, and admired the successes of the Villas Boas brothers. So Brigadier Aboim was enthusiastic about the new idea of a closed national park. It was a coup for the Xingu Park's proponents to have the support of this dynamic and very senior officer and public servant.

Brazil had taken note of the national park movement in the United States, and created a few small nature reserves in imitation. There was also growing respect for endemic Brazilian nature and wildlife, an awareness that the Amazon region had the world's richest biodiversity, and an embryonic environmental movement. But the new idea of a national indigenous park of the Xingu was radical and ground-breaking in four ways: it would be the first indigenous area to embrace a cluster of different tribes in their homelands; it would combine protection of both natural environment and indigenous peoples; it would be closed to all but invited researchers; and, most importantly, it was on a vast scale. If enacted, it would be a pioneer and by far the largest such protected area in all South America.

In 1951, soon after becoming vice-president of Brazil, João Café Filho convened a round-table in Rio de Janeiro about the national park proposal. The four drivers of the project were Brigadier Aboim, Dr Heloisa Torres of the National Museum, Darcy Ribeiro (the Indian Protection Service's (SPI's) leading anthropologist), and Orlando Villas Boas. Others at the round-table were the director of the SPI, José Maria da Gama Malcher; Orlando's friend the great doctor Noel Nutels; and Major Souza Leão, head of the FBC. Orlando dug out a suit and tie for this meeting—the first time for many years that he had worn such city dress. The round-table was a success. It decided 'to organize a commission to study the creation of a National Park at the headwaters of the Xingu in a location previously and appropriately chosen.' The four main proponents 'were charged with this task'.

The enthusiasts worked fast, and by 27 April 1952 their draft law was ready for Brigadier Aboim to send to Vice-President Café Filho. The law began by defining the boundaries of the proposed Xingu Indigenous Park. These were enormous. To the west they ran along the Teles Pires river as far north as a great waterfall of Sete Quedas ('Seven Falls') at 9.5°S; then its northern limit following the boundary between the states of Pará and Mato Grosso—far downriver of the Von Martius rapids; then up the entire Liberdade river (an eastern tributary of the Xingu) to its source, with the eastern boundary from there to the source of the Suiá-Missu river (another eastern tributary); thence to a southern boundary far up the fan of the Xingu's headwater rivers; and completing the circuit with a line from 12.4°S on the Von den Steinen headwater westwards to 11.7°S on the Teles Pires. Most of these points were unexplored, and the area they embraced was vast: 205,750 square kilometres (almost 80,000 square miles)—the size of England and Wales.

The draft law went on to give sweeping protection to the area's indigenous peoples. Article 2 declared that all these lands and their natural resources 'are reserved for the indigenous tribes who live on them or will come to live there, as a patrimony for their perpetual use.' This wording contained two new concepts: that an indigenous territory could embrace a cluster of tribes, not just one; and that the proposed park could be a sanctuary for other peoples 'who will come to live there'.

The draft stressed that natural resources could be used 'solely by the Indians to provide for their subsistence'. The park would be 'the inalienable patrimony of the tribes who inhabit it', and any attempt to dispose of it would be null and void. Also, the entire area would be 'interdicted against any [unauthorized] penetration, on any pretext whatever'.

A section of the draft law was a 'justification' for its protection of 'some of the last survivors of pre-Columbian Brazil from the certain destruction that has already destroyed millions [of them].' It admitted that the Roncador–Xingu Expedition had, for all its good intentions, brought change through new machinery and diseases against which Indians had no organic resistance. But 'an even greater evil threatens the Xinguano peoples: the extension of our social system into their lands'. If the territory were sold off to colonists, this would lead to compulsory employment of Indians at the very bottom of frontier society and their degradation and debasement. Another great innovation was to give total protection to the area's flora and fauna, and to make these available only for scientific study. The four authors realized that they were often breaking new ground. So their draft concluded: 'The proposals set out here recommend the creation of a novel type of Park, one that differs from both so-called national parks and from indigenous reserves in Brazil and other countries.'

The next move was to sell this idea to President Vargas. So in May 1952 Vice-President Café Filho took a delegation across to the presidential palace. In addition to Orlando and Claudio, this contained the venerable champion of Indians, the eighty-seven-year-old General Cândido Rondon. He made a rapid summary of the Xingu situation—which the president found interesting. But the meeting then went wrong. The director of the SPI, Gama Malcher, criticized his parent Ministry of Agriculture's treatment of Indians in southern Brazil—forgetting that its minister was President Vargas's son. Darcy Ribeiro then stressed that only Indians could 'preserve a living sample of Brazil's original nature', thinking that this would appeal to the president, who was known to love wildlife more than Indians—but Orlando felt that his left-wing friend Ribeiro had been too aggressive. It was the charming doctor Noel Nutels who saved the day. He talked about health, and then broke the ice with a joke. The president laughed, and thereafter wanted only Nutels to do all the talking. As Orlando and Claudio recalled: 'Noel Nutels then made a very clear, very simple exposition—because he was an extraordinary man.' Old Rondon agreed that violent and rapid integration of Indians into national society would really be the end of them, so the Xingu Park could be a testing ground for gradual, controlled change. The Villas Boas brothers were delighted to hear their mentor Rondon say this, because he had previously appeared to favour more rapid integration of indigenous people.

During the remainder of 1952 and 1953 the park proposal was scrutinized by committees of the Senate, which generally approved it—financially, legally, and for indigenous rights. President Vargas also seemed to support the Xingu Park. But in August 1954, two years after it was presented to him, he committed suicide. Pressure from the military caused him to resign the presidency; and within hours he shot himself, leaving a note to the nation blaming unnamed foreign influences. President Vargas's death did not, however, damage the progress of the park legislation, because Vice-President Café Filho succeeded him for the remaining year of the presidential term—and he was a committed supporter of the plan.

But in 1954 violent opposition emerged from a different quarter. The governor of the state of Mato Grosso, Fernando Correa da Costa, woke up to the fact that the gigantic proposed park would occupy and interdict almost a quarter of his state. So he had a map of the upper Xingu drawn up, divided into a mass of rectangular plots for sale to colonists or land speculators. On 31 October 1954 local newspapers carried full-page advertisements by a property company called Ypiranga that offered 'a magnificent colonization opportunity approved by the Government of the State of Mato Grosso' in a new town to be called Cafeara City, with land 'rich in timber, precious metals, diamonds, rubber trees and oil plants … exceptional lands with perfect conditions for growing coffee'. These claims were all untrue: apart from timber (which was too remote to be commercially logged) none of these commodities existed in the upper Xingu. And all but the most gullible knew that weak soils, hot climate, heavy rains, and voracious insects made growing coffee there impossible. Other colonization companies touted similar fantasies.

In rebuttal, the SPI had its senior ethnologist, Roberto de Oliveira, write a report about these property offerings. He published a map and a detailed inventory showing that the state had indeed reserved huge areas 'for colonization', from the Teles Pires in the west right across to Xavante lands in the east. It had actually sold concessions, of 200,000 hectares (almost 500,000 acres) each, to eighteen property companies, which he listed. Mato Grosso claimed that these unexplored forests were 'unoccupied' by Indians or others—but some concessions were within the Xinguano heartland. Oliveira argued that these awards damaged the Indians (because some plots were in tribal areas), individual colonists (who would have to buy land from big property speculators), and national security (because one company was Japanese owned).

A distinguished BBC broadcaster, Kenneth Matthews, was there at that time. He met Brigadier Aboim, and found him to be gentle, charming, imperturbable, and, passionate about the Xingu National Park. But Aboim doubted whether the bill would ever get approval because of the powerful local opposition. 'The situation was very serious. The land was being resold by speculators in small parcels, and was changing hands practically every day.'

Aboim now launched a public counter-attack. He got his friend, the editor of the *Correio da Manhã* (Morning Post) in São Paulo, to publish, on 2 November 1954, a long exposé he had written. In it, the brigadier revealed that the state government was selling or awarding its 200,000-hectare plots of Xingu land to colonists while the National Congress was actually still considering the law for a Xingu Indigenous Park. He wrote that because the state was 'illegally trying to benefit a privileged few before the creation of the Park was approved', if it became law the government would have to compensate these bogus colonizers. A counter-argument came from a local senator who argued, in the newspaper *O Globo*, that the state of Mato Grosso was thinly populated 'so it seems just and reasonable that we want to increase our population by attracting people and capital to our wilderness'. The fight raged in the media throughout 1955. The popular and influential picture magazine *O Cruzeiro* on 23 April showed Jânio Quadros, the dynamic young mayor of São Paulo (about to become state governor), being welcomed in the Xingu by Aboim, Orlando, and Chief Krumare. Then on 11 June this magazine xenophobically denounced a Japanese–Brazilian tycoon called Matsubaru who hoped to get very rich from sales of Xingu land. On 9 August the Villas Boas brothers published an impassioned article in the *Correio da Manhã* praising the harmony of the Xingu Indians and condemning the 'pseudo-colonizers' who wanted to destroy these cultures by selling their land. On the other side, the *Tribuna da Imprensa* (also in São Paulo) on 6 July published an outrageous claim by the state governor that the park's proponents only pretended to be interested in protecting Indians but were actually seeking a fantastical gold mine called Martírios in the Xingu forests. On 8 August the same newspaper wrote that the people of Mato Grosso were 'prepared to take up arms' to prevent the park and supported the governor's plan 'to transform an empty wilderness into a hothouse of population'. The FBC entered the fray under an opportunistic new director Arquimedes Pereira Lima—who may well have been in corrupt cahoots with the governor. Claiming to be true to its original brief, the FBC now supported colonization and saw indigenous peoples as an obstacle to progress. An acrimonious dispute between the FBC's director and its employee Orlando Villas Boas was played out in the press—and led to the foundation launching a disciplinary enquiry against Orlando.

There was also constitutional debate as to whether the federal government had the right to give protected status to such a large area within a state. The lands bureau of the state of Mato Grosso argued that it did not, because Brazil is a 'Federative Republic' in which states have considerable autonomy. This led in June 1955 to a parliamentary commission of enquiry into the legality of 'Alienation of Lands in Mato Grosso', which heard testimonies from many witnesses, including Brigadier Aboim and Gama Malcher of the SPI, and against the bosses of property companies. In the upper house, senators gave passionate speeches for and against the park, and many amendments were proposed. On 28 October 1955 there were votes on amendments to each clause of the draft, which was presented in revised form at the end of November.

During these debates, both sides exaggerated wildly. Some of the park's advocates depicted the Xinguanos as 'noble savages' living in pristine harmony in an original Amazonian environment. In fact, these Indians had undergone some change, and their society had some blemishes by modern standards. Also, the upper Xingu, located in transition between *campo* savannah and the mass of Amazonian forests, was not a paradigm of rich nature. In the other camp, the Mato Grosso elites generally viewed Indians as 'savage, indolent and, ideally, destined for extinction'. Progress and development could come only from industrious white men farming 'legally acquired' lands. This was all wrong—Indians were not savage, they worked hard, and if not molested they would survive. And, as we have seen, the notion of white men succeeding in tropical rainforests was absurd: they had always been defeated by the climate, poor soils, overpowering vegetation, and voracious insects and pests. At that time, only indigenous people could live within forests without destroying them. And indigenous lands bought from the state government would not be 'legally acquired'.

At the end of 1955 Brazil elected a new president, Juscelino Kubitschek. His passion was the creation of a new national capital called Brasilia deep in the interior of the country; but he was uninterested in the proposed Xingu Park. Nevertheless, the parliamentary inquiry about it continued to hear witnesses, although many of these were hostile. The state governor suggested greatly reducing the size of the park, or even moving it away from the Xingu altogether—to the north-western corner of his state. Gama Malcher was replaced as director of the SPI by a series of incompetent and sometimes corrupt military men. One of these proposed that the park be reduced to 4,800 square kilometres (1,850 square miles)—a tiny fraction of the original proposal of over 200,000 square kilometres (77,000 miles)—because his service was too poor to manage a huge area, ignoring the facts that these natural forests needed no husbandry and the self-sufficient Indians cost the SPI very little. Opponents kept trying delaying tactics. In April 1956 one of these succeeded: they persuaded the Chamber of Deputies to refer the matter to the Commission of the Constitution and Justice, a move that paralysed the entire process. When Orlando went to seek help from President Kubitschek he found him indifferent. The president at first claimed that he could do nothing because he did not have a majority in the Chamber. Later, in 1959, he argued that the next election was too imminent for him to act.

Everything changed at the end of 1960. Jânio Quadros, the governor of the state of São Paulo, was elected president with the largest landslide in Brazilian history. In his early forties, thin and with a black moustache, bursting with energy, incorrupt, efficient, and effective, he was a liberal with right-of-centre pragmatism.

Quadros was a personal friend of the Villas Boas, and he had seen the wonderful world of the Xingu. He promptly sacked the head of the FBC. He sent a plane to fetch Jorge Ferreira, the reporter for *O Cruzeiro* who had done so much to publicize the brothers' achievements, to Brasilia, and said to him: 'I want you to be president of the Central Brazil Foundation, which is about to create what you and the Villas Boas have been dreaming about for so long: the National Park of the Xingu. I attach only one condition. You must first go to converse with the governor of Mato Grosso' to get his consent. So Ferreira went to the state capital Cuiabá, spent four hours with the newly re-elected governor Correa da Costa, and got him to release 25,000 square kilometres for the park. On 5 April 1961 Ferreira wrote to President Quadros about his meeting (already signing himself as director of the FBC). He reiterated the unique qualities of the Xinguanos compared to wretched tribes in other parts of Brazil, and of the region's natural environment. He felt that colonists who had been granted lands must be compensated, but only for the minimal value of their title deeds, and with nothing going to the property companies. Ferreira then reported that the governor 'would not oppose, for an instant, the creation of the Indigenous Park of the Xingu *on the proposed terms*'. The most significant term was a drastic shrinking of its size from the 1952 proposal—as Ferreira had been instructed to concede by the president. Ferreira then defined new boundaries for a far smaller park, which would embrace little more than the heartland of the Xinguano peoples on the fan of headwaters and those on the main Xingu around Diauarum.

The park legislation should have been passed by Congress, but the machinations of the previous eight years showed that the national legislature might never have approved it. So Quadros made use of his presidential fiat. He issued Decree 50,455 of 14 April 1961 (ratified as Decree 51,084 of 31 July 1961) which 'Created the National Park of the Xingu'.

These decrees placed the park directly under the presidency of the Republic—unlike any other indigenous territory. Its area was roughly 22,000 square kilometres (8,500 square miles), and its boundaries were as agreed between Jorge Ferreira and the governor of Mato Grosso. The northern limit at 10°S was just above the Von Martius rapids; and the southern at 12°S included much of the Xingu's headwaters. It was the western and eastern sides that were dramatically truncated from the 1952 draft law. Instead of stretching west to the Teles Pires and east into Xavante lands, the park just included much of the upper Xingu headwaters and a stretch of the main Xingu around Diauarum. The sources of all the southern headwaters and western and eastern tributaries lay outside the park's protection. At that time this did not seem to matter, because the entire region was covered in pristine forests and *campo* watered by unpolluted rivers; but decades later this omission was deeply regretted.

The second decree listed the five admirable objectives of the Xingu National Park:[†]

1. To preserve the pristine flora and fauna of the region against any form of damage, 'because these are an example of Brazilian nature and are of aesthetic and scientific value to the national patrimony';
2. To ensure for the indigenous peoples living there the possession of the areas they occupy, according to their rights in the Federal Constitution;
3. To guarantee the indigenous peoples the medical, social and educational assistance they need for their survival, but while preserving their cultural heritage;
4. Promote research in all natural and social sciences within the Park's area;
5. Superintend tourist activities in the area, ensuring that these avoid any form of harm to the indigenous groups or the natural patrimony that they preserve.

[†] In these 1961 decrees it was called the Xingu National Park, whereas in the draft Act of 1952 it had been the Xingu Indigenous Park (PIX). In 1968 it reverted to the 'Indigenous' title, and it is still known as this. Of course, it was never a 'national park' that could be visited by tourists, but a closed indigenous reservation of massive size.

The decree went on to define the duties and remit of the administrator-general. He would be appointed by and answer to the president of Brazil, although he would also be a special delegate of both the SPI and of the National Bureau of Hunting and Fishing. Other clauses dealt with the park's finances (which came directly from the presidency) and its administration. All sales of land within the park area were invalidated; and surveyors, prospectors, or any other intruders would immediately be expelled. The Brazilian Air Force would sign an agreement with the park concerning its installations within and services to it.

* * *

State legislators and property speculators of Mato Grosso were not the only critics of the Xingu Park. Helmut Sick, the scientist on the Roncador–Xingu Expedition, noted that 'the Church did not regard the idea of a reserve with favour, since it was intent on prosecuting its missionary work for the conversion of the natives'. Missionaries knew that they would not be allowed to proselytize in the Xingu Park. Other critics claimed that it was wrong to keep Xingu indigenous people isolated from outside society, which they would have to enter sooner or later. Still others deplored Indians being paraded as glamorous curiosities for the delectation of visitors. Then there was the opposite objection: that the Indians were not as pristine or isolated as was depicted, so that they would just be artificial curiosities. Some conspiracy theorists thought that the new park was a sham, a cover for a clandestine air force and army base. Another, later, criticism was that the Xingu Park denied the Xavante to the east the large territory that was their constitutional right—they got only an 'archipelago' of small reserves surrounded by farms and ranches. This was deplorable, but it was not the fault of the Xingu activists, who had included much Xavante territory in their original 1952 proposal.

The various critics of the new Xingu Park were a minority, and their objections were easily refuted. Most commentators were highly enthusiastic about this bold experiment, the first vast national park in South America, created for the benefit of both indigenous peoples and unspoiled nature. Helmut Sick felt that it was a humane plan, done out of pity for the Indians whose forests would otherwise have been stolen from them. The anthropologist George Zarur was delighted that it was based on two principles: 'cultural relativism' as propounded by Franz Boas (the influential German anthropologist who applauded cultural diversity, but opposed racist notions that some cultures were superior to others); and Rondon's humanist tradition of Brazilian respect for indigenous peoples. For Zarur, the park was 'a fundamental advance in human rights'. Another anthropologist, Antonio Carlos de Souza Lima, reminded readers that 'the idea of an indigenous park did not exist in legislation at that time'. So he hailed it as a new model for defining indigenous lands, with its immense area. He ridiculed the notion that the park had been created to be a military base, because the idea for it came from anthropologists and scientists. Above all, it was a tribute to the Villas Boas brothers and to the Xinguanos themselves. Thanks to the airstrips built by the brothers, politicians and journalists had seen the beautiful region and its admirable peoples. President Quadros knew, when he rammed the park into law, that he could rely on his Villas Boas friends to administer it humanely and efficiently. They and their colleagues had triumphantly weathered eight years of political and public relations wrangling—for which they had as little training or experience as they had had for exploration or anthropology or social science.

7

POSTO LEONARDO

In 1954 the Villas Boas had to leave their once-happy Jacaré camp. This was because the Brazilian Air Force (FAB) had decided to make it their permanent base in the region. They eventually constructed military buildings and an improved runway, and renamed it simply 'Xingu'. Inevitably, some purists condemned this move, arguing that it is wrong to establish a military installation in the heart of what was to become the first protected indigenous park in South America. But the brothers were pragmatists who appreciated the huge advantages of having an air force base there.

During what proved to be the next twenty years, they enjoyed regular *free* transport on a military service known as CAN (Correo Aéreo Nacional: National Air Mail). Skilled air force pilots mostly flew the wartime workhorse Douglas C-47 military transport planes.* These wonderfully versatile twin-propeller aircraft could take up to thirty passengers on metal benches along the sides, with a mass of freight in the middle. They could land on unlit dirt airstrips. CAN's weekly service in this part of central Brazil eventually consisted of hopping along a chain of bases from Aragarças to Xavantina (two towns where the Roncador–Xingu Expedition had its original camps), to Xingu, then Cachimbo, and on to Jacareacanga on the lower Tapajós.

Air became the only means of access to the upper Xingu—nobody used the long overland and river trail any more. Also, because this was a military service, its planes took off from air force bases so that it was easy to exclude

---

* From 1942 onwards, the Douglas Aircaft Company in California built a staggering 16,000 C-47 Skytrains (also called Dakotas). These helped win the war as the basic transport aircraft, and continued in civilian service all over the world for the next thirty years. Douglas merged with McDonnell Aircraft Corporation in 1967, and was absorbed by Boeing in 1997.

the adventurers of the Amazon forests—rubber-tappers (*seringueiros*), fur trappers (*gateiros*), mining prospectors (*garimpeiros*), land-grabbers (*grileiros*), or loggers (*mateiros*). In time, the Xingu base did create a problem as an unregulated source of goods for the indigenous people; but the transport benefits far outweighed this. Orlando knew that regular free flights were the key to everything. Without them the Villas Boas could never have operated permanently in the Xingu. So he made sure that the pilots were welcomed with coffee and gifts of Indian bows and feather-work, joked with them, and listened to their stories of postings and past friends. The pilot officers generally liked and admired the Indians, and were therefore pleased to be able to help them.

Having ceded Jacaré to the air force, the brothers had to find a new base. In 1954 they started to build a wooden hut on the Tuatuari tributary of the Culuene, about 20 kilometres (12 miles) due south of their earlier camp. They called this new installation Posto Capitão Vasconcellos, after the Indian Protection Service (SPI) official (and later its director) who had mapped and reported on these rivers in 1924–5. Tragically, in 1961, the year in which the Xingu National Park became law, the dashing Leonardo Villas Boas died. This was during a heart operation in São Paulo. One of the three cardiologists performing this was their great friend Dr Murillo Villela, who decades later told me in great medical detail how he and his colleagues had worked for hours but had been unable to save the forty-one-year-old. Orlando and Claudio were grief-stricken at the loss of their beloved brother, with whom they had shared so many adventures. They had long since forgiven his liaison with the beautiful Kamaiurá Mavirá. As a tribute, they immediately changed the name of their new post from Vasconcellos to Leonardo—which it has remained ever since.

Throughout the 1950s, the Villas Boas had a curious triangular working arrangement: the Central Brazil Foundation paid their modest salaries and those of their workmen, in return asking them to build airstrips and cut trails; the air force used these landing grounds and provided free transport; and the SPI appointed the brothers as its representatives, providing tools and presents for Indians, but actually paying the wages of only a handful of helpers at the post.

What was to become the Xingu Indigenous Park came to be administered, from 1955 to the present, from two posts: Leonardo (originally Vasconcellos) for the Xinguano peoples of the headwater rivers; and Diauarum for tribes downstream on the main Xingu—Juruna, Metuktire, Kaiabi, and Suiá. The two posts were 170 kilometres (106 miles) apart, which meant either an agreeable rapids-free river voyage that lasted two days, or flights of twenty minutes between the two grass airstrips. The journey from Leonardo started on the Tuatuari, which soon joined the Culuene, flowing between banks of low woods, stretches of *campo*, or burned patches, with broad sandbanks at the end of the dry season. The scenery changed at the sacred site Morená, where the headwaters merge to form the main Xingu river. This is an expanse of waters that disappear into a maze of mysterious lagoons and channels. Beyond, the Xingu is 200 metres (650 feet) wide with lucid velvety green waters reflecting banks of high rainforest festooned with creepers. Its surface can be glassily smooth, broken by occasional fish leaping. There is vibrant bird life, hundreds of species from skimmers on the surface, falcons gliding along the treeline, fishing herons and egrets, and flights of ducks and toucans or macaws high above. The forest walls are unbroken, apart from some clearings for travellers to sling their hammocks. The few small indigenous settlements are usually located away from the river, to escape seasonal flooding.

During the two decades until 1975, Orlando Villas Boas was at Posto Leonardo and Claudio downriver to the north at Diauarum. In the early days, a few malcontents who were frustrated by being excluded from the Xingu—missionaries, adventurers, tourists, and fantasists—spread rumours that the Villas Boas were living in luxury, or that they had stumbled across gold that had eluded seventeenth-century *bandeirantes*, or that they indulged in orgies. The reality could not have been more different. By the late 1950s, Vasconcellos (later Leonardo) was still just a clearing in low woods, with charcoal-burned or rotting tree-stumps strewn around its five or six small huts and one large one. The main building was a log palisade with a matted thatch roof supported by three great tree trunks. Within, there was an earth floor but no windows—such light as there was entered through cracks between the log walls. The interior was dank and gloomy, with no furniture other than hammocks. The surrounding huts were for storage, utilities, and housing workers, and some had corrugated-iron rather than thatched roofs. There were farmyard pigs, dogs, and chickens. Local pets—parrots, a macaw, a woodpecker, a stork, and a black mutum curassow—wandered in and out of the main hut.

Orlando often lay in his hammock with the tame macaw grumbling on his shoulder. The atmosphere was very quiet. Indians came at any time to chat to Orlando, who would joke with them and pass on gossip from other tribes. An Indian might paddle up the Tuatuari, with his wife, son, hammock, and pot, just to pass time and tell some story to Orlando. This informality was deliberate. The Villas Boas had realized, almost instinctively, that hours of idle conversation were more effective than 'the usual missionary trilogy—religion, education, sanitation'. So there was no bustle. At this early stage, Orlando felt that 'schools and religion could be as destructive to Indians as the bullets of pioneers. ... What seem to us the benefits of civilization [could] be the tools of destruction for the Indians.'

In the post, food was as simple as the accommodation. It always included the staples of the Brazilian interior: black beans known as *feijão*, rice and corn (grown by some SPI-employed workmen), and manioc (supplied abundantly by Indian women). The indigenous people regularly caught fish. For Brazilians and visitors there was coffee, sugar, salt, and meat, with a few other luxuries such as guava jelly or fresh fruit, all flown in on air force planes. Orlando later reminisced that 'We ate very well. ... The staple diet was corn, manioc, and lots of fish. The fish was so fresh it flapped its tail in the frying pan. I loved not only the food, but the way of life. Everything was very healthy.'

There were always Indian volunteers working at the post and in its kitchen. The Kaiabi were the best, because they were hard-working, efficient, and cheerfully cooperative, and also because they had experienced white men's ways when they were on the Teles Pires. Their chief, Sabino, had helped to build a post for the SPI when he was there. Thus, when he migrated into the Xingu in 1955, he spent a year or two with Claudio in Diauarum, and then supervised a team of his people improving Posto Leonardo's huts and opening its manioc clearings. Sabino then became Orlando's right hand in running the post. When the Villas Boas contacted the Metuktire and in 1954 boldly took their chief, Krumare, upriver to meet his former enemies, Krumare's sons, the half-brothers Bebcuche and Rauni, remained in the upper Xingu for many months. They were hopeless at cooking rice in the kitchen, but they learned much by watching the more sophisticated Xinguanos, and they picked up some Portuguese.

The other post, Diauarum, downriver to the north, was just as basic as Leonardo. It had a lovelier location, raised on a bluff in a curve of the Xingu so that it had views along the river and to forests on the far bank. The Villas Boas completed its airstrip as early as 1948, and Claudio developed a very modest camp there in 1954. But it was only after his arduous trail-cutting and opening airstrips from Cachimbo to the Teles Pires, in 1957–8, that Claudio returned to reside permanently at Diauarum. By the end of that decade Diauarum was still just a few log-and-thatch huts. Adrian Cowell likened these to medieval serfs' hovels, with the chinks in their wattle walls daubed with mud. The main hut was far smaller than the one at Leonardo, containing just a table, little carved stools, home-made racks for the few dishes and mugs, and a clay pitcher of water. Outside was a sunlit rack of dried fish and meat. The 400-metre (1,300-foot) red-earth airstrip lay beyond the straggly line of huts, and also ran parallel to the river. This landing ground was rarely used. A small plane was supposed to come every two months with food and supplies such as petrol or tools; but on the rare occasions when it did, the pilot usually forgot one or other of these cargoes. So the post often went hungry. This was exacerbated when vampire bats flew in from the surrounding forest and killed a few domestic chickens and pigs. Vampires (*Vampyrus auritus*) are the only bats that attack large animals: they drink their blood, at night, without waking the victim thanks to anaesthetic and anti-coagulant saliva. Diauarum boasted some pequi-fruit trees (the Indians' great favourite) planted by the Suiá; but an attempt to grow European fruit trees failed because of voracious *saúba* (leafcutter ants).

In 1960 the Villas Boas were in political trouble, and Orlando was even banished from his new Posto Vasconellos. Both were threatened with dismissal from the SPI. This was partly because of their outspoken condemnation of their boss, the director of the Central Brazil Foundation (FBC), Arquimedes Lima, whom they accused of conniving with the governor of Mato Grosso in the sale of indigenous land. They were also in trouble for having helped a fugitive Indian, who was accused of having killed an oppressive official, to return to his people. The man was a Je-speaking Krahó, a tribe who lived far to the east on the upper Tocantins river and who had been in contact with frontier society for over a century. The brothers never actually left the Xingu. However, what really saved them at the end of that year was national politics: the election as president of their friend, the dynamic Jânio Quadros. Quadros immediately sacked the corrupt FBC director, and reinstated the admirable brothers at their Post. The new head of the FBC was another great friend, the journalist Jorge Ferreira.

By 1961, when the Xingu Park became law, the Villas Boas had come a long way from the city boys looking for adventure, who in 1944 had joined the FBC. Now in their late forties, they were famous as explorers who had spent fifteen years in the wilds and were known to be wonderfully kind with the Indians. Not only did they look very different to one another, but they were developing distinct and eccentric characters. Orlando was short, at 1.65 metres (5 foot 6 inches), stocky, often half-naked with a small pot belly bulging over home-made shorts of bottle-green parachute silk. His strength was in his powerful face, the sort chosen by movie casting directors. He had a hawk nose, imperial-style beard, and leathery skin with lines of hardship—and humour. Adrian Cowell thought that he looked like a saint or a pirate, but overall 'he might have been an attendant in a Turkish bath'. Although well educated at school and highly intelligent, Orlando's reading was simple: popular books, detective novels, and even comics that were regularly brought in by the transport planes.

By contrast, the indomitable explorer Claudio did not look the part. He had a strange, slightly tubby shape, and would wear an ordinary shirt hanging out of cotton trousers or old jeans or denims cut into shorts. Both brothers wore flip-flop sandals, as did most people in central Brazil. When Claudio returned from one of his tremendous expeditions, he would carry only a bag of manioc over his shoulder, and his complexion would be pale from all those months in the forest shade. He wore glasses, either round granny spectacles or sunglasses. Unlike Orlando with his strong face and extrovert personality, Claudio had a mild, modest, and gentle manner. He was happiest lying in his hammock for hours on end, chatting to Indians. Men and women (particularly women) knew that they could wander in at any time, and often let their babies crawl over the small bearded man. They would converse quietly, in the endless monotony that is normal and polite in Xingu society. I remember him as affectionate but dignified with the Indians. He knew when to joke or have horseplay with them, although with less jocularity than Orlando. He was firm about commands, and received complete obedience. With outsiders, however, he was different, more diffident.

A keen reader and amateur philosopher, Claudio loved dipping into the piles of books in his scruffy hut, and would then lie gazing up at the roof and pondering sociology. Already in the 1950s his reading included Jacques Maritain about Aquinas, Bertrand Russell's history of philosophy, a pamphlet by Stalin, and propaganda about the Great Leap Forward in Mao's China. Between silences he might launch into hours of talking about his half-digested theories. For Cowell, this was 'the enthusiasm of an undergraduate at his first vision of a Socialist Utopia.' This emerged as 'rushing, cascading, pouring talk. He spoke very quickly, digressing through philosophers. ... He argued, thundered, exhorted ... metaphysics at breakneck speed.' I recall him using his hands expressively as he talked, eloquently and quickly, with sudden stress on individual words as though he was reciting poetry. The Indians would watch, bemused by a style that was so different to their own formal speech-making.

Sydney Possuelo (who was to become the last of the great *sertanista* indigenist–explorers) spent months alone with Claudio as his young assistant at Diauarum in the late 1950s. Sydney remembered starlit nights lying on a sandbank beside the Xingu conversing with this 'quiet, introspective and solitary' man. 'It was at these moments that his soul seemed to float into infinity in philosophical considerations—that I could not follow.' But even if outsiders failed to grasp Claudio's political theories, 'we were all deeply impressed by his clear thinking about indigenous affairs and his grasp of individual Indians' attitudes, identities and beliefs'.

Claudio seemed able to go for long periods without either food or sleep, and when he did eat it might be at night, contentedly munching leftovers in the cooking pans. There were a few hens at Diauarum, but these were being killed by the vampire bats from the surrounding forest. So Claudio made a pen to protect his poultry: a henhouse of 3 x 4 metres (10 x 13 feet) whose walls of upright posts with daub in the cracks were considered bat-proof. 'He made it with such skill and care that, when it was finished, *he himself* moved into the hen house, saying: "It's too good for hens." He lived in that tiny hut until he left the Xingu, on retirement.' I recall this cluttered bedroom, with an iron bedstead in the midst of shelves of dusty boxes, cardboard suitcases, and piles of books. These Spartan surroundings were not done for effect, but were because Claudio was an unpretentious man who had other priorities in life. His only luxury, books aside, was a most surprising hobby: collecting guns. He had fifteen fine revolvers and rifles, all scrupulously oiled, which he occasionally used when hunting.

In those years before and after the Xingu Park became law, each brother continued learning more about the indigenous peoples in his area. It is worth recalling that neither had any training in dealing with Indians, nor anthropological or other relevant academic studies. As they were not linguists, they relied on words of indigenous languages they were learning, or on interpretation by the few Indians who had picked up some Portuguese. Yet they managed to understand the inter-tribal politics of each people and the characters of its chiefs, shamans, and other important people. They also learned (and later wrote popular books about) the ethnography and mythology of the tribes. And they evolved a totally new philosophy about how to help these fascinating but vulnerable peoples.

The Villas Boas did enjoy some unique advantages. In the headwaters plateau, they had stumbled across a federation of tribes with identical elaborate cultures, who by geographical accident had survived intact into the twentieth century. Then, fourteen years after their arrival in the region, the 1961 law creating the Xingu Indigenous Park meant that they and their budget came directly under the president of Brazil. So they answered to no one else—their earlier employer the FBC (which had never had any brief for helping Indians) was abolished in 1963, and although they had accreditation from the SPI they were not its employees. Another unique advantage, as we have seen, was that the park enjoyed regular and free movement of goods and passengers in air force planes. So the brothers were the first non-missionaries able to reside permanently with indigenous peoples within tropical rainforests.

The planes also brought journalists and politicians. Already well known as explorers from the Roncador–Xingu Expedition, the Villas Boas now gained renown as humanitarians caring for the very photogenic 'original Brazilians'. They were savvy enough to welcome visits by politicians of every political persuasion, and did not reveal their political or religious feelings (although Claudio was certainly left wing). All that mattered to them was the Indians, whose survival ultimately depended on politicians, who answered to voters, who were influenced by the media. So by cultivating journalists and politicians the Villas Boas were greatly helping the indigenous cause. At this time in the mid-twentieth century, everyone was aware that there were still scores of tribes throughout the Amazonian forests who remained isolated, uncontacted, and potentially hostile. Most of those Indians were very remote and difficult to reach; and none enjoyed the unique advantages of the Xinguanos.

The Xingu peoples were hunter-gatherers and fishermen with only rudimentary agriculture—little more than manioc, the only major food crop that can grow within tropical forests. Because of the bio-geographical isolation of the Americas and the lack of pasture in forests, they had no domestic or draught animals. They used no metal, and very little pottery or stone. But, unlike African or Asian hunter-gatherers, they were not threatened by large predators—jaguars were the only big cats, and they rarely attacked humans. It is now accepted that pre-agricultural, pre-pastoral, pre-literate, and pre-metal societies could enjoy good lives in terms of social stability, cultural development, and personal happiness. This was certainly the case with the Xinguanos.

The day in a Xingu village starts with bathing. An hour before dawn, every naked man, woman, and child leaves a cool hammock, having slept without covering but above a fire. All run joyfully the few hundred metres to their lake or river, often shouting out its name. They plunge into the water, slightly warmer than the night air, with ecstatic yelps of sheer delight. They never cease to marvel at the pleasure of being back in the luxury of water. Scrupulously clean, Indians bathe three or four times a day, and if they see a stream or pond on their travels they cannot resist plunging in. As dawn rises, the men may swim out like porpoises, the women soak and then stride out with jerking steps like a chorus line. They smooth water off their gleaming bodies and down their long black hair, and some may then anoint themselves with juice from a vine. The children play endlessly in the shallows, jumping and splashing, or diving in repeatedly from tree branches.

After this the day begins, and every creature's main concern is food. This is a constant task, taking up most of their time, skill, and energy—particularly for the women. After the delicious dawn swim, the men might paddle off into the morning mist to fish or hunt. Every visitor to the Xingu has sublime memories of watching canoes glide into the middle of a stunningly beautiful lake, or down a river, with one man paddling gently and the other standing motionless as a statue in the prow. Most fishing was by bow and arrow. The prow-man could see a fish in the clear waters, instantly calculate its speed and the angle of refraction, and then shoot with uncanny speed and accuracy. His arrow, attached to a liana cord, would suddenly be bobbing and wriggling in the stricken fish. Other fish might be caught in spindly traps fixed in weirs and rapids, but there were few of these in the flat upper Xingu. At the end of the dry season, when waters are low, it is possible to douse a small stream with the sap of a liana called *timbó* (*Lonchocarpus utilis*), whose rotenone poison stuns fish but does not make them inedible. This *timbó* fishing is a joyous communal effort, with men and women smashing the sap out of the creepers, then gleefully catching basketsful of unconscious fish as they rise stunned to the surface. The great funerary ceremony *kuarup* is always held at this time of year, because the host village has to accumulate vast quantities of sun-dried fish to feed all the visiting peoples. The end of the dry season is also the time when thousands of turtle eggs may be dug up from sandbanks, and provide important added nutrient to a simple diet.

As noted, the upper Xinguano tribes ate fish, supplemented by a few monkeys and forest birds—unlike the omnivore Juruna, Metuktire, Kaiabi, and Suiá downriver on the main Xingu, who avidly hunted and consumed any forest game. But all indigenous men adored hunting. This was their great skill, the main topic of conversation around the men's hut in the evening, and the ambition for all boys. Adrian Cowell decided to learn something of this art. He became friends with a young Aweti called Kaluana, and the two would plunge into the forest, sometimes for several days, with only hammocks, salt, and guns. Cowell gradually learned some of the tricks: understanding and imitating bird calls, calculating where flocks of monkeys were heading as they swung through the trees so that they would crash towards the waiting hunters, knowing the likely perches of different birds, or the tracks of larger animals. Of course, the young Englishman could never match an Indian in the speed and grace with which he flits through the forest, nor in his acute hearing and vision, or the ability to freeze on an instant in any position. But in a few months Cowell became fairly proficient and successful as a hunter. He also found himself behaving like an Indian, becoming as thrilled as they by the

93

excitement of hunting. He lapsed into an unthinking rhythm in those hot months, rising at dawn, stalking in the forest for hours on end, shooting, killing, eating as much as he could when food was available, and then retiring to his hammock in a state of oblivion. He found that he lost interest in the minutiae and motivation of his earlier existence, thinking like an Indian and taking each day as it came. Cowell's life revolved around this hunting for food. He was untroubled by insects or other irritants, and no longer appreciated in the beauty or scientific importance of his surroundings. Rivers became just a source of fish, the forest of interest only for its potential game, and sunshine or rain significant just for their effect on hunting.

Cowell's lack of ambition during this period made him more acceptable to the Indians; and it gave him greater understanding of and sympathy for people 'whose only goal was existence' rather than some purposeful pursuit of progress. For a while he felt that the difference between the two societies was not primitive versus modern, but rather 'the chasm between men who live in the jungle and those who live in our civilization'.

There was nothing new about this contrast. Brazil's indigenous peoples had always been hunter-gatherers with some agriculture, who kept their populations small and knew that the forests, savannahs, and rivers would always be their larder whenever they chose to hunt or fish in them. As long ago as the 1550s the French had founded a colony on the bay of Rio de Janeiro—from which the warlike Portuguese and their native allies soon expelled them. But during that period a wise old Indian told the French pastor Jean de Léry that he thought that those strangers were crazy to cross the ocean to seek wealth from dyes in logs of brazilwood (*Caesalpinia echinata*). 'Is the land that nourished you not sufficient to feed your children also? We have fathers, mothers and children whom we love. But we are certain that the land that nourished us will also feed them. We therefore rest without further cares.' This lack of materialist greed inspired Michel de Montaigne in his famous essay 'Des cannibales', then Jean-Jacques Rousseau's vision of the 'noble savage', and from them other philosophers, including even Karl Marx.

Adrian Cowell's immersion in indigenous thinking, his hunting skills, and his personal rapport with individuals such as the Metuktire half-brothers Rauni and Bebcuche endeared him to the Villas Boas brothers. 'Adriano' was their favourite of all the foreigners who visited the Xingu. After he left, Orlando often wrote to him with candid views about his treatment by the authorities and about politics and politicians. (Surprisingly, copies of these letters are in the archive of the indigenous service Funai in Brasilia—which seems unaware of how violently they criticize it.) As we shall see, Orlando later lured Cowell back for an important contact expedition.

Manioc is the staple food of Amazonian peoples, accounting for three-quarters of their consumption. It is the men's task to open clearings in the forest (known as *roças*) in which to plant manioc bushes. In the past this had been a huge task, because it could take weeks to cut down a large tree using blunt stone axes. (This changed dramatically with the advent of steel axes, so that men gained more leisure time and the gender balance was changed forever.) The felled trees and vegetation in a *roça* were allowed to dry during the hot months, then burned, and manioc cuttings were planted amid the ashes. These cuttings were set into mounds of loose earth a metre or so apart, with up to 15,000 bushes per hectare (2½ acres). At any time, a village would have up to 40 hectares (100 acres) of clearings around it, so it might have 60,000 manioc plants. Each *roça* lasted about three years. The men built fences in a vain attempt to keep out packs of pig-like peccary, who caused massive losses by routing up the growing tubers. (The peccary were not poisoned by the manioc's prussic acid (cyanide) because this was released by an enzyme only after the roots had been dug up and had dried.)

Daily tasks are divided between the sexes, and neither would dream of doing the other's work. As we have seen, men fish and hunt, they fell forest to make clearings, they build houses (a major, but infrequent, communal effort), and they make bows, arrows, and other weapons or tools. But women work far more than men. They have to fetch water every day. This is a hard and monotonous chore, for it is always a fair distance from the lake or stream to the village, and the vessels (of gourds or pottery) were so heavy that older women could damage spinal columns or lower limbs. (In modern times, this has improved slightly with lighter aluminium pots; and some villages now have wells or pumped water.)

The women's main concern is with manioc. During the long dry season they work on this from dawn to dusk. The manioc *roças* can be up to 6 kilometres (almost 4 miles) from the village. Women usually go to the clearings in the early morning before the midday heat, dig up manioc roots, and carry the thick tubers back, in huge baskets on their heads or on their backs, stooped and with a strap around their foreheads. They then scrape the roots with a clam shell, and grate them on a board studded with sharp bones, slivers of palmwood, or stones. There follows a long process of washings over a sieve, wringing out the pulp, and successive boilings to remove cyanide. Squeezed lumps are dried in the sun. The result of this work is a pure flour called *tepeac* (*farinha* in Portuguese) that is the basis of all tribal food, and a secondary powder called *teparaté* that is stored in great silos. Lumps of dry flour are moistened with water or fish juice, beaten flat with a paddle, and

95

baked in a broad pan into pancakes like unleavened bread called *beijús*.
Otherwise the flour is boiled in water to make *cauim* gruel, perhaps flavoured
with fruit; or it is roasted into granules. Women thus spend hours every day
processing manioc, stopping only to care for their children or prepare
meals. This work is particularly intense in the dry months, when they labour
to accumulate a large surplus. Each village likes to store great quantities of
flour, to see it through the rainy season and to be generous hosts. But Indians
had to allow for the depredations of *saúba* (leafcutter ants), who carried
masses of *farinha* grains back to their underground anthills—before whites
brought in ant-proof metal containers.

The garden clearings might also contain a few other crops such as corn or
beans, or the cotton which was used for arm-bands and hammocks, along
with annatto bushes (*Bixa Orellana*) for their dazzling red dye and genipap for
black, gourds for containers, or straight arrow-canes for arrows. Later came
a few imported fruits and vegetables. But manioc was always the plant that
really mattered.

One of the few delicacies in the monotonous Xingu diet is the fruit of the
pequi tree (*Caryocar brasiliensis*), one of the giants of the forest. Indians adore
this fruit, which ripens in November and December. There is great excitement when the fruit falls from the tall trees. But processing pequi is laborious
work—another chore for the women. Women and children gather it, and
then work late into the night to boil it before rot can set in, then scrape the
pulp off each seed, and pack them in cylindrical baskets of woven bark and
leaves. Some pequi is eaten raw, but most is processed for storage, placed in
baskets in streams for many months, and the yellow pulp then mixed with
water or manioc gruel to produce an excellent cold soup. The fruit can be
roasted, to taste like egg yolk or devilled eggs. Or it can be fermented, causing the anthropologist Ellen Basso to comment that 'the Kalapalo prize fermented pequi pulp, since its vinegary taste is a welcome change from their
usually bland diet'.

Despite all this work, Aritana Yawalapiti, the genial paramount chief of the
Xinguanos, claimed that the status of women was generally good. 'All women
are respected,' he declared, 'especially the older ones. ... Women have the
same authority as men and they are not ordered around. In some villages,
women have the same positions as male chiefs.' But the reality is rather different. Although women are the basis of village economies, and relations
between the sexes can be affectionate, their status is lowly. For a start, they
do not join in the men's evening discussions in the village plaza, and thus have
no say in tribal policy. They are forbidden to see the sacred flutes or enter the

men's hut. They take no lead in ceremonies or dances or sporting competitions, and generally wear fewer feathers or ornaments than males. (There are, however, occasional festivals only for women.) Perhaps as a reaction, they often form a collective bond in a village, gossip happily with their peers, and can tease the men about such matters as their performance as hunters or lovers. The women are strong, both mentally and physically. Marriages are loving, and domestic violence as we know it would be unthinkable in a communal house: any man behaving like that would be despised by his peers. Women can have influence through sex and, as Aritana said, there are occasionally highly respected matriarchs and female shamans.

But, although men do much work, the women are born to drudgery. As Adrian Cowell noted, 'Men may rest, sport, or philosophise after the day's work is done, but women are seldom seen away from tasks.' The American anthropologist Thomas Gregor echoed this view, in his perceptive study of the Aruak-speaking Mehinaku. Back in the village after a morning of hunting, fishing, or wandering in the forest looking for medicinal plants, the men have a meal of fish and manioc, and might then play flutes, work on making artefacts such as bows and arrows, or simply relax in their hammocks.

On fine days, mid-afternoon could be a time for wrestling. The men gather in front of the men's house in the centre of the village, decorate themselves with red *urucum* and black charcoal or genipap sap, and have a few bouts of tough but friendly *huka-huka* wrestling. Men pair off, crouching, and try to grab an opponent's upper leg and throw him to the ground. The name *huka-huka* is onomatopoeic from the wrestlers' grunts. It is fast and furious, but all over in a moment and no pain is inflicted. There is no triumphalism, either by the victor or by his watching fans: after a bout, the fighters embrace and simply stroll off. This muscular sport helps give Xinguanos their beautiful physiques.

In the late afternoon husbands and wives might pair off to tend their forest gardens, gather firewood for the night (they sleep with no covering, just a small fire near their hammocks), and have sex either in the forest or in their part of the communal house. Then, if there is fresh fish, they could have another meal. At dusk the older men sit and chat in the middle of the plaza, smoking cheroots of some tobacco-like leaves. Younger men stroll around, often arm in arm, or might have sex with their girlfriends. In the village where Gregor lived, 'by eight o'clock the smokers return to their houses to chat with their wives and families. Sometimes one of the men will tell a story, or two of the older women will join in singing songs about forest animals. Gradually the conversation dies out and the Mehinaku sleep.'

8

HEALTH

The Villas Boas were understandably shattered by the mortality in the influenza epidemics of 1947–8 and measles after 1954. They had also learned how all the Xingu's indigenous peoples had been devastated during the sixty years before their arrival. So health was of the utmost importance. There was no point in trying to help Indians if they died of disease.

Some fine doctors had tried to stem the epidemics of the late 1940s and 1950s; but their visits were temporary. Then there was the legendary Dr Noel Nutels. Born in 1913 in a Ukrainian Jewish family, Nutels was brought to Brazil as a boy and studied medicine at Brazilian universities. He joined the Roncador–Xingu Expedition at its outset in 1943 as a malaria specialist, with his entomologist wife Elisa. During a quarter-century he then treated Indians and settlers throughout the Brazilian interior. Nutels created a flying-doctor service known as SUSA (Service of Aerial Health Units) with four teams, travelling in DC-47s, tirelessly vaccinating, X-raying, and treating tuberculosis and all the other diseases of the poor colonist frontier. Their workload was prodigious, covering 200,000 kilometres (125,000 miles) a year by every form of transport, performing tens of thousands of X-rays and an even greater number of vaccinations. Noel Nutels loved Indians, and they adored him. He knew every Indian by name and joked with each. Whenever he flew in, the Xinguanos would run joyfully to the airstrip to welcome him, and laugh at his comic greetings. 'He seemed a giant ... with his vast white head of hair, thick dark eyebrows, immense grey moustache, high forehead, firm nose and jutting chin, lively eyes ... and booming voice.' He wore a short-sleeved shirt, and his skin was white but his face sunburned. I experienced his charm, exuberant vitality, and wisdom. For Orlando he was a kindred spirit, both in his extrovert good humour, repertoire of jokes, and rapport with Indians, and in his sensible ideas about indigenist policy. Orlando named his second son Noel after his great friend, and was heartbroken when Dr Nutels died in 1973.

The only drawback about Noel Nutels was that he had such a workload that his visits to the Xingu were sporadic. The Villas Boas needed permanent resident medical attention for their Indians. In 1963, when Orlando was on one of his visits to São Paulo, he asked his personal doctor, his friend Dr Murillo Villela, where he could find help, and was introduced to the doctor's twenty-six-year-old nurse, Marina Lopes de Lima. Orlando used his considerable charm to persuade her to go to the Xingu. She accepted, and proved to be a perfect candidate. Petite and pretty, Marina was efficient and practical, undaunted by the primitive conditions, adaptable and calm. She was immediately sympathetic to the Indians, and within a year had won their confidence—not easily done. This young trained nurse had to tackle every branch of medicine on her own. She explained: 'I do as much as possible: common cures, extraction of teeth, difficult births, and even minor surgery. Because the needs here are so great and the means so difficult, I just have to rely on the little I know.' The norm was for sick Indians to get themselves to Posto Leonardo, where there was a dispensary and a rudimentary dentist's chair. For more serious cases, Marina herself would have to hurry to a village, by canoe or on foot. In later years, serious cases could be evacuated in a small plane given by a benefactor, together with its resident pilot, and using a network of simple dirt airstrips that were opened beside some villages.

Tireless and versatile though Nurse Marina was, the Xingu needed more sophisticated medical help. The Villas Boas dreaded a repeat of the lethal influenza, pneumonia, and then measles epidemics of the 1940s and 1950s. A young doctor called Roberto Baruzzi from the São Paulo Medical School (EPM: Escola Paulista de Medicina) had volunteered to join a 'medical caravan' treating Indians and settlers on the Araguaia river, east of the Xingu. On a return flight in 1964 the plane containing Dr Baruzzi touched down at Posto Leonardo. People there asked for his urgent help in treating a sick Mehinaku adolescent called Monain, which he did successfully. (Monain went on to become a prestigious shaman.) Baruzzi recalled that 'this visit aroused my interest, since I had heard much about the Villas Boas ever since their first expedition'. Soon after, Baruzzi sought out Orlando when he heard that he was in São Paulo. This was just what the famous Indianist was seeking, so he promptly invited Baruzzi back to the Xingu.

Young Dr Baruzzi flew there in the dry season of 1965 with seven medical-school colleagues—volunteer doctors and orderlies. The team's three months of treatment of the Xinguanos was a success. So they themselves recommended a continuing medical programme, both curative and preventive; and

Orlando eagerly welcomed this. The result was a formal agreement between the Xingu Indigenous Park and the Preventive Medicine Department of the São Paulo Medical School, signed in July 1966. This was a simple document. It committed the EPM to send volunteer doctors once or twice a year (or immediately, in the event of an epidemic), to visit every village, administer inoculations, perform basic treatments, and if they wished to use this as part of their medical research and training. The agreement was not exclusive—the park authorities could continue to use services such as Dr Noel Nutels's flying-doctor teams, and there was always the back-up of hospitals in São Paulo for serious cases. Everything of course depended on the air force's free weekly flights.

Health provision for indigenous people was different to that for other Brazilians. On the plus side, Indians lived very healthily—with an excellent diet, plenty of exercise, and no smoking, alcohol, sugars, or fatty foods. They were not at risk from the accidents, pollution, or the stresses of urban life. But, as we have seen, these handsome and fit people could be fatally vulnerable to imported diseases against which they had no inherited immunity, even simple ones like influenza or measles. So curative medicine for them was different, and a priority was inoculation, which was why the 1966 agreement was with the teaching hospital's Preventive Medicine Department.

Another great difference was that the indigenous people believed in faith healing by their shamans. In colonial times, the priority for Jesuits and other missionaries had been to ridicule, undermine, and destroy shamans and their beliefs. The Villas Boas had always insisted that this must not happen in the Xingu. 'The shaman is the link binding the community to the supernatural— which in the Indians' concept is the source of all ills.' Shamanic ritual was thus an essential part of any cure. It was effective because of its

> important psychological impact on the patient. [Western] doctors agree that this symbolic effect is a catalyst in a cure. … Also, when an Indian is close to death he undergoes a ceremonial that makes him think, not of cure, but to prepare himself for his own death. So the rituals must be respected, even if at times we find them difficult to comprehend.

The Paulista doctors readily agreed. They were intelligent and humane enough to appreciate that they got best results by working with, not against, shamans (known as *pajés* by Tupi speakers such as the Kamaiurá, Juruna, or Kaiabi, and often by outsiders). Dr Baruzzi knew that his 'challenge was not just to install health assistance based on western medicine by merely transferring technology and resources. The real challenge was to take health benefits

101

to the Indians without causing irreversible damage to their culture, without destroying their belief in traditional medicine.' He appreciated that immediately imposing modern medicine could cause long-term harm. Mental and social well-being mattered as much as physical health. Each year he would say to his team of doctors: 'The pajé cures one part, we cure another.'

The agreement between the Xingu Park and the EPM hospital was a symbiotic one from which everyone benefited. The Villas Boas got the doctors they craved for their indigenous peoples, at no cost; the volunteer doctors often sacrificed holiday time, but they were enchanted by the Xingu and its peoples, proud to be able to help, did some research, and had delightful adventures; the Indians enjoyed superb medical treatment. The *pajés* had no difficulty in working alongside Western medics, and they took some credit for the cures. Most Indians instinctively felt that alien diseases were best cured by outside medicine, whereas for their own ailments they relied on the smoke and incantations of shamans to combat the sorcery or malign spirits that had caused these. With Western doctors, Indians tended to prefer injections to pills, because of the fussy ritual and the stab of pain involved in the jabs.

In 1970 the International Red Cross was invited to report on the health of Brazilian indigenous peoples. Its team of three European doctors and an anthropologist visited twenty indigenous posts, including the Xingu. They were impressed by its villages as 'a good example of preserved culture due to isolation and non-interference', and they liked Nurse Marina's 'three-bed clinic with dispensary facilities and a reasonably well-stocked pharmacy'. But they commented disapprovingly that people wore no clothing, and that their hygiene was generally poor—apparently unaware that all Indians bathed throughout the day and kept their huts and village plazas scrupulously clean, even though they might have no sanitary plumbing.

The inspectors noted that some tribes had been vaccinated against measles and smallpox, but complained that no records were kept of who had been inoculated. This was unfair. Xingu people did not have the identity cards or electoral registers of Europeans, but the volunteer doctors did strive to record the name of every vaccinated person. In Xinguano villages, they entered each hut and asked to treat everyone in it. At that time, 1971, I travelled with Claudio, Dr Roberto Baruzzi, and four other young doctors to inoculate recently contacted Metuktire. We reached this group in a temporary forest meeting-place on the Jarina river, a western tributary of the Xingu far down near the Von Martius rapids. Conditions were as remote from a gleaming European hospital as one could possibly imagine. A throng of naked Kayapó flitted among the dead leaves and gloom of pristine tropical forest. The doctors had no furniture or equipment—there was no room for any in the canoes that had taken us there. But they were dedicated and efficient, and did try to record the identity of everyone they inoculated. All the Metuktire were eager to get their jab of white men's magic. They expressed their thanks by holding a farewell ceremony, with the men stamping a ritual dance, and the women and girls lined up to sing for us, melodiously but without musical instruments—all in the dark forest lit only by camp fires. Although there were no creature comforts, this was an effective expedition among the most delightful travelling companions one could wish for.

In 1969, after six years of splendid work among the Xinguanos, the nurse Marina Lopes de Lima decided to return to urban Brazil. During the previous four years there had not been a single indigenous death, not even any infant mortality. Orlando was jubilant about this success, but in despair at the thought of losing Marina. So the fifty-six-year-old bachelor proposed marriage to the attractive nurse twenty-three years his junior. They had worked together closely at Posto Leonardo so that there was great mutual admiration—which had developed, without their realizing it, into love. She accepted, and they were married in a registry office in the old town Goiás. It was a very successful marriage, with a son, Orlando, born a year later and another, Noel, three years after that.

The initial vaccine, which was applied first by Dr Nutels and then by the EPM doctors, was against tuberculosis. This was totally successful. The doctors had been given an X-ray apparatus which, together with PPD tests, showed that by the late 1960s there was no TB in the Xingu. But a greater killer of indigenous peoples had always been measles. We have seen how measles arrived in 1955 and tragically killed 114 people—almost a fifth of the 660 Xinguanos at that time. The survivors did acquire some degree of immunity through antibodies. Then, in 1968, a measles vaccine called Edmonston B was finally developed. The Paulista doctors eagerly applied this—although they had difficulty in keeping it refrigerated on boat journeys, and it was later found to be rather too powerful for indigenous people. This vaccine was superseded in the 1970s by BCG against measles, polio, and tetanus; and in the 1990s by MMR (for children) against measles, mumps, and rubella. Influenza had also been a great killer; but it was often treatable by penicillin, which became available after the 1940s. There was also DPT against diphtheria, tetanus, and whooping cough—in case these diseases ever struck the Xingu.*

---

* In these tests and inoculations, BCG stands for 'bacillus Calmette-Guérin'; PPD is a 'purified protein derivative' (or Mantoux) screening test for tuberculosis; rubella, in MMR, is chicken pox; P in DPT is pertussis or whooping cough.

Although Baruzzi's doctors came from the medical school's Department of Preventive Medicine, they also did much curative treatment. By the 1970s the worst disease was malaria. Over 80 per cent of examined Indians had enlarged spleens from it. There was no vaccine or cure for malaria, just quinine-based febrifuges that alleviated its symptoms. So these were applied—in concert with the *pajé* shamans, of course. There was also spraying of the great thatch huts with DDT—before that chemical was shown to be too noxious for the natural environment. (There was no hope of persuading Indians to put mosquito nets over their hammocks.) Some British doctors who visited in 1968 confirmed that most of the cases they were asked to treat were malaria. By that time, thanks to the EPM doctors and Nurse Marina, these doctors found none of the lethal imported diseases such as influenza or measles, just 'mixed anaemias due to infestations, diarrhoeas, upper-respiratory-tract infections, and various skin conditions'.

Contrary to the Red Cross mission's report, the EPM teams did try to keep a medical record of every single Indian. This soon developed into a full-page fiche, with a picture of the man or woman at different ages, their name (which sometimes changed), a reference number, date of birth, parentage, spouse, children, measurements—weight, height, pulse—and then every illness, inoculation, or medical treatment of any kind. Most indigenous people were delighted to have these cards, and went to get them; but the doctors also visited every hut to ensure that no one was missing. As the decades went by, this register of indigenous health became the finest record of its kind in South America, if not in the entire world. It is a goldmine for medical, demographic, or anthropological researchers.

Dr (later Professor) Roberto Baruzzi was an excellent and dedicated doctor, a gentle man with the patience and amiability to endear him to Indians. I watched him in action on many occasions and saw how greatly every man, woman, and child loved him. This was helped by his knowing all their names and medical histories, often from the time they were born. Baruzzi (as he liked to be called: his wife and I were almost the only people he allowed to call him Roberto) was not as ebullient as Noel Nutels or Orlando, but invariably calm, modest, and enthusiastic about his work. He developed from a handsome young doctor to a senior academic with gravitas, a strong face, and bushy black eyebrows—but with tremendous charm and a sense of humour to endear him to both Orlando and the Xinguanos.

In 1982 the distinguished Professor Alexander Leaf of the Harvard Medical School reported to the Brazilian National Research Council how hugely impressed he had been by Baruzzi: 'His is dedicated labour, more generous in its motivation than any other I know.' Baruzzi had by then visited the Xingu as a volunteer at least four times every year throughout the previous eighteen years (and he continued to do this for almost three further decades). The result was excellent general health and well-being among the Xinguanos, their superb physiques, an end to serious epidemics, and a population growing faster than the national average. Stephen Hugh-Jones, professor of anthropology at Cambridge University, reported that the EPM's 'programme of vaccinations is the oldest and most successful in all indigenous populations throughout lowland South America'. Orlando paid tribute to the outstanding doctors who had participated as volunteers—including the world-class ophthalmologist Rubens Belfort and the admirable Douglas Rodrigues, who eventually succeeded Baruzzi. Orlando appreciated that 'the programme would long ago have ceased, but for the tireless work of Baruzzi in keeping it alive and inspiring the School's current students and future doctors. In truth, these doctors were making history.'

9

TWO SOCIETIES

The legislation creating the Xingu National Park stated that, in addition to protecting its indigenous peoples, it could be used for study by natural scientists and by anthropologists. A few ornithologists, zoologists, and botanists did visit, but its location in transition between savannah and tropical rainforests meant that it had fewer attractions for them than did the richer Amazonian ecosystem to the north-west. With anthropologists it was another matter: for them it was a paradise.

Brazil's vast Amazonian forests are home to scores of indigenous peoples, but these are difficult to locate or reach. Any who lived on major rivers had long ago been captured by slavers, converted by missionaries, oppressed by rubber barons or other bosses, or extinguished by disease. So any survivors had retreated deep into forests or up tributaries blocked by rapids. Some were still uncontacted and therefore forbidden to social scientists, missionaries, or adventurers, and a few were dangerously hostile. The Xinguanos were different, as almost the only easily accessible forest peoples still in fairly pristine condition. They were also remarkably tolerant about anthropologists intruding into their lives or invited visitors taking their pictures—provided, of course, that the strangers were generous with presents. Some even seemed to welcome the outsiders' interest in their customs and beliefs.

There were academic riches for anthropologists in these well-ordered societies emerging from hunter-gatherer and early agricultural development, with their spiritual beliefs, mythology, ceremonial, and long-established societies. Berta Ribeiro also saw change itself as a research opportunity: 'This process is seductive for us anthropologists, because we see in miniature how a homogenous people reacts when its cultural remnants are under pressure from a dominant society: ours.' And, as we have seen repeatedly, the nature and rate of change were fundamental elements of the Villas Boas' unique management style.

Another attraction for accredited anthropologists was the working conditions in the Xingu Park. The Villas Boas brothers provided basic infrastructure and modest comforts, while the host tribe gave food and lodging. Importantly, anthropologists enjoyed medical care, with radios and, in later years, airstrips at most villages for emergency evacuations. There was complete safety, because inter-tribal warfare had ceased, unauthorized outsiders were rigorously excluded, and there was not even interference or competition from rival anthropologists or missionaries. But the greatest luxury of all was regular, easy, and free travel on air force planes. Few anthropologists studying indigenous peoples anywhere in the world enjoyed such superb conditions in such an idyllic realm.

A steady stream of anthropologists got permission to work in the Xingu—these are listed chronologically in Appendix 3. Many expressed their gratitude. A typical tribute came from Thomas Gregor, who studied the Mehinaku, the Xingu's largest Aruak-speaking group, during four periods after 1967. Gregor wrote:

> I was privileged to meet the administrators of the Post, Claudio and Orlando Villas Boas. These courageous brothers virtually single-handedly established the Xingu Park and protected its frontiers from [undesirable intruders]. ... They generously gave me the hospitality of the Indian Post, the help of their staff, and their encouragement for my work.

For their part, Orlando and Claudio tolerated the anthropologists, preferring those with exuberant personalities like the American Kenneth Brecher with the Waurá, or Adrian Cowell (not a trained anthropologist, but his writings were valuable), who could empathize so well with Indians. They particularly liked Anthony Seeger and his wife Judy, not just for an admirable study they made of the Suiá, but because as relatives of the famous folk musician Pete Seeger they could play the guitar and sing. Orlando's favourite was the Cuban revolutionary song 'Guantanamera', and he got the Seegers to perform this every evening. I have a vivid memory of their beautiful rendering of that ballad with its soaring high notes, in the dimly lit main hut at Posto Leonardo, to an audience of slightly bemused Indians and an enraptured Orlando.

The Villas Boas themselves acquired a profound understanding of indigenous people through decades of living with them. They may have lacked academic training, but (in books written later) they comprehensively described Indian society and mythology. They wrote in simple language for a lay audience, as well as special books for children. They could also be sceptical about some academic studies. Claudio, for instance, told me that he disapproved of those anthropologists who tried to classify native society in neat pigeonholes or to squeeze the Indians' broad conception of life into their own Western experience. For him, the worst were the few who wrote in academic jargon and were obsessed with such minutiae as parentage and sibling relationships. These 'form a little gang, write theses that no-one reads, copy what others have written, and are all a group of frustrated failures.' In truth, however, the Villas Boas rarely bothered to read academic studies of the tribes they knew so well, any more than anthropologists read their more popular books. But the brothers helped anthropologists, and were happy to have them in the villages, and sometimes on their expeditions—so long as the Indians themselves liked the researchers. Writings by social scientists could help the indigenous cause. Anthropologists were professionals who grew to love and respect the people they were studying. Most became fluent in an indigenous language, lived for months embedded in communal huts, wrote sympathetically about societies, and provided a record of those that were about to change forever.

There was also a stream of other visitors who got permission to see the Xingu and fly there in air force planes: politicians of every political persuasion, journalists, military personnel, Indian service officials, and some VIPs. One of the latter was ex-King Leopold III of Belgium, who came in 1964. The Villas Boas liked the charming king (disgraced and forced to abdicate because of his capitulation to the Germans during the war) because he had a good knowledge of the environment and established a dignified rapport with the Xinguanos. All these visitors were invited or welcomed for one reason: they could help the indigenous cause through their political clout or writing.

A code of conduct was drawn up for visitors, 'so that they would not make fools of themselves'. They were advised not to try to imitate Indians in their body paint, haircuts, ornaments, or nudity. They should not attempt to join in ceremonies, hunting, fishing, or wrestling, because no visitor could match the skill and grace of indigenous peoples. Outsiders were warned off *huka-huka* wrestling because they would not grasp its subtleties—and might actually be too violent. With food, good practice was to attempt to eat whatever Indians offer, but not to try to make them eat something they dislike—which was virtually everything other than their standard fish-and-manioc diet. Important advice was not to trade aggressively, demanding artefacts in return for manufactured goods, because Indians do not understand bargaining or commerce. They will, however, be generous to those who are good to them. Avoid physical contact, for although Indians are too polite to say 'no' they might dislike an embrace or caress from someone they do not know well. And of course there must be no sex.

Most aspects of upper-Xingu society are admirable by modern liberal standards, but a few are incomprehensible or disagreeable—just as Indians find much in our way of life abhorrent because it is too aggressive, noisy, undignified, greedy, mean, or selfish.

The indigenous birth rate is low for various reasons. One is that, even though a baby starts eating ordinary food after its first year, it is not fully weaned until aged about five, which inhibits another pregnancy by the mother. Another reason is infanticide. During labour, a mother sits in her hammock with her feet on the ground. As soon as the infant is born an older woman midwife places it on the ground where it is carefully examined by a group of attendant women. If there is any defect (or even suspected bad magic), it is stifled. Small groups of hunter-gatherers cannot afford to carry disabled passengers. Third, with no obstetric medical skills, there are miscarriages and infant mortality—but no more than in the rest of Brazil. A fourth reason is fairly late marriage and no desire for large families.

Once a baby has survived the perils of birth, it sleeps in its mother's hammock, often with her breast in its mouth so that if its wakes during the night it can suckle until it falls asleep again. Children are adored by their parents and the entire community. As the great chief Aritana Yawalapiti said, with pride: 'We never hit children or even scold them. We like to pick them up and ask what is wrong. Because if we punish them they will grow up being difficult and bad-tempered.' The Brazilian anthropologist Carmen Junqueira noted that parents hated to see a child cry, and would therefore give it whatever it wanted. 'Its wishes are orders and its crying is an alarm caused by a lack of love or attention.' Punishment is very rare indeed, and might consist of gentle scarification—as a preventive against the evil spirit that caused the bad behaviour, and done only when the parents are calm and not angry. As the Villas Boas noted, parents demanded nothing from their children. 'A child is an entity and should be respected as such. Indians think that they should never be contradicted.' Orlando once watched a mother making pots shaped like birds, but as soon as she finished one her four-year-old daughter broke it. It never occurred to the mother to stop making pots, or to prevent her child breaking them. It was only when the child decided to move away that she finally finished the eleventh pot. On another occasion, a group of five-year-old Ikpeng children set fire to a communal house, one of only eight that constituted their village. The adults lost most of their belongings in the conflagration, as well as the great thatched *maloca* itself. 'But they did not grieve because of this, nor reprimand the culprit. The most they did was to tease the child as "the captain of the fire" or "the smoke boy".' The entire community then embarked on the task of rebuilding the hut. This attitude explains why, back in 1925, the Indians had been so affronted when they saw Colonel Fawcett hit a boy. It also explains why you never hear indigenous children shouting or misbehaving, or their parents scolding them.

In this unmaterialistic and pre-literate society, there is of course no formal schooling. Children play happily and do small chores if they feel like it. When aged about seven they start imitating their parents. Girls might do some spinning or grind manioc; boys shoot little bows at birds, learn to fish at the river's edge and to move stealthily through the forest, and they start *huka-huka* wrestling with one another. Whenever there is a festival, you will see a ragged line of children copying the grown-ups. There is a close bond between fathers and sons, mothers and daughters. But when Orlando asked a father whether he was teaching his son, he replied: 'No, because I do not know whether he wants it. When he does want to know something, he will ask and I will teach him.' Children mature fast in this uncomplicated world. By the time a boy is ten or twelve he almost has an adult's knowledge and skills in hunting, fishing, and other male tasks, as does a girl with women's work.

At the opposite end of Xinguano society is the chief. He enjoys prestige and authority, but no power. No one gives orders to others in a village. Orlando observed that 'the chief of a village is just an intermediary, a link between daily life and the supernatural world. ... His function is purely social. He has no executive power to command: he is a mediator.' The position of chief can be hereditary, passing to the son or grandson of a former chief. But more important than ancestry is that 'a chief must be a fine orator, a person of great goodness. He is comprehending and counselling, giving advice but not orders.' Although his authority is symbolic, he must have these qualities and be dignified, understanding, and tranquil. In the village he is the first among equals. The men sit outside the men's house each evening, often smoking a cheroot of tobacco-like grasses, gossiping and discussing tribal affairs in a totally democratic way. It is rare for there to be any new policy in that simple and conservative society. But if the men do agree on some matter of collective interest, the chief proclaims it to the entire village, at the door of his *maloca* and always with his bow in his hand. This lack of power was ever thus. In the sixteenth century, the French philosopher Michel de Montaigne asked a young chief of the warlike Tupinamba of Brazil's Atlantic seaboard what advantages he gained from his rank. He answered simply: 'To march first into battle.'

Despite their lack of power, many chiefs were revered and respected. Washington Novaes (one of Brazil's most influential columnists) regarded

Chief Malakuyawá of the Waurá as 'the most impressive human being I met in almost seventy years of life'. Some chiefs used their prestige to influence their people's attitude to outsiders. Chief Kanato of the Yawalapiti combined being a zealous champion of tradition with welcoming those whites whom he judged to be true friends of the Indians. In an obituary, it was said that he 'always maintained relations of impeccable friendship, solidarity and admiration for the Villas Boas brothers'. It was Kanato's vision, 'wedded to tradition, but open to strangers and researchers who respected that dignity', that later influenced Brazil's Indian Protection Service to portray the Xingu Park as an example for other indigenous posts to emulate. This chief educated all his children to be intermediaries between the two societies, and he trained his son Aritana to succeed him. Orlando also appreciated Aritana's political and management potential, and therefore groomed him for leadership. Orlando's instinct was, as usual, right. Aritana matured from being a serious and handsome young man, and a champion wrestler, who revived and inspired his Yawalapiti people, to becoming the genial, gentle, and hugely respected paramount chief of all Xinguanos and living into the third decade of the twenty-first century.

Aritana had an Edenic vision:

> The beauty of our lives here is that we still live in the same way as we have always done, with the same legends, festivals and beliefs of our ancestors— unlike so many other tribes who have put aside their old way of life. Everyone here is the same: we have no rich or poor. We ourselves make most of the things we need, and what we don't make we trade from other neighbouring tribes. We don't like to fight or quarrel. Why should we? What purpose does it serve? We prefer to live in peace in our villages and on friendly terms with everyone. This is why I call this land of ours Paradise.

All his people prided themselves on their virtues, particularly for being gentle, hospitable, and generous. The corollary was that if Indians ever criticized others it was because they were considered to be quarrelsome, lazy, weak, or thieving.

In the tough world of the Brazilian frontier, Indians were thought to be idle wastrels. But anyone who experienced tribal society would know that, although they might have no material ambitions, they were anything but lazy. We have seen how hard they work in hunting, fishing, and growing and preparing manioc and other food. Also, indigenous peoples used to make every artefact, utensil, and ornament they needed, and they did this with consummate skill. There was beauty in their productions, and also in their body paint and featherwork. But this art was conventional and static, rarely creative. And although Indians have huge knowledge of the flora and fauna of their world, partly in order to hunt and gather successfully, they have no scientific, aesthetic, or intellectual interest in it. However, in their mythology and legends animals rank equally with human beings.

It was easy to be beguiled by this harmonious culture. The anthropologist Darcy Ribeiro said that 'no-one is unaffected by the experience of seeing the world through the eyes of an Indian. You will never again be the same person.' Washington Novaes agreed. He almost envied indigenous people because they could scarcely be 'much simpler, happier, to sing more, dance more, wear plenty of decoration, know the intricacy of the world around you, co-exist with spirits, work less, and not be preoccupied by money, property or transport'. For Orlando:

> This is a stable and harmonious society, where no-one orders anyone, each man owns his household, the aged own history, and children own the world. … Power as we understand it does not exist in an Indian tribal community: it is diluted for the community's benefit. No-one may profit from power nor exploit it, just as no-one wants to command.

This 'freedom' of each individual man was, however, ambiguous. True, the notion of working *for* a master was unheard of. But everyone in a tiny community was strictly bound by its conventions and unwritten rules. There was no place for nonconformists. For the Villas Boas, 'What maintains tribal unity is the force of a culture born from their traditions.' Such small communities were how human beings had always lived, from the evolution of our species until very recent times. In his study of the fifty-seven members of the Mehinaku people, Thomas Gregor stressed how everyone was interrelated, both in the family sense and in domestic, working, spiritual, and other contacts. They all knew one another's footfalls, voices, ways of making arrows or other objects, and even which whoops each man made to show that he had caught fish or game. People cheerfully greeted one another when passing, even if the other was asleep. There was no privacy, for conversations could easily be overheard. It was hard for married couples to keep their sexual encounters secret except in the darkness of a hut or deep in the forest. Most Indians enjoyed sex: it was fairly open and natural. There could be joking banter about an individual's performance, but there was no prurience or obscenity.

There was 'a great need for co-operation for a small tribe to survive as a unit. Despite this need, village cohesion can be tenuous, and hostility and fear

113

may threaten its fabric.' There was no privacy, and conservative conformity with all social customs. One antidote to this constant contact came from living in ritual seclusion behind a partition in the communal hut, in such strict isolation that the secluded person virtually ceased to exist. There were three stages in life when people would be secluded. At the birth of a first child both the mother and father were secluded for up to a year; and the infant was not seen until aged about eighteen months, when a godfather cut its first hair. For later babies, only the mother was secluded, and only for a few weeks.

The next big seclusion came when boys were aged about ten and had their ears pierced, and when girls started to menstruate. This puberty seclusion lasted for at least a year for both sexes; but for chiefs' sons it could be for up to two years, followed by a six-month lull, and then a further year of seclusion. Aritana was groomed to be an important chief, and he recalled how 'I myself spent five years in seclusion. This is an important period of learning for us, rather like going to school. My father and uncle taught me tribal myths and legends and also how to make things like arrows and bows or [mollusc-shell] necklaces. Above all, they taught me how to behave, how to treat others, and especially how to converse'—both formally for chiefly functions and casually for everyday chatter.

A boy in seclusion talked to no one other than his male relatives. If he watched other young people at play, it was just wistfully through cracks in the thatched wall of the hut. Like all Indians he washed or bathed several times a day, either by having water brought to him or by going to a secluded part of the river. He urinated into a bamboo tube through the wall, and went out to defecate in the forest after dark. One young Mehinaku described the boredom: 'Look at how I live. I sit on my bench all day, working [at making things]. Little boys tease me from outside. But I can't leave the house: witches would shoot me with magic arrows if I did. I must stay in seclusion. This is the way to become a man.' These initiation rituals also involved elaborate food taboos, periods of violent fasting, and worst of all having to vomit after drinking poisons—all to demonstrate manly courage. Some boys did not survive. Roberto Baruzzi, the great doctor of the Xingu peoples, told me that once his doctors had got imported diseases under control, the greatest killer of young males was from these extreme initiation ordeals. When the seclusion finally ended a father would tear down the partition, and the boy had become a man. With girls, seclusion lasted for a year but was less punishing than for boys. I once saw a father bring his pale daughter back into daylight, with unforgettable looks at one another, of parental pride in the father and adoration in the girl.

The third seclusion came after the death of a spouse. This was very rigid. The surviving husband or wife disappeared for up to a year and was seen by none but immediate family.

A visitor to an indigenous *maloca* would have no inkling that there were people secluded behind partitions in its recesses. The stranger would be equally unaware of the magical forces that govern indigenous society. An important role for a chief is to be an intermediary between ordinary life and the world of the spirits, the province of the shamans. In a Xinguano community there was much talk about witchcraft, with lurid stories of evil magic and spells—all of which was readily believed. Although the Indians did not worship a living god, their myths often involved heroic ancestors and creators. They did not believe in protective deities, but in malign spirits who wanted to dominate people by hurting them—but never by killing. There were four main evil spirits. Jacuí lives deep in rivers, and causes severe pains and fevers. This spirit is placated by a special flute also called *jacuí*—which is stored in the men's hut and may never be seen by women on pain of death: if they hear its sound they and their children must hide. Anhangu lives in wetlands and can also cause intense pains. Early missionaries used 'anhangu' as the name of the devil, in order to frighten people into converting to Christianity. Then there was Olei, a spirit associated with manioc gardens: anyone who hears its song falls ill. Acacu is the embodiment of howler monkeys, whose lugubrious droning echoes through the forest. Acacu's sound drives people crazy, causing them to run back and forth or to try to climb houses. After a trance, a man describes his visions, which may involve having seen dead ancestors or unknown villages.

If an Indian hunting in the forest hears a strange noise he knows that it is an evil spirit and fears that he will fall ill. So back in the village he will seek a shaman who can oppose the spirit's influence, perhaps by smoking a cigar of a wild tobacco called *airi* wrapped in a special leaf and bound with *buriti*-palm fibres. The faith-healer blows smoke over his patient, and may then organize a ceremony or a massage to remove the spirit. In the 1960s the greatest shaman in the upper Xingu was Sariruá, brother of the Yawalapiti chief Kanato. He described how he worked with smoke from two big, long cigars. 'Then, when the cigar is finished I run and I "die", breathing rapidly.' Someone standing behind catches him as he falls in a trance. 'Suddenly awake, I run into the forest. I can only remember running. Then I return, with a charm I find in the forest and place this beside the hammock of the sick man. Then the patient gets better.' Aritana, Sariruá's nephew, recalled how his uncle had once cured him of a headache. The shaman puffed smoke over the part that ached.

He then held my head with his hand and extracted the illness 'from inside', showed me a white object and said: 'This is what is causing your pain. I have removed that pain and will now remove one more, so that you will no longer feel anything.' He repeated the same words ten times, always holding my head at the place where it ached. After a short while the headache went away.

Each shaman underwent a long initiation into the secrets of his craft, and he enjoyed considerable prestige in the community. But his position could be precarious. We have seen how in 1947 the shaman Maiuri was executed immediately after Chief Izarari of the Kalapalo died of influenza. The Villas Boas liked another shaman, Uarru, who was a calm and thoughtful man and a leader of ceremonial. But it appeared that Uarru knew too much about the spirit world for his people's comfort, so 'the others decided to kill him. They tried hacking him with machetes, but he remained impassive and did not react. ... He calmly said to his persecutors: "You will not be able to kill me. The best would be to dig a grave and bury me alive." Which is what they did.' Similarly, in 1970 a Kamaiurá told Carmen Junqueira that in the past his people had had many sorcerers, and used to get them to bewitch enemies with their spells. 'But today if someone uses black magic he is immediately killed. Therefore we no longer use evil magic.'

Although shamans risked death if their sorcery failed, the uninitiated could be even more vulnerable. The Villas Boas once feared that a Mehinaku boy called Maxumare might suffer because his father had been considered evil and killed; so they brought the lad to live with them. When Maxumare was twelve he wanted to return to his village, and they of course allowed him to do what he wished. But within a few days, when he was playing in the river with other boys, three grown men appeared on the bank, took him when he emerged from a dive, and clubbed him to death. The other boys ran off, no one reported this execution, and Maxumare was buried nearby. On one occasion, I myself was sitting beside the Curisevo river with a Mehinaku man, who told me that the two boys with us were orphans whose fathers had been killed because they were 'quarrelsome'. My fishing companion told me that he had twice killed men for suspected witchcraft because teenage boys (one his own son) had died. In each case the tribe had agreed on the killing; a group pursued the suspect when he was hunting in the forest; they told him that he was to be killed; and, even if he asked for mercy, they finished him off with a club blow. Whenever a young man is dying mysteriously, he is constantly asked who bewitched him: whomever he names will be executed.

Suspected sorcery was not the only reason for killing. Kenneth Brecher (an American anthropologist, at Oxford) described the fate of a lovely Waurá girl, who was one of his best friends in that tribe's village. She had many lovers, but would not marry, and Brecher described her as a free spirit. But her nonconformity was considered too disruptive. She ignored warnings to behave with decorum, so the chief told her she must die, and her mother agreed. The girl was sewn into her hammock and buried alive. Once she was gone, the tribe greatly missed her.

The Villas Boas told an equally tragic story of a twelve-year-old Yawalapiti boy called Pooyoo, who had been naughty. But because he was a little unbalanced, and particularly because he had lost both parents and had no family, the women decided to kill him. So they painted him with red *urucum*, adorned him with a few feathers, and put him in a grave. Claudio told how 'the woman who had raised him said: "Go and see your father. He is a long way away," and she threw the first earth into the grave, until they had covered the body leaving only the face exposed.' The boy kept saying that he did not want to die, but they filled the grave and buried him alive. When Claudio told the Yawalapiti women that what they had done was wrong, some showed remorse. But most explained that it had been done because having no parents was an ugly defect; so killing him was similar to eliminating a newborn baby with physical or spiritual blemishes. They would not have done this to a boy with parents to protect him. Shamans also needed the support of a family. 'Sometimes when they come to kill a sorcerer, he just calls "Come. I have no beauty. I have no brothers or children. You may kill me now."'

Tribes downriver near Diauarum felt just as compelled to kill for suspected sorcery as did the Xinguanos. After the Villas Boas had gained the friendship of the Juruna, in 1950 they took two Juruna, who had been kidnapped by the Suiá and then transferred to the Kamaiurá, back to their original people. These were Tamacu—the man who had dramatically helped the brothers at the first contact by remembering his original Juruna name—and Tutuná, and both went with their Kamaiurá wives. But it was not a happy repatriation, because the Juruna were suspicious of the two men who had been away for so long. Tragically, two men and three women in the village died mysteriously, and the repatriated pair were blamed. It seemed certain that the two 'knew sorcery that the Kamaiurá had taught them. They cast spells on a house so that everyone in it fell ill' and died. The two realized that they were in mortal danger and tried to flee with their wives; but three Juruna (including the 'Tarzan' Pauaide) pursued them to their clearings and killed them with clubs. Juruna women then planned to drown the two Kamaiurá wives, but the Villas Boas moved quickly and whisked these widows back to their original village.

117

When Adrian Cowell was at Diauarum in 1967 he witnessed a number of killings—some for revenge, others pointless. He described a wretched case that involved three tribes, the Trumai, Kamaiurá, and Suiá, as well as subtle intervention by Claudio Villas Boas.

Eighty years previously, when Karl von den Steinen first entered the upper Xingu, the Trumai had been a considerable people whose warriors manned a fleet of canoes. But during the ensuing decades they had been ravaged by disease and inter-tribal warfare. In 1960 the remnant of this tribe had to flee from a village near the sacred place Morená and take refuge at Diauarum— because a Kamaiurá chief had died, this large people blamed the Trumai for bewitching him, and they threatened to massacre them.

By 1967 the Trumai at Diauarum were reduced to a mere twenty people, but these included four beautiful unmarried women and two remarkable young men: Javaritu and his brother Aruyave. Javaritu had married a Suiá girl and became in effect leader of her people during the difficult period after their contact. The Suiá had been so traumatized by this contact that they stopped planting manioc, and were in acute danger of starvation. But Javaritu's common sense, steadiness, and experience at Diauarum guided them in their relations with the outside world and restored their morale and will to survive. Javaritu had also become a trusted aide of Claudio, who saw him as 'reliable and watchful, a man of obvious moral strength'. His younger brother Aruyave had been adopted by Claudio as an orphaned boy, and lived in Diauarum as one of Claudio's best helpers in running the post.

One day in 1967 Javaritu went fishing in his canoe and never returned. After a desperate search it was found that he had been murdered by a Kaiabi called Tapiokap. He had been hit by a 0.22 rifle from a distance, and the killer had then paddled over and killed him in cold blood with another shot. When Aruyave brought his brother's body back for burial at Diauarum, the young Trumai found himself torn between the tribal need for revenge against the Kaiabi and Claudio's teaching of compassion. Claudio also had to use his skills in dealing with the murderer Tapiokap—a strange misfit, known to have killed six people when the Kaiabi were still on the Teles Pires, and whom Prepori had expelled from their Xingu village because of his homicidal tendencies. Claudio spent two long nights talking to Tapiokap, who said: "In the lake I talked to Javaritu. Then I went and killed him. Just so, Claudio." When told that this was wrong and evil, Tapiokap answered: "Claudio, such I am. I am just like that."

A frightening triangle of vengeances now ensued, an example of how difficult it was for Claudio to navigate within a web of tribal honour and loyal-

and 2. Orlando, Leonardo and Claudio Villas Boas rapidly became field leaders of the oncador-Xingu Expedition of 1945-46. The media started to notice their glamour, and ey became Brazil's most famous explorers.

The first months of the Expedition were ross the territory of the hostile Xavante ople, in *cerrado* bushland.

4. Entering the forests in late 1946, the brothers met Kalapalo people and became good friends of their chief Izarari, who posed with them beside a headwater of the Xingu river.

5. Jânio Quadros, a dynamic politician, family friend of the Villas Boas, and future President of Brazil, was enchanted by a visit to the upper Xingu. Orlando, on the right, introduces him to a Kamaiurá chief.

6. Claudio welcomes the splendid doctor Noel Nutels. A regular service by Brazilian Air Force DC-47 Dakota planes was a crucial factor in the success of the brothers' work in the Xingu.

8. Claudio developed a deep understanding of indigenous affairs. Here, Metuktire love listening to his long conversations, delivered from his hammock or simple hut.

7. The media asked Orlando to investigate the disappearance of Lt.-Colonel Percy Fawcett in the upper Xingu in 1925. Orlando holds a skull that the Kalapalo said was the lost English colonel's, but when sent to London it proved not to be his.

. A crucial meeting in the creation of the Xingu Indigenous Park. In 1952 the nthropologists Darcy Ribeiro (on the left) and Heloisa Torres (director of the National Museum in Rio de Janeiro, in the centre) present this radical plan to Vice-President João Café Filho (on the right). The two other proponents, Air Force Brigadier Raymundo Aboim nd Orlando Villas Boas, were also at this meeting.

0 and 11. The author with Claudio n the Jarina river, and the brothers' reatest foreign friend Adrian Cowell vith him in Diauarum.

2. From 1965 to the present, olunteer doctors from São Paulo ave provided excellent medical reatment for the Xingu's peoples. heir leader was Dr Roberto Baruzzi, n the background of this picture of noculations of Metuktire.

13 and 14. Orlando with the young Rauni Metuktire and a Yawalapiti child; and in a Juruna dugout canoe with their chief Bibina during an attempt to contact the Suiá, in 1958.

15. Orlando and Claudio during the second Panará contact expedition in 1972, when in their late fifties.

16. Xinguano families could go to visit Orlando whenever they wished. This family slung their hammocks in the main hut of Posto Leonardo for such a visit — their own maloca in their village would have had far stronger walls.

7 and 18. Xinguano peoples are extremely loving parents, who never chastise their children. A proud father brings his adoring (but paler) daughter out of months of puberty seclusion, an important coming-of-age ritual after which she is recognised as a woman in her tribe.

9 and 20. A man would normally wear only a necklace of fresh-water molluscs and possibly brightly feathered ear plugs. Making these prized *urapeí* necklaces was a speciality of Kuikuro and Kalapalo men.

21 and 22. Women work constantly to make and cook the staple food manioc. One pours *cauim* brew, and another kneads manioc to make *beiju* pancakes. Both use broad *camalupe* pans, which were made only by Waurá women potters.

23. With no formal schooling, children are either with their parents or playing happily together, like these Kamaiurá in their beautiful Lake Ipavu.

24. There was time-honoured distinction between genders, with men dominant in tribal society. But women were morally tou[g] and sure of themselves. This Kamaiurá wom[a] wears only a necklace (of imported beads) and a girdle to hold her *uluri* cache-sexe.

The Xinguano peoples love coming together for ceremonies. The greatest of these is the kuarup, held only in memory of very important chiefs. Orlando and Claudio each had a kuarup in his honour, as did the great doctor Roberto Baruzzi.

25. Shamans spend the first day of the kuarup decorating a pole to represent the dead chief. Every aspect of this decoration, and the wood of the pole, conform to strict liturgical customs.

26. The two-day kuarup ceremony starts with a summons by flute players trotting into each hut in the village of the host people. One of these magnificent maloca huts is seen, behind the two flute players each with a girl behind him.

27. Each visiting people performs dances and mock charges. The men wear their finest headdresses and body decorations, and are often in long lines during the rituals.

29. Both sexes paint one another for ceremonial and, for men, wrestling. They mainly use two common berries: red *urucum* (annatto) and black genipap.

28. Wrestling was the favourite sport of Xinguanos, performed daily in each village and in inter-village contests. (Football is now competing with it among the young.) Bouts of *huka-huka* wrestling (onomatopoeic after the grunts made by wrestlers) are rapid and not painful. This exercise helps to give Xinguanos fine physiques, and a champion wrestler gains kudos among his people.

30 and 31. Indigenous society is interwoven with the spirit world, and shamans enjoy prestige as the interpreters of spirits and as faith healers. These masks and straw costumes are very rarely seen vestments of Mehinaku shamans.

ties. Claudio had raised three fine young men to be his helpers in running Diauarum—Aruyave, Pionim, and Mairawé—and all three became tragically embroiled in the consequences of this killing. The Trumai Aruyave was the brother of the murdered Javaritu. The Kaiabi Pionim was married to Aruyave's and Javaritu's sister. And by a cruel twist Mairawé, another Kaiabi, was Aruyave's best friend but was also the brother of the murderer Tapiokap. After a few weeks, the psychopath Tapiokap suddenly appeared at Diauarum: he had to be hustled away before Aruyave could get to a gun with which to kill his brother's murderer. Later that year, when both Orlando and Claudio were away, it was Pionim who wrought vengeance on his Kaiabi kinsman—he had an obligation to do this because he was married to the sister of the two Trumai brothers. So Pionim went to his Kaiabi village, lured Tapiokap into a canoe on the pretext of taking him to get ammunition, shot him dead during the voyage, and cut his stomach so that he would sink without trace. When Claudio returned, he had to deal with the honour killings that should now have ensued between the three young men—all of whom he had reared and loved, who were efficient assistants, and who had been great friends of one another. Claudio hated to intervene in purely Indian affairs, so his solution was to hustle Pionim and Aruyave upriver to Posto Leonardo, leaving Mairawé at Diauarum. The friends, now avowed enemies, could talk on the radio but never meet. And Pionim could not return to his Kaiabi people, even though everyone knew that Tapiokap, whom he had killed, had been dangerously mad.

The Villas Boas were deeply saddened by this complicated case, but it was just one example of the sort of problem they confronted throughout their years in the Xingu. Its resolution required sensitive understanding of indigenous thinking, rather than the application of outside laws. In Brazil indigenous people living in communal societies were then, and still are, legal minors—this means that they are not subject to Brazilian law for acts committed within tribal custom, even murder. As well as getting tribes to stop fighting one another, the Villas Boas also sought to end vendetta and sorcery killings. But they had to move slowly and with tact. Claudio had learned that Indians were very loving to one another, but only within their own village (or in the upper Xingu with kindred villages). 'Outside the village clearing is the forest where they kill meat for food or gather [useful plants]. Killing is the essence of forest existence. ... Within an Indian mind there is a complete division between duties within their group and an absence of duty in the killing world outside. ... In this context they feel that men have no greater right to life than animals.'

Shortly after Javaritu's murder, three canoes of Kamaiurá came downriver to Diauarum. This was the first contact between the more sophisticated

119

Kamaiurá and the depleted Trumai, since these had fled from them in 1960.* The Kamaiurá were led by Chief Tacuman, son of the chief whose death seven years previously had been blamed on Trumai sorcery. Now, the visitors brought presents and there were days of ceremonial dances. Nonetheless, Claudio suspected that the visit was not just for reconciliation, but partly motivated by the Kamaiurá being short of women and wanting the Trumai beauties. They achieved this later that year when they persuaded the remnant of the Trumai people to come upriver and live in their village—Tacuman himself got one of the girls as an additional wife.

Chief Tacuman had another objective in going to Diauarum. He felt threatened within the Kamaiurá by a younger man called Tuvule, who was also the son of an important chief. Tacuman had obeyed a request by Orlando not to kill endangered giant otters; but Tuvule's men had caught otters, and taken their skins to the air force base at Xingu to trade for guns and revolvers—which gave his faction an advantage. Tacuman wanted Claudio to stop this tribal power play; but Claudio refused since it was his policy to intervene if necessary between Indians and predatory whites, but almost never between Indians themselves. Tacuman later shrewdly turned this policy against Claudio, when he was reprimanded for absorbing the Trumai in order to get their women. That this was how Indians behaved, Tacuman told him, so Claudio should not try to impose his white values.

These manoeuvres were another example of the diplomacy and persuasion that the Villas Boas were deploying on a daily basis. They never saw themselves as colonial-style district commissioners, bringing the rule of law to the natives. They had moral authority, helped by being the source of imported goods, but they did not use force.

The dynamic younger Kamaiurá chief Tuvule did wrest control of his people from Chief Tacuman—thanks in part to the guns traded from the air force personnel. One day in 1971 Tuvule went with friends to fish in the river. On the way they stopped in a hut being built beside Posto Leonardo by a man called Kalucumã of the tiny Aweti people, and they ate some of his *beijú* bread. But soon after the group set off in their canoes, Tuvule felt ill and was rushed back to Posto Leonardo. The resident nurse Marina (who had recently married Orlando) diagnosed a haemorrhage of the oesophagus—a very serious condition for which he would have to be evacuated to a hospital. But the young chief died on the following morning. The despondent Kamaiurá

* There are now about a hundred Trumai, living in three small villages near the banks of the Xingu, midway between Posto Leonardo and Diauarum.

assumed that their popular Tuvule had been bewitched by Kalucumã of the Aweti, and it was decided that he must die. As Orlando explained: 'When this happens, it is humanly impossible to reverse the situation.' The executioners waited for Orlando himself to leave. A regular air force plane arrived, bringing among others the anthropologist Thomas Gregor; and Orlando left on it for work with the authorities. Orlando described the tragic drama that happened as soon as he had flown away. 'The Kamaiurá, who were hiding in the forest beyond the airstrip, invaded the Post. There were quite a few of them, perhaps ten, led by [Orlando's old friend] Maricá armed with a carbine. They ran towards Kalucumã's hut.' When he saw them coming, he fled into Orlando's own house, where there was just his wife Marina with their infant son in her arms. Once there he hid in a small cupboard. The passengers from the plane were arriving at the house as the Kamaiurá approached, so Marina handed her baby to an appalled Indian Protection Service official and told him to run off—which he did, with two air force officers.

> The invaders entered the house, seized Kalucumã, and started to kill him by cutting his throat. Marina advanced and tried to pull the poor man from the hands of his executioners. The anthropologist [Gregor] … desperately cried 'Stop! Stop!' The nurse managed to snatch the bleeding and half-dead Indian from the hands of his killers. She even tried to take him to the dispensary, but it was impossible: he died on the way there. The invaders had disappeared, taking the end of a finger they had cut off when he was still alive, and a fistful of hair.

They then burned his half-built *maloca*.

Casual killings were not just of other Indians. The normal indigenous reaction to the few unauthorized outsiders who penetrated the upper Xingu, and who presented a threat or behaved badly, was to kill them. We saw how this was probably the fate of Colonel Fawcett in 1925 and of Albert de Winton in 1934. Then, in 1967, a short, black rubber-tapper managed to escape from oppressive *seringueiro* bosses on the Teles Pires. With his wife and children he dodged pursuing gunmen, crossed the forests, and fled down the Manitsauá river towards the Xingu. The first indigenous village he reached was that of a Kaiabi known as Cuyabano, so named because he had been to the provincial capital Cuiabá. The fugitive asked this Kaiabi to help him reach Diauarum. Halfway there, however, they paused on a bank for food. The man alighted first, but as he bent to do so Cuyabano hit him on the head with a paddle, and when he fell into the water killed him with an axe. The woman and children cried and waved their arms, so

121

Cuyabano also killed them with his axe. But when Adrian Cowell asked the Kaiabi whether the fugitive had done anything wrong or insulted him, he said not. Asked why, in that case, he had killed the entire family, Cuyabano said, 'We don't know.' Claudio later told him that it was wrong to kill anyone: intruders should be informed that they cannot remain, but should then be taken to Diauarum for expulsion. The Kaiabi were normally well behaved and, like the black fugitive, they themselves had suffered from cruel rubber bosses. Despite this, the tribe held its traditional 'necklace dance', which celebrates the killing of an enemy. Claudio was just able to make them use a straw dummy instead of the corpse of the actual victim.

These killings for spiritual, vendetta, or inexplicable reasons were deplorable, and the Villas Boas very gradually tried to stop them. They had already put an end to inter-tribal warfare, which had caused more deaths.

In the early days, most visitors to the Xingu had been welcome because the Indians saw them as bringers of wonderful tools, machines, and presents. Individual whites were even admired because it was thought that they had somehow made all their belongings themselves, as the indigenous people did. Before long, it became obvious that visitors could not manufacture anything, and most were hopelessly incompetent in forest skills. Then, a few Indians were taken out to the great cities—either evacuated for serious medical treatment, or for chiefs to be paraded in spectacles to represent 'the Indian race'. When these returned, they told their peoples about the gigantic gulf between their tranquil villages and the unimaginably crowded, noisy, and dirty cities. They took manufactured marvels, planes, radios, cars, and skyscrapers for granted—without needing to understand their mechanics any more than other users do. But they never envied modern society. When the American anthropologist Kenneth Brecher took a young Waurá to São Paulo for medical treatment, his friend pitied him for the terrible noise, ugliness, and anxieties of his way of life, as well as for his Brazilian girlfriend, who never looked straight at him. He urged Brecher to come and live quietly with the Waurá, where they would find him a proper wife.

Indigenous society has many great qualities, but also blemishes in our eyes. It is not altogether Rousseau's idealized world of the noble savage. But the Villas Boas were adamant that the outside world was not superior or inferior to the indigenous one, just different. In this they subscribed to the view of the great French anthropologist Claude Lévi-Strauss and many others: that these were simply two distinct societies.

10

CHANGE

In addition to healthcare, the Villas Boas' greatest concern was change, or rather the *rate* and *nature* of change among the peoples of the upper Xingu. During the sixty years between von den Steinen's first contacts and the arrival of the Roncador–Xingu Expedition, visitors had introduced a trickle of manufactured presents. The most sought-after in that forest realm were of course metal blades—machetes, axes, knives, hoes, and sickles—as well as fish-hooks and line, and beads for ornament.

This changed radically with the arrival of regular air force planes. Here again, the upper-Xingu experience was unlike that of some two hundred other functioning tribes in Brazil. By the late 1960s the Xinguanos had become dependent on the blades and fishing tackle, which led to 'an increase in productivity with less effort needed for it'. But a Kamaiurá interviewed at that time noted a paradox: that in the past Indians had danced more and worked less, even though they had struggled to cut trees or even thick lianas with blunt stone axes.

> Now there is a lot of work. We have many roças [clearings] and plant many [new] things—bananas, pumpkins, sugar cane. In the past we hardly even ate beiju [manioc bread], and fish was served [instead] on a leaf. ... Now we Indians have more tools and work more, and we have more food. Metal is better than stone.

This man was grateful to whites for their axes, pans, and glass beads—even though he knew that they also brought the diseases from which many Indians died.

The Villas Boas had to devise a strategy for dealing with imported goods. They knew that tools contributed to irreversible change; but once people were accustomed to these it became impossible to deny them. They were also aware of the Xinguano tradition of generosity: there was no private property, but admiration for magnanimous leaders. Much of the brothers' managerial authority stemmed from being the providers of these wonderful presents. In the early years, administrators at Posto Leonardo and Diauarum used to distribute essential tools freely to villages on a quota system. They tried, however, to avoid importing objects that would compete with any particular tribe's speciality. An example of this was the Waurá women's monopoly of making huge round pottery pans for roasting manioc; so the brothers allowed the import of smaller aluminium cooking pots, but not metal roasting pans. They also tried to restrict guns and ammunition, because in the hands of expert hunters these might deplete game resources—or even be used in inter-tribal warfare or casual killings.

This free quota system led to a rapid turnover in manufactured goods, and a failure to care for them. So it could not last. The administration then decided to distribute articles on demand. Any individual could go to a post with requests, but these tended to be presented collectively by a village's best spokesman. When asking for goods, Indians of course could not know the monetary value or scarcity of objects, and their knowledge of outside goods extended to more exotic items brought in by anthropologists or other visitors keen to make a good impression. A typical Mehinaku list in 1965 included, in addition to the tools essential for cutting wood, farming, or fishing, 'gunpowder and a primer, shirts, trousers, macaroni, an umbrella, a flashlight with bulb and batteries, matches, red cotton yarn, scissors, razor blades, small knives, a drill, and adze, sugar, and a small bag'. A list from the Kuikuro at that time also included 'a comb, mirror, a large kettle and ammunition'. Acquiring such non-essential items as red clothes, bags, umbrellas, and, later, radios and batteries for them, and even tape recorders or movie cameras, raised a group's prestige. Requests that could not easily be met were noted for future purchase, or the administrator might try offering a substitute. 'On such occasions the principle followed is to adopt a solicitous, gentle attitude, to try to satisfy the Indians' expectations.' The Villas Boas knew that these imports were changing indigenous society, even corrupting it; but they could not isolate the peoples in the park from having goods that they needed or desired. All that they could do was to regulate the type of import and, above all, the *rate* of change. So they evolved a policy of 'change; but only at the speed the Indians want'.

The air force base at Xingu presented a minor threat to Posto Leonardo's attempt to control imports. But the Villas Boas hesitated to criticize or control its military personnel, because they knew that the success of the park was heavily dependent on weekly air force transport, and they liked the pilots, who were generally pleased to help the Indians. By 1970 there were about eight military personnel at Xingu base, and perhaps fifteen civilian workers, local frontiersmen who farmed and hunted, maintained installations, and did some building. The park authorities tried to forbid Indians from visiting the base, and air force officers generally helped in this exclusion. But it was easy for Indians to walk or paddle there in secret and trade with the civilians. They could barter artefacts, feather ornaments, or feline and giant-otter skins for things that their own post would not give them: fancy foods, some aluminium pans, guns and ammunition, even alcohol (for the few tribes who liked it). Attractive Indian women could be a temptation for the workmen, although such sexual relationships were strongly disapproved of by the officers, and could be punished. A Kamaiurá told Carmen Junqueira that the post forbade visits to Xingu base because people going there might catch diseases such as influenza or measles, and because the personnel might want to have sex with Indian women. But some Indians liked going there, or even further afield, to farms beyond the outer limits of the park. This Kamaiurá thought that the prohibition was because the post authorities were jealous of his people having commerce with outsiders. 'This is rotten, because Indians need many things and also want to get to know towns, to travel and trade. ... The solution is to go secretly to Xingu [base]. It is wise not to quarrel with the Post; but Indians like to trade.'

Most indigenous people appreciated all that the Villas Boas were doing for them, in stopping attacks by neighbouring tribes, and particularly in providing excellent medical treatment. Another Kamaiurá added that 'some say that the Post prevents other whites from coming here to take our land. This is possible—there are already many whites near here [in surrounding farms].' So the consensus was that 'We Indians like the Post very much, because we greatly need axes, machetes, scythes and medicine. If the head of the Post [Orlando] were to leave, all of us here would end up dying. But he does not go—he will remain until he is very old.' Indians were not sure who paid for the goods—it might have been Orlando himself on his journeys to São Paulo, or his superiors in the Indian Protection Service (SPI), or the doctors buying medicines. (It was in fact all three of these providers, but mostly government funds.) 'What is certain is that the Post has many things. But these are no longer distributed by the head of the Post [Orlando] but by Indian workers—Kaiabi, Trumai, Metuktire.' This was thought to be unfair. The Kamaiurá imagined that his people lost out because they had no one working in the post. The anthropologist Thomas Gregor added another benefit provided by the post: that it 'opened up a new social world for the Xingu Indians'. Previously, contact between villages had come through occasional formal ceremonies. 'Today the Post serves as an interactional free zone where the Xinguanos can make casual contacts with their neighbours in a [neutral] setting. Intertribal news, gossip, and communication are facilitated as never before.'

Imported goods may have helped in clearing *roças* and the resulting agriculture, but they inevitably wiped out handicraft skills. Xinguanos used to make bark canoes shaped over fires. Then they learned from the Juruna how to make dugouts—of course using metal axes, adzes, and planes; and in later years came aluminium boats. Outboard motors replaced paddles. Hunters started to use 0.22 rifles instead of bows and arrows. An Indian noted that 'girls do not wear uluris now, except for dances, after which they remove them. In the past they were all naked, now they have clothes'. Clothing of course needed imported cloth, needles and thread, and soap—and it supplanted artistic body paint. Hammocks changed from open fibre to more comfortable cloth: 'The whites have much wool, and women now make hammocks only of wool.' Metal pans replaced handsome manioc-roasting pans—despite the Villas Boas' early attempt to protect Waurá women's pottery skills. Discarded boxes or barrels of plastic and metal were now used as seats, instead of beautiful carved and painted stools. Indians forgot traditional skills, either from making things more easily using knives and tools, or because artefacts such as stone axes became obsolete, or because metal replaced pottery and wood.

Most indigenous people felt that such imports made only a minor impact, and would not destroy their culture:

> It is good to live as Indians, as we do now. ... We Indians do not want change. He who is born an Indian lives as one. He could change if he wishes, but it is not good to do so. Indians remain here, working, wrestling, dancing. It is good to study, to learn to read and know everything. Study, but keep one's skills as an Indian: it is good thus. ... Indians cannot live in cities. We like to visit, to learn about them and see how caraibas [whites] make all these things that caraibas have. But do not get used to it: return quickly. Indians die right here. It is good for caraibas to live in cities and Indians here.

Anthropologists reacted differently to these changes. Most researchers gave credit to the administrators for slowing the rate of change. 'Today, thanks to Orlando and Claudio Villas Boas, Indian lands and culture remain essentially intact.' Change 'is less violent because it is guided by the wisdom, intuition, and generosity of men like Claudio and Orlando'.

Some anthropologists worried that the Villas Boas were changing too much. Renate Viertler (who worked with the Kamaiurá in 1967) wrote that although the brothers sought to preserve many indigenous customs, their 'intense economic and medical assistance' and their ending of inter-tribal conflicts would 'lead to profound transformations in the positioning of villages throughout the upper-Xingu region'. Rafael Bastos even claimed that it had been wrong to contact warlike peoples and then stop them from fighting one another, to produce what has been called the Pax Xinguana. Bastos wrote that this peace was imposed 'arbitrarily and brutally' and was unnatural for indigenous warriors whose belligerence was a 'dramatic factionalism' between their peoples. Orlando's son (of the same name, who became a brilliant professor of jurisprudence simultaneously at São Paulo's two best universities) commented that this nonsense was like deploring vaccinations because they prevented 'natural' diseases. He also pointed out that the twelve Xinguano peoples had ceased inter-tribal fighting and merged peacefully in the nineteenth century, long before contact. Darcy Ribeiro stressed the courage of the brothers who risked their lives to contact hostile tribes and then persuade them to stop fighting. He admitted that 'this was a sad business for those peoples. But it was less bad because this pacification was done by the Villas Boas, who knew how to defend them and guarantee them a better chance of survival than [was done] for other peoples summoned to cohabit with us.'

Others criticized from the opposite flank. The *sertanista* Francisco 'Chico' Meirelles[*] felt that the brothers were moving too slowly. In an interview in 1973 Meirelles 'did not accept the working methods of the Villas Boas brothers, and he was suspicious of anthropologists. The greatest crime committed against the Indians was their segregation in the Xingu Park.' The policy of gradual change left Indians unprepared for the 'fatal' arrival of modern civilization—which was inevitable. Meirelles argued that Brazil should be training Indians for this confrontation. 'Either we should prepare Indians to par-

---

[*] Francisco Meirelles (1908–78), a former cavalry officer, was an explorer and *sertanista* almost as famous as the Villas Boas. He had contacted one group of warlike Xavante in 1946 (just after the Roncador–Xingu Expedition), then a series of potentially hostile Kayapó peoples west of the Xingu, and the Xikrin Kayapó (at the same time as Leonardo Villas Boas), and later—with his son Apoena (named after a Xavante chief)—peoples like the Suruí, Pakáa Nova (Uru-eu-wau-wau), and Wari in Rondônia. He and the Villas Boas liked and respected one another, despite their diametric disagreement about indigenist policy.

127

ticipate in our competitive society—which is where they will be as soon as they are contacted by us—or they will remain marginalized, transformed into beggars.' He even argued that unless indigenous peoples were rapidly integrated they would be exterminated. The anthropologist Pedro Agostinho da Silva agreed to some extent. He admired the work of the Villas Boas and accepted that their Indians were surviving well in an 'isolated and sealed environment'. But he argued that 'if we wish to ensure the survival of Xingu society, it must be prepared for ecological reality.' It was essential 'to prepare for gradual transition from a subsistence to a consumer economy, without the loss of ethnic and social cohesion'—which was precisely what the Villas Boas strove to achieve, but easier said than done.

Some missionaries tried to introduce the concept of working for pay. In 1967 Claudio went to visit Chief Bebgogoti's large village of Mekragnoti Kayapó on the Iriri river—these were related to the Metuktire who had chosen to remain within the Xingu Park. Claudio was quite impressed by a Canadian Protestant missionary called Dale Snyder, who hardly interfered with tribal customs but did try to prepare his Indians for contact with frontier society by teaching them Portuguese, reading and writing, and elements of commerce. He insisted that they bring food or other objects as token 'payment' before being given tools or medicine. Claudio, however, preferred his system of generosity in the Xinguano tradition, rather than barter.

Claudio argued that, despite Snyder's gentle approach, missionaries would inevitably seek religious conversion and, if this were done too soon after contact, it shattered indigenous culture. 'It's like an operation on their minds—a lobectomy. You force them to change all the unconscious data through which they view the world.' Orlando felt that conversion to Christianity was unnecessary because

the Indians have a rich religion. Teaching them catechism would be madness: it would overthrow all their cultural values. With what object? To tell them not to believe in [the malign spirit] Jacuí but to accept that the whale swallowed Jonah, when they know neither what Jonah nor a whale is?

This was why missionaries were banned from the Xingu Park.

The integration argument was taken further by people who pretended to care for the Indians' interests, but actually wanted their land and its natural resources, or their cheap labour, or simply to be rid of them as a nuisance. Such critics claimed that keeping indigenous people in a 'primitive' state was inhuman because it denied them enjoyment of the prosperity of Brazil's 'economic miracle'. General Frederico Rondon (no relation or soulmate of the great Indian protector) condemned 'segregating them from contact with the most advanced national elements, and helping to retard their incorporation into Brazilian society.' This and the other rapid-integration arguments were flagrantly disingenuous. The general knew full well that Indians leaving protected territories or communal villages had no contact with 'advanced elements' and did not enjoy Brazil's economic miracle—they just sank below the millions of desperately poor backwoodsmen at the base of frontier society. Another general, Oscar Jerónimo Bandeira de Mello (who was, amazingly, later put in charge of the SPI), claimed that indigenous reserves were impeding national 'progress' in the form of road-building and deforestation. 'The Indian is not a guinea pig, nor the property of half-a-dozen opportunists. You cannot stop the development of Brazil on account of the Xingu Park.' Orlando's answer was that defending indigenous peoples' right to their lands was not impeding progress. 'What do the fazendeiros [ranchers] want to do with the land? Remove two hundred Indians and put in their place one caboclo [peasant woodsman] and one mare looking after two hundred cattle for them. To them an Indian is worth less than a steer. I will not debate with that sort of people.'

When he considered whether Indians should be integrated, Orlando looked back at the four centuries since the Portuguese started to colonize Brazil. He observed that, since then, most of the world's population had exploded, whereas Brazil's several million indigenous peoples had almost been extinguished (largely by alien diseases, of course). There had been repeated experiments to integrate Indians into national society; but every attempt had failed, and continued to do so. There were two stages in this process: acculturation and integration. Acculturation is any form of change, any import of tools or knowledge. Just changing a stone axe to a metal one is an act of acculturation. Orlando admitted that this process is inexorable, and it must happen. 'You cannot leave the Indian with his stone axe because it is folklore.' The Villas Boas were just trying to *slow down* acculturation to a rate that the Indians wanted and could handle without damaging their stable and balanced society. However, many politicians and a few anthropologists wanted the next step: full integration into Brazilian society. This would be catastrophic, 'because integration involves complete change or the substitution of values. You cannot integrate by half.' The two societies could and should co-exist. Some fine democracies contained minorities who were allowed to continue their separate existence.

Another criticism of the Xingu Indigenous Park was that it was a 'human zoo' that kept Indians as attractive curiosities to be 'a showcase for pseudoscientists' or for the delectation of visitors, including the military and their families. This jibe came from people who had never seen the Xingu Park or were jealous of it. A zoo is a place to which animals are brought from their natural habitats and confined in cages, often inside cities. The park is 26,000 square kilometres of pristine forests and rivers that are the habitat of peoples who have lived there for millennia and continue to do so freely. It is as far from a zoo or a cage as one could get.

In 1971 the Brazilian government invited Robin Hanbury-Tenison to report on the treatment of its indigenous peoples. He went on behalf of Survival International, a charity to help indigenous peoples that he, this author, and two others had founded two years previously (initially with a different name). Hanbury-Tenison visited nine of the peoples in the Xingu and fourteen in other parts of the country, and he concluded that, despite some good efforts elsewhere, 'The Indians of the Xingu Indigenous Park were the healthiest in mind and body of those we saw in Brazil.' He totally disagreed with the integrationist critics, feeling that Xingu peoples 'were better able to cope with their present problems and had a better chance of eventual adaptation to the twentieth century.... This is entirely due to the Villas Boas brothers and the total dedication of their lives to this work over the last twenty-five years.'

In the following year, 1972, the Brazilians invited another such inspection, this time bt the Aborigines Protection Society (one of the world's oldest NGOs, founded in 1837), and provided planes and other transport for this team. No group, Brazilians or foreigners, has been given such sweeping access, before or since then. I had the great good fortune to be one of four investigators in that team. We presented our report to the recently formed indigenous agency Funai, and published it as a 186-page book. After visiting scores of indigenous territories all over Brazil, we were as impressed as Robin Hanbury-Tenison (and many others) had been by the unique approach of the Xingu Park. We wrote:

> It was refreshing to escape the paternalism we have noted at so many other posts. Moreover, we felt that the [indigenous] leaders were more capable of meeting the outside world on equal terms than many of those more strenuously 'civilized' Indians we had met elsewhere. ... The Xingu Park must be the only region in Brazil to enjoy [so many] advantages and to have had a single and continuous policy under the same leadership since the 1940s. The Park is famous as an example of what slow acculturation can mean. ... [Most impressive] is the self-confidence of the Indians and their lack of that inferiority complex that characterises other tribes with long contact.

CHANGE

This was the achievement of the Villas Boas.

* * *

By the 1970s the two surviving Villas Boas brothers were also changing, becoming increasingly different to one another in looks and foibles. Orlando was now slightly pudgier, short but now weighing 80 kilograms (175 pounds). Like everyone in the Brazilian interior, he wore minimal clothes—an open shirt or none, tough cotton trousers, often flip-flops with no socks. His hair was long and unkempt, his goatee beard greying. He often had his glasses on top of his head, but lowered them for reading. One journalist admired Orlando's 'bright, black and expressive eyes, and an easy laugh as wicked as a caboclo's [backwoodsman's]. Actually, he *is* a caboclo. Twenty-five years in the forest have burned his skin and made him at home in nature.' Despite his formidable intelligence, Orlando's tastes remained those of an ordinary Brazilian—fiction by all the popular Brazilian authors, light reading in magazines (particularly popular history) and even photo-novelas (picture romances) and gossip, Vila-Lobos music, passion-fruit juice, plenty of cigarettes. Orlando was quiet and serious when dealing with the day-to-day administration of the park—and often irritated when things went wrong. He had no secretarial assistant or office staff, and he flew out to São Paulo or Brasilia perhaps twice a year to see the authorities and expedite park affairs.

There were a handful of workmen on the SPI payroll who tended a kitchen garden and kept machinery functioning and buildings repaired. Much management was done by Indians—another innovation by the brothers: 'An Indian father will let his son live at the Post and learn things from "civilized" men, provided that this doesn't interfere with his education as an Indian.' Most youngsters started in the kitchen as helpers, then progressed to dealing with food supplies, and then became cooks; or they might work in the infirmary. They could then choose to learn a speciality such as carpentry or machine maintenance, with a few becoming highly proficient as mechanics, radio operators, or drivers of the post's tractor and jeep. In the mid-1960s there were twenty helpers—twelve efficient Kaiabi, two Kamaiurá, and one each from six other Xinguano villages. Three of the Kaiabi had their wives and children with them, partly because their villages were farther away. At the end of that decade these volunteers were led by the Kaiabi Pionim 'who substitutes for Orlando in his absence' and had been a key member of every expedition, and by the radio operator Aruyave Trumai. (Pionim and Aruyave were the two promising young men who had had to be exiled from Diauarum to Leonardo in 1967, because of Pionim's revenge killing of the Kaiabi psychopath Tapiokap.) There was a driver–mechanic called Kaniko, the head cook Sabino (helped by his wife and her sister), and a charming twenty-year-old Metuktire driver called Megaron—who was destined for greater things. Aritana, the young Yawalapiti chief groomed by the Villas Boas, helped smooth and interpret inter-tribal relations. 'The efficient helpers at the Post are most solicitous to all visitors, helping with their every need' in a friendly, amiable, and dedicated manner.

Orlando could be an extrovert charmer, spellbinding when he embarked on tales of his adventures—as I often heard him do. Indians loved his expansive, jokey manner. He embraced them and called them by nicknames such as 'baby face' or 'hairless monkey'. The English photographer Maureen Bisilliat, who revealed the beauty of the Xinguanos in dazzling photographs, knew Orlando as 'sturdy and exuberant, generous, gregarious—a mighty mountain of a man with all-seeing eyes and a splendid sense of humour, forever translating the twists and turns of life into acutely perceptive anecdotes'.

The brothers were determined to interfere as little as possible in indigenous customs, to be nothing more than intermediaries between that society and the potentially threatening outside world. They of course knew all the villages and their hierarchies; but they stayed in their posts and visited tribes rarely—usually only when invited to a ceremony. Even then, the famous British photographer Don McCullin 'noticed that when the Indians performed their ceremonies and dances, the brothers kept their distance. They had discretion. There was a tranquillity there: a kind of spiritual blessing about the atmosphere that they created in the depths of that forest.'

Indians were kings in their land. Whenever some wandered into the administrative building, conversation turned to them. Orlando listened with the infinite patience they expected. David Nasser, one of Brazil's foremost commentators, remarked that 'The Xingu Indians observed that Orlando seemed instinctively to understand their secrets, without even speaking their language'. When the British doctor Philip Hugh-Jones and other scientists came upriver from Diauarum to Posto Leonardo in 1968, Orlando warmly welcomed the Indians who were with them, but scarcely said a word to the strangers he didn't know. 'He has a variable temper, but is often very helpful—and his word is law around the Xingu Park. ... He tolerates visitors who are prepared to help him, so is sympathetic to doctors, scientists, etc.' Doors were never shut in the post. Indian children called Orlando 'Tamoin'—'grandfather' in Tupi and treated him like one; or he was 'Lando' (short for Orlando). At dawn, a child might come to his hammock, pull his hair and say,

'Wake up Tamoin, the sun is rising,' but he would gently answer, 'Tamoin is sleeping: leave him alone. We can play later.' The writer Rachel de Queiroz remembered seeing a Trumai boy who had been sent for treatment to a hospital in Rio de Janeiro leafing through the picture magazine *O Cruzeiro*. He came across an article about Orlando. 'He hugged and kissed the pictures, laughing with tears in his eyes and exclaiming "Vira Boa! Vira Boa!"' (Years later, this boy became famous as the artist Amati Trumai.)

Posto Leonardo gradually grew into a little hamlet of some twenty houses. There was the all-important infirmary, a small guest house, stores, and workshops. In addition to the main meeting and refectory hall, Orlando built a home for himself: a modest stone house with a sitting room, two bedrooms, and a broad veranda.

Diauarum, the other post, downriver to the north, also grew into a little camp of similar size. Its three rows of tidy thatched houses were for resident Kaiabi and for Indian or white visitors. There was no large hall, but there was an infirmary, workshop, storerooms, and the modest dwelling for Claudio— based on his bat-proof hen house. Claudio's qualities and idiosyncrasies became more pronounced. Thin and slight, weighing only 50 kilograms (110 pounds), with granny glasses (often tinted), and completely white hair, moustache, and beard, he was still a far cry from the macho stereotype of the great explorer that he was. As he entered his fifties, Claudio still lived like a monk, in the hut with mud-and-wattle walls, earth floor and *inajá*-palm roof. The furniture was just his hammock, a rickety table, and overflowing bookcases. Claudio did not conceal his shyness, saying: 'I am an extremely timid person, with many doubts about the values and directions of our so-called civilized world.' He loved Stravinsky and Beethoven, but not Vila-Lobos. His reading was still an eclectic jumble of philosophy and political theory. He could quote Hegel, Kierkegaard, Ludwig Feuerbach, Thomas Aquinas, Lévi-Strauss, Freud, and Marx—although I and others found his thinking often difficult to follow. In a rare revelation about his politics, he said that he 'defended a largely egalitarian regime of socialism (almost Christian, but not communist) that valued man'.

Claudio was just as attuned to indigenous people as his brother, but in a different way. He knew much about tribal mythology and beliefs, and he shared the Indians' love and knowledge of the forests. He profoundly understood indigenous thinking, was adept at tribal politics, and had infinite patience in hours of quiet conversation. Every afternoon, men, women, children, and tribal elders would come to chat, argue, or laugh with Claudio. He clearly preferred being with them to the company of other Brazilians or foreigners. Few non-Indians got as close to him as they did.

Like his brother, Claudio relied on immensely efficient Kaiabi to administer Diauarum. Chief among these was Mairawé. Born on the Teles Pires, and the son of Chief Ewafuá, he migrated into the Xingu with his family in the early 1950s. He later recalled:

> I have accompanied Claudio Villas-Boas ever since I was a boy. I was practically raised by him. I learned many things from him, to speak Portuguese, the affairs of the reserve, and what it means to be chief of a post. One day he felt that I was competent to be chief [of Diauarum] and stay in his place. So now I am here. When he leaves to travel, I remain in his place and stay to take charge.

The anthropologist Darcy Ribeiro's ex-wife Berta met the famous Mairawé in 1978 when he was twenty-eight, now with a house at Diauarum, a Suiá wife, and four children. She found the young Kaiabi to be very handsome, well educated in Portuguese, a self-made man, dignified in his position as manager of Diauarum, and never asking for anything. Mairawé travelled constantly as 'factotum of the northern part of the Park'. He was a proficient boatman who knew every inch of the river, and 'he alone can drive a tractor, pilot a boat, and also converse with his people'. He could bridge the gulf between the two societies, being well attuned to white men's ways, mature and calm, and helpful and loyal towards them. Funai officials treated him as an equal, because 'his seriousness commands respect'. But Mairawé was also totally Kaiabi. He participated in all his people's ceremonies and shared their beliefs. He was aware of his status as an indigenous leader, recorder of all births, marriages, and deaths among the Kaiabi within the Xingu Park, and his people had invited him to write their history.

Claudio's forays to the cities were very rare—and when he did emerge, he could not wait to return to the peaceful Xingu. I flew out with him on one such excursion, in 1971 when he was going on a hopeless attempt to reverse a decision by the then military government (about which more later). He was deeply worried and more than usually quiet. He had with him another little boy he had adopted, Tauaru, the son of a Trumai woman. Claudio raised him as he would a fostered child. He was pleased when I played with the boy, in the unfamiliar surroundings of a São Paulo apartment, and surprised me by suddenly inviting me onto his next big forest expedition—which I sadly could not accept because of other commitments.

The Villas Boas brothers were very close to one another, despite their radically different natures. They spoke on a crackly short-wave radio almost daily. Once Claudio apologized for some complaints he had made to his older brother. He said: 'These are just the gripes of old age. As you know, I am in a sort of menopause. So, don't be cross with me. Everything here is fine. All positive. Over …' At which, Orlando jokily said to people who were listening: 'I cannot stand more of these sentimental confessions by Claudio. What is worse is that they happen at the wrong times!' Claudio came up the Xingu to visit his brother quite often, giving a howl like a monkey as he approached from his boat. Orlando would have some light-hearted comment like: 'Claudio is a rascal. He comes to visit me just to pinch guns. He has a collection of revolvers and is always denuding my stock. The latest he took was a Biretta 007 that I had won!'

The brothers were totally agreed about policy towards indigenous peoples and about the administration of the Xingu. The Indians loved and respected both men. But they disliked some restrictions that were placed on themselves. Claudio confessed: 'I am fully aware that at times the Indians resent me, with a kind of repressed hatred. … In truth, both Orlando and I are their friends, companions, and "big fathers". Then they love us. But we also represent their castrators, advisers against contact with white men, who forbid them to go and see the great new roads' that were being hacked into the forest. Later, looking back on his decades in the Xingu, Claudio told how he and Orlando came to admire indigenous culture so much. 'We appreciated its value, so that we grew to respect Indians as authentic men. They, far more intelligent than us, discovered that we viewed them thus. So they also grew to respect us.'

11

CONTACTS AND RESCUES

The tranquillity of the upper Xingu was still violated by surprise attacks. The strapping but generally pacific Xinguano Indians lived in fear of a mysterious warlike people who lived far up the Ronuro—the westernmost of the fan of rivers that converge to form the main Xingu. For many years these elusive raiders were known as Txikão (pronounced 'shik-aun'), which means 'hostile people' in Tupi; but we now know that they call themselves Ikpeng.

There were numerous reports of their ferocity. In 1942 the Ikpeng killed a dozen Nahukwá, and a further four of them in 1944; in the following year they attacked the Waurá and burned a communal hut. (The Waurá retaliated by burning an Ikpeng village.) They harassed the Indian Protection Service's (SPI's) Culiseu Post on the Batovi in 1946. Within the Xingu Park, they attacked Mehinaku canoes on the Curisevo river in 1948, and their village in the following year—the Mehinaku repelled this onslaught but feared a repeat. In 1949 Dr Pedro Lima (one of the first medics in the Xingu) found the Waurá terrified after another skirmish with the Ikpeng, so that throughout the following year they posted sentries during the men's evening smoking session and protected their women when they fetched water from the river. Another early doctor, Kalervo Oberg, was at the Villas Boas camp in Jacaré when there was panic because of a rumoured Ikpeng attack. 'The apprehension of the Indians, especially the fear on the faces of women and children, was unmistakable evidence of the reality of war in their lives.' Then, in 1950 Chief Kamalive of the Nahukwá, 'a tall, thin, brave man', ran to Orlando in a state of agitation, pointing to the west and crying out: '"The Txikão [Ikpeng] are fierce."' ... He told us a long and dramatic history. We learned that the [Ikpeng] gave no rest to his peaceful and good-natured people. Every year, during the dry season, they appeared, shooting arrows, setting fire to huts, seizing children.' The Ikpeng also turned their attention back to the Mehinaku, launching an

137

attack that was repelled by Chief Aiuruá wielding a Winchester 0.44 rifle. The chief was wounded, and Orlando recalled that 'He staggered in, covered in blood with an arrow buried in his ribs. Immediately brought to our post on the Culuene, Aiuruá was operated on and saved.' In the wet season of 1952, the Ikpeng again raided the Waurá and kidnapped some of their children, including the chief's daughter. In retaliation, Waurá and Kamaiurá men paddled up the Batovi, walked across savannah for a day and a half, and killed two men in an attack on an Ikpeng village.

All these skirmishes demonstrated that the main motives for inter-tribal warfare were revenge, and the capture of women and children. The French anthropologist Patrick Menget later established that the panic among Xinguanos had been exaggerated. In some twenty raids between 1942 and 1960 the Ikpeng actually killed between ten and fifteen people. They captured seven children or adults, of whom only three survived to adulthood within their tribe: two Waurá women and one Nahukwá man. 'The Xinguanos, on their side, managed to capture only one Ikpeng woman—who succeeded in fleeing after two months and returned to her village.' The Xinguano warriors killed three Ikpeng and twice burned their village.

In 1952, Claudio decided that he must try to contact these dangerous people. Not knowing what language the Ikpeng spoke, he took with him five Indians, each of whom spoke a different tongue. After twelve days' journey south-westwards up the Batovi river, his eagle-eyed guides spotted an Ikpeng trail leading into the forest. They investigated this, before returning to the river and hiding their boat among the vegetation. Next day, they advanced cautiously along the trail, pausing frequently to listen. After three hours, Claudio recalled:

> We heard the chatter of men, women and children. Treading gently, we advanced a few paces until, peering through the foliage, we could see the [Ikpeng] camp. There were [about eighty] people gathered unconcernedly. Between their hammocks, various curassows, parrots and macaws wandered tranquilly. Here and there were half-lit small fires: you could see that these were alight only by wisps of blue smoke that rose from them.

The sun was at its zenith. This was the quiet hour when all of nature, animals and men, rests. Although he appreciated that it was a difficult moment to make contact, Claudio

> resolved to attempt the impossible. So, accompanied by two Kaiabi Indians called Acuchim and Koá, we entered the camp. An old man was drowsing, half seated, in a hammock. The people he saw when he opened his eyes

caused him shock. ... He confronted us. We took a step forward and held out a fine machete with a red handle. Standing and straightening his body, the old man started to shout. As if shaken by thunder, they all rose and the camp was plunged into tremendous confusion. Women cried out and ran to hustle their children into the forest; men, bellowing incomprehensible words, seized their weapons, and the sound of clustering arrows reached our ears. Although we felt that it was useless, we resolved to persist in our demonstrations of friendship for a little longer. All in vain. When arrows started to whistle [towards us], we managed to take refuge behind a thick tree that grew at the edge of the camp. There, making a rapid assessment, we concluded that simple flight was no longer possible. This was because there was an open area of the camp to be traversed before reaching our return path [and] none of us would escape the arrows.

Claudio later admitted that surprising the Ikpeng in their camp 'was the stupidest mistake I ever made. ... I would be dead if Cerilo Kaiabi had not been following behind me. He fired [a gun] into the air, and with just that one shot they were gone.' The expedition raced back to their boat before the Ikpeng could cut them off. On the riverbank they left presents of four boxes of axes, one of scythes, and four dozen machetes, and then fled downstream. Claudio had learned the hard way a basic rule of contact: you must let Indians observe you from concealment, but never catch them unawares.

Three years later, in 1955, both Villas Boas brothers tried again. With seven Indians they went up the Batovi to the place where Claudio had survived the shower of arrows; but they saw no Ikpeng. Back at the post, some shamans had had a vision of the Villas Boas being killed by the fierce tribe, so all the Xinguano peoples 'lamented and wept copiously'. They were delighted when their great guardians returned unscathed.

The elusive Ikpeng lived south-west of what was soon to become the Xingu Indigenous Park. In 1958 and 1959 they raided near an SPI post far south of the Batovi. So agents from that reserve borrowed an American missionary's plane, located a village, and started their own contact by dropping presents; but this endeavour ceased when funds ran out. Chief Melobo of the Ikpeng later admitted that, having never seen flying machinery, they thought that the plane was a huge bird. So, when it dropped a present of *rapadura* brown sugar (a Brazilian favourite), this seemed to be the bird's excrement, and therefore poisonous.

In 1960, the Ikpeng snatched two Waurá women in another audacious raid. This was the moment when the Villas Boas were expelled from the post (then called Vasconcellos) and from the SPI, because they had fallen out with the head of the Central Brazil Foundation (FBC), who was plotting with the state governor to sell Xingu lands. A 'Brazilian adventurer' was temporarily in charge of the post, and he encouraged ten Waurá and Mehinaku warriors to launch a reprisal raid, for which he armed them with guns and ammunition. 'They surprised the [Ikpeng] in their village and [boasted that they] killed twelve adults, but did not manage to recover the [kidnapped] girls.' (This death toll does not tally with what the anthropologist Patrick Menget later learned.)

With the election of their friend Jânio Quadros as president in 1961, the Villas Boas were soon back in charge of the newly legalized Xingu Indigenous Park. More years elapsed until 1964, when first the Aweti and then the Yawalapiti reported that Ikpeng had been prowling around their small villages immediately alongside Leonardo administration post. There happened to be two small planes in the Xingu at that time (one donated to the park, the other belonging to the University of Brasilia), and these managed to locate an Ikpeng village, forty minutes' flying time—about 150 kilometres (over 90 miles)—south-west of Leonardo. The next day, when the planes buzzed that village and dropped presents, Indians were seen, hiding in the undergrowth with their bows and arrows, ready to shoot. The university's pilot boldly succeeded in landing nearby on a dry floodplain of baked mud. The attraction team—Orlando and Claudio, the anthropologist Eduardo Galvão, the photographer/ethnographer Jesco von Puttkamer,* and the young Kaiabi

---

* Jesco von Puttkamer was the son of a German baron and Brazilian mother, born near Rio de Janeiro in 1919. After education in Brazil and Switzerland, he returned to Germany with his family to secure an inheritance. When in 1942 Brazil joined the war on the Allied side, the Germans interned Jesco and his brother as enemy aliens—even though a relative of the same name was a naval adjutant to Hitler who remained with the Führer until the bitter end. After the war Jesco worked as a photographer for the Bavarian government at the Nüremberg trials. Back in Brazil with his family in 1947, his photographic career often involved indigenous peoples. In 1960, aged forty-one, he joined the Villas Boas in the Xingu and loved it there: he was unpaid, but was given accommodation at the post and took part in several expeditions, including this one to the Ikpeng. But von Puttkamer fell out with the brothers, possibly because of his overfamiliarity with Indian boys. I first met him in his house in Goiânia in 1971: a tall blond man, very amiable and with a deep knowledge of Indians. Throughout that decade he was a leading writer and superb photographer of Brazilian Indians for *National Geographic* magazine. He was active as an ethnographer and archaeologist for the Catholic University of Goiás for the rest of his life. The university has now made his house in the provincial city Goiânia into a cultural centre in his name, full of 130,000 photographs and 400 artefacts from

Pionim—equally bravely moved from the plane towards a group of Ikpeng. More Indians emerged from the forest. It was a tense moment. Orlando and Claudio remembered how,

> gesticulating nervously, shouting, all talking at once in a strange language, they gave the impression that they were sending us away. With our arms raised [to show that they were unarmed], also saying whatever occurred to us at that moment, we continued to advance across the floodplain towards them. Some—doubtless the boldest—held their ground; others fled. However, even the bravest almost jumped backwards when we attempted to touch them. At one moment we had the impression that the contact had failed: they all beat a retreat and disappeared from our view. But their absence did not last long. They returned, shouting and gesticulating, a minute later. Suddenly, twenty or thirty Indians, arranged in a line, energetically brandishing their bows and arrows, came running to our side. They stopped a short distance away but did not remain in one place: they started walking agitatedly from side to side as if they were treading on a brazier, but their sharp eyes did not miss any of our movements. Step by step, we walked towards the group. We felt that this was the decisive moment. If they withdrew it would be necessary to start everything again. But the [Ikpeng] did not withdraw. Talking incessantly, gesticulating, dancing, they held their bows and arrows out towards us or simply threw them at our feet. We could not have hoped for a more obvious demonstration of peace.

With so many passengers in a small plane, they could carry few presents; but the Ikpeng seemed pleased with the few they had dropped. This contact involved only thirty Indian men and eight women.

In September of the following year, 1965, the Villas Boas returned to try to complete the Ikpeng contact. This time they went by boat, a five-day journey down the Tuatuari and Culuene and then up the Ronuro and lower Jatobá rivers. Finally, they spotted an opening in the riverbank forest. They followed a broad trail that led to the open space where their plane had made the risky landing in the previous year. A young doctor, Murillo Villela,[†] said that

---

46 indigenous peoples in all parts of Brazil. This Puttkamer Centre is not far from another museum and huge archive of another outstanding expert and photographer of Indians, Jesco's (and Orlando's) close friend Adrian Cowell. These two great archives make Goiânia a mecca for indigenous researchers.

[†] Dr Murillo Villela was a close friend of the Villas Boas, and their personal doctor from the 1950s until well into the twenty-first century. He loved adventure, so took leave of his cardiac practice in São Paulo (which was not connected to

'Orlando and Claudio reckon that the Indians had made this trail in the hope that the whites would revisit.' But, although the brothers and two skilled Indians—Koá Kaiabi and Megaron Metuktire—bravely explored along this and another trail deeper into the forest, there were no answers to their calls.

A few miles further up the Jatobá, they spotted a canoe moored to the river bank. Dr Villela recalled:

> We steered our canoes to the left bank, and with great emotion and anxiety tied up and waited. After five minutes, Orlando, Claudio and I discussed the situation. I dived in and swam underwater across the 50-metre-wide [110-foot] river to the moored canoe. Reaching it and protected by it, I bobbed up slightly and peeked into the boat and saw human footprints, still damp, and an arrow. I swam back across the river. We started to call out in various languages for about half an hour, but with no reaction. We then heard a shout, followed by others from different parts of the forest along about 200 metres [650 feet] of river bank. A few Indians started to emerge, quite agitated, holding bows and arrows that they brandished repeatedly, talking much but with no sign that they wanted to descend to meet us. Claudio and Orlando decided that they and I should cross the river in a canoe paddled by a Park worker, completely unarmed and with our hands raised.

A journalist who was watching noted that they, and Koá and Megaron, had no protection other than small aluminium bowls among the presents, which they might have tried to use as shields against arrows. So 'anything could happen. ... We could only wait, confident in the tremendous understanding of Indian psychology that Claudio and Orlando had acquired in twenty years of living with them.'

On the far bank, 'our landing provoked some agitation but no aggression. We offered the presents with our arms outstretched.' The brothers repeated

---

Baruzzi's school of preventive medicine) whenever the brothers asked him to join an expedition. He was a valued expeditioner because, as well as being a versatile field doctor, he doubled as a good shot, a fisherman, and a cook. He was on the Metuktire, Suiá, Ikpeng and, later, Panará contacts as well as the Geographical Centre Expedition of 1959. In 1961 Villela was one of three heart surgeons who operated unsuccessfully on Leonardo Villas Boas. Over half a century later, as a sprightly bearded old man, he told me exactly why they had been unable to save the forty-one-year-old explorer—but I was unable to follow or record his detailed medical explanations. In 1963 Orlando recruited the nurse Marina, his future wife, from Dr Villela's surgery.

the word 'friends' in the various languages they knew. The least nervous Ikpeng approached the boat and finally started to take presents. 'Once the initial tension was over and we were fraternizing, we climbed the bank with them. We were surprised by the great number of Indians with bows and arrows who started to emerge from the forest, gradually as if obeying some strategic manoeuvre.' As the expeditioners started along the trail a chief appeared, naked apart from an egret-feather headdress and holding a bow in one hand and many arrows in the other. 'The shouting behind him rose to an infernal pitch, transforming the calm of the river and forest into a veritable pandemonium.'

This was the moment to offer more presents. The Villas Boas knew from experience that it was important to have gifts for women and well as men. They therefore indicated that these should appear, so that they could hand them theirs in person. But the women were acutely aware that they could be vulnerable as spoils of war. So they

> arrived gradually, almost dragged by their husbands and relatives. They were trembling so much and their babies were crying so loudly, that we had difficulty in calming them. If one of us approached, a mother and child would retreat, trembling. We finally started distributing the presents. ... The first tools we handed over were immediately hidden in the thickets and the recipients came back for more. Axes and machetes, because of their extraordinary utility, provoked exclamations of joy. Matches caused laughter and amazement: such an easy fire, for people who had to struggle so hard to light one [by twirling sticks]. Aluminium pots were also distributed; these would replace gourds and segments of taquaruçu bamboo. ... The women, who had been so reserved at first, revealed themselves as more brazen than the men. They seemed almost possessed. Talking, pulling at our clothes, they tried to obtain more objects than they could carry in their hands.

Dr Villela said that the women 'started to make noisy remarks, presumably about us'. The presents included sweets for the children, which the Indians at first thought were beads for necklaces.

As always in Brazilian history, a first contact with a hostile people had been achieved through the distribution of presents, particularly of irresistible metal blades. All contact events were potentially traumatic for the Indians. But the journalist Arley Pereira, who had been invited to cover the expedition, noted that 'the tremendous power of psychology and leadership of the Villas Boas made itself felt immediately after the contact'. The Ikpeng responded in an unusual manner. They graciously tried to return the generosity by giving a gift to each of the fourteen men on the expedition—bows and arrows, a headdress, a gourd for water, or a basket—and they rapidly learned their names. The expedition knew that it was wise to leave immediately, in a spirit of friendship, with its mission accomplished.

The contact team could see that the Ikpeng were suffering severely. It was later learned that they had been devastated by a lethal epidemic of influenza, which had possibly been brought by one of the kidnapped Waurá women. In just a few months the tribe had lost over half its population of several hundred. The remnant had fled to the Jatobá river (an eastern tributary of the Ronuro) where they 'entered a period of precarious existence ... without manioc, so that a maize-based diet provoked serious vitamin-deficiency (a form of pellagra, with erythema and buboes) which in turn made them more vulnerable to traditional parasites'. A further threat came from some mineral prospectors who had entered the region in search of diamonds. Although these adventurers did not initially clash with the Ikpeng, they may have introduced malaria and other diseases. So some of the once-fierce Indians now looked like skeletons, covered in ulcers and racked by fevers.

In 1967, two years after the happy first contact, the Villas Boas decided that they must rescue the weakened Ikpeng by bringing them within the boundaries of the Xingu Park. This was a controversial decision. Moving the Ikpeng from their village on the Jatobá would cause them to forfeit their constitutional right to that territory. But the Villas Boas justified this exodus on the grounds that the tribe was dangerously reduced in numbers and facing extinction, its wretched health required attention by the post's doctors and better food, and it was threatened by a clash with the diamond *garimpeiros*. Also, the land they were leaving was environmentally impoverished, and it had not been theirs for long. (It was later learned that the Ikpeng were related to the Carib-speaking Arara people hundreds of kilometres to the north-west, and had been migrating for many years.) Also, the founding charter of the Xingu Indigenous Park declared that it should be a sanctuary for distressed indigenous peoples—which the Ikpeng certainly were.

Adrian Cowell was on the expedition that went in June 1967 to bring the Ikpeng by boat into the Xingu Park. This team found that one fear had been realized, for 'a horde of diamond prospectors had invaded the Rivers Jatobá and Batovi and were prostituting the [Ikpeng] women and intimidating their men'. Claudio gathered what was left of the tribe for the exodus, just fifty-six adults and children—about a sixth of their original population. Five secret policemen of Brazil's military government had come, ostensibly to persuade the *garimpeiros* to leave; which they apparently did. But when the boats returned down the Jatobá with the Ikpeng, Cowell noticed that the police agents stayed behind. He bumped into their leader, José, by chance a few years later and was told that 'a small party of "friendly" prospectors had very conveniently remained behind to "co-operate" with José and his police agents.' José readily admitted that he had prospered hugely by a sweetener from the prospectors. So the Ikpeng lost their land immediately after they left, to invaders helped by secret police connivance.

In advance of the Ikpengs' transfer into the Xingu Park, the Villas Boas had conducted a public-relations campaign among the Xinguanos so that they would welcome their former enemies, whom they feared as 'valiant warriors, indefatigable giants, stoical in the face of a shower of arrows, and sowing death wherever they passed'. On the day of their arrival, some five hundred muscular upper-Xingu warriors had assembled to welcome the strangers, painted, adorned with brilliant feather ornaments, singing and dancing. A watching journalist told how:

> Suddenly from the side of the Post's administration building came a loud, high shout. All were paralysed, and then ... as if following a drill order, fewer than a hundred small and rickety Indians emerged. Some people shouted 'It is the Txikão!' The atmosphere became tense. Once the initial impact was over, this small contingent moved towards the other far more numerous group composed of taller and stronger men, in a clear demonstration of people about to kill or die. Another loud shout came from Orlando Villas Boas and the two groups stopped, but maintaining a hostile glare.

Fighting was avoided, despite the legacy of past aggressions.

The once-feared Ikpeng were lodged in a site beside the Tuatuari river, only half a kilometre (550 yards) from Posto Leonardo. The Villas Boas felt that the refugees would be safer from reprisals this close to the base. The plan worked well. The weakened and disoriented Ikpeng proved to be remarkably resilient and industrious. They immediately built a great communal thatched hut like those they had had on the Jatobá—which fortuitously was similar to those of other Xinguano peoples. They gradually came to resemble the Xinguanos in other ways—in their style of hammocks, keeping a caged harpy eagle in the central plaza, women adopting the *uluri* vagina-guard, and in some ornaments and body paint. But the Ikpeng retained features from their past among the Arara far to the north-west, such as more elaborate feather ornaments, basketry, and textiles, and they continued to be diligent farmers. Unlike the Xinguanos, they used *tipiti* basket-tubes to leach poison from manioc. They also hunted and ate more game animals than the nearby fish-eaters. But they feared malign magic as intensely as other Xingu peoples, and

145

would kill anyone suspected of such evil. Patrick Menget wrote that 'hostile witchcraft directly provokes deaths among the [Ikpeng], and they then take captives to substitute for the deceased'.

The Ikpeng are very short, almost pygmies: men average 1.56 metres (5 foot 1 inch) and women 1.46 metres (4 foot 8 inches). Once when I was talking to a standing woman I had to kneel to be at her level. Dr Baruzzi medically examined the newcomers a year after their arrival. Six had died from disease, so there were now only fifty. But although thin, they were in generally good health, thanks to some medical attention, and better food— provided by the post and, remarkably, from generous former enemies. Their main physical problem was enlarged spleens, from malaria contracted when they were on the Jatobá. Their old chief, Pabulu, was very active, and his people were soon growing their own food. A visitor reported that in 1969, two years after their exodus, the Ikpeng were 'always cheerful, smiling and joking at any time of day. No-one ever seems sad: someone is always making others laugh.' So the Ikpeng rescue was a success. They have survived as an entity, with some intermarriage into other tribes. Most then moved to a village down on the Xingu; but a few returned far away to the south-west corner of the park near their former Jatobá village.

* * *

As we have seen, the Kaiabi (or Kawaiweté) differed from other Xingu peoples because they had lived for many years among settlers, rubber-tappers, and missionaries. Although oppressed by some of these intruders, the Kaiabi had become familiar with Brazilian ways. They were by nature an efficient and industrious people who became indispensable to the Villas Boas' administration and expeditions. They also moved into the Xingu in an unusual way, migrating in six contingents over a twenty-year period, and coming of their own accord, not as refugees rescued from a crisis.

Although those Kaiabi who reached the Xingu prospered and were invaluable helpers to its authorities, their tribal culture remained strong. They had powerful shamans, and they retained an intense love for their spiritual homelands on the Rio dos Peixes ('River of Fishes'), a tributary of the Arinos headwater of the Tapajós. That river is 450 kilometres (280 miles) west of Diauarum, a huge distance in densely forested terrain. Over a third of the tribe had been driven out of that homeland on the Peixes by land-grabbing ranchers, and had settled on the Teles Pires river (another headwater of the Tapajós, but closer to the Xingu). Canisio, chief of a Kaiabi village in the

Xingu, used to make the long journey back to the Teles Pires every year. He was profoundly saddened by what he saw:

> Every time, I see that the garimpeiros [mineral prospectors] are invading more and the timber men are finishing everything, destroying the trees, the forest. … I am sad, and think: 'Will they leave us anything? Will we have anything for the future? … Will we have no more game, no more monkeys, mutum [curassows], or above all fish?'

Worst of all, the loggers and farmers polluted the river—whose water the Indians drank and bathed in—with their sawdust and effluents.

In 1966, the year after the Ikpeng contact, some Kaiabi begged the Villas Boas for help in bringing more of their people into the park 'to rescue them from the advance of the national [Brazilian] society'. They wanted to get Indians from the Kaiabi heartland on that distant Peixes river, where their only support came from an effective Jesuit mission. So Claudio organized 'Operation Kaiabi'. He took Prepori and six of his Kaiabi, eleven air force parachute troops, and two journalists. They started by locating a now overgrown airstrip that the Villas Boas had built beside the Teles Pires seventeen years earlier. Military parachutists dropped onto this and cleared it for planes to land. Kaiabi Indians then took weeks to cut a trail for 40 kilometres (25 miles) westwards to the upper Peixes, through dense forests, feeding themselves by hunting and fishing as they progressed. More weeks were spent felling trees and building canoes so that they could descend the river. They finally reached Tatuí, village of the important chief, Temeoni. Moving on for two more weeks by trail and canoe down the Peixes river, they reached another village and met a great expert on the Kaiabi, the Austrian anthropologist Georg Grünberg. It took time to persuade him and most of the people he was studying that it was in their interest to move. After tough walking back down the trails, forty-four Kaiabi and the expeditioners were airlifted into the Xingu. Twenty residents of Tatuí village refused to go, preferring to remain on the Peixes to tend ancestors' graves and 'because they loved their homelands and got on well with the Jesuit Father Dornstauder and his Mission'.

Although Chief Temeoni's village had been fairly small, he himself was a figure of great prestige. With his group's arrival, Xingu Park contained 180 Kaiabi, and it could be said that the Operation 'legitimized the migration of the Kaiabi into the Xingu'. As always, moving people from their territory was controversial. The anthropologist Dr Grünberg gave three reasons why he had finally approved it: heavy pressure by settlers and rubber men (in the absence of protection by the moribund SPI); the cultural disposition of the Kaiabi to roam and seek new lands; and, above all, the charismatic personalities of the shaman Prepori and Claudio Villas Boas, both of whom wanted to unite as much as possible the tribes within the Xingu Indigenous Park.

* * *

There was political upheaval in Brazil during the decade after the creation of the Xingu Indigenous Park. In August 1961 Jânio Quadros, the highly popular president (and friend of the Villas Boas), suddenly resigned. The reason for his resignation is still a mystery, for he was young and in good health, and he continued a successful political career within the state of São Paulo. But his sudden departure threw the country into turmoil. A constitutional flaw at that time had the president and vice-president each elected in his own right, and not necessarily of the same party. Quadros was a right-of-centre independent; but his vice-president, João Goulart, was hard left—he was actually visiting Chairman Mao in China at the time he succeeded to the presidency. Brazil was almost plunged into civil war, with the air force threatening to shoot down Goulart's plane if he tried to return. But Goulart did get back into southern Brazil, and he was allowed to become president. His left-wing government was chaotic (and anti-Indian), and it lasted for less than three years. In 1964 the army moved to seize power in a bloodless coup—with encouragement from the United States. President Goulart fled from Brasília. For one day there was a vain attempt to organize resistance by his minister of education—none other than the Marxist anthropologist Darcy Ribeiro, Orlando's colleague in drafting the Xingu Park legislation.

In the event, the military were to rule Brazil for twenty-one years, from 1964 to 1985, with five successive presidents, each a former army general or marshal. The Villas Boas' sole concern was their indigenous peoples and the Xingu Park. So they remained in the Xingu, protected by the park's 1961 legislation, and they never revealed any political bias. They had always got on well with the air force, and they would entertain any politician or military man who cared to visit. The beautiful Xingu and its handsome Indians were thus a showpiece for the military government, just as they had been for earlier, more democratic, regimes.

Rondon's once-great SPI was in terminal decline, with a series of incompetent and often grossly corrupt directors. It functioned in about a hundred small indigenous territories, in the more open southern and eastern parts of the country, with tribes who had long been in contact; but it had almost no presence in the Amazonian forested half of Brazil. In 1967, three years after the military coup, the minister of the interior, General Albuquerque Lima, appointed the procurator-general, Jader Figueiredo, to head a parliamentary inquiry into irregularities within the SPI. His commissioners worked for fourteen months, in eighteen of Brazil's states and territories, hearing 130 witnesses and substantiating most of the accusations that they made.

In late 1967 the Figueiredo Commission produced a massive report of over 5,100 pages in twenty-one volumes. Procurator Figueiredo launched this report in a hyperbolic press conference and series of broadcasts, claiming that he had uncovered 'genocide' and atrocities worse than those of Nazi Germany. In fact, the crimes detailed in the report were almost all financial: embezzlement and corruption; massive sales of timber, cattle, grain, and other resources; the leasing of indigenous lands to farmers and ranchers at suspiciously low rents; outright theft of government property; and personal fraud. There were indeed a few ugly examples of cruelty to Indians, abuse of women and children, and even covert forced labour. But the worst cases, involving torture or murder, had been perpetrated by ranchers, rubber-tappers, or frontiersmen, and did not involve the SPI—except, ironically, when it had tried to bring the criminals to justice.

It was significant that all the wrongdoings and crimes exposed by the commission had occurred *before* the military coup of 1964. The exercise may in fact have been intended to discredit Goulart's and earlier democratic governments. If so, the generals miscalculated badly. They forgot that the world was full of exiled Brazilian liberals, who were often friends of media editors, and that the foreign press was eager to criticize the military regime. The result was an avalanche of articles about abuse of Indians—all based entirely on the Figueiredo report, since foreigners were not allowed to visit indigenous territories without permission. The most powerful, eloquent, and passionate voice was that of Norman Lewis, in the British *Sunday Times* of 23 February 1969. The military government hastily withdrew and destroyed the report, but it was too late: there was a worldwide outcry about the plight of Brazil's indigenous peoples. One result of this concern was the creation later in 1969, by four people, of whom I was one, of an NGO to protect all the world's indigenous peoples. This soon changed its name to Survival International.

Although the Figueiredo Commission indicted three corrupt former directors of the SPI, none were imprisoned. Some SPI employees were sacked, others exonerated (including the great Indianist Francisco Meirelles, accused of false accounting). The disgraced SPI was wound up, and replaced in 1968

149

by Funai (an acronym for National Indigenous Foundation). This had a new constitution, but it of course continued to administer all the existing indigenous territories, and it employed most of the SPI's staff. One change was that the Xingu Indigenous Park was transferred to the new Funai, and no longer answered directly to the president of Brazil.

* * *

Far to the west of the Xingu, beyond the heartland of the Kaiabi, lived a Je-speaking people called Tapayuna. This tribe was about to suffer a series of crippling tragedies, worse than those afflicting any other indigenous people at that time. By brilliant research and intuition, an anthropologist discovered that these Tapayuna had once been part of the Suiá, who live near Diauarum. They had split early in the nineteenth century, and gradually migrated for some 500 kilometres (300 miles) westwards from the Xingu, to forests between the Arinos and Sangue rivers, both tributaries of the Juruena headwater of the Tapajós. The anthropologist reckoned that there had once been four hundred Tapayuna. They were tough warriors, with lip-discs to make them look intimidating—which earned them the name Beiços-de-pau ('Wooden Lips').

Unfortunately for the Tapayuna, their land was coveted as a settlement frontier. Farmers from southern Brazil moved down the Arinos in 1955, and in the following decade an aggressive colonization company called Conamali sold tracts of what was clearly indigenous land. The Tapayuna responded by menacing the settlers and shooting arrows at their boats. In retribution, and to 'cleanse' the land of Indians, the colonists burned a village and killed children. Because it was almost impossible to locate the Indians in their forests, some settlers left them an apparent present of tapir meat. It was a lethal trap. A Tapayuna widow later told Anthony Seeger: 'I tell you how bad white-men *kupen* put some medicine [poison] in the tapir and all my companions died. Almost all of us died. That's what the white men did to us.' Then in 1957 a rubber-tapper placed sugar laced with arsenic on the banks of a stream. This was another attempted genocide, to rid the area of Indians so that it could legally be seized as *terra devoluta* (unoccupied land). In the following year an SPI official, Fritz Tolksdorf, did make peaceful contact with some Tapayuna on the Alegre river (between the Arinos and Sangue rivers); but there were no funds to follow up on this.

In 1964 the situation worsened, when thirty men were engaged to build a road towards a settler's riverbank farm. The Tapayuna resisted, wounding six

150

workmen with arrows; but it is not known how many Indians died from the road-builders' retaliatory guns. A missionary, Father Adalberto Pereira, offered to try to contact and 'pacify' the tribe, on condition that the road-builders stopped using guns. Presents were left on Indians' trails. But these Tapayuna were by now justifiably suspicious, so the presents were either destroyed or left untouched. Father Adalberto returned in 1967 with one of the best Jesuit missionaries, Father Antonio Iasi, and two Irantxê Indians, and they started to build a hut on a river bank. But black-painted Tapayuna warriors prowled round, and then launched a ferocious attack. Their onslaught lasted for eighteen hours, with the missionaries and an Irantxê cowering in a shelter that was pounded by arrows. Father Adalberto was wounded in the leg, and they later recovered fifty of these missiles before fleeing downriver. Iasi did later make contact with some Tapayuna, and compiled a brief vocabulary of their Je-related language.

The newly formed indigenous foundation Funai engaged a *sertanista* called João Peret, who in January 1968 made a brief riverbank contact, with an exchange of presents. Then—following correct procedure—a reserve was interdicted (provisionally protected) for the Tapayuna, in a presidential decree of 8 October 1968. The *sertanista* managed to locate eleven villages from an overflight, and in May 1969 decided to organize an expedition to reach one of these. Funai was avid for good publicity, and knew how much the media loved the excitement of a 'pacification' (as it was then called). So it invited seven journalists from the three leading picture magazines to join Peret as the first to visit a Tapayuna village—just as the Villas Boas had allowed selected journalists to cover their attraction expeditions. But one of these reporters, Heydl Valle of the magazine *Fatos e Fotos*, was infected by the virulent Hong Kong strain of influenza. On their journey downriver towards the Indians, another reporter joked that Heydl had a terrible cold, so that 'if he is not immediately isolated our copy will become: "How we exterminated the 'Wooden-lips' [Tapayuna]."' But Valle was not sent home, nor properly isolated. His bed was merely segregated in a storage shed, and curious Indians visited him there. Valle himself wrote that laughing Indians imitated the noise of his raucous coughing and sneezing, and in the evening he played ring-a-ring o' roses 'with old people, children, adults and women'. Someone recalled that the expedition had doses of anti-flu vaccine; but the ice keeping these cold had long since melted. There was no doctor with the group, and there had been no medical examinations of its members.

For added publicity, two newly contacted Tapayuna were taken to Rio de Janeiro and São Paulo as trophies, to appear on television—which they did, on 21 July 1969—in the same programme that showed the Americans' moon landing. The journey must have been a traumatic experience for these hunter-gatherers; and both men died of disease during this public-relations exploitation. Peret was lauded in the press as the pacifier of a fierce tribe.

But when the 'hero' Peret returned to the Tapayuna village early in 1970, he found a scene of utter devastation. Dead bodies lay scattered on the ground, with the rest of the tribe hiding in the forest, too weak to bury their dead. When Jesuits went there a few days later they counted seventy-three unburied bodies. The press was now hostile. It reported that the journalist's severe influenza had 'contaminated the entire village. [This was] the consequence of the irresponsibility of the leader of the expedition, who permitted the inclusion of the sick journalist and did not make him return when the first symptoms appeared.'

Fighting, genocidal poisoning, and above all the lethal epidemic had literally decimated the tribe by 90 per cent from an estimated four hundred. The situation was so desperate that the only hope seemed to be to transfer the surviving Tapayuna to a sanctuary. As the ancient link between these people and the Suiá in the Xingu had been established, Father Iasi recommended that the remnant be taken there—despite knowing that the Villas Boas would allow no missionary activity in the park, and despite the two tribes being hundreds of kilometres apart. So in May 1970 forty-one survivors of the once-proud Tapayuna were bused to Cuiabá city and then flown by the air force to the Xingu. Chief Megaron of the Metuktire later recalled that 'Orlando brought the "new Suiá" [Tapayuna] because missionary fathers came to beg him to bring them because they were dying. At that time Orlando had much power, he was in contact with the government. People listened to what he said.' The exodus was not smooth, for the Tapayuna did not really understand what was happening to them, and some fled into the forest at the last moment. Most of the forty-one who reached the Xingu were young, aged under fifteen. They were lodged beside the village of their distant relatives the Suiá, not far from Diauarum. Dr Baruzzi's medical team examined the Tapayuna and found that some still had flu, or were feverish or dehydrated. A further ten died during the next four years, four of them from malaria. Thus, the once-formidable Tapayuna were reduced almost to extinction. Thankfully, however, the Suiá welcomed the new arrivals and the two peoples lived in harmony.

This rescue mission was not instigated by the Villas Boas. But, as always, it deprived the migrating people of their homeland in forests between the Arinos and Sangue rivers. The president of Funai made a lamentable boast, that the airlift had 'freed thirteen thousand square kilometres [over 5,000 square miles] of land for the pioneering frontier'. All of it was immediately occupied by colonists or sold by property companies.

* * *

Funai's first president was a well-intentioned but ineffective former journalist, who had to resign in 1970 because of financial irregularities involving his sister. The foundation's second president, General Oscar Jerónimo Bandeira de Mello, was a strange appointment because he had no experience of, or affinity with, indigenous people. I remember meeting him—a short, simian-looking, and aggressive man. He deluded himself that Funai could be run with military efficiency, and reeled off statistics of the number of 'flying medical teams', model pharmacies, doctors and nurses, schools and teachers, even regular boundary markers surrounding every reserve—all pure fantasy. Having previously served in military intelligence, Bandeira de Mello was suspicious of any pro-Indian organization. To Robin Hanbury-Tenison (who made a fine report about Brazilian Indians for the charity Survival International in 1971), the general could not conceal his jealousy of the Villas Boas' fame. He kept repeating that the brothers were 'just Funai employees like any others', and claimed that their method of gradual and gentle assimilation was less effective than violent integration. He cited the Karajá people of the Araguaia river as an example of the latter, unaware that this tribe was wretched and demoralized. On another occasion, speaking for Funai, the general even criticized the Xingu Indigenous Park 'for taking a position contrary to the Federal Government's plans to promote national integration'. He claimed that it hampered 'progress', as represented by colonization and deforestation.

In 1970 the third military president of Brazil, the former general Garrastazu Médici, announced a 'Plan for National Integration' to open the Brazilian Amazon's vast forests to colonization. This echoed President Vargas's vision a quarter-century earlier; but this time integration was to be achieved not by a trail and airstrips but by a grid of 'penetration roads' slicing into unexplored tropical rainforests. It was hoped that these highways would attract thousands of colonists from Brazil's drought-stricken north-east. The military, who loved slogans, proclaimed that this would 'open a land without people for a people without land'. The flagship new road was the Transamazonica Highway, south of and roughly parallel to the main Amazon river. It was planned eventually to run for an incredible 2,200 kilometres (1,350 miles)—the distance from

Lisbon to Moscow—from the Araguaia/Tocantins river, westwards across the lower Xingu, then the Tapajós, to the Madeira (another great southern tributary of the Amazon). The construction of the Transamazonica was a remarkable feat of endurance and engineering by teams of tough woodsmen, who were followed by earthmovers to build the roadway. Some of these penetration roads resulted in massive colonization, mining, and deforestation; others were rarely used. All of them struck isolated indigenous peoples. During the coming decades Funai's elite, known as *sertanistas*, were fully occupied in trying to contact isolated tribes along the routes of the new highways, before those peoples' lands were invaded by the road-builders and their bulldozers.

Surprisingly, Orlando initially welcomed this east–west Transamazonica Highway. He may have done this to please the government, or because he had not fully appreciated the threat it posed to isolated peoples and tropical forests. He was soon more concerned by another new penetration highway, the BR-163 planned to link Mato Grosso's state capital Cuiabá to Santarém, 1,600 kilometres (1,000 miles) due north on the main Amazon river. This BR-163 would run north–south between the Xingu and the Teles Pires/Tapajós basins. On the other side of the Xingu, between it and the Araguaia, the less important BR-158 road was gradually being built north from Xavantina—the place where the Roncador–Xingu Expedition had started a quarter-century earlier.

A diagonal feeder road, the BR-080, was to link the two north–south roads, crossing the Xingu near the Von Martius rapids—north of the park— to join the BR-163 south of Cachimbo. However, late in 1970 someone ordered the team building this diagonal road to change course, so that the BR-080 would reach the Xingu 110 kilometres (70 miles) *south* of the great rapids, thus slicing across the Xingu Indigenous Park itself. Even worse than this incursion was a rumour that all forests north of the new road were to be removed from the park's jurisdiction.

This deflection of the BR-080 must have been ordered from above, because hundreds of woodsmen and engineers cannot quickly be re-routed. Orlando and Claudio were shattered by this violation of their park, which had been enshrined in law only ten years previously and had enjoyed special presidential status. They at first blamed the civil engineering company that was building the road, Sudeco, and the government's development agency for this part of Brazil. They could not believe that President Médici and the general in charge of Funai had betrayed them—because these important men had just told Orlando to be prepared to take Indians displaced by the Transamazonica into his sanctuary, and he could not take refugees if the park had been amputated. The Villas Boas also found it incomprehensible that they, Brazil's most famous champions of indigenous peoples, had not been consulted in any way about this drastic change to the reserve that was the jewel in the crown of Brazil's new Indian foundation.

As the road-builders approached the park, Orlando published an impassioned plea in a newspaper. He said that the Metuktire would be the first to suffer, so that they would abandon their tribe, their villages, and their families, and, intrigued by the engineers' camp, they risked catching the whites' diseases and that, although they were at that time strong, they would become weak and scattered along the road, and could, in time, be wiped out. Pragmatic as usual, Orlando orchestrated a press campaign within Brazil and abroad and a letter of protest signed by seventy leading intellectuals. Claudio was also disconsolate. I flew out of the Xingu with him on one of his rare ventures to the cities, in a forlorn attempt to reverse this change of route.

But it was all in vain. Orlando had been wrong to trust President Médici and the head of Funai. The government allowed the editorial protests to run their course, and then on 13 July 1971 issued a presidential decree that permanently removed from the park all territory north (downriver) of the new road crossing. The excised area was 8,200 square kilometres (3,170 square miles) of pristine tropical rainforests that were home to two groups of Metuktire. In compensation, the decree extended the park south to parallel 13°S, which took it further up the Batovi, Curisevo, and Culuene headwaters of the Xingu. The new area was somewhat larger than the truncated forests; but it was *campo* savannah, marshy lagoons, and low woods—and almost devoid of indigenous peoples.

Far from protesting about this blow to Brazil's finest indigenous territory, the president of Funai, General Oscar Jerónimo Bandeira de Mello, who should have been determined to protect it, openly approved the road's new route. He declared that this could not be changed and, outrageously, that 'it would bring nothing but benefits to the Indians'. He went on to say that Indians who had been in contact for a long time should be 'taught trades such as fireman, carpenter, and motor or general mechanic'. They would then 'rapidly leave the region' and the Brazilian state could redistribute their lands to farmers. In a later declaration, the general praised the planned new network of roads as 'vital to the development and security of the country' and therefore 'the National Park of the Xingu cannot [be allowed to] impede the country's progress'.

Decades later, when the Brazilian government released confidential state papers, it was found that there had been a sinister plot against the Villas Boas at this time. General Bandeira de Mello had, on 19 May 1971, asked his for-

155

mer colleagues in military intelligence for any dirt they had on the brothers, and they showed him the testimonies by FBC employees about Leonardo Villas Boas snatching his baby daughter from her Kamaiurá mother Mavirá, twenty years earlier in 1951. However, the general had evidently decided that this slur was not sufficiently serious to damage the brothers of whom he was so jealous.

Orlando was now firmly opposed to all the new roads. At a conference at the University of São Paulo in 1972, he declared that 'as the Transamazonica advances, those responsible for it are killing Indians and putting cattle in their place. There will thus be no room for people.' It is now known that Funai and its parent Ministry of the Interior were keeping close watch: their agents at this conference ordered students to turn off their tape-recorders when Orlando spoke. Other Funai officials queried every detail of Orlando's financial accounts, but found nothing amiss. General Bandeira de Mello[‡] ceased as president of Funai in 1974 and was succeeded by a far more sympathetic general, Ismarth de Araújo Oliveira, who hugely admired the Xingu Park. Then, as we shall see, the warlike Metuktire Kayapó took matters into their own hands and waged a long struggle to regain protected status for their forests north of the new road.

---

‡ General Oscar Jerónimo Bandeira de Mello was later shown to have done corrupt land deals while running Funai. The journalist Memelia Moreira recalled being sexually molested by him, at the ceremony opening the re-routed BR-080 link road. A Truth Commission in 2014 named him as an official responsible for serious violations of human rights when he was in the military secret service.

12

PANARÁ

I first met Orlando Villas Boas in Brasilia in May 1961. The law creating the Xingu Indigenous Park had just been passed, so our meeting was in the offices of the Central Brazil Foundation (FBC) in the half-built new capital city. Brasilia's great architect, Oscar Niemeyer, had created two lines of green-glass ministries flanking a central avenue that led towards the iconic white Congress, Senate, and Presidential buildings. I found the FBC's modest office in one of these ministerial blocks. The forty-six-year-old Orlando looked uncomfortable, because he was wearing a suit and in an office far from his beloved forests, rivers, and Indians. At the time, I described him in my diary as squat, plump, with a straggling Ho Chi Minh beard, and his face deeply lined and toughened to a swarthy yellowish colour of old leather, from malaria and exposure. He was certainly charismatic, but had a disconcerting habit of sometimes talking directly to you, then addressing other people in the room, or strolling off to leaf through papers. He was with his friend, the equally dynamic journalist Jorge Ferreira—the man whom President Quadros had recently appointed director of the FBC and who had struck the deal with the governor of Mato Grosso that made the Xingu Park a political reality.

My Oxford friend Richard Mason and I had gone to consult Orlando, as Brazil's leading explorer and indigenous expert, about an expedition we hoped to undertake. We were both twenty-five—younger than Orlando himself had been when he and his brothers joined the Roncador–Xingu Expedition, and with very little more exploration experience than they had had then. Richard Mason was one of those people everybody liked, not just because he was athletic and handsome, but because of his infectious enthusiasms—about everything from modern art (which he already collected quite seriously), to fast cars, travel, literature, science, and medicine (he had just finished his studies as a doctor)—and because he was such fun to be with. Girls adored Richard; but he was about to marry his love, Penny Knowles.

The venture that brought us to consult Orlando in Brasilia was an attempt to make the first descent of the Iriri river, which Richard reckoned to be world's longest unexplored river. The Iriri rises somewhere in the Cachimbo hills (where the Villas Boas had built the Cachimbo airstrip) and flows northwards for some 1,000 kilometres (over 600 miles) before joining the lower Xingu near its junction with the main Amazon. The Royal Geographical Society in London supported this expedition, it was sponsored by the *Sunday Times*, and we had raised all the necessary funding and support in kind—including passages to Brazil, an inflatable rubber boat, outboard motor, field medical kit, and other supplies. Once we had arrived, the Brazilian national mapping agency, IBGE, welcomed our plan to do a traverse (rough survey) of the Iriri, because it was totally unexplored and they wanted it mapped. There was not even aerial photography of the river at that time, and of course this was long before the invention of satellite imagery or GPS. So the IBGE sent its best rainforest surveyor, Durval Aragão (who had been with the Villas Boas on the Geographical Centre Expedition three years earlier), with two assistants. It also gave us the rare privilege of naming minor features we discovered, such as waterfalls, rapids, lakes, or small rivers.

We had thought of approaching the Iriri from the Xingu; but Orlando and Ferreira rightly said that this would be very difficult, through dense forest and crossing several rivers. They explained that the obvious starting point would be the air force base Cachimbo. Orlando mentioned rumours of a warlike uncontacted people known as Kren-Akrore, but these were thought to be in forests far to the south. He assured us that no Indians had been seen near Cachimbo during the decade since its creation. He warned that halfway down the Iriri we would pass through the territory of the potentially dangerous Mekragnoti Kayapó, contacted recently by Brazil's other great Indian expert, Francisco Meirelles, whom we also consulted. But these Kayapó were poor boatmen, so he advised us to camp on islands on that part of the river. Armed with this advice to start at Cachimbo, we approached the air force, and were delighted to find that they were as keen on our plan as the IBGE had been. As one colonel explained, this was because 'our pilots keep getting lost over that part of Brazil, so we want it mapped'. The air force therefore offered every help, with flights, use of Cachimbo base, and some equipment.

After another meeting with Orlando, we went to Cuiabá, capital of Mato Grosso state, to hire five woodsmen and buy food, tools, hammocks, revolvers (for signalling), cooking pots, ant-proof metal boxes, and all other supplies. The woodsmen made sure that we bought plenty of the only food they would eat: black beans, rice, manioc, and jerked beef, with some salt, sugar, and coffee as luxuries. Then we all flew into Cachimbo in the regular air force C-47 transport plane. In addition to the three surveyors from the mapping agency, and the five hired hands, we had another Oxford friend as the expedition's cameraman: Kit Lambert, the son of a distinguished composer and later famous as the impresario of the pop group The Who. So we were eleven men, eight Brazilians and three Englishmen.

The Iriri River Expedition went well. For two months we cut a *picada* trail north-eastwards from Cachimbo towards the supposed source of the Iriri. We soon moved from the natural clearing of *campo* and scrub around the airstrip, into beautiful tall rainforest. I learned how tough trail-cutting was, so could later admire Claudio's achievements—his was the only other group to cut out from Cachimbo, in his case westwards. Each day three men took turns as the cutting party. One of us led, taking a compass bearing to the next tree, then pushing and slashing forward towards it while the other two opened a small trail behind. While the main trail advanced, the rest of us carried heavy loads up from Cachimbo. This was arduous work, more boring than cutting trails, but we had to carry forward everything we needed for that exploration and the eventual descent of the Iriri river. We moved our camp every few weeks, always to the bank of a small stream, with a circle of hammocks slung around a camp fire, in deep shade far below the forest canopy. There was plenty of game in this uninhabited forest, but it was never easy to hunt—our best shot would often return empty-handed; so we had just one dish a day of black beans, rice, and manioc. We became thin, pale from seeing direct sunlight only when back at Cachimbo, and covered in scratches and insect bites. But it was rewarding work, and we loved living in the church-like twilight of majestic rainforests.

We were able to take accurate star-fixes, using radio time-signals and a theodolite—sometimes having to fell a tree to see the stars we were going to need. But although we knew our coordinates, the lie of the land emerged only gradually from a network of exploratory trails. There was the excitement of breaking through a screen of vegetation to be the first non-Indians to see a lovely river, flowing gently and reflecting the green foliage and dappled sunlight. We set our woodsmen to work making two big dugout canoes, each of which took the five men five days with their axes and adzes. These were beautiful craft, fashioned by the illiterate men entirely with biblical measurements—hand-spans, forearm cubits, knuckle inches. Meanwhile the rest of us continued to carry stores forward, including an inflatable rubber boat, an outboard motor, and petrol for it.

By August 1961 we had located the Iriri—after mistakes with other rivers in that totally unmapped and unexplored forest. We launched the two dugout canoes, and had carried forward almost all the supplies for the descent and surveying traverse of the unknown river. Then tragedy struck. Richard Mason's body was found lying on our main trail a few kilometres from our last camp. He was carrying a load of food and had walked into an Indian ambush. He had been hit by eight arrows, and his skull and thigh were smashed by club blows. Some forty arrows and seventeen heavy clubs were ritually arranged around the body. The attack was a complete surprise, since both Orlando Villas Boas and Chico Meirelles had told us not to expect Indians near Cachimbo; and we had seen no signs of any during those months in the now-familiar forest. Also, it was almost unheard of for Indians to kill before any form of contact. Had there been any converse, even by sign language, Richard would have convinced them of his good intentions, since he was a fine man, an excellent leader, and clearly sympathetic to indigenous people.

The shattered remainder of the expedition hurried back to Cachimbo, unsure whether there might be an attack on our camp. After a few days, three teams were flown in by the Brazilian authorities. The Indian Protection Service sent an experienced *sertanista* and Bepunu Kaiabi to confirm that Richard had been killed by an Indian attack (and not by one of us), and to try to ascertain which people had done it. The air force sent a squad of jungle troops to protect against possible attack—heavily armed chaps who knew less about forests than we did. Then there was an excellent medical team, who embalmed the body and wrapped it in canvas. We carried Richard back, slung beneath a pole; and his body was flown to Rio de Janeiro for a funeral and burial in the British cemetery.

Our expedition was carrying machetes as presents for Indians we might encounter. I left a pile of these at the site of the ambush, to show that we had been well-intentioned—this was a technique used by the legendary Rondon. Richard Mason was the last Englishman ever to be killed by a totally uncontacted and unknown tribe. We could tell from the way the Indians had rummaged his belongings that this was the first time they had ever seen clothing or metal, or anything from the outside world.

When the Villas Boas reached the Teles Pires in 1950 the Kaiabi had told them about a warlike tribe of big men with powerful voices, who lived to the east of them. Various Kayapó groups confirmed that they feared attack by a fierce people from that same region. As Orlando told us when we met in Brasilia, the unknown people were known as Kren-Akrore ('Men with Heads

Cut Round') because of their pudding-bowl haircuts; but it was later learned that that tribe referred to itself as Panará, and I will call them thus. The fearsome strangers were thought to be gigantic. This was because the Metuktire Kayapó had captured a boy from them and he grew into a man 2.06 metres (6 foot 8 inches) tall, called Mengire. There is a photograph of Orlando measuring this giant, but coming up only to his shoulder; and Dr Murillo Villela recalled that 'to reach his deltoid region to give him an injection I had to raise my arm far above my head'.

Six years later, in June 1967, there was an unfortunate setback in relations with the unknown tribe. A group of indigenous people appeared at the edge of the Cachimbo airstrip. They were apparently seeking presents. The few servicemen on the base saw ten Indians with bows and clubs, and there seemed to be more hidden in the forest behind. The regular weekly cargo plane happened to be approaching Cachimbo, and when the base radioed its pilot that there were Indians on the airstrip, he assumed that it was an attack. So he twice buzzed the strip at low level, sending the frightened people fleeing into the forest; and he then radioed for urgent reinforcements. The air force overreacted. Four planeloads of heavily armed troops were flown in, and these established trenches and machine-gun nests around Cachimbo. One plane tragically became lost and crashed: a massive search-and-rescue operation finally found the wreckage, but only five survivors of the plane's complement of thirty. As Orlando said at the time, the tribesmen had obviously come peacefully or they would not have filed onto the open airstrip. 'Shout "Indian" and the whole world goes crazy. The *civilizados* shoot. They fly airplanes all over the jungle. A brigadier is photographed crouched behind a machine-gun.' The Indians concluded that the whites were extremely ferocious and dangerous.

In November of that year, 1967, there was a disaster for the Panará. The Mekragnoti Kayapó, who had moved from the Xingu to the Curuá (a tributary of the Iriri) far to the north, had for many decades been bitter enemies of the Panará. These Kayapó had been contacted again by Francisco Meirelles, and he had given them some guns. They tricked Dale Snyder (the Protestant missionary in their village who had favourably impressed Claudio) into giving them ammunition 'to facilitate a ceremonial hunt'. But their real purpose was to settle old scores with the Panará. Thirty-five warriors, almost all the young men in the village, set off on a week-long journey through the forest until they located their prey. 'The Mekragnoti party surrounded the [Panará] village before dawn and attacked by firing guns into the houses. The [Panará] were taken totally unawares. ... Resistance was brief in the face of the gunfire, with most of the inhabitants fleeing into the forest.' Adrian Cowell later watched twenty black-painted Mekragnoti re-enact their murderous onslaught, onto a mock village. They charged out of the forest, screaming and firing into the air. Cowell concluded that 'it was obvious that many [Panará] must have been shot down in their huts, and that only one of two would have had time to fire back with their bows. It must have been sheer butchery.' But the attackers were proud of their victory. One warrior recalled jubilantly:

> We were onto them, coming down on them in the houses. I shot and missed, hitting only a gourd. The enemy ran after me. I dodged an arrow I saw coming—by twisting and falling aside. So I knocked the enemy down with a shot. He sat there and my older brother, Kayti, shot him right down. 'Ha! Kren-Akrore [Panará], I just killed one of you!'

Another attacker, called Ayo, shouted his recollection: 'I killed this enemy and beat him. There was one that I shot with his child, and he fell so.' Kanga said that it was revenge for the Panará having killed his and other young men's parents, in a murderous raid forty years previously. 'My uncle and I took our guns and shot two of them dead. *Be!* There they lie. And there one tried to hide in the grass. *Be!* I got my gun and killed him.' Other Mekragnoti retold different killings, including the clubbing of women captives because they resisted and bit too much. Twenty-six Panará may have been killed in this slaughter.

A Panará woman later described the horror:

> Everyone died, my father, my uncles; and I was crying, yes. There, the Kayapó killed my uncle Tausinko. There they killed Pengsura, who was a boy. They killed Sungkrekyan. ... They killed my husband and nephew, they killed my eldest brother, Peyati, my son Yosuri, my brother Kyotisura. ... The Kayapó massacred these people. For this I am angry: I remain angry and I do not forget.

In 1968, Claudio felt that he must try to contact the tribe of warlike 'giants'. He started with reconnaissance flights from Cachimbo to locate their villages. On one sortie they spotted circular plantations of banana trees in the midst of the unending expanse of forest, with a burned village nearby (possibly the one destroyed by the Kayapó). On another flight they saw an inhabited village, alongside gardens amazingly organized in geometric patterns. 'The outer rings consisted of single rows of banana trees, in beautiful curves and circles. The crosses and double avenues were straight lines of maize, looking like paths over lawns of grass [possibly sweet potatoes].' It was agricultural symmetry never seen in any other Amazon tribe. By contrast with the sophisticated plantations, the village's huts were small and shabby. Its men showed their defiance by shooting arrow after arrow up at the circling plane—a photograph of them doing this was published all over the world. During the ensuing months, further flights located more villages, all roughly 100 kilometres (60 miles) south of Cachimbo, close to a tributary of the Teles Pires called Peixoto de Azevedo. This was where Orlando had located the unknown tribe to Richard Mason and me seven years earlier.

Having located villages from the air, Claudio now prepared a contact expedition. He decided to approach from the Xingu Park to the east, rather than from Cachimbo to the north—since the latter had been the direction of the murderous Kayapó attack. His expedition moved from Diauarum for five days up the Manitsauá river, and spent a month making an airstrip. Meanwhile heavy supplies such as petrol had been brought down the Culuene and Xingu on motorized rafts. Orlando and Claudio recruited many Indians at their respective posts, with the majority being reliable Kaiabi. All came for fun and adventure; but each man's wife and village had to agree to his going; he was then given a hammock, clothes, and ammunition for hunting—but no pay, since the Xingu operated without money. Leaving the river, they cut northwestwards towards Panará territory—rather than due west as the Villas Boas had done when they had explored towards the Teles Pires river twenty years previously. This proved to be a terribly exhausting 150-kilometre (90-mile) *picada*, because they had to traverse two unexpected ranges of low hills in that dense unexplored forest. Prepori Kaiabi led the cutting party, in his trademark red railwayman's cap on long curly black hair (his unknown father was not Indian), and Claudio followed in a floppy hat and dirty shirt. The Villas Boas had lured Adrian Cowell back, to join this tough venture.

In September 1968 the expedition finally reached the Peixoto de Azevedo river, which flows from near Cachimbo into the Teles Pires. The men cleared another airstrip and Orlando flew in with twenty-eight more Indians, the bearded young Dr Murillo Villela, and some invited journalists. Their Juruna built three dugout boats and three canoes—they alone had this skill. In October the big expedition set off down the narrow and tortuous river for what they hoped would be contact with the tribe of 'giants'. After a week, when near the Panará villages that Claudio had seen from the air, they made a more permanent camp. Lanterns were lit at night so that the Indians could watch them, and men from different tribes were told to sing in their respective languages. Lines of presents were suspended on trails—coloured balls, saucepans, machetes, axes, sickles, mirrors and beads. The Panará were evidently watching, but there was no contact.

The Villas Boas decided to try to reach a village whose coordinates they knew from the overflights. The contact group bravely opened a trail, and walked along this for five hours. They saw constant signs of indigenous presence, such as broken saplings or other trails that could be spotted only by other Indians. All that they knew about this uncontacted people was that they were extremely warlike and powerful bowmen (when they had shot up at the plane) so that even the tough Kayapó were scared of them. The expeditioners finally reached a clearing, shouting lustily to show that this was not an attack. They then entered an abandoned village, aware that at any moment they could have been hit by a barrage of arrows. Adrian Cowell described this incursion:

> Orlando's bare belly led the way, forming the spearhead of what must have looked a very odd procession. In his hand he swung an aluminium pot like a thurible, [the Metuktire chief] Kretire came next waving a mirror, and Claudio made benedictions with his saucepan, as if we were some religious order about to exorcise the devil.

No Indians were seen, but the intruders left presents suspended from a cord like a washing line.

Some days later, presents that they had left on another trail had been taken and—very promisingly—a few clubs were left in exchange. Orlando decided to follow that Indian path, walking for several hours until they reached an open space. 'It was a village. The Indians, seeing our approach, abandoned everything and departed so hurriedly that they left bows and arrows, clubs and stone axes.' Dr Villela recalled finding

> banana skins, manioc, beiju [manioc pancakes], little nut-shell vessels for holding water, remains of meals and food being prepared, fires with cinders still hot, straw mats inside and hanging at the entrances of very primitive huts— but no Indians!! What we found indicated that we were dealing with people at a very primitive stage of development—although they did use some tools such as stone axes.

The village was littered with massively heavy logs, hunks of tree-trunk stripped of their bark, and there were two parallel paths leading in from the surrounding forest. These phenomena had been noticed during the overflights. Anthropologists realized that they were signs of log racing, a custom that has for centuries been common among Je-speaking peoples in distant parts of Brazil, but not with the Kayapó in the Xingu. I have watched log racing among Je-speaking Timbira peoples, 1,200 kilometres (750 miles) north-east of the Peixoto de Azevedo river. In this traditional custom, teams of athletic young men from the two halves or moieties of the village pound in from the forest, kicking up a small cloud of dust. One runner carries the hugely heavy log on his shoulder and then rolls it onto that of another man in his relay, as they run at full speed. Arriving in the village, each team drops its mighty log with a thud, and then strolls off—as with *huka-huka* wrestling among the Xinguanos, there is no triumphalism by the winners. This evidence of log racing showed that the uncontacted people were Je speakers, but that they must have migrated from a distant region.

Depressing weeks of waiting ensued, in the downpours of the rainy season. As Cowell recalled:

> The rain was so heavy that it muffled voices, and the surrounding walls of jungle looked as dark as a catacomb. ... Rain is the black mood of the jungle ... it either pounded on the roofs of the camp or wrapped it in a grey drizzle. ... We breathed, we ate, we moved in rain. Storms and the passing of storms were what marked the time of our waiting.

Much of the forest was flooded, and the camp cook built little dykes to keep the water from his fires. But there were no contacts. Claudio insisted that there must be no attempt to coerce the tribe: it must come to accept contact of its own volition. The expedition was finally abandoned, in January 1969, seven months after it had left the Xingu. But when another approximation team revisited its camp a few months later, everything left there was found to have been smashed by clubs.

At the end of 1969 the Metuktire Kayapó in the Xingu thought that they would imitate their Mekragnoti cousins by slaughtering some Panará. They secretly took all their guns and went from their village, Poiriri, on a long trek westwards through the forests. The Villas Boas were understandably furious when they learned about this raid: the Metuktire tried to excuse it by claiming that they had gone to 'pacify' the elusive giants. Fortunately for the latter, the Metuktire returned in mid-January 1970, tired and thin, and with no captives or dead warriors to boast about. They had entered three Panará villages but found them abandoned and overgrown. There was an ominously large burial mound in one village—possibly a sign that white men's diseases had destroyed the Panará before the Metuktire guns.

In 1970 President Garrastazu Médici of Brazil announced his grandiose 'National Integration Programme' to open Amazonia with a network penetration roads. One of these highways threatened the 'giants' whom the Villas Boas were trying to contact. This was the BR-163, from Cuiabá north towards

Santarém on the Amazon, running between the basins of the Xingu and the Teles Pires/Tapajós. Army engineers pushed this highway northwards, with 2,000 men, 210 earthmoving machines, and 350 trucks in a massive construction effort. By late 1971 the new road was approaching the Peixoto de Azevedo river and the forests of the Panará. So another attempt to contact the threatened tribe was becoming increasingly imperative.

Funai was short of funds, so the Villas Boas were again asked to attempt this new contact. This time Claudio decided to approach from Cachimbo, which he left on 15 January 1972 with twenty-six Indians. As he explained: 'We went not so much to pacify the [Panará] as to prevent their being victims of a clash with the road workers.' January was the height of the rainy season, so 'rain was the greatest obstacle we had to overcome. The trail progressed slowly.' They cut with only machetes, since chainsaws are useless for this, and they moved their camps forward every few weeks—just as we had done on the Iriri River Expedition eleven years earlier. Claudio and Orlando paid tribute to their magnificent Kaiabi workers during this and other expeditions:

> There is nothing to compare to the spirit of these Indians. They are always ready for whatever is to be done or whatever happens. They do not lose heart, and nothing blunts their good humour and cheerfulness. ... Cold rains, exhaustion, unexpected but inevitable falls, painful hornet stings, hunger and thirst resulting from setbacks and dry stretches [of forest]—in short, everything is cause for gaiety and laughter.

Even the veteran explorer Claudio complained of the heavy rains, high streams to be forded, flooded trails, and slippery mud.

After a punishing four months of cutting they saw increasing signs of Indian presence, so paused to clear an airstrip. By mid-June 1972 the new airstrip could take a light plane. One brought Orlando and other men. This plane was then able to reconnoitre by air, and it located several villages, each with fifteen to twenty huts and surrounded by farmed clearings. A journalist on one such flight recorded a village where 'Indians, many Indians, follow the plane's manoeuvres with interest. I throw down a packet of presents, and a race starts: one man managed to get the packet and runs off, pursued by the others. The impression is one of happiness.' People in another village were apparently assembled for a festival. Meanwhile, on the ground, the expedition found trails and left presents. These were sometimes taken, and occasionally offerings of clubs, feather headdresses, and arrows were given in return—a very promising gesture. So the canoes pressed on down the river towards the villages seen from the air, hoping to achieve a contact.

Then the atmosphere changed abruptly. In late July the pilot saw that the Indians had burned one of their villages and, two days later, that a second was also a charred ruin. The Villas Boas decided that they must investigate, and set off with twenty Indians and six whites. Orlando was in poor health. He had just suffered an attack of hypoglycaemia with sudden loss of blood-sugar content and very high blood pressure, he was overweight, and he had had two cataract operations. But this did not prevent him from going with the others. On 1 August they entered the first village seen from the air, but it was 'all burned, the framework of the huts blackened, ashes. A desolate panorama.' In sad silence, they moved on to the second village and passed through its clearings of banana trees and vegetables, planted in the curious geometric patterns. But this main village, which had once 'looked like a paradise from the air, was nothing but a heap of charcoal and ash'. A baby tapir appeared, clearly tamed and kept as a pet, with one of the bead necklaces left by the expedition around its neck. But there were no people. Everyone felt deep sympathy for the unknown tribesmen, so obviously traumatized that they had burned their villages and fled into the forest. Having abandoned their *roças*, they must have been suffering hunger. Yet at each burned village the Villas Boas found a stone axe and bows and arrows that they assumed were meant as presents for the visitors, because the Indians had collected the gifts left for them. Some presents were wrapped in plastic and contained pictures of the Villas Boas brothers embracing Ikpeng—because these people's round haircuts were similar to those of the men seen from above.

Years later, after it was learned that the elusive people called themselves Panará, they explained how deeply confused they had been by the behaviour of the strangers. In their language the words for 'stranger' and 'enemy' were the same, so that in a sense this small, bellicose people was at war with the rest of humanity. This could have explained their unprovoked ambush of Richard Mason in 1961. Their sense of isolation and insecurity would have been heightened by the hostile reception they received at Cachimbo, Claudio's flights over their village, and the Mekragnotis' murderous attack, all in 1967. Perhaps convinced that planes were their enemies, they burned their villages because these had now been observed by the light plane. The Mekragnoti had destroyed their northernmost village, Sonkanasan, and its inhabitants who survived the attack took refuge further south in a village called Sonsenasan; but this was now also burned. These exoduses put great pressure on the food grown in the garden plantations of the remaining five or six villages.

As in most indigenous societies, Panará men of each village regularly debate tribal affairs. Understandably, there had been desperate discussions about how to react to the outside forces that were closing in on them. A Panará warrior, Teseya, later described the anxious debates:

'Many whites have come! The whites have come! What will happen to us? Will they be hostile?' Then I [Teseya] said: 'They hung up machetes, so they are not hostile.'... On the whole, it was younger men who wanted to have friendly contact with the strangers, while the elders insisted that they were dangerous and untrustworthy and should be killed. The old men advised us not to mix with the white men, to leave them alone or they would kill us.

The attraction expedition now had a substantial camp beside the Peixoto de Azevedo river: four huts full of hammocks, roofed either in blue plastic or grey *inajá* palm fronds, with an airstrip nearby. Orlando had to leave for medical treatment, but Claudio remained, waiting week after week for something to happen, because 'the logical thing for a sertanista to do is to await [the Indians'] return. We cannot force them. Our weapon now is patience.' Orlando agreed. Contact with Indians, he insisted, is achieved by patience and resignation. 'Haste achieves nothing, and it can lead to death.'

Claudio's diary recorded two acts of personal courage during the weeks of inaction. First, on 27 September 1972:

In the morning arrows were shot from the far bank over our hammocks. I saw that we were surrounded in our camp with a great number, perhaps fifty, hidden in the forest. I recommended calm. I gathered some bead necklaces and machetes and went towards the perimeter, in the place where the forest seemed thickest. The [Panará] disappeared, just as they had arrived—making little noise.

Then, on 15 October, some twenty Indians appeared on the far bank and signalled.

I told our Indians to remain quiet. We calmly answered their signs, showing them knives, necklaces and machetes in our raised arms. We beckoned that they should come to our camp; but they gesticulated, calling us to their side. I reckoned that they were all armed. One who appeared to be the leader spoke loudly, with authority, and appeared older than the others. Six of us crossed to their side, taking necklaces and machetes. We landed and could see that they were in the forest, watching. We suspended the necklaces and machetes on a rope, and returned to our bank. They reappeared ten minutes later, with the necklaces on their necks, and shook the rope as a sign that they wanted more. We crossed again with more presents. But they again hid in the forest.

One thing learned from these fleeting glimpses was that the elusive people were lean and agile, but not giants. Mengire, the boy captured from the

Panará who had grown immensely tall, was a genetic aberration, a freak who sadly died quite young.

Three more months of waiting ensued, during the misery of another rainy season. Then at long last the conciliatory view of the younger Panará prevailed, and the tribe decided to accept contact. Finally, on 4 February 1973, the Villas Boas' patience was rewarded. A group of twenty or thirty Panará suddenly appeared among the trees across the river from the camp, at a place where presents had frequently been left for them. Claudio took a canoe and crossed the river with some Kaiabi. Removing his shoes, he waded ashore holding a machete, and called out in the various native languages he knew. Claudio then tried to hand the machete to one of the Indians; but they indicated that he should leave it on a tree trunk. So, in the words of a journalist watching from the far bank: 'This enigmatic man went forward, with dark glasses covering his eyes, dishevelled, with a greying beard hanging from his chin, his fragile body covered in torn clothes. And the lords of the forest, both fearful and happy, went towards the tree trunk.' But Claudio withdrew the knife. Finally a young man advanced and, despite the tension, accepted the offering from the white hand. 'It was contact, at last.' Teseya Panará later described that decisive moment, from the Indian point of view:

We told [a young man called] Hawkene to pick up the machete and he did so. Hawkene approached Claudio, and Claudio embraced him and said: 'I am not hostile. Do not be afraid of me.' Our men said 'We will all come.' Hawkene was a small man, and he remained there quietly.

In another version of the contact, Claudio sat and pretended to have a painful foot. The Indians were curious about his injury and crowded around to see what was wrong. 'Claudio rose with difficulty, helped by the [Panará] and ... he embraced them and was embraced for a long time.'

Five days later there was a second contact, after Orlando had flown back from his medical treatment. Two young Panará appeared across the river, shouting and beckoning. Most of the people in the attraction camp jumped into a boat and paddled towards the Indians; but at the far bank the two Villas Boas decided that they alone should land. They held out presents, and Orlando managed to place a bead necklace on one of the warriors. The brothers lit a fire and conversed, quietly to reassure the apprehensive Panará. Orlando said that they then joked with the Indians. 'We laughed, even guffawed, tapped them on the backs, everything that people do instinctively when they want to show friendship. We could understand nothing that they said, and vice-versa.' Dr Rubens Belfort (of the São Paulo Medical School) took a famous photograph of Claudio advancing with an axe held out in front of him, and with a black-painted warrior just visible among the forest trees.

The next day there was another, far larger, encounter that ended with an aged Indian making a long speech, after which they withdrew gradually and vanished into the forest; 140 Panará were counted at that meeting, 'some totally covered in black genipapo [vegetable dye], and with symmetrical scars on both sexes that indicated age'. Apart from these rows of little cuts on their chests, men and women were totally naked and unadorned in any way. Almost twelve years after their first attack on a white man in their ambush of our Iriri River Expedition, tactile contact with the feared 'giants' had finally been achieved.

Two months later, in April 1973, the attraction expedition withdrew. Claudio and his team had been in the forests non-stop for over fifteen months (480 days), including two rainy seasons; Orlando was with them for part of the time. They were exhausted, and their forty-two Indians were eager to return to their villages. But before they left, a young Metuktire, Megaron, made a disturbing denunciation: that some men in the contact camp, including him, had influenza. A nurse was brought from Cuiabá to treat the sick in the camp. But after the Panará visited several times, they themselves tragically caught this disease, against which they had no immunity. Megaron reported: 'They came to our camp and went away. When they returned home they were ill, they had flu, they were already thin. Good grief! Who took the disease to them? It was we.' When this was leaked to the press, a Funai official in Cuiabá sent police to remove all journalists—not because some might be infected, but to stop them writing about illness among the Panará. Orlando, however, asked Megaron to conceal one of his favourites, a reporter from the *Estado de São Paulo* newspaper who was in good health. So 'I hid the chap in the forest and stayed there with him in the forest. Once the police from Cuiabá had left in their plane, we emerged from there.'

The Villas Boas were replaced as leaders of the Panará contact mission by Apoena Meirelles. This dynamic young man was the son of the Indianist Francisco Meirelles, who named him after the Xavante chief he had contacted in 1946. Apoena Meirelles spent his boyhood in the Xavante village, and now looked like a seventies radical: lean, with a thin black beard and moustache, and a mane of curly black hair. His team approached other Panará villages from a different direction. There were more exchanges of presents, more fleeting encounters; a small group visited the expedition's camp, then a large group, and finally, in August 1973, an invitation to visit a Panará village. So Apoena, four Xavante, and the portly camera-festooned Jesco von Puttkamer marched for a punishing 38 kilometres (24 miles) through the forest, until they finally passed through neat plantations to a circle of rough huts covered in banana leaves. Once the elderly Puttkamer had recovered from the march, he reported their reward: 'Now what we take to be welcoming ceremonies begin. A medicine man blows breath upon us. ... Warriors deliver orations that sound like prayers. And they weep great tears!' Women painted Apoena and Jesco's faces. In the evening, they ate bananas and manioc cakes cooked on fire-heated stones and wrapped in banana leaves. After eating 'by the light of the cook fires, the dreaded [Panará], faces wreathed in beatific smiles, sing for us—strange chants, simple lines each ending in shouted "*Ahow!*" Then they dance.' When the visitors tried to sleep, 'warriors watch us all night, and every few minutes they pound the earth with enormous war clubs'.

All was not well with these isolated Panará. They looked undernourished, because road-builders and attraction teams had interrupted their usual farming and hunting, and the abandonment and burning of some villages had swelled others with refugees. 'Almost all the Indians have skin infections. Several are too sick with fever to walk.' The visitors were able to give some simple medicines they were carrying. As had been noted from overflights, the Panará village was primitive. It was a circle of seven or eight huts of very rough construction, roofed with interwoven broken branches covered in banana leaves. The Indians slept on the same banana leaves (not in hammocks), near small fires, and they had no household utensils of any kind.

When linguists later studied the Panará, they were surprised to discover that these were Je-speaking Kayapó. But they were not related to the many Kayapó tribes in the Xingu Park and the rivers and plains to the north: they were found to be the last surviving remnant of the *southern* Kayapó—as had been indicated by their practice of log racing. Their ancestors had once dominated a plateau far to the south-east of the Xingu, near the Paraguay river and outside the Amazon basin. These southern Kayapó were thought to have been extinguished in the eighteenth century, by disease, warfare, and colonization. The Panará version of Je was largely incomprehensible to the *northern* Kayapó (who included their enemies the Metuktire and Mekragnoti). The Panará retained many traditions such as the log race, bellicosity, preferring to fight with war clubs than with bows and arrows, sleeping on ground mats or leaves rather than in hammocks, eating any meat they could hunt, dislike of alcohol, tobacco or hallucinogens, painting in black *genipapo* for battle, no ceramics, and an unfamiliarity with canoes. When I later wrote a history of Brazil's indigenous peoples, I found an eighteenth-century report by a Portuguese official about the southern Kayapó. This said that they were very belligerent, preferred to attack from ambush, and after a killing every warrior left his weapons arranged around the victim's body. This was exactly how they had behaved when they killed Richard Mason two centuries later.

Following the two successful contact missions, the Panará suffered a crushing succession of disasters, almost as if the gods were determined to destroy them. Some were curious about the BR-163 Cuiabá–Santarém road being driven through forests to the west of theirs, so they drifted into the camps of army engineers who were building it. They ate too much unfamiliar fare—particularly sugar, a new treat for them—so stopped planting altogether and lived off food handouts from the road workers.

Apoena Meirelles was transferred away from the Panará contact in September 1973 and replaced by another Funai official, Antonio Campinas. But Campinas was then removed because he was accused of having homosexual relations with Indian men: another official said that confused Indians had come to his hammock, thinking that this was expected of them by all whites. It was also alleged that Campinas was sleeping with young Panará women. Campinas stoutly denied both accusations, which might possibly have arisen from misunderstandings of Indian behaviour. But the press reported these lurid stories, and Campinas was removed. There were also allegations of impropriety by army engineers: some were said to be keeping Indians as curiosities in their camps, others of bribing the bewildered tribe to admit gold- and diamond-prospectors to its rivers.

When the southern stretch of the BR-163 (some 700 kilometres (440 miles) north from Cuiabá) opened to traffic in December 1973 some Indians drifted towards the road, readily accepting trinkets from passing truck drivers and bus passengers. The road-builders made a huge camp with many barrack buildings, a mere 4 kilometres from the Peixoto de Azevedo river. One Funai official commented angrily: 'They didn't give a damn about the Indians—their camp could easily have been farther north.'

All this promiscuous contact led to the inevitable diseases. There had been some inoculation of Panará after contact but, as so often, insufficient medical preparation. Fiorello Parise, the next leader of the attraction campaign, reported that 'they went to the road and caught colds. I removed the ill ones to their villages, but many died. They were like skeletons. ... When we followed their trails, there were only burials.' Another Funai official said that many went into the forest to die, of pneumonia, and of malaria which was rampant among the road workers. He recalled that he pulled corpses of Indians from the river, into which they had jumped to alleviate their malarial fevers. Stephan Schwartzman, an American anthropologist who later became a great champion of the Panará, heard about these terrible times from the Indians themselves. Akè, a short, barrel-chested, and forceful chief, had been a boy at the time. He later remembered:

> When the whites came, the Panará all died. Coughing, catarrh and chest pains killed virtually everybody. ... My mother died then, there in Yopuyupaw village. My brother and my mother died, there in the new houses [we had built to replace burned villages]. The others left, and everyone died on the road. ... They were too weak to bury the dead. ... They all rotted on the ground. Vultures ate them all, on the ground, since they had not been buried.

This failure to bury the dead was unknown behaviour for Indians, and a tragic sign of how frightened and weakened the tribe had become. Another chief, the tall, dignified Teseya, later told Schwartzman:

> Then my grandfather Sewakri died. On arrival [at the new village] my mother died, from fear of the white men. ... Then our people started to get ill, ill. Everyone was lying there, prostrate. The others went into the forest, one here, another there. One died, died, died, everyone was ill. 'What is happening to us? Perhaps the white man is to blame,' they said. Everyone died there.

In desperation, they returned to an abandoned village; but the situation did not improve. 'We slept in the forest. Children, adults, all were dying. ... People died from every family. "What will happen to us?"' Some survivors congregated at a village called Topayurõ, and the less weakened or ill survived by gathering honey and bananas. But the deaths continued.

The two anthropologists who first studied the Panará pieced together the location and size of their villages before contact. One, Richard Heelas, estimated that their population had been 425–525 people in seven villages; whereas Stephan Schwartzman reckoned rather more. He deduced from interviews that one of the worst epidemics had struck the Panará *before* the moment of contact with Claudio Villas Boas. Already catastrophic, the depopulation had been exacerbated by the abandonment of villages because they were contaminated by the evil magic of disease or from fear of overflying planes. Those who fled failed to take seeds to plant elsewhere. Other deaths were from ritual executions of shamans suspected of having brought the epidemics. The extreme mourning required of survivors of dead relatives could also cause fatal debilitation. Thus, sixty people died immediately after contact. Schwartzman appreciated that 'it is difficult to imagine the degree of social disorganization that accompanied the arrival of the road, the contacting expedition, and the sudden deaths of so many people.' In addition to the bewildering shock of contact, social collapse, and fearful suffering from alien disease, there was tragic depopulation, for by the end of 1973 the Panará were reduced to 110 people, and a year later to eighty-two. Schwartzman asked Teseya and three older women to list the names, clans, and approximate ages of all who perished in the terrible two years from 1973 to 1975. They did this readily, because indigenous people mourn their dead perpetually, and in a non-literate society their memories are acute. It was a chilling roll-call of 176 deaths, of all ages and both sexes.

Funai tried to react to the catastrophe. There was a campaign of inoculations and attempts to give medical treatment, but this was confused, fragmented, inadequate, and too late. The task was almost impossible, because some Panará were still uncontacted, others were fleeing into the depths of their forests or, conversely, were lured towards the new road. Suddenly, the fierce and proud 'giants' of the previous year's stories were being portrayed and photographed as sickly, starving, and dirty Indians, some begging from traffic on the new road and degraded by civilization's diseases, alcohol, tobacco, and sexual interference. (The Panará later vigorously denied that they had accepted alcohol, tobacco, or prostitution; but such emotive words added to the impact of the press reports.) As the anthropologist Valéria Parise reported, 'a great sadness and melancholy is evident among these Indians. They live in a state of expectancy, with artificial behaviour, continually having to adapt to the ways of the [Funai] camp and the decisions of its sertanista.' In June 1974 Valéria's brother Fiorello Parise, Funai's new head of the Panará contact, moved survivors to a new village called Inkonakoko, 50 kilometres (30 miles) east of the road, to get them away from its harmful influence.

When the Panará had first been observed in the 1960s, there had been a suggestion that they should eventually be moved into the Xingu Indigenous Park. But in January 1972, just as Claudio was setting out on what proved to be the successful contact expedition, his brother Orlando dismissed this idea as crazy, because the Panará deserved by law to have their ancient homeland protected, because the Xingu Park would be an unfamiliar habitat for them, and because it contained their bitter enemies the Metuktire. In November of that year, before the final contact, both Claudio and Orlando formally asked the federal government to interdict all the Panará homeland, carefully defining its geographical boundaries. (Interdiction means secluding an area prior to obtaining permanent reserve status.) They warned that mining companies were eager to invade the area, which was rumoured to contain gold or diamonds. Such 'an invasion of the [Panará] lands would be "disastrous" and would cause serious problems for Funai.' So, in 1974, Funai did finally obtain a decree interdicting some 400,000 hectares (almost 1,000,000 acres) of land for the Panará—although the designated area was in the wrong place: it omitted five Panará villages, and even Funai's own post.

Everything changed during the eighteen months after the first contact in January 1973. By mid-1974 the situation of the Panará was deteriorating so fast and so catastrophically that the Villas Boas made a dramatic U-turn. They and others abandoned the idea of protecting Panará territory. Instead, they started to argue that the tribe would face extinction if it were not moved. Funai's new president, General Ismarth de Araújo Oliveira, greatly admired the work of the Villas Boas in the Xingu. In his instructions to Funai's new regional agent, Fiorello Parise, he told him to see whether the Panará could remain in their lands, which was what he wanted. But he added: 'If you find no way for them to survive and you cannot get them away from the road, I shall start the transfer plan.' Claudio also now agreed that a rescue operation was 'the only way to prevent these Indians from disappearing. ... Even if a large reserve were demarcated for them, it would not be a satisfactory solution' since they were too nomadic. Parise's report on the deteriorating health and social disintegration of the tribe was devastating. So General Ismarth de Araújo Oliveira decided that he must act immediately. He personally removed the interdiction on the 400,000 hectares that had been earmarked as a Panará homeland. The general justified not going through the correct channels of informing the Ministry of the Interior (Funai's parent ministry) and obtaining presidential approval for cancelling the interdiction. He wrote: 'That was an emergency, a necessity that could not be subordinated to bureaucracy'—by which he meant the Statute of the Indian (recently published in 1973) which guaranteed every tribe protection of its homeland. So at the end of 1974 he ordered: 'Orlando, transfer them!'

The decision to remove the Panará for their own salvation was highly controversial. Fiorello Parise and another Funai official opposed the move, as did Father Antonio Iasi of the nearby Jesuit Anchieta Mission. (Father Iasi was a dedicated radical missionary of the 'liberation theology' wing of the Catholic Church, whose mission had for many years helped the Kaiabi, and who had in 1970 personally asked the Villas Boas to take in the shattered remnant of the Tapayuna.) Parisi argued that the Panará were coming to understand that the road brought disease, and were losing their fascination for this sinister invader. He later said: 'For me, the move was a disaster. ... You cannot take a people and transport them from one place to another' like cattle. He, Father Iasi, and others realized that the transfer would largely benefit the colonization and mining companies who were greedily eyeing the forests along the Peixoto de Azevedo. Such fears were justified. In 1976 a study done for the

175

Ministry of the Interior tendentiously claimed that the area could house some 1,500 families of settlers, amounting to 8,500 people. A decree of June 1979 formally nullified the area's interdiction, and Funai awarded it to the government's colonization agency, Incra. Some sceptics now suspect that the president of Funai, General Ismarth, might not have been as pro-Indian and disinterested as Orlando thought, and that he was obeying orders from superiors in the military government. He may deliberately have used the Panarás' catastrophic decline as a pretext for taking their land.

Ranchers, settlers, and prospectors poured in. The beautiful forests of this part of Brazil were destroyed forever and their rivers polluted. Twenty-three towns eventually sprang up along the BR-163, including Matupá on the site of a Panará village. All this was technically illegal under the constitution and the Statute of the Indian, which guaranteed a people the land on which it had always lived and hunted. Some critics would later see the migration as ethnic cleansing. But in the crisis atmosphere of 1974 it was felt that any delay would be fatal—there would soon be no Panará alive, either to be rescued or left in their habitat. The tribe's fate had actually been sealed a few years earlier when the government ordered the building of the BR-163 Cuiabá–Santarém highway that passed beside its land.

Claudio took the aged Chief Kreton and another Panará chief to see the Xingu, and they were impressed by the friendly reception given them by the tribes around Posto Leonardo. They also liked the hens and other domestic animals they saw there, which were of course new to them. Back on the Peixoto de Azevedo, there was a hasty consultation with the tribal elders. Orlando called this a 'plebiscite', after which everyone agreed to move eastwards to the sanctuary of the Xingu Park. Megaron Metuktire said that he had also told Orlando that he must do something or the Panará would become extinct. 'So Orlando got the Air Force to transport them, so that they would not be finished. But the [Panará] lost their land, their region. It was such a rich area, with Brazil-nuts and good earth for farm clearings. They lost all their land.' A young Funai official tried to warn the Panará leaders that they were being moved permanently; but they assured him that it was an excursion, just going to have another look at the Xingu. They therefore left all their meagre possessions behind, and had not even harvested their beloved peanuts, which were ripe for picking. (The Panará still grow very large peanuts, which perform a central role in their tribal customs.)

The exodus took place on 1 January 1975. All the Panará had by now been contacted, and they were only seventy-nine people. These were transported in three forty-minute flights of a C-47, with each of the tribe's clans travelling together. Although one journalist reported that the Panará seemed as relaxed as seasoned travellers during this extraordinary experience, one Panará later told Stephan Schwartzman that some of his people cried from fear during the flight—even though they had been told that they must go, to escape the diseases and fevers killing them in their homelands. Sokriti, the warrior to whom Claudio had offered an axe at the first meeting, said: 'We thought we were going to meet relatives. I was trembling with fear in the plane and clung to the seat.'

Landing at Diauarum, the Panará were welcomed with a night of celebrations. Their leaders were embraced by Rauni of the Metuktire and Prepori of the Kaiabi—both peoples who had fought the Panará in the past. One observer felt that these greetings by avowed enemies were 'a violent humiliation' for the refugees. However, they seemed to enjoy a banquet of roast peccary, papaya, and bananas. The warrior Sokriti was pleased with a headdress given him by Rauni. Next day, they were taken to a clearing nearby on the edge of the Xingu, where the Kaiabi had prepared two huts and a small plantation of corn for them, and they smiled when they saw this.

Soon after their arrival at Diauarum, the seventy-nine Panará were given thorough medical examinations and further inoculations by Dr Baruzzi and his team from the São Paulo teaching hospital. (This examination of a newly contacted people was unique, and was therefore published in an important medical journal.) The doctors found that the surviving Panará were in generally satisfactory physical health, although most were underweight and some were anaemic. All suffered from hookworm and all had evidence of malaria, in their blood and enlarged spleens. But the doctors concluded that their psychological state was wretched. 'The group that entered the [Xingu] National Park had been decimated beyond the most pessimistic calculations. They were profoundly socially disorganized and there was not the necessary cohesion among them to resist the hostile forces of the new environment. A growing apathy affected their already weakened state of health.' Despite this medical attention, the tribe continued to suffer from influenza and pneumonia, and above all from frequent, severe attacks of malaria. During their first eighteen months in the Xingu, a further eleven Panará died, a decline of 14 per cent to a mere sixty-eight people.

The move into the Xingu was not a success. The Panará had never seen a river as large as the Xingu, they could not use canoes, and they came to dislike the huts and clearing prepared for them by the Kaiabi. The garden of maize ran out in a few weeks. But their greatest problem was that the woodlands of the upper Xingu were lower and drier than the magnificent tropical forests of the Peixoto de Azevedo, so they had less of the game and forest fruits that had abounded in that verdant valley. Years later, the Panará chief Akè complained in a filmed interview:

> I do not enjoy being here on the Xingu. It is wretched being in a place you don't like. ... On the Peixoto we had good land, we had fruit trees, much game to hunt—there was plenty. I have great nostalgia to be back in such a rich place. I greatly miss the Peixoto, my land, where I was born.

To Schwartzman on another occasion, Akè named some of the riches he missed:

> There on the Peixoto there are many fruits—açaí [a palm with fruit rich in vitamins], papaya, cupuaçu [the delicious fruit of a tree related to chocolate-making cacao], cashews, pupunha [fruit of the spiny peach-palm *Guilielma speciosa*]—many kinds of honey, abundant peccary, much fish, much game, plenty of mutum [curassow wild turkey]. But it has all ceased. ... On my river there were plenty of Brazil-nuts: we used to eat them during hunts, when we were hungry while returning to our village.

Because the Panará were unhappy near Diauarum, they were soon moved far down the Xingu to Kretire village (previously Porori) of the Je-speaking Metuktire. This almost destroyed them. They were arbitrarily divided among the huts of their former enemies, who were now far tougher, more numerous, self-confident, and prosperous than they were. It soon became clear that Chief Rauni wanted to absorb them altogether, particularly since his people had an excess of young men and there were unattached women among the newcomers.

Luckily Claudio rapidly realized that this move had been a mistake. So he transferred the Panará yet again, in October of that same year, 1975, back up the Xingu to a former Suiá village not far from Diauarum. Some Panará women and children stayed with the Metuktire, but the remainder now resided in a circle of four small huts that was a semblance of their traditional village layout. They were learning to fish with boats and fish-hooks, they planted gardens, and they hunted. Claudio gave them clothing (which they requested), and even guns and ammunition—distributed by night so that others would not be jealous, and with strict instructions that the firearms were for hunting and not for use against other Indians. So their morale and health improved and, from a nadir in 1976, their population also recovered slightly. We shall see, in a later chapter, how two decades later life for the Panará improved dramatically, with a return to part of their homeland and an unprecedented apology and financial compensation from the Brazilian government—because of their tragically mismanaged contact.

13

RETIREMENT

In late 1974 the chiefs of all the tribes in the Xingu Park gathered at Posto Leonardo to bid farewell to the Villas Boas brothers, who had announced that they intended to retire. The new president of Funai, General Ismarth de Araújo Oliveira, praised the remarkable achievements of their thirty years with the indigenous peoples. Orlando made a speech urging the Indians to maintain a solid alliance against threats from roads and settlers, lest they face total extinction. The Indians themselves were deeply saddened to lose their champions—who had also been father figures and playful friends. Some were almost angry at this perceived betrayal, and they could not imagine why the brothers would want to leave the tranquil beauty of the Xingu for the ugly clamour of the cities.

Orlando later said that they had decided to retire because, although relatively young at fifty-nine and sixty-one, they had been in the forests for a long time and had done much tough exploration, and Orlando was in poor health. They had achieved their greatest contact, with the Panará, and the rescue of that people's remnant into the Xingu Indigenous Park. Also, they felt that it was time to pass the management of the park to a younger generation. Orlando's successor as director was a Funai anthropologist called Olympio Serra—a short, quiet man with a full black beard, who supported the Villas Boas' indigenous policy. But the brothers did not leave immediately: for several months Claudio carried on living in spartan simplicity at Diauarum, and Orlando in a new house at Posto Leonardo. Hundreds of Indians of all ages were on the riverbank when Claudio finally left Diauarum. Some wept, others waved their bows and arrows, some even waded out and tried to hold back the boat that was removing their beloved 'white father'.

General Ismarth asked the Villas Boas to use their skills to contact the elusive Arara people, who were in the path of the new Transamazonica highway, in forests far to the north-west of the Xingu Park. He was very disappointed when they refused.* The brothers also declined a suggestion that they might succeed the admirable *sertanista* Gilberto Pinto, who had been killed at the end of 1974 by the Atroari-Waimiri peoples whom he was contacting. In each case, the Villas Boas felt too weary to embark on another dangerous contact in dense, remote, and unfamiliar forests with none of their excellent Indian helpers. Also, their hearts were with the peoples of the Xingu, and their contacts and rescues had all been of nearby tribes.

So, in January 1976, the brothers moved to São Paulo. Their pay in the Xingu had been minimal and their pensions were correspondingly meagre. Had they retired altogether, as some of their enemies wanted, they would have been poverty-stricken. But to their surprise a new military president, ex-General Ernesto Geisel, declared that retirement was out of the question because 'the Villas Boas are untouchable'. He therefore arranged well-paid work for them as consultants to Funai, and more reasonable pensions.

In São Paulo, Claudio had a small apartment on the top floor of a block of flats on the noisy Rua Augusta, in the residential centre of the city. He lived alone, but quite often had visitors—preferably Indians. He had shaved off his beard but kept a white moustache, often wore his trademark dark glasses, and smoked constantly. There was no television, but of course plenty of books, and taped classical music. Claudio hated restaurants, so after a while he installed a cook–housekeeper called Maria and established a new routine in his flat. His fifteen-year-old adopted son, a Trumai called Tauaru, boarded in a school outside São Paulo but came to his foster father at weekends. Once a year Tauaru's loving mother Jenie Trumai and some of his siblings came from the Xingu to stay with Claudio and see their relative. The boy had a good Brazilian education and grew up well. But, to Claudio's despair, he was tragically killed in a car accident a decade later, in 1986.

---

* The Arara were not finally contacted until 1981, after a long attraction campaign by the Villas Boas' protégé Sydney Possuelo. They proved to be Carib speakers, distantly related to the Ikpeng who had been brought into the Xingu Park in 1967. The Atroari-Waimiri, also Carib speakers, lived in the path of another new road, the BR-174, which was being opened from Manaus north towards Roraima. This people had in 1968 killed Father João (Giovanni) Calleri, an Italian missionary entrusted by Funai to undertake their contact, together with his eight companions, including two nuns. Gilberto Pinto achieved the contact with tact and skill, but he was killed, largely because of a feud between two chiefs, one of whom he had befriended more than the other.

Orlando moved into a small house with Marina and their two boys, Orlando and Noel. But in 1980 he was awarded the State of São Paulo Prize and used this windfall to buy an attractive house and large garden in the city's leafy Lapa district. The brothers remained close. Whenever they were writing a book together, a car would take Claudio the short distance to Orlando's house. They would sit side by side at a cluttered desk, with Orlando writing a page on an old typewriter, and then passing it to Claudio for correction because he was 'a perfect editor'. Claudio would lunch with his brother's family every Sunday; but, always shy, if there were other guests he might quietly disappear. Claudio also kept in touch with his sister and their youngest brother, Álvaro, who had also devoted his life to Indians. Álvaro was not a *sertanista* or forest explorer, so he worked for Funai in charge of acculturated peoples in the interior of the state of São Paulo. He was a quiet, intelligent, and charming man, and in 1985 was briefly president of Funai.

When the Villas Boas left the Xingu in 1976 they were at the height of their fame. One crowning glory of their careers had been the contact of the Panará 'giants' after so many months of punishing exploration and danger—all extensively reported in the media. Praise came from all sides. As early as 1973 Orlando was described as 'a living legend', but one who carried this accolade with the greatest elegance. The academician Antonio Callado praised the 'magic brothers' for their achievements as explorers which had culminated in the Xingu Indigenous Park, 'a creation of love, and as such I think that it will endure for a long time, or perhaps will never end'. The great anthropologist Darcy Ribeiro declared that 'Orlando, Claudio and Leonardo had the most extraordinary and beautiful lives of which I know. ... Their daring and generous adventures would have been unimaginable had they not lived them.' He admired the courage with which they contacted or pacified various tribes—'a sad business for those peoples, but less bad because it was conducted by the Villas Boas'. Some journalists were even more effusive, describing the brothers as

> these lovely indianists and above all brave humanitarians, worthy heirs ... of Rondon ... who are now known, respected and loved by all Brazil, thanks to their uninterrupted work of forty years. ... It is an indefatigable and intrepid struggle in favour of our sacrificed indigenous peoples and for their right to cultural and physical survival.

I witnessed this fame. I once went with Orlando and a dozen Brazilian friends to lunch in a small São Paulo restaurant. He started talking about his amazing adventures. Soon the entire restaurant fell silent to hear this spellbinding raconteur; then the kitchen staff tiptoed out to join the listeners. Later, when we asked for the bill, the proprietor said: 'No charge. It is such an honour to have Orlando Villas Boas in my restaurant that I am giving you all lunch on the house.'

Thanks to President Geisel, Orlando continued to work for Funai as a counsellor. His job was to advise the foundation's president and to give lectures, broadcasts, and interviews. He joked that he was dealing with scores of calls every day, and had enough invitations to dinners or speeches to occupy every evening. He particularly enjoyed talking to students. One journalist appreciated that 'he is superb at public relations, expansive, with a gift for expression that it would be hard to equal. But he knows how many benefits this gift has given to his indigenous cause.' This was the key. The brothers, particularly the extrovert Orlando rather than the shyer Claudio, did not mind the publicity thrust upon them. They may even have courted it because they knew how all their lectures, interviews, articles, and broadcasts influenced the public, that these were the voters who elected politicians, who in turn had the power to protect or abandon Indians.

The Villas Boas constantly spoke on the same themes. They showed how indigenous society was complex in beliefs and rituals but simple in customs and possessions. Its generosity, family life, and dignity were admirable. This communal way of life was different, but not inferior, to that of other Brazilians. The Indians had a right to their separate cultures and to the lands that sustained them. Nevertheless, the brothers admitted that eventual assimilation of indigenous peoples within the rest of Brazil was inevitable. But they insisted that such a massive transition must be done as slowly and gradually as possible. 'Change, but only at the speed the Indians want' was their mantra, because full or rapid integration into tough frontier society would be disastrous and criminally wrong. Neither side would gain by having detribalized Indians joining the lowest level of unemployed, marginalized, or trafficked backwoodsmen.

Amid the adulation, there was criticism—sometimes born of jealousy. One controversial issue was the movements of threatened peoples into the Xingu Park, because these refugees lost their homelands forever. This was particularly true of the Ikpeng in 1967, the Tapayuna in 1970, and the Panará in 1975—although, to be fair, the Villas Boas were not prime movers in the last two of these rescues, and the Ikpeng lost some weak *campo cerrado* rather than a richly forested homeland. Some supporters of indigenous people saw these moves as betrayals.

Another onslaught came in 1980 from Mário Juruna, a Xavante who later became the only Indian ever to be elected to the National Congress. Juruna was a fiery and effective champion of indigenous rights. He was angry with Funai for trying to prevent his going to the radical Russell Tribunal on Human Rights in the Netherlands because it was feared that he would unfairly attack Funai's treatment of Indians. Juruna accused Orlando of 'profiting at the expense of indigenous people. ... He is isolated among Brazilian anthropologists and indigenists because of his unqualified defence of Funai, of which he is a functionary.' It was true that Orlando often spoke well of Funai after his admirer General Ismarth became its president, and that he was employed as its counsellor. But, for all its shortcomings, Funai was the main defender of Indians and their territories. Also, Orlando did constantly criticize those within the indigenous foundation who favoured integration rather than his policy of gradual assimilation, or those who were incompetent. Juruna's attack was short-lived because, thanks to pro-indigenous lawyers, he did get a passport and went to the tribunal, where he was indeed highly critical of Funai.[†]

The quarter-century of the brothers' retirement, from the mid-1970s to the end of the millennium, was a period of intense activity for Brazilian Indians. Following on from the Transamazonica, other 'penetration' roads were cut into the Amazon forests, using two devastatingly destructive inventions, the chainsaw and the earthmover. These roads brought swarms of settlers, land speculators, ranchers, farmers, loggers, prospectors, and adventurers into Amazonia, in the greatest internal migration in South American history. The 1980s became known as the 'Decade of Destruction' because of the resulting deforestation. The brothers' friend Adrian Cowell told the world about this environmental onslaught in a series of prize-winning television films and books, whose impact influenced the United States Congress,

[†] Mário Juruna's name was a corruption of his Xavante name Dzururã, and had nothing to do with the Juruna tribe on the Xingu. He had long since left his Xavante people, in the Mission of São Marcos in Mato Grosso. He became a national celebrity through his writing and speeches. His trademark was a tape-recorder, on which he wittily claimed to record all the lies told by politicians. A close ally of Darcy Ribeiro, Mário Juruna was a passionate defender of indigenous rights, particularly of his own people and of the Yanomami. In 1982 he was elected to Congress—in Rio de Janeiro (then called Guanabara), ironically the only state that actually contained no Indians—and he was an effective politician. After Deputy Juruna lost his seat in 1986, he also went onto the Funai payroll, and he made his peace with Orlando. But by 2000, aged fifty, he was living in poverty, reduced to a wheelchair by rheumatism and chronic diabetes, and he died in hospital two years later.

the World Bank, and the viewing public in many countries, particularly where it mattered most—in Brazil itself.

In response, indigenous peoples formed scores of interest groups to protect their lands and fight for their rights. Their associations were either for a single large indigenous people, or a cluster of peoples, or by all those living in a particular region or river basin. By the end of the century there were well over a hundred of these NGOs. They were helped by Funai, by activist sympathizers in Brazil and abroad, missionaries, anthropologists, and public opinion. The philosophy and methods of the Villas Boas guided these campaigns and groupings. They were also the inspiration for the British NGO Survival International, which actively championed campaigns by indigenous peoples all over Brazil. Thus, the 1980s and 1990s, when Brazil suffered accelerating destruction of its tropical rainforests, also witnessed a series of splendid victories in indigenous land rights. (This author was one of the founders of Survival International, in 1969, together with the anthropologist Francis Huxley and the activists Robin Hanbury-Tenison and Nicholas Guppy. After fifty years of campaigning, Survival is acknowledged as the world's leading defender of indigenous peoples.) The brothers were often asked to support particular causes, and frequently did so in their speeches, broadcasts, and interviews.

One of the most important campaigns came in 1978, against a bill proposed by the military government's hard-line minister of the interior, Rangel Reis. His bill was called Emancipation of Indians, whereby any individual Indian or entire tribe could choose to leave communal indigenous society and the tutelage of Funai, in order to become ordinary Brazilian citizens. The seductive word 'emancipation' was a trap. A similar law in the United States, the Dawes Act of 1887, had divided Native American reservations into plots for individual families. Speculators had immediately picked off these smallholdings, so that any Native American territory could be fragmented and its tribe's cohesion and society demolished. The Villas Boas lent their prestige to the chorus of protest, with Darcy Ribeiro leading the anthropologists' condemnation of 'emancipation'. This campaign succeeded. In 1979 the next general to become president of Brazil cancelled the proposal.

The result of all the campaigning, political lobbying, legal work, demonstrations, and even armed confrontations was the establishment of scores of new indigenous territories and national parks, particularly in the Amazonian forests. Some were larger than many member states of the United Nations. Three of the biggest were created, respectively, for the Yanomami on the Venezuelan border in the extreme north, for peoples of the Upper Rio

Negro on the frontier with Colombia, and for Indians of the Javari valley in the far west of Brazil beside Peru. The prototype and inspiration for these vast new indigenous territories was of course the Xingu Indigenous Park. As we shall see, the Xingu Park was eventually linked to Kayapó territories to the north, forming a gigantic 800-kilometre (500-mile) indigenous and environmental corridor in the heart of the country.

* * *

During their retirement, the brothers produced a series of books. They wrote as laymen, without academic training but drawing on decades of experience, and they aimed at a general readership. No one else could have written these vivid and readable books, which were of course wholly sympathetic to the Indians. They started in 1970, before their retirement, with the publication of *Xingu: Os índios, seus mitos*, an important book translated three years later as *Xingu: The Indians, their Myths*. In this, they stressed how much myths mean to Indians as the basis of their material and spiritual worlds and as the justification for their actions. Mythology is 'the psychological basis, the common experience, the definitive kinship, and the higher authority of Xingu culture'. To appreciate the myths, a reader must merge the boundaries between mankind and animals, night and day, and the natural and supernatural realms. In a perceptive introduction to the English version, the anthropologist Kenneth Brecher stressed that no one could equal the brothers' formidable knowledge gained from thirty years of observation. 'They make no claim to scholarship or scientific technique, which is possibly what makes the book so readable,' and their descriptions of the Xingu environment impart 'a gentle authority which [explains] why so many people have fallen under their spell.'

Then in 1979 the two brothers wrote a short text for a book called *Xingu: Tribal Territory*—a vibrant introduction to the Xingu's environment, seasons, nature, and peoples that is an essential introduction for anyone visiting that magical place for the first time. This text was an introduction to a collection of stunningly beautiful photographs of Xinguanos, by the English photographer Maureen Bisilliat—lyrical close-ups of their bodies and faces gleaming in vivid body paint, taken on eight visits at Orlando's invitation. Bisilliat followed this in 1995 with *Guerreiros sem Espada* ('Warriors without Swords'), a lively scrapbook compendium of interviews, articles, and pictures about the Villas Boas.

The extrovert Orlando liked writing about colourful people—Indians and backwoodsmen. He published a series of small, chatty books: a history of his people by an old Juruna chief called Káia, in 1984; adventurers on the Rio das Mortes, in 1988; stories about Indians and woodsmen, in 1992; and in 1997 *Almanaque do sertão* ('Almanac of the Wilderness'), amusing anecdotes about visitors to the Xingu, *caboclos*, and Indians. He delighted in the homespun wisdom, humour, and bawdy campfire songs of the woodsmen; the culture and dignity of Indians; and visitors who made fools of themselves with their machismo, inexperience, or pomposity.

Orlando loved to communicate with children, which he did in 1978 in a history of Indians written in the way that tribal elders would tell traditions to their grandchildren. In 1986 there was a tale told by a boy called 'Tamoin' (a nickname for his own son, also called Orlando). Another collection of stories for young children was published in 2013, long after his death, as *Histórias do Xingu*.

The longest book by the Villas Boas was *A Marcha para o Oeste* ('The March to the West', but never translated) in 1994. This told the saga of the Roncador–Xingu Expedition of 1943–6 and the brothers' introduction to the Xingu and its peoples. It was a great book, written as if dictated by Orlando and Claudio, with vivid recollections and exciting stories (sometimes embellished, out of sequence, or near-libellous) but a thrilling account by the leaders of a unique adventure. It won the Jabuti literary prize as the best reportage book. Then, late in life. Orlando started to write an autobiography, which was unfinished when he died in 2002. The first part of this, with a medley of other anecdotes, was published posthumously as *História e causos*. In 2002 Cristina Müller and others edited *O Xingu dos Villas Bôas*, a compendium of papers and lectures by and about the brothers, by a dozen authors including their great friend Adrian Cowell and myself. Another fine collection of papers and reminiscences was written and compiled in 2015 by his brilliant son Orlando Villas Boas Filho, a professor of law simultaneously at two of the most important universities in São Paulo. He called this *Orlando Villas Bôas and the Construction of Indigenism in Brazil* (a translation of the title) because the young Orlando stressed his father's contributions to the theory about and policy towards indigenous people.

* * *

In addition to praise, the Villas Boas won awards. One of the first, the gold medal of the Royal Geographical Society (RGS) in London, came in 1967. This was given jointly to Claudio and Orlando, the only Brazilians ever to win it. For the RGS they were perfect candidates, with their combination of first explorations of untrodden lands and humanitarian struggle for indigenous peoples—this reminded the society of its mentor Dr David Livingstone, who used his fame as an African explorer to combat slavery (largely by Arabs). The Explorers Club of New York also gave them its Citation of Merit at that time.

In 1970 it was felt that the Indians' cause would be hugely strengthened if the Villas Boas could win a Nobel Peace Prize. Robin Hanbury-Tenison, of the new charity Survival International (initially called Primitive Peoples Fund), took up the cause with vigour. Only parliamentarians, senior academics, and institutions could make such nominations, so all of us involved with Survival enrolled a galaxy of supporters. In the UK the main nominees were the minister Lord Boyd and Sir Julian Huxley (the first director of UNESCO and father of the anthropologist Francis) and we enlisted some forty senior politicians, Members of Parliament, and three Nobel-prize-winning scientists; in France the famous anthropologist Claude Lévi-Strauss and the Société des Américanistes de Paris; in the USA the American Anthropological Association under Charles Wagley; and luminaries from other European and South American countries. In Brazil itself, the Museu Nacional in Rio de Janeiro wrote that 'without any doubt all Brazilian anthropologists support [the nomination] without reserve'. Even General Bandeira de Melo grudgingly lent his support, because it would be a source of pride for all Brazilians and an endorsement of Funai, of which he was then president. Claudio alone was nominated in 1970; but he was unsuccessful, so we tried again in 1972 for both brothers, again with many distinguished supporters. However, 1972 was one of nineteen years in which the Nobel Committee decided to award no Peace Prize, because it felt that no candidate was sufficiently important in peace-making on a world stage.

A galaxy of other awards continued during the ensuing decades: in 1972 Brazil's Medal of Indigenist Merit; in 1973 they travelled to Japan for an award; 1975 the Rio Branco Medal of Merit; 1976 the Boilesen Prize for education and science; 1977 to the United States for the Humanitarian Commendation of the Lions Club; in 1980 Orlando received the State of São Paulo Prize (which came with prize money of $100,000, with which he bought the house in the Lapa district); in 1984 to Hamburg for the Geo Prize plus more prize money, handed to him by ex-Chancellor Willy Brandt; and in 1998 both the Freedom of the City of São Paulo and the Medal of Human Rights personally from the president of Brazil. In 1999 a congressional edict awarded the octogenarian brothers pensions for life for 'exceptional services to the Brazilian indigenous cause'; and in 2000 (the 500th anniversary of the Portuguese discovery of Brazil) Orlando was named as a National Hero. He was also delighted by a peculiarly Brazilian accolade: to 'dance', aged eighty-six, on a float in Rio de Janeiro's great Carnival parade, wearing the green-and-white colours of the Paulista Samba School; and in the following year that school had both a float and that year's samba song in his honour. Finally in 2003, immediately after Orlando's death, he appeared on a postage stamp, and the National Congress passed a law officially adding 'Orlando Villas Boas' to the name of the Xingu Indigenous Park.

14

LEGACY

In 1985 Brazil returned to democratic rule after twenty-one years of military government. At the end of 1986 there was a special general election to choose a constituent assembly, with a mandate of one year in which to draft a new constitution. Every special-interest group argued its case, and most clauses were hammered out in weeks of negotiation; but the end result was a political triumph. Human-rights activists, non-government organizations (NGOs), lawyers, liberal intellectuals, and the Indian leaders themselves lobbied and fought ferociously to get favourable terms for indigenous peoples. They were arguing against commercial interests that coveted Indian lands and the resources on and under them, and against some political theorists who thought that tribal societies must merge into the rest of Brazil. The Villas Boas brothers joined many others in signing a manifesto addressed to the constituent assembly in May 1988. This passionately defended indigenous rights, but wanted Indians to play a distinct role in Brazil's *future*, not just its past. This manifesto, together with all the other bargaining and protests, succeeded in getting excellent wording about Indians in the constitution that was passed later that year.

This 1988 constitution had only two articles about indigenous peoples, but it contained radical innovations. It declared that these were descendants of the original Brazilians so that in a sense it was their land. There was no mention of integration or even assimilation, which meant that Indians had the right to remain different. The constitution guaranteed respect for their way of life, in its society, customs, languages, and beliefs. It also gave a sweeping definition of indigenous lands, as 'those traditionally occupied by Indians ... on which they live, ... those used for productive activities and those indispensable to the preservation of the environmental resources necessary for their wellbeing and their physical and cultural reproduction'. This Article 231 also prohibited, under legal penalty, the occupation or degradation of any indigenous lands or reserves. Article 232 reiterated the rights of Indians over the lands they inhabit and the exclusive use of the goods and resources on those lands.

Indians and their territories remained in the tutelage of Funai. The constitution raised indigenous people to the status of citizens with full rights, while still enjoying the security of state protection. They remained legal minors under the protection of the *ministro público* (attorney general), who had the right and duty to bring prosecutions, individually or collectively, against any who might harm them. As minors, they were not subject to national law for their actions—even killing or infanticide—if these were done in the context of tribal custom or spiritual beliefs. They could act collectively, and were not liable to taxation, military service, state education, or other obligations. They did not have voting rights—although a few individual Indians have since left tribal society and been elected in local or in one case national politics. All this was a triumphant vindication of the policy of gradual change devised by the Villas Boas, of the concept of two parallel societies, and of the huge protected indigenous areas as pioneered by the Xingu Indigenous Park.

Within the Xingu Park itself, every people without exception decided to continue to act collectively and practise its traditional way of life. During the sixty years since the creation of the park, all its Indians have coped well with the gigantic transition from being hunter-gatherers with simple agriculture to an awareness of modern Brazilian society.

Some tribal leaders deplored change. In 1981 the Xingu peoples combined to produce a newsletter that was a lament for vanishing traditions:

In the old days, we Indians used to perform rituals at all times. But the rituals are gradually disappearing, because the whites have arrived. .... There's an end to all the rituals, languages, and food because people stop making garden [clearings]. The Indians also stop making ornaments and all the things that they need to live: baskets, sifters for manioc and corn flour, manioc graters, clay pots, drills for fire, mats ... and *tipitis* to squeeze [poison out of] manioc dough to make flour, canoes, paddles, basketry fish-traps, houses, hammocks, and gourd dippers. They don't poison fish with *timbó*, hunt, use herbal medicines, make poisoned arrows, bark blankets, necklaces of monkey teeth, large painted baskets with fringes to carry hammocks, or tattoo themselves and apply body paint of [red] anatto and [black] genipapo, or practise shamanism and witchcraft, and other things as well. ... Why is it important not to lose our customs? Because if we cease being Indians, we are neither white nor Indian. [This would lead to miscegenation] and if this happens, we will lose our land.

190

Yet, because the Indians were running their own affairs, they were better able to confront the dilemma between tradition and modernization, thereby fulfilling the Villas Boas' cardinal policy that they should change only at a speed that *they themselves* wanted. Individuals thus chose whether or not to wear clothes. They made greater use of outboard motors, chainsaws, radios, cameras, solar-powered television, bicycles, and a few vehicles and tractors. Brazil's national sport, football, is now played on every dusty village plaza, with the goalposts beside the men's hut. Among Xinguanos, this game is played alongside traditional *huka-huka* wrestling.

Villages are essentially unchanged, with their handsome circle of great thatched huts. Life within these communal houses continues in gentle harmony and silence. Ceremonies are performed regularly. Both sexes love these, with their dances, parades, and blaze of colour from body-paint and feather ornaments. There is nothing sham about them, since every move conforms to tradition and ritual—as in all the world's religions. The routine of daily life is scarcely changed, with the delicious dawn swim for all ages, fishing or hunting for men, and manioc preparation for women.

A school was started in the Xingu in the mid-1970s, to teach reading and writing in Portuguese, numeracy, and information technology. As always, there was debate about whether pupils should be taught in indigenous languages or in the national tongue, Portuguese. The São Paulo doctors, under Baruzzi and his equally admirable successor, Professor Douglas Rodrigues, devised regular courses in healthcare and basic medicine for young men and women from every village. I obtained some foreign-aid funding for these week-long residential courses, and attended one at Diauarum. In a session on sexually transmitted diseases, the class was asked what to do if a young Indian visited a frontier town outside the park and returned with AIDS. One warrior gave an answer that was logical to him, but not what the instructors expected: 'Kill him.'

While maintaining all the fine customs of their society, the peoples of the upper Xingu continue practices that would have been illegal had they been full Brazilian citizens. Their doctor Roberto Baruzzi told me that the greatest cause of death among adolescents was their violent initiation rites, which involve taking poisons during the months of seclusion. Random killings, which had so distressed Adrian Cowell in the 1950s, still happen occasionally, as do infanticides if a newborn baby suffers from any physical defect or evil omens. The anthropologist Michael Heckenberger spent 1993 sleeping with his hammock amid those of the family of Chief Afukaká of the Kuikuro. He loved and admired the chief and his kin. But Heckenberger was alarmed that during that year an 'epidemic of witchcraft' took the lives of seven people, including three from the chief's own household.

Demographically, the Xingu peoples reached a nadir in the 1960s. When von den Steinen first entered the upper Xingu in the 1880s he reckoned its population at three thousand, but epidemics in the ensuing sixty years ravaged tribes. Then came more influenza and measles soon after the arrival of the Roncador–Xingu Expedition and the air force base. This changed, thanks to the advent of preventive and curative medicines, the ministrations of Nurse Marina, and from 1965 onwards regular visits by volunteer doctors from the São Paulo Medical School (EPM, later renamed UNIFESP—Federal University of São Paulo). Every people trebled or quadrupled during the half century after the low point. Thus, by the millennium, numbers had recovered to their original size in Steinen's day, and as the twenty-first century progressed the demographics forged ahead, as a result of a high birth rate and dramatic reduction in infant and other mortality. The total is, of course, still a tiny fraction of Brazil's 208 million people. In the most recent census, only 850,000 people considered themselves to be indigenous—0.4 per cent of the national total. And those living in the Xingu are just 0.3 per cent of that indigenous number.*

The Xingu Indigenous Park retains the boundaries it was given after the BR-080 sliced across it in 1971 (with the addition of small territories for the Suiá (Kisêdje) to the east and for the Ikpeng in the south-west corner). There seems no danger of its being damaged again—despite turbulence in Brazilian politics and economy. The Xingu was the pioneer. Brazil now boasts half a dozen other huge indigenous 'parks'; and these have also been replicated in most South American countries. That model of combining swathes of tropical rainforest with homelands for indigenous peoples is a proud legacy for the Villas Boas and their colleagues. The first five presidents after Brazil's return to democratic rule in 1985 each added further indigenous territories, so that virtually every forest tribe now has its land protected. This means that a mere half-million Brazilian Indians are guardians of some 11 per cent of all Brazil, or 25 per cent of 'Amazonia Legal' (the states that comprise the northern half of the country). These forests and rivers are not only home to the richest terrestrial ecosystem on earth, but they generate rain for half a continent, and their vegetation is the repository of unimaginable quantities of carbon. To paraphrase Winston Churchill, rarely have so many—we in the rest of the

---

* This book's appendix 'Populations of Xingu Peoples' gives the exact number in each tribe at different dates.

world—owed so much to so few. This stewardship is because indigenous people are the only ones who can flourish *within* the forests that they cherish. If they were evicted, outsiders would fell the forests and the population of invading ranchers could be less than that of tribal peoples. There would be catastrophic and irreparable damage to Earth's environment.

Three outstanding leaders of Xingu society understood this fundamental difference. Megaron Metuktire knew that Indians love and live successfully within the rainforest, whereas other Brazilians fear and destroy it:

> The whites are always getting closer to our lands. These people think only of felling forest and planting pasture for their cattle to graze. The whites need money to live, for without money whites cannot survive. We Indians need the forest to live. But many whites do not understand our way of life. This is why it is very difficult for each group to understand the other.

Mairawé Kaiabi deplored the damage done by ranchers with their thoughtless deforestation. He declared that 'to be an Indian is to live in the forest, to know all its sounds. It is different to the life of a white man.' Chief Aritana Yawalapiti agreed. He was deeply saddened by the destruction surrounding the park, where 'the beautiful forest has been cut down, and with it the birds and animals have disappeared. ... *We* use our lands without destroying them.'

The scale of that deforestation could never have been conceived by the Villas Boas or other activists in the 1950s. Nor could they have foreseen the expanses of soya plantations, cattle ranches, and desolation that would surround and stifle the Xingu Park during the coming half century. In those early days, Brazilian Amazonia was covered in an unbroken canopy of trees, the largest expanse of tropical rainforests in the world. By 2010 half the land of the upper Xingu basin immediately around the park had been totally deforested—some 60,000 square kilometres (23,000 square miles), which is more than twice the size of the park itself. This uncontrolled destruction locks the Indians' homeland in a lethal embrace. Everyone who flies into the Xingu is struck by the stark boundary between its green luxuriance and the brown waste outside. This is as sharp a contrast as Hyde Park or Central Park make in the midst of their grey cities.

When the Xingu Park was created, back in 1961, last-minute horse-trading with the governor of Mato Grosso resulted in its being far smaller than originally proposed. As a result, the sources of every headwater and tributary of the Xingu lie outside its protected area. This did not matter when the entire region was undisturbed forest. But now that the park is surrounded by agriculture on all sides, toxic pesticides, fertilizers, and sludge pollute the waters on which the Indians rely for fishing, drinking, and daily bathing. Other problems are caused by a hydroelectric dam on the Culuene before it flows into the park, and by indiscriminate fishing in those upper waters. Afukaká Kuikuro lamented: 'When I see soya I do not understand. It worries me greatly. They harvest it, then spray poisons. Harvest, spray poisons. Every year, they spray poisons, harvest. What can we do? The white man comes there and says "This is mine, my land". That is how he treats the land.' This chief praised the Villas Boas for alerting his people to these threats. 'Orlando said to me: "Afukaká, you must fight for the Kuikuro, but you must also fight for every village here. You must all be united." We are fighting together.' There have been several campaigns to protect those rivers. One was 'Y Ikatu Xingu' ('Save the Good Water of the Xingu'), which deplored the way that water, the source of life, was being treated as sewerage. Within the park itself there are dramatic posters about the campaign for cleaner rivers, so that young Xinguanos are aware of the problem. But, without criminal prosecutions, few of the surrounding farmers have been forced to curb their pollution.

One surprising reason why Xinguanos cling to their traditional way of life was that some Indians who travelled out into modern Brazil found the experience so disagreeable. The sophisticated Mairawé Kaiabi was appalled that whites 'live in cities, surrounded by walls, with times for everything, and never thinking of others. ... For us, all are equal. ... In the cities there is misery and hunger: I saw poor whites and rich ones, the one exploiting the other.' The Waurá were baffled that white men, who produced such great material wealth, were so disagreeable. They 'do not know how to share and seem to lack human compassion. Whites can ignore the suffering of others who are hungry, even children. ... The white man is bad: he is angry, violent, and dangerous. ... He even beats and kicks his own children, this too I have seen. This is not how human beings behave.' Abused children may grow up 'filled with anger'. A white man shouts at another. 'Foolishly he spills angry words like water slopped on the ground. He becomes violent and has no control over himself.' The anthropologist Kenneth Brecher once took a Waurá to São Paulo for an operation. It was the first time that the young man had worn clothes or left the Xingu. But after a week, he looked sadly at his friend Brecher and asked: 'How could you return to this world after seeing how we live? How can you breathe this foul air or sleep with these terrible noises?' Asked whether he would tell his people what he had seen, the Waurá said: 'No, they would not believe me, and they would be unhappy to think of you having to live here. Our chief is an old man and it is better that he doesn't know.'

194

Another reason why Xingu Indians are handling change so well is that the Villas Boas trained and then trusted them to perform non-indigenous aspects of management. The Aborigines Protection Society mission in 1972 was impressed that the Xingu was the only post where Indians were actually in charge. They did everything, from talking-in the arriving plane, to handling commissariat, the buildings themselves, and internal transport. They were self-assured and there was no sign of paternalism towards them. Orlando retired as director of the park three years after that visit, and he was succeeded by successive Funai officials who continued Villas Boas' policies. Then, in 1984, the leaders of the Indians themselves were invited to nominate the next director. Surprisingly, they chose Megaron, the nephew of Chief Rauni of the Metuktire Kayapó from the northern edge of the park; and he proved to be an excellent director. (Their choice of Megaron was another tribute to the Villas Boas, because they had brokered peace between the Xinguanos and their former bellicose Kayapó enemies.) Since Megaron, Funai's director of the Xingu Park has always been an Indian, usually a Yawalapiti or Kaiabi. Aritana, the young Yawalapiti groomed by the Villas Boas, has for many decades been the genial paramount chief of all the Xinguano peoples, alongside the park's administrative directors (one of whom was his brother Piracumã).

The Xinguanos—those twelve peoples living in the fan of headwaters of the Xingu—have survived and flourished. Most of the young have learned skills of the outside world. They speak Portuguese and are literate, both on paper and with computers—many have lively internet pages and are active on Facebook. They have most of the outside crafts they need, from driving tractors and outboard motors, to handling radios and camcorders, basic engineering and medicine, and playing football. This is on top of traditional skills in fishing and hunting, basketry and pottery, wrestling, archery, running, swimming, and the rituals of festivals. There are now regular Olympiads for all Brazilian indigenous peoples, in which the Xinguanos win plenty of medals. All this is their own achievement, helped by conserving their robust society with its emphasis on generosity, dignity, and moderation. But it is also a vindication of the Villas Boas' determination to control and slow down the pace of change.

What became of the other indigenous peoples living within the Xingu Park, but further north down the main Xingu river? These are the tribes administered from Diauarum, all of whom were either contacted by the brothers or who migrated or were rescued into the park. They could have declined into extinction, or become so demoralized that they ceased to have children, or lapsed into drunkenness or drugs, or espoused an extreme religious sect, or been riven by missionaries from rival faiths, or lost all faith, or left their villages to become roadside beggars or farm labourers in debt-bondage, or lost their lands and had them invaded by adventurers, or drifted into the bottom layer of the coloniza-tion frontier and its towns. There are tribes in Brazil who have suffered every one of these afflictions—although happily these are exceptions, since most are adapting to change with dignity and resilience. The other peoples along the Xingu all avoided these pitfalls. They have survived and increased in numbers. But they have had varying degrees of success and happiness.

The Kaiabi (or Kawaiweté, as they now prefer) had been contacted by the Villas Boas on the Teles Pires river in 1950 and then migrated into the park in five groups between 1954 and 1969. These were the most successful people in the Xingu economically. This was partly because they had already experi-enced outside life on the settlement frontier on the Teles Pires and farther west on the Arinos, because their migrations were voluntary and planned by themselves, because they had charismatic leaders such as Prepori, Canisio, and Mairawé, and above all because they were naturally efficient and hard-working.

After the Villas Boas left the Xingu in 1975, Kaiabi such as Mairawé con-tinued to administer Diauarum, others were the mainstay at Leonardo, and two served as directors of the entire Xingu Indigenous Park. The Kaiabi also thrived because they had a strong culture. Prepori, for instance, trained to be a shaman and maintained his people's spiritualism. Even Mairawé, who spoke and wrote Portuguese and was proficient in modern management, declared: 'I have not lost my pride in being an Indian. I am an Indian! I am a Kaiabi! At festivals I paint myself, dance and run. I have not lost my customs.'

By 2010 the Kaiabi had eighteen flourishing villages, situated along the main Xingu river above and below Diauarum and on its Manitsauá and Arraias tributaries. Each village has plenty of agriculture in its *roça* clearings. There is now a football field in each central plaza, and this is the favourite sport. (I once watched a World Cup final (in which Brazil was playing but lost) with some Kaiabi at Diauarum, on a small television powered by a solar panel.) The Kaiabi population has relatively soared, to 1,200 people, partly as a result of inward migrations but mostly from a high birth rate.

* * *

The once-warlike Metuktire Kayapó, who were contacted in 1953 and 1954, had a turbulent history but were ultimately even more successful than the

196

Kaiabi. The few Metuktire who had chosen to remain on the Xingu above the Von Martius rapids suddenly found in 1971 that their lands were outside the park. They were victims of the government decision to have the BR-080 road slice across the Xingu Park and to remove land north of the new crossing. These were the forests inhabited by the Metuktire, and they contained that tribe's most sacred place, Capoto. The Villas Boas and others had tried desperately to reverse the decision about the road; but when their efforts failed they asked all Metuktire to move south in order to remain inside the park. Most refused, unable to grasp the magnitude of the threat to their forested homelands. The only group to accept the invitation was that led by Rauni, once the naughty but engaging teenager whom Adrian Cowell had known in the 1950s, but now matured into a forceful chief. His people built a village called Porori (later renamed Kretire after the dead chief) 20 kilometres (12 miles) south of the road and therefore within the Xingu Park.

Rauni's half-brothers, Chiefs Krumare and Kremoro, came with him, but spent only a short time in the new village. They soon took their people back to the Jarina river to be near sacred Capoto, in their beloved—but now unprotected—forests outside the park's new northern limit. As their nephew Megaron passionately argued, 'Capoto is our true village and our true land. It is white men who come to our land. It is white men who invade our land. We have been living in that land for a long time. ... The whites have taken almost all the land from the Indians; do they now want to take what is left to us?' Repeated requests were made to Funai for the Metuktire to recover their sacred Capoto region and have it demarcated. But Funai and the Villas Boas were powerless to countermand the decree by President Médici.

So the road was built, and with it came settlers and an aggressive ranch called Agropexim that started to deforest the amputated area. Workers on the road and ranch introduced alien diseases. As Megaron later complained, 'from 1971 to 1975 the Park officials did not help my people. In 1975 about 74 people caught measles from outside contact on the road and brought it in to Jarina. Measles killed many people.' It attacked Megaron's father Kopre's village as well as his uncle Rauni's village, Kretire. 'Many Indians caught measles, including I myself. I don't know why I didn't die.' Then when the road opened to traffic it also brought influenza and malaria.

All the Metuktire, within and outside the park, were outraged by the BR-080. Being warlike Kayapó with strong leaders, they took direct action. When in 1974 the Indians felt menaced by a new hamlet called Piaraçu near the river crossing, four residents of this roadside halt were killed, and during the next four years men from Kretire village expelled its last settlers. In 1976 ninety-one warriors from six villages (including some non-Kayapó) united to show their anger. They sank the pontoon raft that ferried traffic across the Xingu, and ransacked some trucks and cars on the new road. Two labourers from the Agropexim ranch were killed later that year. But the Metuktire could do nothing about São José do Xingu, a shanty town 40 kilometres (25 miles) east of the crossing that became known locally as 'Bang-Bang' because of its many brothels.

The Indians' protests and belligerence gradually won them concessions. In May 1976 a Funai edict created a reserve called Jarina for one group of Metuktire living north of the road. This Jarina reserve was a 40-kilometre (25-mile)-wide swathe of forest, running for 80 kilometres (50 miles) north from the road towards the Von Martius rapids—but only on the west side or left bank of the Xingu. It gave protection to some two hundred Indians, most of them in the village under Chiefs Krumare and Kremoro near the mouth of the Jarina.

The eastern or right bank of the Xingu north of the road was still unprotected, and it was here that tensions again degenerated into open conflict. A ranch called São Luiz was advancing towards the river, with its men felling forest ever closer to the Xingu. In June 1980 Rauni warned the ranch owner to desist and leave; but in August his woodsmen were back, clearing land only 5 kilometres (3 miles) from the river. When Rauni was informed, he enlisted Suiá, Kaiabi, and Juruna allies to help his Metuktire expel the invaders. Megaron said that his uncle Rauni told his men 'to hit the farm workers so that they would not return. But the warriors hit the workers too hard.' That was an understatement. Bedjai, a Metuktire whose father had been killed by whites, wielded his club in a frenzy of revenge. 'Because of this, and because the workers were very badly hurt, the warriors decided to kill the wounded workers, and that's how they died.' As reported by a labourer who escaped, Indians suddenly appeared in their clearing and ordered them to leave; five did so; the warriors told the remaining twelve 'to strip and kneel, then bludgeoned ten of them to death. Another was killed by an arrow when he tried to escape. Only one of the labourers managed to get away, running through the forest until he reached a fazenda twelve hours later.' This killing of eleven unarmed farm workers was a cruel mistake, a reversion to the Kayapó's war-like past when they thought nothing of taking lives. There was understandable anger in the press, but no punishment of the Indians because of their legal immunity. The farmer produced a certificate signed by General Bandeira de Mello as president of Funai, claiming that he had owned the 2420-hectare (6,000-acre) property since 1968 (three years before the road was built). But

Rauni was unimpressed and unrepentant, warning that 'warriors will kill all whites who continue to enter our lands'.

Yet, despite the massacre and warning, twenty colonist farmers did move into the 'vacant' area and invested heavily in it, attracted by 'negative certificates' that declared the forests to be empty of Indians. Orlando denounced Funai's irresponsible action in issuing these certificates, because he recalled that when he himself first entered the area twenty years previously there had been uncontacted Indians on *both* banks. 'All that stretch of land [north of] the BR-080 was always considered as an area of perambulation for Indians moving in search of better hunting grounds.' The *fazendeiros* were therefore illegal invaders, and the Indians had every right to defend their lands. Now, in 1980, the Indians demanded a 40-kilometre (25-mile)-wide reserve on the right bank of the Xingu opposite their Jarina reserve on the left bank.

The months and years dragged by. There were further meetings with Funai officials in the Xingu, and petitions; but no protection of the east bank of the Xingu north of the road. In February 1984 Rauni went to Brasilia to demand action from a new president of Funai. This official promised to address a meeting of all the interested parties at Kretire village; but he failed to attend. Chief Megaron met farmers at São José do Xingu to assure them that the Indians' quarrel was with Funai, not them. Both sides admitted that they were frightened of one another. A typical settler's attitude was that 'Indians and peccary are the same thing. If either comes onto my land, I don't think twice—I kill them.' Whenever Indians left the Xingu Park, by road or air, they witnessed the devastation right up to its edge:

> A desert of ashes and charcoal tree trunks ... where nothing moves except an occasional herd of cattle in search of scattered tufts of grass. ... 'If we lose our land,' said Rauni, 'the whites will destroy the whole forest. Where will we go to hunt tapir, coati [ant-bears] or jaguar? What will we eat? There will be no game left.'

Frustrated, the Indians decided to act again, but this time in a bloodless manner that would achieve the greatest publicity. So in March 1984 they embarked on what became known as 'the War of the Xingu'. They started by seizing a big new metal raft that ferried traffic across the Xingu river. The Metuktire then demanded the dismissal of the president of Funai, as well as the recovery of their disputed land. Later that month they raised the stakes by kidnapping the director of the Xingu Park, Cláudio Romero, when he went to Kretire village to negotiate. Romero and other white hostages were treated well, fed large quantities of fish and monkeys, and entered into the life of the village by fishing and bathing with the Indians. The ferry raft was occupied for weeks, with trucks paralysed along the BR-080, in deep mud since this was the end of the rainy season. Local police were unsure what to do about the Indians. Newspapers carried dramatic pictures of a hundred muscular Kayapó warriors on the raft, wearing black warpaint and boxer shorts and brandishing their clubs and bows, as well as of their tough women wielding machetes 'as proof that they were also ready to fight'. Other Xingu tribes lent their support. A Kaiabi, Ipó, recalled that 'our war lasted for almost two months. It was hard, but it was great to see all the Xingu tribes fighting together, all united. Everyone helped: the Suiá, the Kaiabi, the [Mebengokre and Metuktire], the [Ikpeng] and the [Panará].'

The Indians gradually won their public-relations 'war'. The press was generally sympathetic, and non-government and missionary organizations clamoured for Funai and the government to give the Metuktire what they wanted. On 14 April two senior Funai officials and the passionately pro-Indian *sertanista* Sydney Possuelo went to parley at the guard post where the new road entered the park. But they too were seized, threatened, and held as hostages.

The Metuktire chiefs Rauni, Kremoro, and Krumare together with the Xavante congressman Mário Juruna now negotiated directly with the minister of the interior, Mário Andreazza—Funai's parent politician and one of the most powerful men in Brazil. They got swift action, for on 16 April 1984 Funai interdicted a strip on the *right* bank of the Xingu. This was only 15 kilometres (9 miles) wide, because it was claimed that a 25-kilometre (15.6-mile) reserve would be too expensive since twenty incumbent ranchers would have to be compensated. The Indians threatened to send armed warriors to demarcate the reserve as they defined it; the settlers said that they had mined the land with explosives. Whenever Rauni and the other chiefs met the minister they wore headdresses, lip-discs, and *genipapo* warpaint—for maximum publicity impact. Finally, however, advised by the pragmatic Megaron, they settled for the narrower 15-kilometre band. They did gain the sacking of the president of Funai. They then released their hostages, after three weeks' captivity, and they freed the ferry on condition that Indians would in future control the Xingu crossing. Although the released hostages were bearded, tired, and ill, they magnanimously applauded the Indians for being so steadfast, for remaining united, and for their effective campaign. On 3 May 1984 the minister signed an agreement giving the Metuktire the new 15-kilometre strip on the east bank, as well as the Capoto sacred area, north of the Jarina reserve and west of the Von Martius rapids. In a televised gesture during the signing ceremony, Rauni playfully pulled the ear of the embarrassed but smiling Minister Andreazza, to show that he needed to show better judgement in future.

A few days later, a new president of Funai appointed Rauni's thirty-four-year-old nephew Megaron as director of the Xingu Indigenous Park. He had been a crucial negotiator in ending the 'War of the Xingu' and, more importantly, he was the choice of all the park's indigenous leaders—even though his Metuktire people now technically lived beyond its northern limit. This appointment was a triple vindication of the policies of the Villas Boas. No Indian had previously held such an important position in Funai, and this promotion was because the brothers had so effectively trained indigenous leaders to manage their communities. Megaron himself was Orlando's protégé: a child when his Metuktire people were first contacted, he had gone aged fourteen to help at Posto Leonardo, where he learned Portuguese, management skills, and white men's ways—as Rauni had done before him. Third, it was remarkable that the Xinguano chiefs chose a fierce Metuktire—their bitter enemies before the Villas Boas achieved inter-tribal peace. The incumbent director Cláudio Romero was happy to hand over the running of the park to Megaron, and declared that 'the important thing is to celebrate their conquest', while Sydney Possuelo rejoiced that 'for the first time the Indians have won without having to kill'. A newspaper headline called this appointment 'the greatest victory achieved by the Indians'.

In October 1984 work started on the demarcation of the reserve areas. The new director, Megaron, recalled that his Metuktire people had struggled for these lands for thirteen years, ever since the BR-080 had truncated the park. 'We nearly lost the Capoto, our best land, our sacred land. These things need not have happened, had the whites from the outset respected and demarcated our lands. From now on we want the fazendeiros to honour our boundaries and we will respect their farms.'

* * *

We should pause here to consider the amazing transformation in Rauni's Kayapó people during the previous three decades. When the Villas Boas contacted the Metuktire in 1953, they were lean, tough, and ruthless warriors, and their society was primitive compared to that of the elegant and conservative Xinguanos upriver. But the Metuktire and related Mekragnoti were vibrant, energetic, likeable, and, above all, quick and even eager to learn. These forest-dwelling Kayapó were wilder than larger northern groups of their nation, seven tribes who live on great plains of forest and *campo cer-*

rado between the middle Xingu and Araguaia rivers, and had been in contact with Brazilian society for over a century.

In 1980 the lives of these northern Kayapó changed dramatically when gold was discovered on their lands. Thousands of wildcat *garimpeiro* miners poured in to pan feverishly for the precious metal. But after months of defiance and occasional aggression, stunts (such as hijacking a plane and vehicles), publicity, and hard bargaining, these Kayapó negotiated a hefty 5 per cent royalty on exported gold dust and became rich. But they spent their windfall wealth sensibly, buying supplies collectively for all the tribe.

Rauni was just one of several charismatic Kayapó chiefs. More than any other indigenous people, the Kayapó developed a flair for public relations and political activism. They rapidly learned that television cameras would home in on Indians in headdresses waggling their lip-discs, particularly if they were doing something outrageous like invading the president of Funai's office and expelling him from it. When Brazil was drafting its new constitution in 1987–8, the Kayapó exceeded all other indigenous peoples in their attempts to influence legislators. They maintained a lobbying bureau in Brasilia, staged well-publicized demonstrations, and even chartered a plane to bring congressmen to see how beautiful their village was. All this helped to achieve the pro-indigenous clauses in the 1988 constitution.

At the end of that year the Kayapó and other sympathizers organized another great protest. This was to prevent a gigantic hydroelectric dam at the Xingu's other major rapids, Belo Monte, close to that river's junction with the main Amazon and 1,150 kilometres (720 miles) downstream of the Von Martius rapids. The protest culminated in February 1989 in a huge demonstration at Altamira, the town on the Transamazonica Highway nearest to the proposed dam. Sixteen Kayapó chiefs attended this colourful gathering, including Rauni and Kremoro from the upper-Xingu Metuktire, in a display of harmony that would have been impossible before the Villas Boas and others persuaded tribes to stop feuding. There were also representatives of other indigenous peoples, a media frenzy of 121 reporters, television coverage from all over the world, ecologists, politicians, human-rights activists, and celebrities. When the electricity company tried in vain to 'sell' the dam to the Indians, these would have none of it. TV cameras showed a feisty Kayapó woman swinging a machete and tapping a hapless engineer on the face. With devastating logic, she told him: 'You are a liar. We don't need electricity. Electricity won't give us food. We need the rivers to flow freely—our future depends on them. We need our forests to hunt and gather in. We do not want your dam.' She described the miserable lives of people living in the dirt, ugliness, and poverty of Altamira. 'Is this what you are offering us? Is this progress? Don't talk to us about relieving our "poverty." We are not poor. We are the richest people in Brazil. We are not wretched. We are Indians.' The protest was a total success. All foreign funding was denied and the dam was cancelled—at least for then.

In December 1987 the British pop star Sting gave a concert in Rio de Janeiro's gigantic Maracanã football stadium, to a rapturous audience as numerous as the entire indigenous population of Brazilian Amazonia. Sting and his future wife Trudie Styler were then rewarded by being taken to see the Xingu. For three hours their plane flew over 'a land mutilated by progress', a desolation of dust and ashes, the ghosts of burned trees, scorched earth, and the raw wounds of mines and landing strips. Suddenly this wasteland ended in the wall of trees of the Xingu Indigenous Park. Like all other visitors, Sting and Trudie were enchanted by the virgin beauty of the Xingu's tropical rainforests and the romance of its Indians. They particularly liked the forceful and charming Chief Rauni, now a tall, dignified man of about fifty 'with shoulder-length hair, ceremonial beads, a lip-disc and Levi's'. So, in October 1988, at another huge concert in São Paulo, Sting defied a law that prohibited foreigners from interfering in Brazilian affairs by making an impassioned appeal for the rights of indigenous peoples.

Sting now determined to help the Indians by doing more than just singing for their environmentally fashionable cause. So, back in Britain he founded a charity called the Rainforest Foundation, with Chief Rauni as the honorary president and Dr Roberto Baruzzi as the chairman of its Brazilian branch.

Back in Brazil in 1989, Sting took Rauni to meet President José Sarney, who confirmed to them a promise to create and demarcate a reserve called Menkragnoti. This was a massive victory. It embraced a gigantic stretch of forests from the middle Xingu westwards beyond the Curuá and Iriri rivers almost as far as the new BR-163 road (the one that shattered the Panará). The area of this new Menkragnoti reserve would be 49,143 square kilometres (19,000 square miles), which was almost twice the size of the Xingu Park. Crucially, it joined the Metuktires' newly won Jarina and Capoto reserves to the extensive territories of other Kayapó peoples to the north. It was thus the missing link to create an unbroken 'Kayapó corridor', a great north–south swathe of protected land—an area larger than England—running northwards from the Xinguanos' villages, down much of the Xingu river basin, in the geographical heart of Brazil. This would give the various tribes of the Kayapó nation territories covering 133,240 square kilometres (51,450 square miles). It also created a haven for wildlife and a natural barrier to forest destruction, in a critical zone surrounded by cattle ranches, colonization projects, mining camps, and sawmills.

Sting knew that his pop-idol celebrity gave him access anywhere, and he recognized Rauni's charisma. So in 1989 Sting and Rauni made a highly successful fund-raising journey, visiting sixteen countries in five continents. The highlights were a televised meeting with President François Mitterrand of France and an audience with Pope John Paul II. The resulting picture of a Brazilian Indian standing between the pope and a pop star gave Brazilians a glamorous new image of their indigenous people, in sharp contrast to a stereotype of poverty-stricken tribals at the margin of frontier society.

There were many hurdles before the 'missing link' Menkragnoti reserve became reality. It took three years of legal action to register all this land. An even greater problem was the demarcation and marking of hundreds of kilometres of new boundaries in extremely tough terrain. This task was supposed to do be done by Funai, but it was years behind in demarcating other indigenous lands, and its finances were always precarious. So Sting's charity donated $1.3 million, from his and Rauni's promotional tour and his own concerts, to demarcate the Menkragnoti Indigenous Territory. This was an elaborate operation, involving scores of workmen, a plane, two helicopters, boats and trucks, sensitive surveying equipment, global positioning systems, and satellite imagery. It took three teams three months in late 1992 to cut a perimeter swathe and fix boundary markers.

Rauni and his nephew Megaron helped their Kayapó peoples in other ways, with an institute in his name to preserve tribal culture and arts, market vegetable oils, and even launch a television channel. On another fund-raising tour with Sting, Rauni appeared on French television shaking hands with President Jacques Chirac, in a fine headdress of white egret feathers and flapping his trademark lip-disc. On another tour in 2001 Rauni appealed for funds to help expel illegal loggers. He declared: 'We do not have the resources to protect this immense forest *that we are guarding for all of you,*' thus becoming the first environmental campaigner to remind the world that Brazil's indigenous peoples were doing a great service by protecting a substantial proportion of Earth's surviving tropical rainforests. Megaron secured the building of two schools in the Capoto–Jarina Indigenous Territory, explaining that 'We prefer to remain isolated and to live as we have always lived. But with the interference of white men, we need the help' of education in order to stand up to them.

In 2003 the government announced a plan to revive the Belo Monte hydroelectric dam on the lower Xingu—the 'pharaonic' project that had been crushed by the Altamira meeting fourteen years previously. The struggle against it raged for the next twelve years, and Rauni was constantly at the head of indigenous protests. Scientists, environmentalists, anthropologists, international organizations, many engineers, lawyers, and most of the media opposed this and other hydroelectric dams as an environmental catastrophe. The problems with them were that the Amazon basin is so flat that the great Xingu river has a relatively short drop at its rapids; the reservoir behind it would spread to drown a vast area of forest and the lands of many indigenous peoples and other riverbank dwellers; many fish species would be destroyed because the dam would stop their migration far up rivers in their spawning cycle; and in the heart of the Amazon there might be too few buyers for the resulting electricity, which cannot be stored. However, the years of protest were in vain. President Dilma Rousseff was stubbornly determined to get the dam built. Earthmovers churned hundreds of square kilometres of forest near Altamira, and the dam finally started limited operations in 2016.

* * *

The Suiá were another people who formed part of the Villas Boas legacy. As we saw, this warlike tribe was first seen by von den Steinen in 1884, but then became hostile to the outside world for seventy-five years, before being re-contacted by the Villas Boas in 1959. By that time they were severely depleted in numbers and almost starving; but they gradually recovered their identity and pride. Since most of their elders had died, younger Suiá abandoned some traditional customs of Je-speaking peoples, such as wearing lip-discs. They adopted a few upper-Xingu practices, imitating their round haircuts, headdresses, leg-binding, and feather ear-tufts. Suiá thatched communal huts that came to resemble Xinguano *malocas*, albeit smaller and with over twenty of them arranged in their traditional broad cartwheel circle. Most ceremonies, sports, spiritual beliefs, and decorations remained as in their past. Being Je speakers they continued to eat every type of game meat as well as fish; and from the Juruna people downriver they adopted mildly alcoholic *caxiri* made from fermented manioc and maize. So they evolved an interesting new hybrid identity.

In the mid-1990s the Suiá formally changed their tribal name to Kisêdje. Many were by now living far up the Suiá-Missu on a headwater river that they call Wawi. The problem was that this Wawi river lay just outside the eastern boundary of the Xingu Park. This caused friction with encroaching farmers, who claimed this land and wanted to clear and burn it for crops or pasture.

With Funai's help, the Kisêdje won. In 1998 the new 1,500-square-kilometre (580-square-mile) Wawi Indigenous Territory was passed into law and, in effect, enlarged the eastern side of the Xingu Park. Now, with a healthy birth rate, the Kisêdje population is approaching four hundred. They have a school with textbooks and teachers in their own language and idiom, an excellent medical dispensary, and even a film unit to record their traditional customs.

* * *

Another people whose survival may be considered as a legacy of the Villas Boas are the Tapayuna. As we saw, the once-powerful Tapayuna had almost been extinguished, by aggressive land-grabbers who poisoned them, followed by a lethal influenza epidemic caught from a journalist on a hideously mis-managed contact. In 1970 forty survivors were rescued by being airlifted into the Xingu, where they were housed alongside their distant Suiá relatives in a compound near Diauarum. Disease further reduced this people to a mere thirty-one individuals; but these never forgot their tragic past. By 1980 they had recovered sufficiently to create their own village. They then experienced a further setback, from the familiar curse of imagined sorcery. In the middle of that decade, a Suiá killed a Tapayuna whom he suspected of evil magic. Fearing further killings, some Tapayuna fled down the Xingu to join other Je speakers, the Metuktire, while the rest paddled up the Suiá-Missu river to join the Suiá (now Kisêdje) living in their Wawi territory. There are now some sixty of this sad tribe in the two locations.

* * *

The Panará were the final people who form part of the Villas Boas' legacy, in both their contact, finally achieved in January 1973, and their transfer into the Xingu two years later. As we saw in Chapter 12, they suffered terrible depopu-lation and disruption immediately after contact, so that their few survivors had in 1975 been airlifted into the sanctuary of the Xingu. They were unhappy in their new environment, where the forests were weaker and the rivers wider than those of their homelands on the Peixoto de Azevedo. The Panará survi-vors were therefore moved twice during the year after their arrival, before settling in a small village near Diauarum. They started learning to handle boats and to fish. But, as one doctor noted, these 'refugee guests were overcome by a heavy feeling of defeat, so that many became "animated ghosts" who medi-tated for hours on end'. In 1983 they moved down the Xingu to another location more like their former homeland; but there were further deaths, and the Panará feared that it harboured malign spirits. So in 1989 they moved yet again, far up the Manitsauá river to a location at the western edge of the Xingu Park, where they started to create good plantation clearings.

All was still not well with the Panará. In 1991 their tough young chief Akè—a stocky, shortish man, physically unlike his lean compatriots— lamented: 'I do not like being here in the Xingu. It is wretched, being in a place you don't like. ... On the Peixoto [de Azevedo river] we had good land, we had fruit trees, much game to hunt—there was plenty. I have great nostalgia to be back in such a rich place ... the Peixoto, my land, where I was born.' He went on to list the forest fruits and nuts, game animals and birds, and the honey that abounded there.

Activist friends therefore offered to take Chief Akè back to see his lost homeland. In November 1991 his guides—from the Brazilian NGO the Nucleus for Indigenous Rights (NDI) and the American anthropologist Stephan Schwartzman—escorted the chief by bus along the BR-080 (that cut across the Xingu Park) to the new BR-163 highway and then on foot to the Peixoto de Azevedo river. Akè was devastated to see the effects of sixteen years of uncontrolled deforestation, aggressive ranching, and profligate mineral prospecting. The Panarás' former paradise was now desolate, reduced to barren mud, the forests gone, and the rivers gouged and polluted. Six of the original eight Panará villages were obliterated, by cattle ranches or a lunar landscape of mine workings and effluent. A British film-maker, Brian Moser, was there, and he showed the furious chief brandishing his club at miners who had destroyed his boyhood home.

Akè, Schwartzman, and other Panará returned to the BR-163 the following June, chartered an air taxi to fly over some forests that were still intact, and spotted the location for another village. This was to the north, near Cachimbo and the upper Iriri—where the Panará hunting party had ambushed Richard Mason thirty years earlier. There were two attempts to reach the village, overland through 70 kilometres of dense forest, with a tough Funai operative, Lourenço de Mello. Returning again in 1993, they had an armed confrontation with land prospectors who had already opened a clandestine airstrip and were surveying the area in order to claim it. The indigenous sympathizers acted fast, mapping and drawing up a legal claim for a large Panará reserve. They received enthusiastic support from the new president of Funai, who was none other than Sydney Possuelo, the last great *sertanista* and former assistant of Claudio Villas Boas. Funai immediately interdicted the area—a temporary block, prior to full legal registration. It finally became law in

1996, as the 4,950-square-kilometre (1,900-square-mile) Panará Indigenous Territory, with its eastern forests abutting the Menkragnoti territory achieved by Sting and Rauni.

Back in the Xingu there was a three-day meeting in November 1994 to discuss whether the Panará really wanted to leave the sanctuary of the Xingu for the Iriri. This was attended by Mairawé Kaiabi (administrator of Diauarum), and the tribe's erstwhile Metuktire enemies Megaron (as director of the Xingu Park) and his uncle Rauni. Some younger Panará wanted to remain in the Xingu where they had grown up, but the majority decided to move. Their unhappy diaspora in the Xingu had lasted for twenty years.

Chief Akè's supporters hired a plane to take him and some of his people to the airstrip of Kubengokre village on the middle Iriri (the home of the Mekragnoti Kayapó, whose men had gone to shoot up a Panará village eighteen years previously), then by boat up the Iriri, to start to clear land for a new village. The Panará called this place Nansepotiti ('Iriri river'), and gradually moved there during 1995 and 1996. The final contingent had to take nine flights in a light plane small enough to land on a rough strip that Akè and his people had cleared beside their new village. Panará morale soared with this return to luxuriant forests, in a territory where they were masters rather than refugee guests, and in a village of their traditional huts, with their unique geometric plantations in nearby clearings. Nansepotiti is in an idyllic location, on a bluff above a curve of the Iriri. The river's waters are dappled dark green from the reflection of tropical rainforest towering above it. Everyone bathes regularly, and children play all day long in the shallow river.

Shortly after their departure from the Xingu, pro-Indian lawyers launched an audacious claim for compensation to the surviving Panará because of their tragically mismanaged contact. In a landmark judgment—unique in Brazilian history—Judge Novély Vilanova in October 1997 found in their favour. He accepted that government agents had been well intentioned in contacting the tribe and later moving it into the Xingu. But he felt that too little had been done to protect them. So he ordered compensation paid to the family of every Panará who died in the terrible two years between 1973 and 1975, plus substantial 'moral damages' to the tribe as a whole. This all amounted to well over a million dollars. Then, in 2004 President Lula awarded the prestigious Order of Cultural Merit to the Panará people for their gallant struggle to recover from near-extinction.

As the years went by, the Panará chose to adopt many outside practices. Both sexes are now clothed: the women in bright dresses that they make on pedal sewing machines, the men in shorts and T-shirts often sporting brash advertising logos. Men have modern haircuts rather than traditional pudding-bowl crowns; but women retain a fringe in front and luxuriant tresses behind. Most men and many women speak basic Portuguese. Hunters now use guns as well as bows, and they fish with boats, outboards, lines, and hooks. Boys kick balls around a football field in the dusty heart of the village. Electricity, from solar panels and a car battery, powers a public-address system playing Brazilian music or—their favourite—a recording of themselves singing. It also runs a short-wave radio on which the chiefs chat daily to their former enemies, the Mekragnoti, downriver. Food is plentiful, including their favourite, a species of giant peanut. Traditional customs and celebrations have been revived, and flourish alongside the novelties. This difficult but largely successful transition has been described, sympathetically and perceptively, by the Oxford anthropologist Elizabeth Ewart. She spent two years embedded in the corner of a Panará hut, and is one of the handful of outsiders who can speak their version of Je—as once spoken by the southern Kayapó, of whom they are the only survivors.

There were about a hundred Panará when they moved back to the Iriri in the mid-1990s. Their population then grew fast, because of improved morale from having their own land and optimism for the future. Thus, the village is now full of children and mothers with babies. There were 202 Panará by 2000, and 480 in 2010. This healthy birth rate was greatly helped by Baruzzi's São Paulo doctors, who built a dispensary and continued to fly in to give regular medical and natal treatment, even after the tribe moved from the Xingu. Hygiene also improved, with a well and latrines; and there is instruction in a schoolhouse. Nansepotiti village was originally just a row of thatched huts overlooking the Iriri. But to accommodate their explosive growth, the Panará cleverly turned their doors so that these became one side of a far larger circle, inland from the riverbank. An enlarged airstrip now runs between the tribe's traditional village and the small cluster of administrative buildings.

I visited the Panará soon after they started to build Nansepotiti. To my surprise, they remembered every detail of killing Richard Mason almost forty years earlier. This was because it had been their first glimpse of the outside world, with incomprehensible things like a metal box full of sugar that Richard was carrying, his clothing, his gun, and even his beard. I spoke to Chief Teseya, a gentle giant of a man roughly my age, lying in his hammock, with Elizabeth Ewart translating. He confirmed what we had suspected: that a long-range foraging and hunting party (that had not included him) had come across our trail—a simple path to us, but like a highway to them—and had ambushed the first person to walk along it. He told me that the swish of

Richard's approaching jeans had been a novel sound for hunters who knew every noise in their forests. I asked whether they recalled a pile of machetes I left when we removed the body (to show that we had been friendly). An old woman who was listening interrupted excitedly. She said that those machetes had made a huge impact, so that there was competition between the elders and the younger men about who should have them. She was the widow of the last member of the hunting party, who had just died, and said that her husband had mentioned 'something shiny'—and I remembered that Richard's cigarette lighter had been lying near his body, dented from being whacked by a club. Teseya later put his arm around my shoulders and said that it had all happened long ago, when the Panará were at war with all other peoples, and when they used the same word for 'stranger' and for 'enemy'. 'At that time we did not know that there were good white men and bad white men.' He then named the good white men who had recently helped them recover some of their forests. 'You are a good white man: you can come back and visit us whenever you want.'

This meeting with the Panará made me ponder how extremely unlucky Richard Mason had been. It was a tragic fluke that their long-range hunting party had come across our trail, so far from their nearest village, in that infinite vastness of unexplored forests. I now know that the Panará were the most bellicose tribe in all Brazil, feared by all nearby peoples, and the only one that would have killed from ambush without any contact. Richard was unlucky to be the first of our eleven-man expedition to walk into the ambush. The timing was also unfortunate. We had by then spent four months carrying up all the supplies we needed and making canoes for the first descent of the Iiriri, so that a few days later we would have gone.

* * *

In 1998 all Brazil mourned the death of Claudio, aged eighty-two, and in 2002 that of Orlando, aged eighty-eight. They left an extraordinary sixfold legacy. First, everyone identified them with the admirable peoples of the upper Xingu, and knew that they had been the first laymen to live for decades among these Indians and devote their lives to helping them. Second, their vision of that beautiful region had led to the creation of the Xingu Indigenous Park, the first huge protected area for both indigenous people and the environment. This bold experiment was later replicated throughout Brazil and other South American nations, thus leading to the conservation of a significant proportion of the world's tropical rainforests and their teeming ecosystems. Third, through lifetimes of lecturing, writing, and media publicity, the Villas Boas brothers followed Rondon's humanist revolution in changing attitudes to indigenous peoples. The Indians and their cultures became a source of pride for Brazilians rather than being seen as an impediment to progress. As the anthropologist George Zarur wrote: 'The ideas that led to the creation of the Xingu Park transformed relations between Indians and whites in Brazil' and even in the rest of the world. This led directly to the favourable clauses in the 1988 constitution. Fourth, by their tough explorations, brave contacts, and (sometimes controversial) rescues, the brothers protected and saved a score of peoples. They also brought seemingly impossible inter-tribal peace to the region—the so-called Pax Xinguana. Fifth, they did their best to shield the Xingu from being engulfed by the settlement frontier with its violent behaviour, religions, aggressive economy, and environmental degradation and pollution.

Lastly, they devised a new approach to relations between indigenous people and whites, based on non-interference in tribal society, respect and friendship with chiefs and shamans, preparing young people for management roles in a non-Indian context but without diminishing their pride in their heritage, the judicious and *gradual* introduction of manufactured goods and alien ideas, and care for health and sustenance. This bought time for Indians to confront the momentous change from tranquil tribal life to the turbulent modern world. Proof of this is the physical and moral survival and the relative prosperity of the Xingu peoples. All of them want to continue their customary communal lives, within modern Brazil. Influential chiefs were grateful for all that the Villas Boas had done. The Kuikuro Afukaká declared that 'had Orlando not come to the Xingu it would not be as good as it is today. He helped to secure our traditions, and to demarcate the land to prevent the arrival of whites, farmers.'

All these successes became critically important when in 2019 Jair Bolsonaro became president of Brazil. He had declared a dislike of indigenous peoples and their agency Funai, and threatened to dismantle their protected territories in order to release the forests and the natural resources on these for commercial exploitation. He even revived the absurd notion that Indians *wanted* to be released from communal societies so that they could prosper as ordinary citizens—despite every tribe vehemently denying this. Thanks to the Villas Boas and many other well-wishers in Brazil and abroad, and to the 1988 constitution, the Indians and their leaders are girded for a fierce struggle to combat these threats. But it will not be easy.

Claudio and Orlando each had his praises sung in eloquent obituaries. But the tributes that the brothers would have appreciated most were *kuarup*

211

memorial ceremonies given in their honour by the Xingu Indians. I was the only non-Brazilian to attend both of these: for Claudio in the Kamaiurá village in 1998, and for Orlando in that of the Yawalapiti in 2003. As explained in Chapter 2, every detail of a two-day *kuarup* is governed by norms as rigid as those for a Christian funeral. Before Claudio's *kuarup*, I remember Orlando saying that it was so long since he had last been in the Xingu that people there would have forgotten him. But he was, of course, completely wrong. Every man and woman of every age welcomed him as a returning father figure. Indians are not normally emotional, but so many embraced Orlando that he was covered in red *urucum* body paint, and there was weeping in sympathy for the death of his beloved brother Claudio. He stood among a throng of Indians and made a passionate speech, about the need for them to maintain their societies and customs, and to defend these against outside pressures.

On the first morning of the *kuarup*, the men and woman of each visiting people decorated one another in brilliant body paint and donned dazzling headdresses and other featherwork. During that afternoon, while the shamans were carefully decorating the *kuarup* post, Orlando, Marina, and their sons Orlando and Noel—the family of the dead 'chief' Claudio—stood in the middle of the village plaza while each of the visiting tribes performed dances, parades, and mock charges around them. This was a glorious spectacle, but I worried about the four grieving relatives standing for several hours in strong sunshine without hats. That night a small fire was lit below the *kuarup* post, and relays of two or three shamans chanted behind it, softly but with occasional rhythm from their gourd *maraca* rattles or tapping the ground with canes. I sat for hours, in the circle of great thatched *malocas* lit by a full moon and a heavenly canopy of stars, silently contemplating Claudio's personality and great achievements. Orlando's *kuarup* five years later was in the rather larger Yawalapiti village with a broad central plaza. There were more visitors at this ceremony, but each was personally invited by the Villas Boas family or the Xinguanos, so that there were relatively few—considering that Orlando was one of the most famous people in Brazil. I flew in, in an air taxi with Professor Roberto Baruzzi, and witnessed the intense welcome he received from all the Indians whom he had tended for so many years. This time, the widow Marina and their sons sat in a little stand with an awning, to receive the salutary parades by visiting peoples. A more emotional time came that evening, when anyone could sit on benches around the *kuarup* post, gazing at it and thinking about the man it represented. Baruzzi sat for hours, in silent grief, remembering almost forty years of adventures and joyful times with his dear, ebullient friend. On the second morning there were traditional *huka-huka* wrestling matches, with pairs of fighters surrounded by a throng of warriors glistening in body paint. The final, very moving, moment at each ceremony came in the middle of the second day, when the ornate *kuarup* pole was carried down to the river and formally launched into it. Everyone watched the pole float downstream, carrying the spirit of the dead man. It disappeared down the Tuatuari, into the Culuene, Curisevo, and possibly for hundreds of kilometres down the mighty Xingu and even mightier Amazon, then out into the Atlantic Ocean. The brothers were not strongly religious, but they understood indigenous mythology well, and they would have known how deeply all the peoples of the Xingu mourned and remembered their dead. They themselves had earned a unique place in that collective memory.

The fiftieth anniversary of the creation of the Xingu Indigenous Park was in 2011. All its peoples celebrated this half-century with a three-day Festival of the Xingu Cultures. This was a magnificent gathering, with dances, sporting contests, parades, and ceremonies in the usual blaze of colour from body paint and feather ornaments. Rauni, Megaron, Aritana, Mairawé Kaiabi, Takuman Kamaiura, and other chiefs made speeches to celebrate their peoples' survival and success, and to inspire young Indians to maintain their way of life. Chief Kuiussi Suiá reminded everyone: 'We are now commemorating the great conquest that was left for us by the Villas Boas brothers. It was they who ensured our lives here.' All the participants endorsed a 'Final Statement', addressed to the heads of Funai and the relevant ministries. This praised the park's founders,

> who had enabled the indigenous peoples of the Xingu to preserve forever their rivers, forests, songs, and their wisdom in living harmoniously. … Orlando, Claudio and Leonardo Villas Boas appreciated our cultural richness, and they governed our peoples in order to further this. They would certainly have been heartbroken to see the present-day building of hydroelectric dams, clandestine tourism, deforestation, and the pollution and silting up of rivers. Now we no longer have the Villas Boas brothers to advise us and help us to influence the governing elite. We must therefore strengthen our own leaders.

This is what indigenous people are doing, to face the future.

Eight years later in 2019, Brazil's indigenous peoples faced a terrible unforeseen challenge. The nation, exasperated by massive corruption in its main political parties, elected a populist, evangelical right-winger, Jair Bolsonaro. The new president was deeply hostile to Indians, whom he regarded as an anachronistic impediment to progress. He and his 'ruralist' lobby in Congress openly coveted the vast indigenous territories and their natural resources of timber, minerals, and potential farmland. Indigenous rights won in the 1988 constitution, the policy of gradual change pioneered by the Villas Boas, and the significant proportion of the world's tropical rainforests of which the Indians were custodians, were all threatened. One of the new president's first actions was to emasculate Funai, by cutting its funding and placing it under the ruralists' Ministry of Agriculture.

President Bolsonaro claimed that Indians really wanted to get rich, and he offered to 'integrate' them into capitalist society by exploiting their lands in agribusiness—in partnership with, or selling out to, local farmers and ranchers. Anthropologists, scientists, jurists, ecclesiastics, and other liberals campaigned against these pernicious policies. So did all Brazil's indigenous spokesmen; the Villas Boas's protégés were at the forefront. The octogenarian Rauni, with his trademark lip-disc and feather headdress, made passionate speeches, as he had on a world stage. Aritana Yawalapiti, a few years younger than Rauni, had been groomed by the brothers to be a chief, and now, half a century later, was the hugely respected paramount chief of all the Xinguanos. Aritana recalled Claudio warning him: 'When the whites come, they will bring papers and coloured charts to convince you [to part with your land]. But on the day you let them, the Xingu is finished.' So the wise old chief, always patient, reasonable and dignified, politely rejected Bolsonaro's fraudulent offer. He said: 'We do not need to plant [the lucrative crop] soya. We have our clearings with manioc and maize, and our fishing and hunting. The government must respect our way of life.' The cornerstone of this was a communal society rather than individual greed and competition. But Aritana appreciated that their successful survival needed computers, lawyers, and social media. He was pleased that his son and heir Tapi was studying for a Master's at the University of Brasilia, as were half a dozen other young Xinguanos. But all would return to their villages with their higher degrees. Orlando and Claudio would have been justifiably proud.

The Villas Boas appreciated that change was inevitable. But they wanted it to be gradual, controlled, and at the speed the indigenous people themselves wanted.

32. Clothing had to be introduced to peoples who had never worn it during previous millennia. These women grapple with needles and thread, while their son looks miserable in his t-shirt.

34. Throughout Brazilian history metal blades were irresistible presents in contacting isolated tribes

33. The Villas Boas were careful not to import utensils that would compete with any individual tribe's speciality. So they admitted aluminium pots, but not large roasting pans that would compete with Waura women's *camelupe* manioc pans.

35. A very Brazilian scene: a Kaiabi father and son watch Brazil play in the 1998 World Cup final, wearing Brazilian national strip, and on a television powered by a solar panel.

36. As well as providing superb medical treatment for all Xingu peoples, the doctors of the São Paulo medical school also organised courses in basic 'barefoot' medicine for men and women from every village. This residential course was at Diauarum.

37 and 38. The Villas Boas recognised leadership potential in a chief's son called Aritana. They helped him revive his Yawalapiti people, whose members were dispersed in other villages. Aritana's Yawalapiti village flourished; he became the highly respected paramount chief of all the Xinguano peoples; had a film made about him; is computer-literate like many of his people; and is a spokesman on a national and world stage.

39. Young men learned how to use cameras, to record their ceremonial and society. Malocas often have large screens, on which the people's favourite viewing is videos of themselves singing at festivals.

40. The Ikpeng flourished after their rescue into the Xingu in 1967. They were recently so proud of their work in surveying their territory that they held a festival to commemorate the maps that resulted from it.

41. The Villas Boas eventually left most of the running of the Xingu to its Indians. These became expert engineers, mechanics and modern farmers.

42. Soon after contact, a Metuktire woman smokes a pipe of wild tobacco while her son is defiant in his body paint and beads.

43. Metuktire women lined up and sang in unison, without instruments, as thanks to the São Paulo doctors who had come to the Jarina river in 1971 to vaccinate their people.

44. A Metuktire Kayapó family faces the future with uncertainty. In the event, they have adapted extremely well, while retaining their once-aggressive vitality.

45. Smiling Metuktire women. When the Villas Boas contacted these people in 1954 they found that their women were remarkably strong towards their menfolk.

46 and 47. Rauni Metuktire had been a young raider before contact; learned western ways as an apprentice in Posto Leonardo; helped the Villas Boas on expeditions in the 1960s (left-hand picture); was a forceful chief in regaining Metuktire forests lost in 1971; was taken on a world tour by the pop star Sting in the late 1990s; and is now (right picture) an articulate campaigner against dams and other threats.

48. When the Kayapó learned agriculture, their women do much of the work in tending forest gardens, always accompanied by their children.

49. Metuktire men wore lip-discs in their lower lips to make themselves look fiercer, and black genipap body paint when prepared for battle.

50. Bebgogoti, chief of the Mekragnoti Kayapó, who led his people away from the Xingu, and then organised the murderous raid on the Panará in 1967.

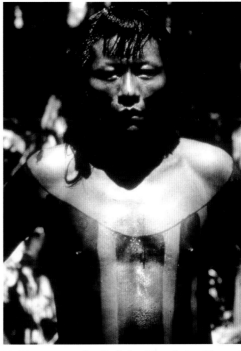

51. Krumare, chief of the Metuktire Kayapó and Rauni's half-brother, who regained his people's sacred Capoto heartland.

52. Orlando and Ikpeng women, at the first brief contact in 1964. He had learned how important it was to have presents for women as well as men.

53 and 54. Orlando at the first encounter with once-feared Ikpeng. He knew that most Indians liked warm friendship and jocularity.

55. The anthropologist Eduardo Galvão and Claudio with the Ikpeng. It was rare for an anthropologist to be invited on a contact expedition: their studies were usually made over a long period, when a tribe was settled.

56 and 57. The Iriri River Expedition of 1961. The author (on the left) helps to launch a dugout canoe made by the expedition's woodsmen; and Richard Mason (in front) and the author carry a rubber boat forward — along the trail where the then-unkown Panará later mounted an ambush that killed Mason.

58. A procession, led by Orlando with Claudio two behind him, bravely enters an abandoned Panará village in 1968, bearing gifts of pans and mirrors, and making noise to show that they were not hostile. Hidden Indians could have fired arrows at the intruders; but none was seen.

59. Orlando inoculating Mengire. Before contact, the Panará were all thought to be giants because this man, who had been captured from the Panará by Metuktire when an infant, had grown to 2.08 metres (6 ft. 8 ins.). But his great height proved to be a freak.

60. Canoes of the second expedition to try to contact the Panará embark on the Peixoto de Azevedo river in 1972. Most of the indigenous volunteers were indomitable and indefatigable Kaiabi.

61. Claudio bravely advances towards unseen Panará holding an axe. Throughout Brazilian history irresistible metal blades were invariably used in first-contacts.

62. The 1972 expedition built an airstrip, from which a light plane spotted a Panará village – whose warriors defiantly shot arrows at this evil bird. Note the heavy tree trunk, bottom left. This was used in log racing – a ceremonial sport used by no other tribe in this part of Brazil.

63 and 64. A dramatic moment: the first sighting of a Panará, among the forest trees. This was Sokriti, seen in black war paint.

65. Forest above the Iriri river, beside the Panará village of Nansepotiti. This was the tough pristine forest into which Claudio in 1957 and the Iriri River Expedition in 1961 cut trails.

66. A bewildered Panará girl climbs into an Air Force plane, when the tribe's few survivors were airlifted into the Xingu Park in 1975.

67. Chief Teseya Panará

68. Panará morale soared with their return to the Iriri after nineteen years' unhappy diaspora in the Xingu. The result was a relative population explosion.

APPENDIX 1

Timeline of the Villas Boas

1914   Orlando born to Agnello and Arlinda Villas Boas, in Santa Cruz in interior of São Paulo state, where the family had farms.

1916   Claudio born in Botucatu, São Paulo state.

1918   Leonardo born in Botucatu.

1924   After farming decline, Villas Boas family moves to São Paulo. Sons and daughters sent to good schools.

1940   Father Agnello struck with hemiplegia paralysis.

1941   Mother Arlinda dies, and five months later father Agnello dies. Villas Boas children sell large house and move to a pension.

1942   Brothers get jobs in São Paulo: Orlando with Standard Oil (Esso), Claudio with the municipal telephone company, and Leonardo in Franchini electrical goods.

1943   June: President Getúlio Vargas launches Roncador–Xingu Expedition, appoints Col. Flaviano Vanique as its leader.
Oct.: Vargas creates the Central Brazil Foundation (FBC), a federal bureau to direct colonization expansion into central Brazil.
Villas Boas brothers leave their jobs, travel inland to join the expedition on the upper Araguaia.

1944   Jan.: Claudio and Leonardo join the FBC, at the future town Aragarças.
March–April: The expedition goes from Aragarças to its starting place (at the future town Xavantina); Orlando arrives by river.

1945   12 June: Roncador–Xingu Expedition crosses Rio das Mortes into Xavante territory, with the brothers in the vanguard.
Aug.–Sept.: Clear first landing strip, 'Campo dos Índios'.
Pass the Roncador hills.
Dec.: Reach a Xingu headwater, make small camp 'Tanguro'.

1946   Jan.: Move from *campo* into rainforests; many men ill.

Feb.–March: Start to build large 'Garapú' base and airstrip.

April–Aug.: Extend airstrip, accumulating supplies, build two boats and a canoe.

29 Sept.–4 Oct.: Descend Sete de Setembro to larger Kuluene river, celebrate complete success of mission.

6 Oct.: Meet first Kalapalo Indians, later visit their village.

Nov.: Build airstrip and camp 'Kuluene', helped by Kalapalo and Kuikuro. Plane takes five chiefs on a flight.

Dec.: Influenza epidemic strikes Kuikuro and Kalapalo villages; many die.

1947   1 Jan.: Chief Izarari Kalapalo dies of influenza.

22 April: Inauguration of airstrip and camp 'Jacaré' (future air force base 'Xingu').

May onwards: Visit Xinguano villages, including Kamaiurá, Meinaku, Aweti, and sacred site Morená where Kuluene and Ronuro rivers join to form Xingu.

Aug.: First sighting of Juruna.

1948   20 March: FBC officially ends Roncador–Xingu Expedition and starts Xingu–Tapajós Expedition.

Marshal Rondon names Villas Boas as SPI (Indian Protection Service) representatives in the upper Xingu.

Ascend Batovi river, meet Waurá.

Aug.: Contact Juruna (Yudjá) where Manitsauá river meets Xingu.

Dr Noel Nutels arrives as official doctor.

Orlando, Eduardo Galvão, and Brigadeiro Raymundo Aboim have the initial idea to create Xingu Park.

Oct.: Start to clear airstrip at Diauarum on the Xingu.

Nov.: first flight lands.

1949   Colonel Vanique removed from FBC and returns to army. Orlando named leader of expedition.

First notices of Metuktire Kayapó.

Deputy (later Vice-President, then President) João Café Filho visits Xingu.

June: Ascent of Manitsauá river, then start to cut trail westwards.

End Sept. Reach Teles Pires river.

1950   Return to bring supplies forward to Teles Pires, open airstrip there.

Contact with Kaiabi (Kawaiweté).

Aerial exploration of Cachimbo hills.

1951   Crash-landing at Cachimbo.

June–Aug. Three brothers spend months creating Cachimbo airstrip.

Cachimbo opened for air force by President Getúlio Vargas.

Exploration of Teles Pires river and Kayabi hills; build 'Kaiabi' airstrip.

Kalapalo chief Comatsi describes killing Colonel Fawcett, shows bones which are sent to Ambassador Assis de Chateaubriand in London.

Kamaiurá woman Mavirá has a daughter by Leonardo, who removes the baby in May.

Prepori brings first group of Kaiabi into Xingu.

1952   Exploration down Xingu to Von Martius rapids: meet some Metuktire Kayapó.

27 April: Orlando, Darcy Ribeiro, Heloisa Torres, and Brigadeiro Aboim present draft law for creation of Xingu National Park to Vice-President Café Filho.

May: Presentation of park plan to President Vargas. Marshal Rondon supports the idea.

Villas Boas help find crashed PanAm plane in hills near Araguaia river.

First attempt to contact Ikpeng, ascend Batovi river.

Claudio builds airstrip and camp at Diauarum.

Nov.: SPI agent Ayres Cunha marries Diacuí Kalapalo in Rio de Janeiro.

1953   Leonardo leaves for the Araguaia, then to contact Xikrin Kayapó on Itacaiunas.

July: Jânio Quadros, governor of São Paulo state, visits Cachimbo and Xingu.

Mato Grosso state government starts selling Xingu land; Villas Boas and others mount media counter-attack against it and the FBC.

Ayres Cunha removes their daughter after Diacuí dies in childbirth.

Brothers have to leave Jacaré post for use by the air force, build a hut on the Tuatuari river (the future Post).

Measles epidemic kills 114 Indians among Kamaiurá and three other peoples.

1954   Villas Boas brief contact with Metuktire Kayapó near Von Martius rapids.

Construction of 'Capitão Vasconcellos' Post (renamed Leonardo in 1962).

Political action for a Xingu Park, and media campaign against sales of land continue.

Measles epidemic controlled by Dr Nutels and Villas Boas.

Orlando takes Metuktire chief Krumare to upper Xingu and to São Paulo for its 400th anniversary parade.

Prepori brings Chief Sabino's contingent of Kaiabi from Teles Pires to Xingu.

Nov.: Villas Boas visit Krumare's village. Rauni and other Metuktire remain as helpers at Vasconcellos (future Leonardo) Post.

1955   Congress committees scrutinize Xingu Park plan.

Exploration of Liberdade river: clear an airstrip there, contact more Metuktire.

Claudio and Orlando ascend Batovi but find no Ikpeng.

1956   President Juscelino Kubitschek elected, but uninterested in park proposal.

Second attempt to contact Ikpeng driven off by arrows: tribe retreats from the Batovi river to its Jatobá tributary.

Mekragnoti and many Metuktire migrate from Xingu to near Iriri river.

Oct.: Claudio starts to cut trail from Cachimbo west towards Cururu.

1957   Cachimbo–Cururu trail continues intermittently.

Claudio moves permanently to Diauarum.

1958   Jan.: Marshal Rondon dies.

June: Claudio's western trail reaches Creputiá; builds airstrips 'São Benedito' and 'Divisor'.

Trail reaches Cururu, Cláudio returns to help Orlando try to contact Suiá.

Flu epidemic among Kaiabi at Diauarum.

1959   Orlando leads expedition to Geographical Centre of Brazil below Von Martius rapids. See another group of Metuktire on Liberdade river.

Villas Boas forced to leave Vasconcellos Post (in dispute with SPI over integration and FBC over land sales) and move to Diauarum.

Contact with Suiá (Kisedje) on Suiá-Missu river.

1960   Second contact with Suiá, by Harald Schultz, some settle near Diauarum.

Villas Boas descend Xingu river to Serra das Coordenadas.

Jânio Quadros elected president.

1961   14 April: Xingu National Park (PNX) legalized in decree by President Quadros.

Leonardo ill, taken to São Paulo, and dies during a heart operation.

25 Aug.: President Quadros resigns, replaced by Vice-President João Goulart.

1 Sept.: Panará ambush and kill Richard Mason near upper Iriri river.

1962 Vasconcellos Post returned to Villas Boas by SPI, renamed Posto Leonardo.

Kalapalo, Matipui, and Nahukua move into new Xingu Park area.

1963 Nurse Marina Lopes de Lima brought to Xingu by Orlando.

Start building airstrips at every upper Xingu village.

Nomadic Metuktire settle in Poiriri village.

FBC abolished. Xingu Park comes under Ministry of Economic Development.

1964 Visit by ex-King Leopold III of Belgium.

Brief contact with Ikpeng on Jatobá river when plane lands nearby.

President Goulart overthrown by the military in a bloodless coup.

1965 Orlando invites doctors from Escola Paulista de Medicina (EPM) to visit Xingu.

Sept.: Boat up Jatobá brings successful contact of Ikpeng.

1966 Formal agreement with EPM for continual medical help, later led by Dr Roberto Baruzzi.

Another group of Kaiabi under Chief Temeoni reach Xingu after long migration from Rio dos Peixes.

1967 June: Ikpeng survivors moved into park to live near Posto Leonardo.

Some Panará appear at Cachimbo resulting in panic reaction and crash of air force plane.

Mekragnoti Kayapó armed with guns attack Panará village and kill twenty-six.

Royal Geographical Society awards gold medal jointly to Claudio and Orlando.

Claudio flight over village of Panará, who fire arrows at plane.

Nov.: Orlando and Claudio mission to Kararao Kayapó near Xingu mouth.

Dec.: Critical Figueiredo report into SPI published; SPI abolished.

1968 May: National Indigenous Foundation (Funai) created, and includes Xingu Park.

Xingu National Park increased in area to 26,000 sq. km.

First attempt to contact Panará: 130-km trail cut from Manitsauá north-west to Peixoto de Azevedo river; three airstrips built.

Oct.: Enter abandoned Panará village.

1969   Jan.: Panará attraction expedition finally returns after months of rain but no contact.

May–July: Funai attempt to contact Tapayuna near Arinos river results in terrible losses from influenza.

Sept.: Orlando marries Marina.

Another Kaiabi contingent migrates into Xingu.

1970   President Médici launches Plan for National Integration and penetration roads into Amazonia.

May: Remnant of Tapayuna from Arinos river airlifted to live beside Suiá relatives near Diauarum.

Villas Boas publish *Xingu: Os Índios, seus mitos*.

Nov.: Orlando Filho born.

1971   Jan.: Claudio nominated for Nobel Peace Prize.

Funai allows BR-080 road to cut across park.

13 July: Decree changes shape of park, removing forest to north, adding *campo* to south.

Robin Hanbury-Tenison report for Survival International.

Kamaiurá kill suspected Aweti sorcerer in Orlando's house.

Oct.: aerial sighting of another Panará village.

1972   Jan.: Start second attempt to contact Panará; trail cut south from Cachimbo towards Peixoto de Azevedo river.

June: Panará contact expedition builds airstrip; overflights of villages.

Aborigines' Protection Society report on situation of indigenous peoples.

Second nomination of Orlando and Claudio for Nobel Peace Prize.

1973   4 and 8 Feb.: Finally make full contacts with Panará.

March: Death of Dr Noel Nutels.

April: Panará contact expedition withdraws; Apoena Meirelles continues attraction.

May: Orlando visits Japan to receive an award.

1974   Oct.: Gathering of many chiefs and president of Funai at Posto Leonardo to bid farewell to Villas Boas.

Dec.: Part of BR-163 road opens to traffic; Panará suffer hunger, disease, and many die.

1975   Jan.: Panará survivors airlifted into Xingu.

April: Orlando awarded Rio Branco Medal of Merit.

Settlers from south Brazil start town Canarana at southern edge of park.

Air force ceases monthly flights to Xingu by its CAN service.

Oct.: Anthropologist Olympio Serra succeeds Orlando as director of park.

1976   Orlando and Claudio leave the Xingu and go to live in São Paulo.

May: Jarina reserve for Metuktire on west bank of Xingu, north of BR-080.

Orlando awarded Boilesen Prize.

1977   Orlando goes to USA for Humanitarian Commendation from Lions Club.

1978   Television series *Aritana* screened.

Dec.: Olympio Serra resigns as director of Xingu Park.

1979   April: Publish *A arte dos pajés*; also *Xingu, Tribal Territory* with Maureen Bisilliat.

1980   March: Orlando awarded State of São Paulo Prize and buys a house in Lapa City, São Paulo.

Rauni and Metuktire kill eleven workers near BR-080 road.

1983   Seizure of a plane by Gorotire Kayapó; negotiate gold-mining commission.

1984   March–May: 'War of the Xingu', Metuktire seize raft over Xingu, kidnap Funai officials, in protest to recover Capoto territory lost in 1971.

April: Confirmation of reserve on east bank of Xingu, north of BR-080.

May: Megaron Metuktire named first indigenous director of Xingu Park.

Oct.: Demarcation of Capoto–Jarina reserve to north of Xingu Park.

Dec.: Orlando in Germany for award of Geo Prize by Chancellor Brandt.

1987   Lobbying of constituent assembly, for indigenous rights.

1988   New Brazilian constitution has good pro-indigenous clauses.

Creation of Batovi indigenous territory, at south-west of park.

1989   Kayapó organize Altamira meeting to protest against Belo Monte hydroelectric dam on lower Xingu.

Sting and Rauni get President José Sarney to agree to huge Menkragnoti reserve.

Sting and Rauni on international fund-raising tour.

1991   Akè Panará revisits devastated Peixoto de Azevedo lands, sees intact forest on Iriri.

1992   Demarcation of new Menkragnoti reserve linking the Xingu Park and Metuktire reserves to Kayapó territories.

1994   Metuktire Kayapó leave Xingu Park for their Jarina and Capoto territories.

Panará sympathisers launch legal actions for return to part of their homeland.

Villas Boas publish prize-winning *A Marcha para o Oeste*.

1995   Panará return to their own indigenous territory on upper Iriri, start village.

1997   Villas Boas publish *Almanaque do sertão*.

Oct.: Federal court awards compensation to the Panará.

1998   1 March: Claudio dies aged eighty-two; *kuarup* in his honour in August.

Ratification of Wawi territory for Kisêdje (Suiá) and Batovi for Waurá.

Orlando awarded Human Rights Medal by Brazilian government.

1999   Special medical district (DSEI) of Xingu created with the Ministry of Health Funasa and UNIFESP.

2000   Brazil's 500th anniversary: Orlando declared a National Hero.

Orlando honoured by a samba school in Rio de Janeiro Carnival parade.

Orlando publishes *A Arte dos Pajés*.

2002   12 Dec.: Orlando dies aged eighty-eight; *kuarup* in his honour in July 2003.

2011   Celebration of fiftieth anniversary of Xingu Indigenous Park, in São Paulo.

2015   Celebration of fifty years of Xingu work by São Paulo Medical School (EPM, later UNIFESP).

2016   Feb.: Death of Professor Roberto Baruzzi; *kuarup* in his honour in 2017.

APPENDIX 2

Early expeditions to the Upper Xingu

1884	Karl **von den Steinen** down Batovi to **Bakairi**, **Waurá** then on to **Trumai**, and **Suiá** and **Juruna** on Xingu.
1887	Karl **von den Steinen** with Paul **Ehrenreich** down Curisevo to **Kalapalo, Meinaku, Aweti, Yawalapiti, Kamaiurá**.
1896	Hermann **Meyer** and Dr Karl **Ranke** to Curisevo and Jatoba rivers see **Kamaiurá, Trumai, Aweti, Nahukwá**.
1899	Hermann **Meyer** and Theodor **Koch-Grünberg** visit **Mehinaku, Yawalapiti**.
1899	**Suiá** kill five Americans seeking rubber.
1897 and 1900	Lt-Col. Paula **Castro** disastrous expeditions seeking mythical Los Martírios mines on Culuene.
1900–1	Max **Schmidt** with **Bakairi** and on Curisevo, visits **Mehinaku, Trumai**.
1910	Max **Schmidt** second expedition.
1913	Commandant **Fontoura** for the Defesa da Borracha rubber service.
1920	Major Ramiro **Noronha** (of Rondon Commission) maps rivers, sees **Kuikuro, Kalapalo, Naravuti**, and makes a post for **Bakairi** south of the Xingu.
1924–5	Captain Vicente de Paula **Vasconcellos** and Thomas **Reiz** of Indian Protection Service, with Dr Heinrich **Hintermann**, map Culuene and Curisevo, meet various peoples.
June 1925	Lt-Col. Percy **Fawcett** with **Bakairi. Aweti, Kalapalo, Nahukwá**.

1926	Leonard **Legters** (American missionary) and a SPI official make reconnaissance.
1926–8	Max **Schmidt** with southern **Bakairi**.
June–Aug. 1928	Commander George **Dyott** on Fawcett search expedition questions **Nahukwá**, **Kalapalo**, **Kuikuro** then flees down Xingu.
1930s–48	Thomas **Young** and wife, nurse Marjorie Clarke, Protestant mission among **Nahukwá** on upper Curisevo (south of the Xingu Park).
1931	Vincent **Petrullo** lands float plane for rapid visit with **Yawalapiti**.
1935	Albert de **Winton**, journalist/actor killed by **Kalapalo** and **Kamaiurá**.
1938	Buell **Quain** among **Trumai** and **Kamaiurá**.
1939?	Italian expedition killed by **Juruna** near Von Martius rapids.
1943	Journalist Edmar **Morel** and film-maker Nilo **Veloso** with **Kalapalo**.
1944–5	Nilo **Veloso** films Roncador–Xingu Expedition.

APPENDIX 3

Anthropologists and Researchers in the Upper Xingu, 1946–88

1946–76	Orlando, Claudio, and Leonardo **Villas Boas** meet **Kalapalo**; then study all tribes during subsequent decades.
1947–52	Eduardo **Galvão**, Pedro **Lima** with **Waurá**, **Kamaiurá**, **Mehinaku**.
1950	Eduardo **Galvão** with **Juruna**.
1950	Kalervo **Oberg** (doctor) with **Aweti**.
1952–3	Jorge **Ferreira** reporter for *O Cruzeiro*.
1952–61	Mário **Simões** with **Mehinaku** and other peoples.
1953–61	Robert **Carneiro** and Gertrude **Dole** with **Kuikuro**, **Trumai**.
1955	Gerhard **Baer** and René **Fuerst** with **Kalapalo** and other peoples.
1955 and later	Terence **Turner** and Joan **Bamberger** with **Metuktire**.
1958	Adrian **Cowell** with **Aweti**, **Metuktire**.
1958	Egon **Schaden** with **Trumai**.
1959–61	Adélia Engrácia de **Oliveira** with **Juruna**.
1959	Dr Murillo **Villela** with Orlando **Villas Boas** on **Suiá** contact.
1960	Harald **Schultz** with **Suiá**.
1961	Richard **Mason**, John **Hemming** on Iriri River Expedition, ambushed by **Panará**.
1962	Eduardo **Galvão**, Mário **Simões** on **Txikão** (**Ikpeng**) contact attempt.
1962–3	Amadeu Duarte **Lanna** with **Suiá**.
1963, 1965	Mário **Simões** reports on all Xinguanos.

1965	Harald **Schultz** and Vilma **Chiara** with **Waurá, Suiá**.
1965–2010	Roberto **Baruzzi** and **Escola Paulista de Medicina** with all peoples.
1965–71	Carmen (Lima) **Junqueira** with **Kamaiurá**.
1965–75	Mickey **Stout** and Ruth **Thomson** linguists with **Metuktire**.
1966–7	Protásio **Frikel** with **Suiá**.
1966–8	Mark **Münzel** with **Kamaiurá**.
1967	Renate **Viertler** with **Kamaiurá**.
1967	Aurore **Monod** with **Trumai**.
1967	Adrian **Cowell** on contact attempt to **Panará**.
1967–8	Murillo **Villela**, Jesco von **Puttkamer** with **Villas Boas** on **Ikpeng** contact.
1967–9 and 1972	Patrick **Menget** with **Ikpeng**.
1968	Ellen **Basso** with **Kalapalo**.
1968	Adélia **Oliveira** with **Juruna**.
1968–9	Philip **Hugh-Jones**, Anthony **Smith**, medical team.
1969–74	Thomas **Gregor** with **Mehinaku**.
1969	Georg **Grünberg** with **Kaiabi**.
1969	Bo **Akerren**, René **Fuerst** and others, Red Cross medical survey.
1970–1	Kenneth **Brecher** with **Waurá**.
1970	Dr Roberto **Baruzzi** medical examination of **Tapayuna** on arrival in Xingu.
1971	Robin **Hanbury-Tenison** survey for Primitive People's Fund (Survival International).
1971	George **Zarur** with **Aweti**.
1971–3	Cláudio and Orlando **Villas Boas** on **Panará** contact expedition.
1971–2	Anthony **Seeger** with **Suiá**.
1972	John **Hemming**, Francis **Huxley**, René **Fuerst** survey for Aborigines' Protection Society.
1972	Pedro Agostinho da **Silva** with **Kamaiurá**.
1974 onwards	Gustaaf **Verswijver** with **Metuktire** and other **Kayapó**.
1974 and later visits	Maureen **Bisilliat** photographed many Xinguanos.
1974–80	Rafael José **Bastos** with **Kamaiurá, Yawalapiti**.

1975	Roberto **Baruzzi** medical study of **Panará** airlifted into Xingu.
1975	George **Zarur** with **Kalapalo**.
1975–8	Richard **Heelas** with **Panará**.
1976–80	Bruna **Franchetto** with **Kuikuro**.
1977	Etienne **Samain** with **Kamaiurá**.
1977	Berta **Ribeiro** with **Kaiabi**.
1980–2, 1984	Mariana K. L. **Ferreira** (teacher at Diauarum) with **Metuktire, Kaiabi**.
1980–94	Stephan **Schwartzman** with **Panará**.
1981–3	Emilienne **Ireland** with **Waurá**.
1982–3	Bruna **Franchetto** with **Kuikuro, Metuktire, Tapyuná, Suiá**.
1983	Vanessa **Lea** with **Metuktire**.
1993	Suzanne **Oakdale** with **Kaiabi** (**Kawaiwete**).
1993–5	Michael **Heckenberger** with **Kuikuro**.
1997–8	Elizabeth **Ewart** with **Panará**.

APPENDIX 4

Populations of indigenous peoples

Upper Xingu, Leonardo	1950	1967	1985	2002	2011
Tupi speaking					
Aweti	27	40	60	127	195
Kamaiurá	110	120	189	419	467
Carib-speaking					
Kalapalo	148	100	225	441	385
Kuikuro	148	130	223	444	522
Matipu	16	30	86	98	149
Nafukwá + Naruvôto	28			108	195
Ikpeng		51	142	305	459
Arawak (Aruak)-speaking					
Mehinaku	56	65	97	220	254
Waurá	95	86	153	338	410
Yawalapiti	12	39	149	214	156
Isolated language					
Trumai	18	26	58	126	97
	658	687	1,382	2,840	3,289
Diauarum-based					
Juruna (Yudjá)—*Tupi*	75	101	260	348	350
Kaiabi (Kawaiweté)—*Tupi*		213	435	958	1,193
Suiá (Kisêdje)—*Je*		73	151	304	330
Tapayuna—*Je*		41	45	58	60
		402	732	1,580	1,933
Later left Xingu Indigenous Park					
Metuktire Kayapó—*Je*	245	376	557	1,010	1,328
Panará—*Je*			100	159	480

Notes: The 1950 estimates are Galvão's, just for the upper-Xingu peoples. The dates of other census figures fluctuate somewhat. Some Metuktire remained in the park after their lands north of the BR-080 road were removed in 1971. They gained their own Jarina and Capoto territories in that area in 1984, and moved into them. There were only seventy-nine Panará airlifted into the Xingu in 1975; and they left for their own territory on the Iriri in 1995–6. After 1985 some Tapayuna joined the Metuktire in Capoto–Jarina territory, others remained with the Kisêdje (Suiá) in Wawi territory.

NOTES AND REFERENCES

CHAPTER 1. THE EXPEDITION

3 *and so forth'*: Interview with Claudio Villas Boas, *Jornal da Tarde*, 26 Aug. 1978. The first mention of the brothers was in an article by Adalberto Ribeiro, 'Na rastro da Expedição Roncador-Xingu', *Correio da Manhã*, 7 Sept. 1945. The school friend who invited Orlando to send regular reports to *A Gazeta* in São Paulo was the distinguished journalist Manoel Rodrigues Ferreira.

The scene at the start of this chapter, of woodsmen signing in for the expedition, is the opening sequence of a movie called *Xingu*, directed in 2012 by Cao Hamburger for O2 Filmes (and also a television series for Globo TV). The signing-in may not have happened exactly as depicted. But Colonel Vanique's ban on literate members was true.

7 *surround them'*: Claudio and Orlando Villas Boas, *Almanaque do sertão* (São Paulo, 1997), 2.

7 *turned tail'*: Villas Boas, *Almanaque do sertão*, 210.

10 *of our mission'*: Orlando and Claudio Villas Boas, *A Marcha para o Oeste: A Epopéia da Expedição Roncador-Xingu* (São Paulo, 1994; enlarged 2nd edn São Paulo, 2012), 150. The modern BR-158 road north from Xavantina is to the east of the Roncador–Xingu trail. But there is now a frontier town at Garapú, and the larger Canarana is near the short-lived Tanguro camp. Both these bustling towns are outside the south-eastern limit of the Xingu Indigenous Park.

10 *ended as grownups'*: Orlando Villas-Boas, in a dedication when he sent me their book *A Marcha para o Oeste* (1995).

CHAPTER 2. KALAPALO

11 *became friends'*: Orlando Villas Boas, in Cristina Müller et al., *O Xingu dos Villas Bôas* (São Paulo, 2002), 150.

11 *authority and goodwill'*: Villas Boas, *Almanaque do sertão*, 99.

14 *equal tranquillity'*: Villas Boas, *Marcha*, 172.

18 *the authorities'*: Orlando Villas Boas, 'Trinta e cinco anos de assistencia', in Roberto Baruzzi and Carmen Junqueira, eds., *Parque Indígena do Xingu: Saúde, cultura e historia* (São Paulo, 2005), 51.

18 *most critical'*: Villas Boas, *Marcha*, 184.

18 *save him'*; *irreparable loss'*: Villas Boas, *Marcha*, 188.

231

20 *coming and going'*: Helmut Sick, *Tukani* (London, 1959), 71.

23 *social life'*: Villas Boas, *Marcha*, 261.

23 *these two points'*: Rafael José de Menezes Bastos, 'Apuàp world hearing revisited: talking with "animals", "spirits" and other beings', *Ethnomusicology Forum* **22**:3 2013, 291.

24 *from a gourd'*: Villas Boas, *Marcha*, 281.

25 *disturbing nothing'*: Villas Boas, *Marcha*, 310.

25 *suitcase'*: Villas Boas, *Marcha*, 333.

25 *about the Xingu'*: Villas Boas, *Marcha*, 277.

26 *in their hammocks'*: Sick, *Tukani*, 115.

26 *wants to die'*: Villas Boas, *Marcha*, 340.

26 *covered her up again'*: Sick, *Tukani*, 116.

27 *of these Indians'*: Antonio Ximenes, 'As cartas de Rondon a Villas Boas', *Jornal do Brasil*, 22 June 1997, in the Villas Boas family archive.

27 *your aged admirer'*: Marshal Cândido Rondon to Villas Boas brothers, Rio de Janeiro, 1 Feb. 1949, in Villas Bôas, *Almanaque do sertão*, 19.

28 *had worldwide relevance'*; *what we did'*: Antonio Ximenes, 'As cartas de Rondon a Villas Boas'.

CHAPTER 3. ONWARD EXPLORATION

31 *into the huts'*; *people inside'*: Orlando and Claudio Villas Boas, *Xingu: The Indians, their Myths* (London, 1973), 35. At that time Suiá was often spelled Suyá; in recent years they prefer to be called Kisêdje.

31 *slaughtered brothers'*: Villas Boas, *Marcha*, 388.

31 *between the knees'*: Villas Boas, *Xingu: The Indians*, 35.

32 *approach further'*; *another step'*; *with his bow'*; *encounter'*: *Marcha*, 389, 431.

33 *want to go'*; *shirts hanging'*; *talk to them'''*; *to be raised'*; *killed us, no'*: Carandine Juruna interviewed in Tuba-Tuba village, 27 Feb. 1990, in Mariana Ferreira, ed., *Histórias do Xingu: coletânea de depoimentos dos índios Suyá, Kayabi, Juruna, Trumai, Txucarramãe e Txicão* (São Paulo, 1994), 175.

33 *suspicion and caution'*; *more amiably'*; *greatest attraction'*: *Marcha*, 431, 441, 442.

36 *in these parts'*; *over rocks'*: Villas Boas, 'Viagem pioneira pela Maritsauá', *Revista de Atualidade Indígena* (Brasília) **3**:15, March–April 1979, 22.

38 *no bounds'*: Sick, *Tukani*, 176.

38 *unpredictable Indians'*; *the grunting of peccary'*; *as if by magic'*; *side of the river'*: *Marcha*, 487.

39 *my brother'*: Mariana K. Leal Ferreira, 'Da origem dos homens à conquista da escrita: um estudo sobre povos indígenas e educação escolar no Brasil' (Master's thesis, Universidade de São Paulo, 1992), vol. 2, 32–5, in Vanessa Lea, *Parque Indígena do Xingu: Laudo antropológico* (São Paulo, 1997) 120. Ferreira recorded these Kaiabi memories when she was a nurse at Diauarum in the late 1980s.

39 *uninterested in barter'*: Villas Boas, *Marcha*, 516.

39 *time and time again*': Sick, *Tukani*, 186.

40 *crash landing*'; *on the planet*'; *delirium*': Villas Boas, *Almanaque do sertão*, 203, 201, 204; *Marcha*, 493–4.

CHAPTER 4. THE MEDIA JUNGLE

44 *ancient Egypt*': P. H. Fawcett, *Exploration Fawcett* (ed. Brian Fawcett) (London, 1953), 285.

44 *of the universe*': David Grann, *The Lost City of Z* (London and New York, 2009), 209. Fawcett's son Brian had found these fantasies among his father's papers.

44 *tribes one meets*': Fawcett, *Exploration Fawcett*, 17–18.

45 *the three Englishmen*': Adrian Cowell, *The Heart of the Forest* (London, 1960), 63. Edmar Morel wrote about this in the *Jornal do Brasil* in 1943 and it was reported in England by *The People*, much later in June and July 1951.

45 *to the east*'; *into the water*': Cowell, *Heart of the Forest*, 64, 65. Antonio Callado, one of Brazil's most distinguished editors and broadcasters, endorsed Canisio's version in 'Esqueleto na Lagoa Verde' (an article of 1953, republished in a book of that name by Paz e Terra, Rio de Janeiro, 1977).

47 *on its bed*': Orlando Villas Boas, 'Fawcett: Orlando guarda ossada do explorador inglês', *Revista de Atualidade Indígena* **1**:6, Sept.–Oct. 1977, 30.

47 *sources of the Xingu*': Capitão Vicente de Paula Vasconcellos, quoted in Luís Donisete Benzi Grupioni, *Coleções e Expedições Vigiadas* (São Paulo, 1998), 99.

47 *recognised in him*': Villas Boas, *Marcha*, 167.

48 *examined*': 'Report on the Human Remains from Brazil', for the Royal Anthropological Institute, by Professor A. J. E. Cave, Miss M. L. Tildesley, and Dr J. C. Trevor, 9 Nov. 1951.

48 *worthy of payment*': Ellen Basso, *The Kalapalo Indians of Central Brazil* (New York, 1973), 4. The anthropologist Etienne Samain dismissed the Green Lake story as nonsense, but without explaining why, in her *Moroneta Kamayurá* (Rio de Janeiro, 1991), xxii. Vajavi Kalapalo's version of 1998 is in Benedict Allen, 'River of no return', *The Independent*, 11 Sept. 1999.

49 *Rio das Mortes*': Ayres Câmara Cunha, *Entre os Índios do Xingu: A verdadeira história de Diacuí* (São Paulo, 1960), 237.

50 *here in São Paulo*': Orlando in an interview with Ethevaldo Siqueira, 'Villas Boas: integrar é destruir o índio', *O Estado de São Paulo*, 4 Feb. 1979; and Orlando Villas Boas, 'Fawcett', 30. Orlando was forgetful about where he had found the bones: he sometimes said the Museu Nacional (in Rio de Janeiro), at others the Museu Paulista (in São Paulo).

50 *a civilized port*': Villas Boas, *Marcha*, 381, and 'As expedições que desapareceram no roteiro de Fawcett', *Revista de Atualidade Indígena* (Brasília) **2**:7, Nov.–Dec. 1977, 52.

51 *between the races*': Kenneth Matthews, *Brazilian Interior* (London, 1956), 199.

52 *husband*': Cunha, *Entre os Índios*, 242.

52 *[whites]'*: David Nasser, 'Índio quer ser índio', *O Cruzeiro*, 2 June 1971.

53 *a daughter'*: Darcy Ribeiro in a report by Geraldo Farinha, *O Globo* (Rio de Janeiro), 26 Sept. 1952.

53 *baby girl'*; *hand over the girl'*: Testimony of Leopoldo Jose da Silva, to an FBC internal inquiry, Xavantina, 8 Sept. 1952. The other testimony was by Antonio Alves dos Santos, also in Xavantina, 2 Sept. 1952. Both men claimed that Leonardo had slept with other Indian women and that his hut was at times full of them. These reports found their way into the files of the ASI secret police during the years of military government. They were released forty years later, and seen by Rubens Valente, *Os Fuzis e as Flechas* (São Paulo, 2017), 216–17. Also, interview with Maialu, *Claudia* magazine, São Paulo, Aug. 2012.

54 *kill you!'*: Jorge Ferreira reminiscing, 'Jorge Ferreira, o grande reporter do Xingu', in Müller et al., eds., *O Xingu dos Villas Bôas*, 46.

CHAPTER 5. THE 1950s

56 *I was not'*: Suzanne Oakdale, paper delivered to the Society for the Anthropology of Lowland South America (SALSA), Belém do Pará, July 2011, citing an interview with Prepori that she had conducted in 1993.

56 *hunt or fish'*: Heloisa Pagliaro, 'A mudança dos Kaiabi para o Parque Indígena do Xingu: uma história de sucesso demográfico', in Baruzzi and Junqueira, eds., *Parque Indígena do Xingu*, 207.

57 *of his people'*: Adrian Cowell, *The Tribe that Hides from Man* (London, 1973), 32.

58 *surprise attacks'*: Claudio and Orlando Villas-Boas, 'Atração dos índios Txukahamãi', in Mário Simões, ed., *S.P.I.—1954* (Rio de Janeiro, 1955), 79.

59 *a later date'*: Villas Boas, 'Atração', 81; Gustaaf Verswijver, *The Club-Fighters of the Amazon: Warfare among the Kaiapo Indians of Central Brazil* (Ghent, 1992), 291.

59 *from their canoe'*; *many days'*: Cowell, *Heart of the Forest*, 177.

59 *young men'*: Villas Boas, *Marcha*, 561.

60 *ears pierced'*; *impossible'*; 61 *following day'*: Villas Boas, 'Atração', 82, 83. This group near the Von Martius rapids was the Metuktire, rather than the Mebengokre, who were contacted farther south on the Jarina, later that year.

61 *infants cried'*: Villas Boas, *Marcha*, 566.

61 *not even tripe'*: Villas Boas, 'Atração', 85.

62 *worthless'*; *reserves of food'*; *to their men'*; *communities'*: Villas Boas, *Almanaque do sertão*, 226–8; Maureen Bisilliat, *Guerreiros sem espada: Experiências revistas dos irmãos Villas Bôas* (São Paulo, 1995), 29; anon, 'Os irmãos da selva', *Veja* **218**, 8 Nov. 1972, 52.

63 *their foreheads'*: Villas Boas, 'Atração', 85.

63 *high'*; *minimum'*: Verswijver, Club-Fighters, 234, 234–5. Verswijver, with characteristic erudition, gave a chronological record of the bewildering splits and moves of these groups, whom he calls Southern Mekrãgnoti: *Club-Fighters*, 291–2. In 1960 Claudio persuaded this group to move from their village on the Liberdade westwards across

the Xingu to a village called Roikore on the Capoto stream between the Jarina and Iriri Novo. But when the Xingu Park was created in 1961, Claudio got them to move again, in order to come within its boundaries: 65 people under Chief Kremoro settled at Porori village, on the Xingu near the mouth of the Jarina river. This village grew in 1964, when 120 people moved to it from the north-west; and another group joined in 1967: Lea, *Parque Indígena do Xingu*, 113–14.

64 *immense dignity'; 65 at our coming'; at the boat'; man and woman too'; still good'; near man';
    much clothes'; we see'*: Cowell, *Heart of the Forest*, 234–5, 237, 183, 186, 184.

66 *interval of time'; Xingu'*: Dr João Leão da Mota, 'A epidemia de sarampo no Xingu', in
    Simões, ed., *S.P.I.—1954*, 132; Eduardo Galvão and Mário Simões, 'Mudança e sobre-
    vivência no Alto Xingu—Brasil Central', *Revista de Antropologia* **14**, 1966, 44. Darcy
    Ribeiro wrote that the measles was caught by Indians visiting the air force base Jacaré,
    where they met labourers who were infected. Ribeiro, citing reports by Doctors Serôa
    da Mota and Leão da Mota, as well as by Claudio Villas Boas, said that 698 Indians fell
    ill and 108 died: 61 in the expedition's bases Jacaré and Kalapalo and 48 at Capitão
    Vasconcellos and in the Waurá and Kuikuro villages: Darcy Ribeiro, *Os índios e a civi-
    lização* (Rio de Janeiro, 1970), 279.

66 *now they have five'*: Villas Boas, *A Marcha*, 364.

66 *was horrible'*: Chief Aritana, introductory speech to a course for indigenous medical
    agents, Posto Leonardo, June 1998.

67 *frequent reminiscences'*: Basso, *Kalapalo Indians*, 5.

67 *crying with hunger'*: Emilienne Ireland, 'Cerebral Savage: The Whiteman as Symbol of
    Cleverness and Savagery in Waurá Myth', in Jonathan D. Hill, ed., *Rethinking History
    and Myth* (Chicago, 1988), 162. The Waurá had previously suffered a terrible measles
    epidemic, soon after contact by von den Steinen in the 1880s.

67 *on the floor'; of the building'; interesting and powerful'; to swallow'*: Cowell, *Heart of the
    Forest*, 203–4.

68 *the toughest'; fever and delirium'*: Villas Boas, *Almanaque do sertão*, 204, 205.

69 *work for him'*: Cowell, *Tribe that Hides*, 79. Also an interview with Orlando, *A Gazeta*,
    6 July 1957.

70 *mythological ugliness'*: Paul Ehrenreich, 'Beiträge zur Völkerkunde Brasiliens',
    Veröffentlichungen aus dem königlichen Museum für Völkerkunde, 2 (Berlin, 1891); trans.
    Egon Schaden as 'A segunda expedição alemã ao rio Xingu', *Revista do Museu Paulista*,
    n.s. 2 1929, 270. Ehrenreich was with von den Steinen on his second expedition to
    the Xingu in 1887.

70 *huts'*: Eduardo Galvão, 'Apontamentos sobre os índios Kamaiurá', *Publicações Avulsas
    do Museu Nacional* **5**, 1949, 35.

71 *no longer fight them'*: Karandini Juruna, talking to Adelia Engrácia de Oliveira, in her
    'Os índios Jurúna e sua cultura nos dias atuais', *Boletim do Museu Paraense Emílio Goeldi*,
    n.s., *Antropologia* **11–12**, June–Dec. 1970, 34.

71 *advance rapidly'; talked ceaselessly'; never seen dogs'; degree of mistrust'*: Dr Murillo Villela,
    in Müller et al., *O Xingu dos Villas Bôas*, 52, 53. Dr Villela spelt the name of the Suiá
    chief's brother as Thaimostotine.

72 *their women*'; *in the boat*': Villas Boas, *Marcha*, 598–9.

72 *peaceful intentions*': Harald Schultz, 'Informações etnográficas sôbre os índios Suyá, 1960', *Revista do Museu Paulista, Antropologia* **13**, 1961/2, 315.

CHAPTER 6. THE XINGU PARK

73 *biological balance*': José Carvalho, Pedro de Lima, and Eduardo Galvão, *Observações zoológicas e antropológicas na Região dos Formadores de Xingu*, Museu Nacional, Publicações Avulsas **5** (Rio de Janeiro, 1949), 7. Manoel Rodrigues Ferreira (not to be confused with Jorge Ferreira) wrote regular articles for the picture magazine *O Cruzeiro*, as well as a book about the expedition: *Nos sertões do lendário Rio das Mortes* (São Paulo, 1946); and a later memoir, *Aspectos do Alto Xingu e a Vera Cruz* (São Paulo, 1983).

76 *appropriately chosen*'; *this task*': *Relatório Anual do CNPI* [National Indigenist Council], *1951*, (Rio de Janeiro, 1952) 35; Carlos Augusto da Rocha Freire, 'Sagas Sertanistas: Práticas e representações do campo indigenista no século XX' (doctoral thesis, Universidade Federal do Rio de Janeiro, 2005), 63.

76 *perpetual use*'; *live there*'; 77 *their subsistence*'; *inhabit it*'; *any pretext whatever*'; *millions [of them]*'; *into their lands*'; *other countries*': Draft Law, 'Proposta para o Parque do Xingu', in José M. da Gama Malcher, ed., *S.P.I.—1952* (Rio de Janeiro, 1953), 98.

77 *original nature*': Darcy Ribeiro, *Confissões* (São Paulo, 1997), 195. Orlando recalled that President Vargas had said, 'This won't do. You have brought me a pocket battleship.' Orlando and Claudio interview, *Banas* magazine, 22 April 1974.

77 *extraordinary man*': Interview with Orlando and Claudio Villas Boas, *Banas* magazine, 22 April 1974, in Bisilliat, *Guerreiros sem espada*, 69.

78 *for colonization*'; *unoccupied*': Roberto C. de Oliveira, 'Relatório de uma investigação sôbre terras em Mato Grosso', in Mário F. Simões, ed., *S.P.I.—1954* (Rio de Janeiro, 1955) 173–84; also in Lea, *Parque Indígena do Xingu*, 172–83.

79 *every day*': Matthews, *Brazilian Interior*, 146.

79 *was approved*': Letter by Brigadier Aboim to the editor of *Correio da Manhã*, 1 Nov. 1954, in the Aboim family archive.

79 *our wilderness*': Senator Sylvio Curvo in *O Globo*, 22 Nov. 1954.

80 *destined for extinction*': Leandro Mendes Rocha, 'A marcha para o oeste e os índios do Xingu,' *Indios do Brasil*, **2**, June 1990, 18; Seth Garfield, 'A nationalist environment: Indians, nature, and the construction of the Xingu National Park in Brazil', *Luso-Brazilian Review* (University of Wisconsin) **41**:1, 2004, 158.

81 *Mato Grosso*': 'Jorge Ferreira, o grande reporter do Xingu', in Müller et al., eds., *O Xingu dos Villas Boas*, 46.

81 *proposed terms*': Jorge Ferreira, president of the Central Brazil Foundation, to President Jânio Quadros, Brasilia, 5 April 1961, in Maria Menezes, *Parque Indígena do Xingu: A construção de um território estatal* (Campinas, 2000) 386.

82 *national patrimony*': Decree 51.084 of 31 July 1961, in Lea, *Parque Indígena do Xingu*, 158.

83 *of the natives*': Sick, *Tukani*, 226.

Brazil': Ribeiro, *Confissões*, 195; Garfield, 'A nationalist environment', 156.

84 *human rights'*: George Zarur, 'A revolução dos Villas-Boas: Os cinqüenta anos do Parque Indígena do Xingu', *Scientific American, Brasil*, 2011.

84 *that time'*: Antonio Carlos de Souza Lima, 'O governo dos índios sob a gestão do SPI', in Manuela Carneiro da Cunha, ed., *História dos Índios no Brasil* (São Paulo, 1992), 168.

CHAPTER 7. POSTO LEONARDO

88 *religion, education, sanitation'*; *for the Indians'*: Cowell, *Heart of the Forest*, 67, 61.

88 *very healthy'*: Orlando interviewed by Adrena Williams, 'A day in the life of Orlando Villas Boas', *The Times*, London, 1991.

90 *Turkish bath'*; *a Socialist Utopia'*; *breakneck speed'*: Cowell, *Heart of the Forest*, 41, 102.

90 *could not follow'*; 91 *and beliefs'*; *on retirement'*: Sydney Possuelo, 'Cláudio Villas Boas, um filósofo no sertão brasileiro', *Parabólicas* (a review published by ISA in São Paulo), April 1998.

94 *goal was existence'*; *in our civilization'*: Cowell, *Heart of the Forest*, 245.

94 *further cares'*: Jean de Léry, *Le Voyage au Brésil*, ed. Charly Clerc (Paris, 1927 [La Rochelle, 1578]), 172.

96 *bland diet'*: Basso, *Kalapalo Indians*, 28.

96 *male chiefs'*: Aritana Yawalapiti, in conversation with Sandra Wellington, 'My tribe, my people', *Observer Magazine*, London, 18 June 1989, 33.

97 *away from tasks'*: Cowell, *Heart of the Forest*, 223.

97 *Mehinaku sleep'*: Thomas Gregor, *Mehinaku: The Drama of Daily Life in a Brazilian Indian Village* (Chicago and London, 1977), 24.

CHAPTER 8. HEALTH

99 *booming voice'*: Carlos Azevedo, 'O Brasileiro Noel Nutels', *Realidade*, Aug. 1968; also profile in *Folha de S. Paulo*, 30 July 1966.

100 *I know'*: Arlindo Mungioli, 'Marina Villas Boas', *Última Hora*, 2 Oct. 1964.

100 *first expedition'*: Roberto G. Baruzzi, 'Do Araguaia ao Xingu', in Roberto Baruzzi and Carmen Junqueira, eds., *Parque Indígena do Xingu: Saúde, cultura e história* (São Paulo, 2005), 66. Orlando gave a different version, with Baruzzi making a miraculous cure of a groaning Indian woman and one of the post's workers declaring that he had 'a saintly hand'; and then recalled meeting Baruzzi again in São Paulo when he was treating a boy desperately ill from poisoning during his initiation seclusion.

101 *all ills'*; *comprehend'*: Orlando Villas Boas, 'Trinta e cinco anos de assistência e pesquisa: a Escola Paulista de Medicina e o Parque Indígena do Xingu', in Baruzzi and Junqueira, eds., *Parque Indígena do Xingu*, 55.

102 *traditional medicine'*: Baruzzi, 'Do Araguaia ao Xingu', 71–2.

102 *cure another'*: Marcos Faerman, 'Aventuras dos pajés brancos', *Jornal da Tarde*, 29 Nov. 1990.

102 *non-interference'*; *pharmacy'*: Bo Åkerren et al., *Report of the ICRC Medical Mission to the Brazilian Amazon Region* (Geneva, 1970). The three doctors came from Sweden, the Netherlands, and Germany, and the anthropologist was the Swiss René Fuerst (with whom I later travelled in Brazil).

104 *skin conditions'*: Dr Philip Hugh-Jones, in Anthony Smith, *Mato Grosso: Last Virgin Land* (London, 1971), 114.

105 *any other I know'*: Report by Professor Alexander Leaf to the Conselho Nacional de Pesquisas (CNPq), 1982, in Baruzzi and Junqueira, eds., *Parque Indígena do Xingu*, 90.

105 *lowland South America'*: Professor Stephen Hugh-Jones and Dr Christine Hugh-Jones, *Report to the Rainforest Foundation*, 1996. Professor Hugh-Jones was the son of Dr Philip Hugh-Jones who reported on the medical situation in the Xingu in 1968. The Escola Paulista de Medicina later became part of UNIFESP (Universidade Federal de São Paulo) and changed its name to that.

105 *making history'*: Orlando Villas Boas, 'Trinta e cinco anos', 55.

CHAPTER 9. TWO SOCIETIES

107 *ours'*: Berta Ribeiro, *Diário do Xingu* (Rio de Janeiro, 1979), 35.

108 *my work'*: Gregor, *Mehinaku*, xiv.

109 *frustrated failures'*; 109 personal communications; *of themselves'*: Interview with Orlando and Claudio by Sérgio Gomes and Joca Pereira, *Folha de S. Paulo*, 23 April 1978.

110 *bad-tempered'*: Aritana Yawalapiti, in Wellington, 'My tribe, my people', 30.

110 *love or attention'*: Carmen Junqueira, *Os índios de Ipavu: Um estudo sobre a vida do grupo Kamaiurá* (São Paulo, 1975), 89.

110 *contradicted'*; *smoke boy'"*: Villas Boas, *Almanaque do sertão*, 214.

111 *teach him'*: Orlando and Claudio Villas Boas, 'A cultura dos índios xinguanos', in Orlando Villas Bôas Filho, ed., *Orlando Villas Bôas: Expedições, reflexões e registros* (São Paulo, 2006), 13.

111 *a mediator'*; *not orders'*: Orlando and Claudio Villas Boas, 'Tribal territory', in Maureen Bisilliat, Orlando Villas-Boas, and Claudio Villas-Boas, *Xingu: Território tribal* (São Paulo, 1990), 45.

111 *battle'*: Michel de Montaigne, 'Des cannibales', *Essaies* (Bordeaux, 1580, and frequently republished).

112 *years of life'*: Washington Novaes, preface to Baruzzi and Junqueira, eds., *Parque Indígena do Xingu*, 16.

112 *the Villas Boas brothers'*; *that dignity'*: Marina Kahn, 'Morreu Paru, o grande embaixador do Alto Xingu', *Notícias Socioambiental*, São Paulo, 5 Nov. 2001.

112 *Paradise'*: Aritana Yawalapiti, in the launch Prospectus for *Kuarup: Organização Indígena do Xingu* (Rio de Janeiro, 1991).

113 *the same person'*: Darcy Ribeiro broadcast in 1985, in Baruzzi and Junqueira, eds., *Parque Indígena do Xingu*, 16.

113 *transport'*: Washington Novaes, preface to Baruzzi and Junqueira, eds., *Parque Indígena do Xingu*, 16.

113 *wants to command'*: Bisilliat and Villas-Boas, *Xingu: Território tribal*, 45.

world': Declaration by Orlando Villas Boas in 2002, in Baruzzi and Junqueira, eds., *Parque Indígena do Xingu*, 110.

113 *from their traditions'*: Villas Boas, *Almanaque do sertão*, 213.

114 *its fabric'*: Thomas Gregor, 'Exposure and seclusion: a study of institutionalized isolation among the Mehinaku Indians of Brazil', *Ethnology* (Pittsburgh) **9**:3, July 1970, 247.

114 *how to converse'*: Aritana Yawalapiti, in Wellington, 'My tribe, my people', 33.

114 *a man'*: Gregor, *Mehinaku*, 237.

115 *breathing rapidly'*; *gets better'*; 116 *went away'*: Julio Abramczyk, 'A medicina mágica dos índios do Xingu', *Folha de S. Paulo*, 30 Aug. 1966; also in Baruzzi and Junqueira, eds., *Parque Indígena do Xingu*, 138, 139.

116 *what they did'*; *situation'*; *hair'*: Villas Boas, *Almanaque do sertão*, 236, 237, 239.

116 *evil magic'*: Junqueira, *Os índios de Ipavu*, 98.

117 *the face exposed'*; *kill me now'*: Cowell, *Tribe that Hides*, 65, 34.

117 *fell ill'*: Oliveira, 'Os índios Juruna e sua cultura', 34. Tamacu was also known as Xatuná.

118 *moral strength'*; *just like that'*; *don't know'*; 119 *than animals'*: Cowell, *Tribe that Hides*, 45, 68.

121 *the situation'*; *hut'*; *hair'*: Villas Boas, *Almanaque do sertão*, 237, 238.

122 *don't know'*: Cowell, *Tribe that Hides*, 151.

CHAPTER 10. CHANGE

123 *needed for it'*; *than stone'*; 124 *small bag'*; *ammunition'*; *expectations'*: Carmen Junqueira, *The Brazilian Indigenous Problem and Policy: The Example of the Xingu National Park* (Copenhagen/Geneva, 1973), 18, 19.

125 *like to trade'*; *surrounding farms]'*; *very old'*; *Metuktire'*: Junqueira, *Os índios de Ipavu*, 101, 100.

126 *the Xingu Indians'*; *as never before'*: Gregor, *Mehinaku*, 20.

126 *they have clothes'*; *of wool'*; *and Indians here'*: A Kamaiurá interviewed by Carmen Junqueira, *Os índios de Ipavu*, 103–4.

126 *essentially intact'*: Gregor, *Mehinaku*, 20.

126 *Claudio and Orlando'*, Berta Ribeiro, *Diário*, 92.

127 *medical assistance'*; *upper-Xingu region'*: Renate Brigitte Viertler, *Os Kamayurá e o Alto Xingu*, Instituto de Estudos Brasileiros, Publicação 10 (São Paulo, 1969), 10.

127 *brutally'*; *factionalism'*: Rafael Bastos, 'Exegeses Yawalapity e Kamayurá da criação do Parque Indígena do Xingu e a invenção da saga dos irmãos Villas Boas', *Revista de Antropologia* 30–32, 1987–9, 395.

127 *cohabit with us'*: Darcy Ribeiro, 'Apresentação—os irmãos Villas Boas', in second edi-

tion of Villas Boas, *A Marcha para o Oeste* (São Paulo, 1994), 11. Orlando Villas Bôas Filho, ed., *Orlando Villas Bôas*, 642.

127 *in the Xingu Park'*: Interview with Francisco Meirelles, *O Globo*, 4 June 1973. Freire, 'Sagas sertanistas', 2.

128 *transformed into beggars'*: Edilson Martins, 'No adeus dos Villas Boas, a orfandade de uma cultura', *Jornal do Brasil*, 8 Jan. 1975. See also *Estado de São Paulo*, 31 May 1973.

128 *sealed environment'*; *ecological reality'*; *social cohesion'*: Pedro Agostinho da Silva, 'Information concerning the territorial and demographic situation in the Alto Xingu', in Walter Dostal, ed., *The Situation of the Indians in South America* (Geneva, 1972), 272.

128 *view the world'*: Cowell, *Tribe that Hides*, 103. The missionary Dale Snyder was from the Unevangelised Fields Mission, which had been working with northern Kayapó groups ever since the 1930s.

128 *whale is?'*: Orlando Villas Boas interviewed in *Veja*, 6 Aug. 1968.

129 *Brazilian society'*: Letter from General Rondon, Villas Boas family archive.

129 *Xingu Park'*: General Bandeira de Mello interview, *Folha da Tarde*, 10 March 1971; Shelton Davis, *Victims of the Miracle: Development and the Indians of Brazil* (Cambridge/New York, 1977), 59.

129 *that sort of people'*: Orlando Villas Boas in *Veja*, 6 Aug. 1968, 51.

129 *folklore'*: Orlando Villas Boas, speech to students of Osvaldo Cruz College in São Paulo, *Jornal do Brasil*, 28 Nov. 1975.

129 *by half'*: Interview with Orlando and Claudio Villas Boas by Sérgio Gomes and Joca Pereira, *Folha de S. Paulo*, 23 April 1978—and many other interviews, lectures, and writings.

130 *in Brazil'*; *twenty-five years'*: Robin Hanbury-Tenison, *Report of a Visit to the Indians of Brazil on Behalf of the Primitive Peoples' Fund/ Survival International, January–March 1971* (London, 1971), 9.

130 *long contact'*: Edwin Brooks, René Fuerst, John Hemming, and Francis Huxley, *Tribes of the Amazon Basin in Brazil, 1972* (London, 1973), 98, 124.

131 *in nature'*: José Maria Santos, 'Villas Boas: um marco na vida do índio', *Diario de S. Paulo*, 12 Sept., 1967.

131 *as an Indian'*: Junqueira, *The Brazilian Indigenous Problem and Policy*, 16.

131 *in his absence'*; 132 *their every need'*: Vivaldo Vieira, 'Retrato do Xingu', *O Popular*, 13 July 1969.

132 *perceptive anecdotes'*: Bisilliat, *Guerreiros sem espada*, 6.

132 *that forest'*: Don McCullin in 1969, quoted in Sue Branford, 'Crusade in the Amazon', *The Guardian*, 7 March 1998.

132 *speaking their language'*: David Nasser, 'Índio quer ser índio', *O Cruzeiro*, 2 June 1971.

132 *doctors, scientists, etc.'*: Diary of Dr Philip Hugh-Jones, quoted in Smith, *Mato Grosso*, 114.

133 *Vira Boa!'*: Rachel de Queiroz, 'Vira Boa', *Folha de Goiaz*, 21 Feb. 1973.

133 *civilized world'*: Edison Martins, 'Cláudio, paz e plenitude indígena', *Jornal do Brasil*, 21 April 1973.

NOTES AND REFERENCES

133 *valued man*': Interview with Claudio, 'O velho cacique branco', *Folha de São Paulo—Folhetim*, 23 April 1978.

134 *take charge*': Mairawê Kaiabi, 'O orgulho de ser índio', *Folha de S. Paulo*, 23 April 1978.

134 *of the Park*'; *with his people*'; *respect*': Berta Ribeiro, *Diário*, 92.

135 *Over …*'; *wrong times!*': Edilson Martins, 'No adeus dos Villas Boas, a orfandade de uma cultura', *Jornal do Brasil*, 8 Jan. 1975.

135 *I had won!*': José Maria Santos, 'Villas Boas: um marco na vida do índio', *Diario de S. Paulo*, 12 Sept. 1967.

135 *great new roads*': Edilson Martins, 'No adeus dos Villas Boas, a orfandade de uma cultura', *Jornal do Brasil*, 8 Jan. 1975.

135 *respect us*': Interview with Claudio Villas Boas, *O Estado de São Paulo*, 16 Dec. 1974.

CHAPTER 11. CONTACTS AND RESCUES

137 *in their lives*': Kalervo Oberg, 'Indian Tribes of Northern Mato Grosso', Smithsonian Institution, Institute of Social Anthropology, Publication **15**, 1953, 6. The anxiety of the Mehinaku is in Pedro Lima, 'Niveis tensionais dos índios Kalapalo e Kamayurá', *Revista Brasileira de Medicina* **7**:12 1950, 6. The 'adventurer' who armed the Waurá and Mehinaku in 1960 was an SPI official who had temporarily replaced the Villas Boas at Posto Capitão Vasconcellos (Leonardo). Expedito Arnaud, 'A ocupação indígena no Alto Xingu', *Boletim de Pesquisa da CEDEAM* (Manaus), **4**:6, Jan.–June 1985, 135–6; Berta Ribeiro, *Diário*, 24–5.

137 *seizing children*'; 138 *saved*': Villas Boas, *Marcha*, 582.

138 *to her village*': Patrick Menget, *Em nome dos outros* (Lisbon, 2001) 102, a translation of 'Au nom des autres: la classification des relations sociales chez les Txikão (Brésil)' doctoral thesis, École Pratique des Hautes Études (Paris, 1977), 87. Menget got this detailed information from the great photographer Jesco von Puttkamer, and from his own interrogations of the Ikpeng during two years of doctoral research in 1967–9. The SPI officials who in 1958 borrowed a plane from an American missionary were from its Culiseu post (on the upper Curisevo south of the park); and attempts at contact in 1959 were by agents from the José Bezerra post on the Paratininga.

138 *from them*'; 139 *escape the arrows*': Villas Boas, *Marcha*, 582, 584.

138 *they were gone*': Cowell, *Tribe that Hides*, 132.

138 *wept copiously*': Jorge Perreira, 'A expedição que não morreu', *O Cruzeiro*, 16 July 1955.

140 *[kidnapped] girls*': Simões, 'Os txikão e outras tribos', 92.

141 *demonstration of peace*': Villas Boas, *Marcha*, 587. Eduardo Galvão and Mário Simões, 'Notícia sobre os índios txikão, alto Xingu', *Boletim do Museu Paraense Emílio Goeldi*, n.s. *Antropologia* **24**, 1965, 5–7; Menezes, *Parque Indígena do Xingu*, 290. Also Orlando Villas Boas interview in Gildávio Ribeiro, 'Txikão foi forte e valente, mas hoje é índio raquítico', *Jornal do Brasil*, 12 Nov. 1967.

241

contact': Arley Pereira, 'Na aldeia com os selvagens', *Diario da Noite* (São Paulo), 17 Sept. 1965.

142 *would revisit'*; *our hands raised'* Villela, 56;

142 *with them'*: Arley Pereira, 'Finalmente o "Tchicão"', *Diario da Noite* (São Paulo), 15 Sept. 1965. The Villas Boas allowed this journalist and his photographer Antonio Moura to go on the expedition to cover the contact.

142 *arms outstretched'*; 143 *strategic manoeuvre'*: Murillo Villela, 'Uma experiência para guarder na memória', in Müller et al., eds., *O Xingu dos Villas Bôas*, 56.

143 *pandemonium'*: Arley Pereira, 'Finalmente o "Tchicão"'.

143 *in their hands'*: Villas Boas, *Marcha*, 587.

143 *about us'*: Villela, 'Uma experiência para guarder na memória', 56.

143 *after the contact'*: Pereira, 'Finalmente o "Tchicão"'.

144 *traditional parasites'*: Menget, *Em nome dos outros*, 105.

144 *intimidating their men'*; 144 *police agents'*: Cowell, *Tribe that Hides*, xii.

145 *wherever they passed'*: Baruzzi, 'Do Araguaia ao Xingu', 80.

145 *hostile glare'*: Gildávio Ribeiro, 'Txikão foi forte e valente, mas hoje é índio raquítico'.

146 *for the deceased'*: Menget, *Au nom des autres*, 87; Berta Ribeiro, *Diário*, 181–90.

146 *making others laugh'*: Vieira, 'Retrato do Xingu'.

147 *above all fish?'*": Canisio, chief of Capivara village, interviewed in Ferreira, *Histórias do Xingu*, vol. 2, 78–9; and Lea, *Parque Indígena do Xingu*, 120.

147 *[Brazilian] society'*; *Xingu'*: Pagliaro, 'A mudança dos Kaiabi', 209, 210.

147 *and his Mission'*: Father Bartolomé Meliá, SJ, 'Os caiabis não-Xinguanos', in Vera Penteado Coelho, ed., *Karl von den Steinen: Um século do antropologia no Xingu* (São Paulo, 1993), 503.

147 *into the Xingu'*: Pagliaro, 'A mudança dos Kaiabi', 120.

150 *did to us'*: The widow of Bentugaruru, recorded by Anthony Seeger in 1973, in Bruna Franchetto, 'A ocupação indígena da região dos formadores e do alto curso do rio Xingu' (1987) in Vanessa Lea, *Laudo Antropológico. Kapoto* (Campinas, 1997) 175. The *Jornal da Tarde*, 14 Feb. 1970 gave a full account of early contacts with the Tapayuna. This included a report by a Kaiabi, Cândido Morimã, who had worked from 1955 as a boatman for the original settlers, at Porto dos Gaúchos on the Arinos 500 kilometres north of Cuiabá.

151 *[Tapayuna]'*: Francisco Nélson, *O Cruzeiro*, 18 May 1969.

151 *adults and women'*: Rubens Valente, 2015 interview with Heydl Valle, in his *Os Fuzis e as Flechas*, 55.

152 *symptoms appeared'*: *Folha de Goiaz*, 19 May 1970. The *Estado de São Paulo* covered these events on 8 Oct. 1968 and 17 April, 22 May, 8 and 20 June 1969; as did other media. Its issue of 22 May 1969 reported the attack on the Jesuit missionaries, which was described by Father Adalberto Holanda Pereira, 'A pacificação dos Tapayuna (Beiço de Pau) até março de 1968', *Revista de Antropologia* **15/16**, 1968, 216–27.

152 *to what he said'*: Megaron Txucarramãe, 'A criação do Parque Indígena do Xingu' (dictated at Posto Leonardo in June 1990), in Ferreira et al., eds., *Histórias do Xingu*, 216.

153 *the pioneering frontier'*: Dr José de Queiroz Campos, president of Funai, *Jornal do Brasil*, 12 May 1970.

153 *any others'*: Orlando Villas Boas, interviewed in *O Globo* (Rio de Janeiro), 5 March 1971.

153 *national integration'*: Oscar Jerónimo Bandeira de Mello, quoted in *O Estado de São Paulo*, 23 April 1971. Junqueira, *The Brazilian Indigenous Problem and Policy*, 12.

153 *benefits to the Indians'*; *general mechanic'*; *region'*: Bandeira de Mello, speech in Campo Grande, *O Estado de S. Paulo*, 22 April 1971. Valente, *Os Fuzis e as Flechas*, 215.

153 *of the country'*: Bandeira de Mello, speaking in Brasilia, *Folha de S. Paulo*, 10 April 1971.

155 *progress'*: Bandeira de Mello, *Visão* magazine, 25 April 1971. The decree of 13 July 1971 is described in Lea, *Parque Indígena do Xingu*, 76–7, with its full text on p. 161. The general's corrupt practice is mentioned in Gerard Colby and Charlotte Dennett, *Thy Will be Done* (New York, 1995); Memelia Moreira described his drunken advances, in her blog 'A cor de asco', 2 April 2013; and he was no. 128 in a list of managers of operations leading to serious violations of human rights during the military years: *Relato Final*, Comissão da Verdade, Brasilia, 10 Dec. 2014.

156 *no room for people'*: Orlando Villas Boas, speaking at a conference of the School of Communications and Arts of the University of São Paulo, reported by the Ministry of the Interior's security department to its equivalent in Funai on 19 Dec. 1972, in Valente, *Os Fuzis e as Flechas*, 225. Valente also found that General Bandeira de Mello had studied the 1951 testimonies against Leonardo Villas Boas.

CHAPTER 12. PANARÁ

161 *above my head'*: Murillo Villela, in Müller et al, *O Xingu dos Villas Boas*, 57. The killing of Richard Mason in 1961 was extensively reported in the Brazilian and British press, notably in 'Morte no Rio Iriri', *O Cruzeiro*, 30 Sept. 1961 and John Hemming, 'Tragedy in the jungle', *Sunday Times*, 18 and 25 Feb. 1962.

161 *machine gun'*: Orlando Villas Boas, in Cowell, *Tribe that Hides*, 73; Villas Boas, *Almanaque do sertão*, 201.

162 *into the forest'*: Richard Heelas, 'The Social Organization of the Panara, a Gê Tribe of Central Brazil' (doctoral dissertation, Oxford University, 1979), 10–11. The massacre was first reported to the SPI/Funai in November 1967 by Richard Roche and Dale Snyder of the Christian Evangelical Mission, who were active at the Menkragnoti post on the Pitiatiá tributary of the Curuá: *O Estado de São Paulo*, 12 Dec. 1967. Verswijver, *Club-Fighters*, 145; Stephan Schwartzman, 'The Panará of the Xingu National Park: The Transformation of a Society' (doctoral thesis, University of Chicago, 1988), 292. The attack was on the Panará village of Sonkanasan.

162 *sheer butchery'*; *one of you!'*; *fell so'*; *killed him'*: Cowell, *Tribe that Hides*, 116, 117, 118.

162 *I do not forget'*: Pèritaw Panará interview in Stephan Schwartzman, *Os Panará do Peixoto de Azevedo e cabeceiras do Iriri: história, contato e transferência ao Parque do Xingu*

(Washington DC, 1992), II.A, 10; and in Ricardo Arnt, Lúcio Flávio Pinto, Raimundo Pinto, and Pedro Martinelli, *Panará: A volta dos índios gigantes* (São Paulo, 1998), 84.

162 *sweet potatoes]*'; 164 *devil*': Cowell, *Tribe that Hides*, 122, 166. The expedition was reported by Valdir Zwetsch, 'Kren-Akárore os índios gigantes da Amazônia', *O Cruzeiro*, 24 March 1971, 54–68.

164 *clubs and stone axes*': Villas Boas, *Marcha*, 515.

164 *such as stone axes*': Villela, 'Uma experiência para guarder na memória', 59.

165 *of our waiting*': Cowell, *Tribe that Hides*, 175, 180. Cowell learned about the Metuktire's unsuccessful 1970 raid from letters by the Summer Institute of Linguistics linguist Micky Stout, who had spent years with that people: see 260–3.

166 *road workers*'; *progressed slowly*': Claudio Villas Boas, interview in *Veja*, 4 April 1973; also quoted in Bisilliat, *Guerreiros sem espada*, 76.

166 *gaiety and laughter*': Villas Boas, *A Marcha*, 517; ESP, 1 Dec. 1972; Arnt et al., *Panará*, 87–8; R. G. Baruzzi et al., 'The Kren-Akorore: a recently contacted indigenous tribe', in K. Elliott and J. Whelan, eds., *Health and Disease in Tribal Societies*, Ciba Foundation Symposium **49** (Amsterdam, 1977), 183.

166 *one of happiness*': Diary of the journalist Luigi Mamprin for 26 June and 5 July 1972, quoted in 'Os Villas Boas e os índios gigantes e outras aventuras', *Veja*, 9 Nov. 1972. The early months of the attraction expedition were reported by Mário Chimanovitch in the *Jornal do Brasil*, 16 May, 30 May, 3 June, 21 June, and 26 June 1972; by Estevaldo Dias and Pedro Martinelli, 'Mais uma vez, os Krain-a-Kore fugiram ao diálogo', *O Globo*, 13 May, 14 May, 15 July, 30 July, and 13 August 1972; by Luis Salgado Ribeiro in *O Estado de São Paulo* and also *O Cruzeiro*, Carnaval issue 1972.

167 *desolate panorama*'; *charcoal and ash*': *Veja*, 9 Nov. 1972.

168 *kill us*': Teseya Panará, talking to Stephan Schwartzman in 1994, in Arnt et al., *Panará*, 104.

168 *is patience*': Interview with Claudio Villas Boas, *O Estado de São Paulo*, 20 Aug. and 12 Nov. 1972.

168 *to death*': Orlando Villas Boas, *Jornal do Brasil*, 6 Feb. 1973.

168 *little noise*'; *in the forest*': Claudio Villas Boas diary, quoted in *Veja*, 9 Nov. 1972, 50, 51.

169 *tree trunk*': Luigi Mamprin's diary, in *Veja*, 14 Feb. 1973; Arnt et al., *Panará*, 90.

169 *contact, at last*': Estevaldo Dias and Pedro Martinelli, 'Os gigantes, finalments', *Veja*, 14 Feb. 1973; also in Arnt et al., *Panará*, 90. Luiz Macopito, 'Amarga renúncia à terra de origem', in Baruzzi and Junqueira, eds., *Parque Indígena do Xingu: Saúde*, 169–70.

169 *remained there quietly*': Teseya Panará to Stephan Schwartzman, 1994, in Arnt et al., *Panará*, 106.

169 *for a long time*': *Jornal do Brasil*, 8 Jan 1975.

169 *vice-versa*': Orlando Villas Boas, in Takao Miyagui, 'Kranhakarore, os machões da selva', *Manchete*, 24 Feb. 1973. José Marqueiz gave an accurate account of this second meeting: 'O novo encontro, uma festa na selva', *O Estado de São Paulo*, 10 Feb. 1973.

170 *indicated age'*; *was we'*; *emerged from there'*: Megaron Metuktire, 'A criação do Parque Indígena do Xingu' (dictated at Posto Leonardo, 1990), in Ferreira, ed., *Histórias do Xingu*, 216–17.

171 *great tears!'*; *they dance'*; *war clubs'*; *too sick with fever to walk'*: Jesco von Puttkamer, 'Brazil's Kreen-Akarores: requiem for a tribe?', *National Geographic* **147**:2, Feb. 1975, 264. Apoena Meirelles, 'A técnica que atraiu os Kreen-Akarore', *Revista de Atualidade Indígena* **3**:18, Sept.-Oct. 1979. Apoena's visit to the village was also reported by Estevaldo Dias and Pedro Martinelli in *O Globo*, 12 Aug. and 14 Aug. 1973.

172 *farther north'*: Odemir Pinto de Oliveira, interviewed in Arnt et al., *Panará*, 97. The Funai official who denounced the homosexual behaviour of Antonio Sousa Campinas was Ezequias Heringer in a report to Funai of 28 December 1973. Campinas was also accused of having sex with Indian women and underage girls. Schwartzman, 'The Panará of the Xingu National Park', 307–9; Arnt et al., *Panará*, 93.

172 *there were only burials'*: Fiorello Parise, *Relatório parcial apresentado ao Il. Sr. Coordenador da Amazônia* (Funai, 1975), in Arnt et al., *Panará*, 96.

173 *had not been buried'*: Akè Panará talking to Schwartzman, 29 Oct. 1991, in *Os Panará do Peixoto de Azevedo*, II B.

173 *died there'*; *happen to us?'''*: Teseya Panará to Schwartzman, 1994, in Arnt et al., *Panará*, 105.

173 *so many people'*: Schwartzman, 'The Panará of the Xingu National Park', 301.

174 *of its sertanista'*: Report to Funai by Valéria Parise, 4 Jan. 1974, in Arnt et al., *Panará*, 112.

174 *problems for Funai'*: José Marqueiz, 'Pedida interdição da região dos "gigantes"', *O Estado de S. Paulo*, 8 Nov. 1972. The request was made to Colonel Olavo Mendes, head of the Transamazonica Sub-coordination, in Manaus.

175 *transfer plan'*: General Ismarth Araújo de Oliveira's instructions to Fiorello Parisi, late 1973, in Arnt et al., *Panará*, 96. Orlando's denunciation of the transfer as crazy was in *O Estado de São Paulo*, 23 Jan. 1972.

175 *satisfactory solution'*: Interview with Claudio Villas Boas, *Opinião*, 25 March 1974; Jane Monahan, 'Doomed tribe', *Sunday Times*, 18 April 1974.

175 *bureaucracy'*; *transfer them!'*: General Ismarth de Araújo Oliveira, speaking in Aurélio Michiles's documentary *O Brasil Grande e os Índios Gigantes* (ISA, São Paulo, 1995); Valente, *Os Fuzis e as Flechas*, 135.

175 *to another'*: Parisi, in Arnt et al., *Panará*, 98; Schwartzman, 'The Panará of the Xingu National Park', 312–13. General Ismarth's 'Ofício' removing the interdiction on a possible Panará reserve was no. 058 of 1975, and the Decree nullifying the reserve was no. 83.541 of 4 June 1979. The report about colonization potential was from the Superintendência de Assuntos Fundiários to the Ministry of the Interior, 6 May 1976: Valente, *Os Fuzis e as Flechas*, 138–9.

176 *all their land'*: Megaron, 'A criação do Parque Indígena do Xingu', in Ferreira, ed., *Histórias do Xingu*, 217.

177 *to the seat'*: Sokriti Panará to Stephan Schwartzman, 1991, in Arnt et al., *Panará*, 116;

Schwartzman, 'The Panará of the Xingu National Park', 316; Baruzzi et al., 'The Kren-Akorore', 186–8. The favourable contemporary report of the transfer was by Mário Antonio Garofalo, 'Os últimos Kren-Akarores', *Manchete*, 1 Feb. 1975, 4–11. Criticism of the airlift came from Father Iasi of the Missão Anchieta, from the journalist Memélia Moreira in an interview with Ricardo Arnt in 1992, and Dr Luiz F. Marcopito, 'Kreen-Akarore: Amarga renúncia à terra de origem', *Revista de Atualidade Indígena* 3:19, Nov.–Dec. 1979. Also: Edilson Martins, *Nossos índios, nossos mortos* (Rio de Janeiro, 1978), 83–8; Luiz Beltrão, *O índio, um mito brasileiro* (Petropolis, 1977), 97–126. Odenir Pinto de Oliveira told Rubens Valente about the Panará thinking that they were just going on an excursion, in an interview in 2013: Valente, *Os Fuzis e as Flechas*, 136.

177 *violent humiliation*': Luiz Marcopito, 'Amarga renúncia à terra de origem', in Baruzzi and Junqueira, eds., *Parque Indígena do Xingu*, 172.

177 *state of health*': Baruzzi et al., 'The Kren-Akorore', 198.

178 *I was born*': Akè Panará, in Brian Moser's film *Before Columbus* (October 1991).

178 *to our village*': Akè Panará, interview in 1991, in Schwartzman, *Os Panará do Peixoto de Azevedo*, IV.

CHAPTER 13. RETIREMENT

180 *untouchable*': Edinilton Araujo, *O Estado de S. Paulo*, 6 Oct. 1976.

181 *never end*'; *lived them*'; *the Villas Boas*': tributes by Antonio Callado (1917–97) and Darcy Ribeiro (1913–97) in 'Apresentação', foreword to Villas Boas, *Marcha*, 13, 11; also in Müller et al., eds., *O Xingu dos Villas Bôas*, 38.

181 *physical survival*': Tatiana Belinki, in *Jornal da Tarde*, 21 July 1984.

182 *cause*': Interview in *O Globo*, 1 July 1973. Some of the many articles when they retired included: 'Os irmãos da selva', *Veja*, 8 Nov. 1972; 'Nos adeus dos Villas Bôas a orfandade de uma cultura', *Jornal do Brasil*, 8 Jan. 1975; 'Memórias dos irmãos Villas Bôas', *Visão*, 10 Feb. 1975; 'Cláudio Villas Bôas, um sertanista longe do sertão', *O Globo*, 16 Mar. 1976; 'Um povo condenado à morte', *A Crítica*, Manaus, 8 April 1976; 'Quando os índios estiverem totalmente exterminados então estaremos mesmo perdidos', *O Estado de S. Paulo*, 6 Oct. 1976; 'O velho cacique branco' (also about Claudio), *Folha de S P/Folhetim*, 23 April 1978; 'Villas Bôas: integrar é destruir o índio', *O Estado de S Paulo*, 4 Feb. 1979; 'Visões de um sertanista', *Istoé*, 21 Nov. 1979. Funai in the early 1970s published the *Boletim Informativo da FUNAI*, from 1976 *Revista de Atualidade Indígena*, and in 2000 it started *Brasil Indígena*—all of which had regular reminiscences by the Villas Boas.

183 *functionary*': Deputy Mário Juruna, *Jornal do Brasil*, 19 Nov. 1980.

185 *Xingu culture*': Kenneth Brecher, 'Foreword' to the English-language edition of Villas Boas, *Xingu:The Indians*, ix. Despite his brilliant writings and broadcasts (on the BBC) about the Waurá, Brecher moved away from anthropology into the theatre, museum, and cultural world of Los Angeles. Maureen Bisilliat (married to a Frenchman) was born and trained in photography in England, but lived and worked in Brazil from

1952 onwards. Her book was published in 1979 as *Xingu: Tribal Territory* with the text by the Villas Boas only in English, then republished in 1990 as *Xingu: Território tribal*, in both Portuguese and English.

185 *so readable'*; *under their spell'*: Kenneth Brecher, in an article by Stuart Wavell, *Guardian Extra*, London, 11 June 1974.

187 *without reserve'*: Letter by Maria Heloísa Fénelon Costa (anthropologist of the Museu National) to the Société des Américanistes de Paris, about the Nobel nomination, 22 Jan. 1970, in Funai's Archive in Brasilia.

CHAPTER 14. LEGACY

190 *lose our land'*: *Memória do Xingu* (a newsletter started by Xinguanos in 1981), quoted in *ARC Bulletin* (Boston), **10**, Feb. 1982.

193 *understand the other'*: Megaron Txukarramãe, 'A história do povo Txukarramãe' (1980), in Ferreira et al., eds., *Histórias do Xingu*, 209. (Megaron later changed his tribal name to Metuktire.)

193 *white man'*; Mairawê Kaiabi, 'O orgulho de ser índio', *Folha de São Paulo*, 23 April 1978.

193 *destroying them'*: Aritana Yawalapiti, Launch Prospectus for 'Kuarup, Organização Indígena do Xingu', Rio de Janeiro, 1991.

194 *treats the land'*; *fighting together'*: Afukaká Kuikuro, interviewed by Carlos Fausto, in Felipe Milanez, ed., *Memórias sertanistas: cem anos de indigenismo no Brasil* (São Paulo, 2015), 92, 95, 92.

194 *exploiting the other'*: Mairawê Kaiabi, 'O orgulho de ser índio', *Folha de São Paulo*, 23 April 1978.

194 *human beings behave'*; *anger'*; *control over himself'*: a Waurá speaking, in Ireland, 'Cerebral savage'.

194 *he doesn't know'*: Brecher, 'Foreword', xi.

196 *lost my customs'*: Mairawê Kaiabi, 'O orgulho de ser índio', *Folha de São Paulo*, 23 April 1978.

197 *left to us?'*; *killed many people'*: Letter by Megaron Txukarramãe [Metuktire], Kretire village, 1 Nov. 1980, *Survival International Review* **6**:2 (34), Summer 1981, 75–6. Megaron also described these events and his role in them in Márcio Souza et al., *Os índios vão à luta* (Rio de Janeiro, 1981), 59–63. The decree that changed the shape of the Xingu Park was 68.909 of 13 July 1971; the creation of P. I. Jarina was Funai *Portaria* 369/N of 26 May 1976: texts of these two edicts are in Lea, *Parque Indígena do Xingu*, 161–2.

197 *didn't die'*: Megaron, talking to Rubens Valente in 2014, in his *Os Fuzis e as Flechas*, 327.

198 *too hard'*; *they died'*: Letter from Megaron to the British film-maker Chris Kelly, 5 Sept. 1980, *Survival International Review* **5**:3–4 (31–2), Autumn/Winter 1980, 27. Rauni helped Kelly to co-produce a documentary film about himself. Its English version was narrated by Marlon Brando and it gained an Oscar nomination.

NOTES AND REFERENCES

198 *twelve hours later*: 'Violence in Xingu National Park', *Time*, 8 Sept. 1980; Stuart Wavell, 'Wounded Indians fight for their land', *The Guardian*, London, 15 Oct. 1980.

199 *enter our lands*: Rauni quoted in *O Globo* (Rio de Janeiro), 13 Aug. 1980.

199 *hunting grounds*: Orlando Villas Boas, *Estado de São Paulo*, 7 Sept. 1980.

199 *I kill them*; *no game left*: Jean-Pierre Dutilleux, introduced by Norman Lewis, 'The tribe that won't surrender', *Observer Magazine*, London, 25 Jan. 1981, 35.

200 *ready to fight*: *O Globo*, 31 March 1984. A blow-by-blow account of the events of 1984 is Vanessa Lea and Mariana Kawall Leal Ferreira, '"A guerra no Xingú": cronologia', in *Povos Indígenas no Brasil / 1984* (São Paulo, 1984), 246–58.

200 *the [Panará]*: Ipó Kaiabi, in Lea, *Parque Indígena do Xingu*, 121; and Vanessa Lea, *Área Indígena Kapoto: Laudo antropológico* (São Paulo, 1997), 105–6.

201 *celebrate their conquest*; *without having to kill*: Marina Wodtke, 'Consenso no Xingu', *Manchete*, 19 May 1984.

201 *by the Indians*: *Jornal do Brasil*, 4 May 1984.

201 *respect their farms*: *Cidade de Santos*, 30 Oct. 1984, in Lea and Ferreira, '"A guerra no Xingú"', 258.

202 *your dam*; 203 *are Indians*: Nicholas Hildyard, 'Adios Amazonia?', *Ecologist*, London, **19**:2, 1989, 53.

203 *mutilated by progress*; *Levi's*: Brian Jackman, 'Singing in the Rain Forest', *Sunday Times*, London, 3 April 1988, 37.

   land: Article signed by Maírawe Kayabi and others, *Memória do Xingú* newsletter, quoted in *ARC Bulletin* (Boston), **10**, Feb. 1982, 7.

204 *for all of you*: Rauni on TV in Geneva, *A Crítica*, 20 June 2001.

204 *we need the help*: Megaron, March 2003, *Povos Indígenas no Brasil, 2001/2005* (São Paulo, 2006), 524.

   Indians: José Uté Gorotire, ESP, 7 Sept. 1980.

206 *hours on end*: Dr Luiz Marcopito, 'Amarga renúncia à terra de origem', *Revista de Atualidade Indígena*, Brasília, **3**:19, Nov.-Dec. 1979, 138.

207 *I was born*: Akè Panará, talking in a documentary film by Brian Moser, 1991.

208 *damages*: Judgment of Judge Novély Vilanova da Silva Reis in favour of the Action for Reparation of Damages, Brasilia, 22 Oct. 1997, in Arnt et al., *Panará*, 125–6. The family of each dead Indian received damages of two *salário mínimo* (the minimum wage, fixed regularly by the government) per month for his full life expectancy, plus four thousand 'minimum wages' as compensation to the tribe as a whole. This unprecedented award was routinely challenged, but upheld by the regional tribunal of Brasilia on 14 September 2000 with the compensation fixed at 1 million reals (about $1 million). Payment of the damages was divided equally between the Brazilian Republic and Funai. Funai's *Parecer* (legal opinion) interdicting the area was no. 179 of 14 December 1994; and the confirmation of the reserve was Funai's Portaria 667 signed by the minister of justice on 1 Nov. 1996. The perimeter of the forest reserve was demarcated with a 6-metre cleared strip cut during 1998 and 1999. The events surrounding the return of the Panará were also given in Stephan

Schwartzman, 'Panará: a saga dos índios gigantes', *Ciência Hoje* **20**:119, April 1996, 26–35; and his 'The Panará: indigenous territory and environmental protection in the Amazon', in Greg Dicum, ed., *Local Heritage in the Changing Tropics: Innovative Strategies for Natural Resource Management and Control* (New Haven, 1995); and Marleine Cohen, 'O caminho de volta: a saga dos gigantes Panará', *Povos Indígenas no Brasil 1991/1995*, 601–613. This contains the lawyer Márcio Santilli's findings of the seriousness of the threat to the Panarás' surviving forests from ruthless land speculators and timber men.

210 *bad white men'*; *you want'*: Teseya Panará talking to the author, Nacepotiti, July 1998. Also John Hemming, 'Return to the Iriri', *The Times Magazine*, 2 January 1999. In another version, told to Brian Moser, the group that killed Mason came from Yopuyupaw ('Village of the Round Fish'). They had gone to gather Brazil nuts, which abound on the upper Iriri, and to hunt.

211 *in Brazil'*: Zarur, 'A revolução dos Villas-Boas'.

211 *whites, farmers'*: Afukaká, interview with Carlos Fausto, in Milanez, *Memórias sertanistas*, 92.

213 *lives here'*: Kuiussi Suiá, June 2011, in *Povos Indígenas no Brasil 2006/2010* (São Paulo, 2011), 594.

213 *our own leaders'*: 'Carta final do 1 Festival de Culturas Xinguanos', Ipavu village, 10–12 June 2011, in Idem, 595.

BIBLIOGRAPHY

ABOIM, Raymundo Vasconcellos, Heloisa Alberto TORRES, Orlando VILLAS BOAS, and Darcy RIBEIRO: Letter to Vice-President José Café Filho, 27 April 1952, enclosing 'Ante-Projeto de Lei, Cria o Parque Indígena do Xingu e dispõe sôbre sua organização', in José M. da Gama Malcher, *S.P.I.*—*1953* (Serviço de Proteção aos Índios, 1953), 98–106; also, with Decreto 50,455, 14 April 1961, in Vanessa R. Lea, *Parque Indígena do Xingu: Laudo antropológico* (IFCH/Unicamp, Campinas, 1977), 148–61.

'A verdade sôbre o Parque Indígena do Xingú', *Tribuna da Imprensa* (Rio de Janeiro, 26 July 1955).

AGOSTINHO DA SILVA, Pedro: 'Geografia e cultura no alto Xingu', *Geografia* **3**:12 (Lisbon, 1967), 20–31.

'Informe sobre a situação territorial e demográfica no alto Xingu', in Georg Grünberg, ed., *La Situación del Indígena en América del Sur* (Tierra Nueva, Montevideo, 1972), 355–80; trans. as 'Information concerning the territorial and demographic situation in the Alto Xingu', in Walter Dostal, ed., *The Situation of the Indian in South America* (World Council of Churches, Geneva, 1972), 252–83.

Kwarip: Mito e ritual no Alto Xingu (EPU and Edusp, São Paulo, 1974).

Mitos e outras narrativas Kamayurá (Universidade Federal da Bahia, Salvador, 1974).

ÅKERREN, Bo, Sjouke BAKKER, Rolf HABERSANG: *Report of the ICRC Medical Mission to the Brazilian Amazon Region* (Comité International de la Croix-Rouge, Geneva, 1970).

ARNAUD, Expedito: 'A ocupação indígena no Alto Xingu', *Boletim de Pesquisa da CEDEAM* (Universidade do Amazonas, Manaus) **4**:6, Jan.–June 1985, 125–59.

ARNT, Ricardo: 'Índios gigantes: uma história com um grande final feliz', *Superinteressante* **10**:12, 1996, 36–45.

and Lúcio Flávio PINTO, Raimundo PINTO, and Pedro MARTINELLI: *Panará: A volta dos índios gigantes* (Instituto Socioambiental, São Paulo, 1998).

BAER, Gerhard: 'Beiträge zur Kenntnis des Xingu-Quellgebiets' (doctoral thesis, University of Basel, 1960, 1962).

BARUZZI, Roberto G.: 'Escola Paulista de Medicina: 16 anos atendendo os índios', *Revista de Atualidade Indigenista*, **21**, July–Aug. 1981, 62–6.

'Do Araguaia ao Xingu', in Roberto C. Baruzzi and Carmen Junqueira, eds., *Parque Indígena do Xingu: Saúde, cultura e história* (Terra Virgem, Universidade Federal de São Paulo, 2005), 59–112.

BIBLIOGRAPHY

'Minha vida e o Parque Indígena do Xingu', in Daisy Peccinini, ed., *Sacralidade da vida: Índios do Xingu e médicos da Escola Paulista de Medicina* (Instituto Victor Brecheret, São Paulo, 2012), 13–19.

and Magid IUNES: *Levantamento das condições de saúde das tribos indígenas do Alto Xingu* (Escola Paulista de Medicina, São Paulo, 1970).

and Carmen JUNQUEIRA, eds: *Parque Indígena do Xingu: Saúde, cultura e história* (Terra Virgem, Universidade Federal de São Paulo, 2005).

and L. F. MARCOPITO, M. L. C. SERRA, F. A. A. SOUZA, and C. STABILE: 'The Kren-Akorore: a recently contacted indigenous tribe', in K. Elliott and J. Whelan, eds., *Health and Disease in Tribal Societies*, Ciba Foundation Symposium **3**:19 (Elsevier North-Holland, Amsterdam, August 1977), 179–211.

BASSO, Ellen Becker: *The Kalapalo Indians of Central Brazil* (Holt, Rinehart & Winston, New York, 1973).

The Last Cannibals: A South American Oral History (University of Texas Press, Austin, 1995).

BASTOS, Rafael José de Menezes: 'Sistemas politicos de comunicação e articulação social no Alto Xingu', *Anuário Antropológico* **81**, 1981.

'"Cargo Anti-Cult" no Alto Xingu: consciência política e legítima defesa étnica', *Boletim de Ciências Sociais* (Florianópolis) **38**, July–Sept. 1985, 1–36.

'O "payemeramaraka" Kamayurá—Uma contribuição à etnografia do xamanismo do Alto Xingu', *Revista de Antropologia* **27/8**, 1984–5, 139–75.

'Exegeses Yawalapity e Kamayurá da criação do Parque Indígena do Xingu e a invenção da saga dos irmãos Villas Boas', *Revista de Antropologia* **30–32**, 1987–9, 391–426; also ANPOCS, Campos do Jordão, 1986.

'Indagação sobre os Kamayurá, o Alto-Xingu e outros nomes e coisas: uma etnologia da sociedade Xinguara', *Anuário Antropológico* (Tempo Brasileiro, Rio de Janeiro) **94**, 1995, 227–69.

BISCH, Jorgen: *Across the River of Death* (Souvenir Press, London, 1958).

BISILLIAT, Maureen, Orlando VILLAS-BÔAS, and Cláudio VILLAS BÔAS: *Xingu, Tribal Territory* (Collins, London, 1979); revised and bilingual as *Xingu: Território tribal* (Cultura, São Paulo, 1990).

Guerreiros sem espada: Experiências revistas dos irmãos Villas Bôas (Empresa das Artes, São Paulo, 1995).

BLANCO, Michel, Júlia MAGALHÃES, Marina VILLAS BÔAS, and Christiane PERES: 'Especial Parque Indígena do Xingu', *Brasil Indígena* **3**:3, July–Sept. 2006, 8–23.

BODARD, Lucien: *Le Massacre des Indiens* (Éditions Gallimard, Paris, 1969); trans. as *Green Hell* (Outerbridge & Dientsfrey, New York, 1971).

BRECHER, Kenneth S.: 'Foreword', in Orlando Villas Boas and Claudio Villas Boas, *Xingu: The Indians, their Myths* (Farrar, Straus & Giroux, New York, 1974; Souvenir Press, London, 2004), vii–xii.

BROOKS, Edwin, René FUERST, John HEMMING, and Francis HUXLEY: *Tribes of the Amazon Basin in Brazil, 1972*, Aborigines Protection Society (Charles Knight & Co., London, 1973).

BIBLIOGRAPHY

CAMARGO, Lúcia Helena de: 'Orlando: Vida em família', in Cristina Müller, Luiz Octavio Lima, and Moisés Rabinovici, eds., *O Xingu dos Villas Bôas* (São Paulo, 2002), 30–7.

CAMPANILI, Maura: 'O entorno do Parque' and 'Panarás: índios gigantes reconquistam a terra original', in Cristina Müller, Luiz Octavio Lima, and Moisés Rabinovici, eds., *O Xingu dos Villas Bôas* (São Paulo, 2002), 78–85.

CAPOZZOLI, Ulisses, ed.: 'Patrimônio cultural do Xingu: O começo do fim?', *Scientific American. Brasil*, edição especial **44** (São Paulo, 2011). This contains his 'A sombra longa do homem branco', 10–17; 'O aperto da Sucuri', 18–21; 'A vida como era há muito tempo', 22–7; 'Os Kayapó mudaram pouco em muito tempo', 74–9.

CARNEIRO, Robert L.: 'Extra-marital sex freedom among the Kuikuru Indians of Mato Grosso', *Revista do Museu Paulista* **10**, 1958, 135–42.

'Slash-and-burn cultivation among the Kuikuru and its implications for the cultural development in the Amazon Basin', in Johannes Wilbert, ed., *The Evolution of Horticultural Systems in Native South America* (Antropológica, Caracas, 1961), 47–67; also in Daniel Gross, ed., *Peoples and Cultures of Native South America* (Doubleday, Garden City, New York, 1973), 98–125.

and Gertrude E. DOLE: 'La cultura de los indios Kuikurus del Brasil Central', *Runa* (Buenos Aires) **8**, 1956–7, 169–202.

CARVALHO, José C. M., Pedro E. de LIMA, and Eduardo GALVÃO: *Observações zoológicas e antropológicas na região dos formadores do Xingu*, Museu Nacional, Publicações Avulsas **5** (Imprensa Nacional, Rio de Janeiro, 1949).

CEDI (Centro Ecumênico de Documentação e Informação): *Povos Indígenas no Brasil [PIB]* (a compendium of articles, reports, media and statistics about Indians) *PIB/1981, PIB/1982, PIB/83, PIB/1984, PIB-85/86, PIB 1987/88/89/90*. CEDI then changed its name to ISA (Instituto Socioambiental) and continued the series: *PIB 1996–2000, PIB 2001/2005*, etc., latterly edited by Beto Ricardo.

COCOLO, Ana Cristina: 'Há 50 anos cuidando da saúde dos povos indígenas', *Entre Teses* (Universidade Federal de São Paulo) **5**, Nov. 2015, 20–30.

COELHO, Vera Penteado, ed.: *Karl von den Steinen: Um século de antropologia no Xingu* (Edusp/Fapesp, Universidade de São Paulo, 1993).

COHEN, Marleine: 'O caminho de volta: A saga dos gigantes Panará', in Carlos Alberto Ricardo, ed., *Povos Indígenas no Brasil 1991/1995* (Instituto Socioambiental, São Paulo, 1996), 601–13.

COSTA E SÁ, Cristina da, Bacellar CORRÊA, Eduardo HENRIQUE: 'Habitação indígena no alto Xingu', *Encontros com a Civilização Brasileira* **12**, Rio de Janeiro, 1979.

COWELL, Adrian: 'Why they killed the Colonel', *Sunday Times*, 21 Sept. 1958.

The Heart of the Forest (Victor Gollancz, London, 1960).

'The dying tribes', *Sunday Times: Colour Section*, 18 Nov. 1962, 3–11.

'Legendary Brothers of the Amazon', *Observer Magazine*, 20 June 1971, 12–25.

The Decade of Destruction: The Crusade to Save the Amazon Rain Forest (Henry Holt & Co., New York, 1990).

BIBLIOGRAPHY

The Tribe that Hides from Man (Bodley Head, London, 1973; Stein & Day, New York, 1973; Pimlico, London, 1995).

'Return from extinction', *Last of the Hiding Tribes* (Nomad, London, 1999).

CUNHA, Ayres Câmara: *Entre os Índios do Xingu: A verdadeira história de Diacuí* (Livraria Exposição do Livro, São Paulo, 1960).

CUNHA, Manuela M. Carneiro da, ed.: *História dos índios no Brasil* (Companhia das Letras, São Paulo, 1992).

CUNNINGHAM, Sue, and Ghillean T. PRANCE: *Out of the Amazon* (Royal Botanic Gardens, Kew, HMSO, London, 1992).

DAVIS, Shelton: *Victims of the Miracle: Development and the Indians of Brazil* (Cambridge University Press, Cambridge/New York, 1977).

and Patrick MENGET: 'Povos primitivos e ideologias civilizadas no Brasil', in Carmen Junqueira and Edgard de A. Carvalho, eds., *Antropologia e Indigenismo na América Latina* (Cortez, São Paulo, 1981), 37–65.

DOLE, Gertrude E.: 'Ownership and exchange among the Kuikuru Indians of Mato Grosso', *Revista do Museu Paulista* **10** (São Paulo), 1958, 125–33.

'A preliminary consideration of the prehistory of the Upper Xingu basin', *Revista do Museu Paulista* **13**, 1962, 399–423.

'Shamanism and political control among the Kuikuru', *Beiträge zur Völkenkunde Sudamerikas* (Hanover, 1964).

'Anarchy without chaos: alternatives to political authority among the Kuikuru', in Marc J. Schwartz, Victor W. Turner, and Arthur Tuden, eds., *Political Anthropology* (Aldine Press, Chicago, 1966).

'Retrospectiva da história comparative das culturas do Alto Xingu: Um esboço das origens culturais alto-xinguanas', in Bruna Franchetto and Michael Heckenberger, eds., *Os Povos do Alto Xingu: História e cultura* (Editora UFRJ, Rio de Janeiro, 2001), 63–76.

DYOTT, George Miller: 'The Search for Colonel Fawcett', *Geographical Journal* (London) **72**, 1928, 443–8 and **74**, 1929, 513–40.

Man Hunting in the Jungle: The Search for Colonel Fawcett (Edward Arnold & Co., London, 1930).

EHRENREICH, Paul, 'Beiträge zur Völkerkunde Brasiliens', *Veröffentlichungen aus dem königlichen Museum für Völkerkunde* **2** (Berlin), 1891; trans. Egon Schaden as 'A segunda expedição alemã ao rio Xingu', *Revista do Museu Paulista* **16**, 1929, 247–75.

EWART, Elizabeth: *Space and Society in Central Brazil: A Panará Ethnography*, London School of Economics, Monographs on Social Anthropology **80** (Bloomsbury, London, 2013).

FAUSTO, Carlos: 'A ocupação indígena do alto curso dos formadores do rio Xingu e a cartografia sagrada altoxinguana', *Laudo Antropológico para o Ministério Público Federal* (ms. Mato Grosso, 2004).

'Entre o passado e o presente: Mil anos de história indígena no Alto Xingu', *Revista de Estudos e Pesquisas* (FUNAI, Brasília) **2**:2, 2005, 9–51.

FAWCETT, Percy Harrison: *Exploration Fawcett* (ed. Brian Fawcett) (Hutchinson & Co., London, 1953); published in the USA as *Lost Trails, Lost Cities* (New York, 1953).

254

BIBLIOGRAPHY

FERRAZ, Iara, and Mariano MAMPIERI: 'Suiá-Missu: um mito refeito', *Carta* (Gabinete do Senador Darcy Ribeiro, Brasília) **9**, 1993, 75–94.

FERRAZ, Silvio: 'Os guardiães do verde', *Veja*, 30 June 1999, 130–43.

FERREIRA, Jorge: 'Kuarup', *O Cruzeiro*, **29**:15, Rio de Janeiro, 26 Jan. 1957, 58–71.

FERREIRA, Manoel Rodrigues: *Nos sertões do lendário Rio das Mortes* (Editora do Brasil, São Paulo, 1946).

'Aspectos do Alto Xingu' e a Vera Cruz (Nobel, São Paulo, 1983).

FERREIRA, Mariana Kawall Leal: *Histórias do Xingu: Coletânea de depoimentos dos índios Suyá, Kayabi, Juruna, Trumai, Txucarramãe e Txicão* (NHII/USP/Fapesp, São Paulo, 1994).

FLEMING, Peter: *Brazilian Adventure* (Jonathan Cape, London, 1933).

FRANCHETTO, Bruna: 'Turbulência Xinguana', *Povos Indígenas no Brasil/1983* (CEDI (Centro Ecumênico de Documentação e Informação), São Paulo, 1983), 180–1.

Laudo Antropológico: A ocupação indígena da região dos formadores e do alto curso do Rio Xingu (Museu Nacional/Universidade Federal do Rio de Janeiro, Rio de Janeiro, 1987).

'"O aparecimento dos caraíbas": Para uma história kuikuro e alto-xinguana', in Manuela Carneiro da Cunha, ed., *História dos Índios no Brasil* (São Paulo, 1992), 339–56.

'Parque Indígena do Xingu', in Ivar Busatto and Maurício Barcellos, eds., *Dossiê Índios em Mato Grosso* (OPAN and CIMI, Cuiabá, 1987), 129–58.

and Michael HECKENBERGER, eds., *Os Povos do Alto Xingu: História e cultura* (Editora UFRJ, Rio de Janeiro, 2001).

FREIRE, Carlos Augusto da Rocha: *Saudades do Brasil ou as lutas pela criação do Parque Indígena do Xingu* (Museu Nacional/Universidade Federal do Rio de Janeiro, Rio de Janeiro, 1987).

'Indigenismo e antropologia: O Conselho Nacional de Proteção aos Índios na Gestão Rondon (1939–1955)' (Master's thesis, Universidade Federal do Rio de Janeiro, 1990).

'Sagas sertanistas: Práticas e representações do campo indigenista no século XX' (doctoral thesis, Universidade Federal do Rio de Janeiro, 2005).

FRIKEL, Protásio Gunther: 'Migração, guerra e sobrevivência Suiá', *Revista de Antropologia* **17**:20, 1972.

FUNAI (Fundação Nacional do Índio): *Parque Indígena do Xingu* (Departamento Geral de Estudos e Pesquisas, FUNAI, Brasília, 1971).

'Parque do Xingu: o chão de muitas culturas', *Revista de Atualidade Indígena* (Brasilia) **2**:7, 1977, 57–8.

GALEAZZI, Marlene Anna, and Frederico MENDES: 'Bye Bye Xingu', *Manchete*, February 1981, 61–71.

GALVÃO, Eduardo Eneas: 'Apontamentos sobre os índios Kamaiurá', *Publicações Avulsas do Museu Nacional* (Rio de Janeiro) **5**, 1949, 31–48; also in his *Encontro de Sociedades* (Rio de Janeiro, 1979), 17–55.

'Cultura e sistema de parentesco das tribos do Alto Rio Xingu', *Boletim do Museu Nacional*, n.s. *Antropologia* **14**, 1953, 1–56; also in his *Encontro de Sociedades* (Rio de Janeiro, 1979), 73–119.

BIBLIOGRAPHY

'Diários do Xingu (1947–1967)', in Marco Antônio Teixeira Gonçalves, ed., *Diários de campo de Eduardo Galvão: Tenetehara, kaioa e índios do Xingu* (UFRJ, Rio de Janeiro, 1996), 249–381.

and José C. M. CARVALHO and Pedro E. de LIMA: *Observações zoológicas e antropológicas na região dos formadores do Xingu* (Rio de Janeiro, 1944).

and Mário F. SIMÕES: 'Mudança e sobrevivência no Alto Xingu: Brasil Central', in Egon Schaden, ed., *Homem, cultura e sociedade no Brasil* (Editora Vozes, Petropolis, 1972), 183–208; also in *Revista de Antropologia* **14**, 1966, 44.

'Notícia sobre os índios txikão, alto Xingu', *Boletim do Museu Paraense Emílio Goeldi*, n.s. *Antropologia* **24**, 1965, 1–24.

GARFIELD, Seth: 'A nationalist environment: Indians, nature, and the construction of the Xingu National Park in Brazil', *Luso-Brazilian Review* (University of Wisconsin) **41**:1, 2004, 139–67.

GIRALDIN, Odair: *'Cayapó e Panará': Luta e sobrevivência de um povo* (Editora da Unicamp, Campinas SP, 1997).

'Renascendo das cinzas: Um histórico da presença dos Cayapó-Panará em Goiás e no Triângulo Mineiro', *Sociedade e Cultura (Impresso)* **3**:1–2, 2000, 161–84.

GOMES, Mercio Pereira: *Os índios e o Brasil* (Editora Vozes, São Paulo, 1988); trans. John Moon as *The Indians and Brazil* (University Press of Florida, Gainesville, 2000).

GREGOR, Thomas: 'Exposure and seclusion: A study of institutionalized isolation among the Mehinaku Indians of Brazil', *Ethnology* (Pittsburgh) **9**:3, July 1970, 234–50.

'Privacy and extra-marital affairs in a tropical forest community', in Daniel R. Gross, ed., *Peoples and Cultures of Native South America* (Doubleday/ Natural History Press, Garden City, New York, 1973), 232–60.

Mehinaku: The Drama of Daily Life in a Brazilian Indian Village (University of Chicago Press, Chicago and London, 1977).

GRÜNBERG, Georg: 'Beiträge zur Ethnographie der Kayabí-indianern Zentral-brasiliens', *Archiv für Völkerkunde* (Vienna), **24**, 1970.

Os Kaiabi do Brasil Central (ISA: Instituto Socioambiental, São Paulo, 204).

HANBURY-TENISON, Robin: *Report of a Visit to the Indians of Brazil, on behalf of the Primitive Peoples' Fund/ Survival International, January–March 1971* (Primitive Peoples' Fund/ Survival International, London, 1971; Quintrell & Co., Wadebridge, 1971).

A Question of Survival for the Indians of Brazil (Angus & Robertson, London, 1973).

HECKENBERGER, Michael J.: 'Manioc agriculture and sedentism in Amazonia, the Upper Xingu example', *Antiquity*, Sept. 1998.

'The wars within: Xinguano witchcraft and balance of power', in Neil Whitehead and Robin Wright, eds., *In Darkness and Secrecy: The Anthropology of Assault Sorcery and Witchcraft in Amazonia* (Duke University Press, Durham, NC, 2004), 179–201.

The Ecology of Power: Culture, Place and Personhood in the Southern Amazon, AD 1000–2000 (Routledge, New York, 2005).

and Afukaká KUIKURO, Carlos FAUSTO, Bruna FRANCHETTO, et al.: 'Amazonia 1492: Pristine forest or cultural parkland', *Science*, 25 April 2003.

BIBLIOGRAPHY

HEELAS, Richard H.: 'The Social Organization of the Panará, a Gê Tribe of Central Brazil' (doctoral thesis, University of Oxford, 1979).

'An historical outline of the Panará (Kreen-Akarore) tribe of central Brazil', *Survival International Revue* **3**:2 (22), Spring 1978, 25–7.

HEMMING, John: 'Tragedy in the jungle', *Sunday Times*, 18 and 25 Feb. 1962.

Amazon Frontier: The Destruction of the Brazilian Indians (Macmillan, London, 1985; revised edition, Papermac, London, 1995).

Die if you Must: Brazilian Indians in the Twentieth Century (Macmillan, London, 2003).

'Tragedy in the jungle', *Sunday Times*, 18 and 25 Feb. 1962.

'The Villas Boas and the Xingu: Contacts, contributions and controversies' (SALSA: Society for the Anthropology of Lowland South America, Florida International University, Miami, January 2004); trans. in Orlando and Cláudio Villas Bôas, *A Marcha para o Oeste: A epopéia da Expedição Roncador-Xingu* (Editora Schwarcz, São Paulo, 2012), 631–38.

'On the death of Orlando Villas Boas and the legacy of the Villas Boas brothers', *Tipiti* (SALSA: Society for the Anthropology of Lowland South America) **3**:1, June 2005, 91–5; trans. as 'O legado de Orlando Villas Bôas e seus irmãos', in Orlando Villas Bôas Filho, *Orlando Villas Bôas e a construção do indigenismo no Brasil* (São Paulo, 2014), 27–39.

'A pax xinguana', in Roberto Baruzzi and Carmen Junqueira, eds., *Parque Indígena do Xingu: Saúde, cultura e história* (Terra Virgem, Universidade Federal de São Paulo, 2005), 25–47.

'Os defensores dos índios brasileiros: os irmãos Villas Bôas', in Orlando Villas Bôas Filho, *Orlando Villas Bôas: Expedições, reflexões e registros* (Metalivros, São Paulo, 2006), 134–47.

HILL, Jonathan, ed.: *Rethinking History and Myth: Indigenous South American Perspectives on the Past* (University of Illinois Press, Urbana, 1988).

HINTERMANN, Heinrich: *Unter Indianern und Reisenschlangen* (Grethlein & Co., Zurich and Leipzig, 1926).

HOPPER, Janice H., ed.: *Indians of Brazil in the Twentieth Century* (Institute for Cross-Cultural Research, Washington, DC, 1967).

IRELAND, Emilienne: 'Cerebral savage: The Whiteman as symbol of cleverness and savagery in Waurá myth', in Jonathan D. Hill, ed., *Rethinking History and Myth: Indigenous South American Perspectives on the Past* (University of Illinois Press, Urbana, 1988), 157–73.

JUNQUEIRA, Carmen: *The Brazilian Indigenous Problem and Policy: The Example of the Xingu National Park*, IWGIA (International Work Group for Indigenous Affairs) **13** (Copenhagen/Geneva, IWGIA, 1973).

Os índios de Ipavu: Um estudo sobre a vida do grupo Kamaiurá (Editora Ática, São Paulo, 1975).

'Pajés e feiticeiros', in Roberto Baruzzi and Carmen Junqueira, eds., *Parque Indígena do Xingu: Saúde, cultura e história* (Terra Virgem, Universidade Federal de São Paulo, 2005), 147–61.

BIBLIOGRAPHY

KAHN, Marina: 'A cara nova do Parque do Xingu', *Povos Indígenas no Brasil—1987/88/89/90* (CEDI, São Paulo, 1991), 468–9.

KRAUSE, Fritz: 'Forschungsaufgaben in Schingu-Quellgebiet, Zentralbrasilien', *Tagungsberichte der Gesellschaft für Völkerkunde* (Leipzig), 1937, 160–72.

LANNA, Amadeu Duarte: 'Aspectos econômicos da organização social dos Suyá', in Egon Schaden, ed., *Homem, cultura e sociedade no Brasil* (Editora Vozes, Petropolis, 1972), 133–82.

LEA, Vanessa Rosemary: *Parque Indígena do Xingu: Laudo antropológico* (Universidade de Campinas, São Paulo, 1997).

Área Indígena Kapoto: Laudo antropológico (Universidade de Campinas, São Paulo, 1997).

and Mariana Kawall LEAL FERREIRA: '"A guerra no Xingu": cronologia', *Povos Indígenas no Brasil/1984* (CEDI, São Paulo, 1984), 246–258.

LEAL FERREIRA, Mariana K.: *Histórias do Xingu: Coletânea de depoimentos dos índios Suyá, Kayabi, Juruna, Trumai, Txucarramãe e Txicão* (NHII/USP-Fapesp, São Paulo, 1994).

'Da origem dos homens à conquista da escrita: um estudo sobre povos indígenas e educação escolar no Brasil' (Master's thesis, Universidade de São Paulo, 1992).

LEAL NETO, Major Av. José: 'Levantamento do Rio da Liberdade (Xingu)', in Mário F. Simões, ed., *SPI—1954* (Serviço de Proteção aos Índios, Rio de Janeiro, 1955), 185–207.

LÉVI-STRAUSS, Claude: 'The tribes of the upper Xingú river', in Julian Steward, ed., *Handbook of South American Indians* **3** (Smithsonian Institution, Washington DC, 1948), 321–47.

LIMA, António Carlos de Souza: *A Expedição Roncador-Xingu* (Museu Nacional/Universidade Federal do Rio de Janeiro, Rio de Janeiro, 1981).

'O governo dos índios sob a gestão do SPI', in Manuela Carneiro da Cunha, ed., *História dos Índios no Brasil* (Companhia das Letras, São Paulo, 1992), 155–74.

Um grande cerco de paz (Editora Vozes, Petrópolis, 1995).

'Os relatórios antropológicos de identificação de terras indígenas da FUNAI: notas sobre o estudo da relação entre antropologia e indigenismo no Brasil (1968–1985)', in João Pacheco de Oliveira, ed., *Indigenismo e territorialização* (Contra Capa, Rio de Janeiro, 1998), 221–68.

LIMA, Carmen S. J. B. (later Carmen Junqueira, q.v.): 'Os Kamaiurá e o Parque Nacional do Xingu' (doctoral thesis, Antropologia, UNICAMP, Rio Claro, SP, 1967).

LIMA, Luís Octávio, Moisés RABINOVIC, and Cristina MÜLLER, eds.: *O Xingu dos Villas Bôas* (Metalivros, São Paulo, 2006).

LIMA, Pedro E. de: 'Os indios Waurá: Observações gerais', *Boletim do Museu Nacional*, n.s. *Antropologia* (Rio de Janeiro) **9**, 1950.

'Distribuição dos grupos indígenas do alto Xingu', *Anais do XXXI Congresso Internacional dos Americanistas* (São Paulo) **1**, 1955, 159–79.

LONGAREZZI, Andréa Maturano: 'Os Kayabi', *Terra Indígena* (CIMI, Centro de Estudos Indígenas, Araraquara) **10**:69, Oct.–Dec. 1993, 40–50.

LUCENA, Eliana: 'Festa para os ministros', *Povos Indígenas no Brasil—85/86* (CEDI, São Paulo, 1986), 333–5.

258

BIBLIOGRAPHY

MARCOPITO, L. F.: 'Kreen-Akarore: amarga renúncia à terra de origem', *Revista de Atualidade Indígena* **4**, 1979, 36–44.

MARQUES, Cesário: *A Vida de Orlando Villas Bôas* (Editora Rio, Rio de Janeira, n.d.).

MATTHEWS, Kenneth: *Brazilian Interior* (Peter Davies, London, 1956).

MEGARON TXUKARRAMÃE: 'A história do povo Txukarramãe' (1980), in Mariana Kawall Leal Ferreira, *Histórias do Xingu* (Fapesp, São Paulo, 1994), 178–222.

MEIRELLES, Apoena: 'Kreen-Akarore, o dificil contato', *Revista de Atualidade Indígena* **3**:18, Sept.–Oct. 1979, 53–63.

MENDES, Gilmar Ferreira: *O Domínio da União sobre as Terras Indígenas: O Parque Nacional do Xingu* (Ministério Público Federal, Brasília, 1988).

MENEZES, Maria Lúcia Pires: 'Parque Indígena do Xingu: as relações entre geopolítica e indigenismo', in Adélia Engracia de Oliveira and Philippe Léna, eds., *Amazônia: A fronteira agrícola 20 anos depois* (Museu Paraense Emílio Goeldi, Belém, 1991), 83–100.

Parque Indígena do Xingu: A construção de um território estatal (Editora da Unicamp/Imprensa Oficial do Estado, Campinas SP, 2000).

MENGET, Patrick: 'Au nom des autres: la classification des relations sociales chez les Txikão (Brésil)' (doctoral thesis, Université de Paris X, Nanterre, 1976); trans. as *Em nome dos outros* (Assírio e Alvim, Lisbon, 2001).

'Les indiens du Haut Xingu', in Muriel Hutter, ed., *Regards sur les Indiens de l'Amazonie* (Éditions Muséum National d'Histoire Naturelle, Paris, 2000).

MESQUITA, Renata Valério de: 'O legado dos Villas Bôas', *Planeta* **519**, April 2016, 14–17.

MEYER, Herrmann: 'Bericht über seine zweite Xingu-Expedition', *Verhandlungen der Gesellschaft für Erdkunde zu Berlin* **27**:3, 1900, 112–28.

'Über seine Expedition nach Central-Brasilien', den *Verhandlungen der Gesellschaft für Erdkunde zu Berlin* **3**, 1897.

MILANEZ, Felipe, ed.: *Memórias sertanistas: Cem anos de indigenismo no Brasil* (Edições Sesc, São Paulo, 2015).

MINDLIN, Betty: 'Prefácio', in Felipe Milanez, ed., *Memórias sertanistas: Cem anos de indigenismo no Brasil* (Edições Sesc, São Paulo, 2015), 11–24.

MOENNICH, Martha: *Fighting for Christ in the Xingu Jungles* (Zondervon Pulishing House, Grand Rapids, MI, 1942).

MOORE, John H.: *Tears of the Sun God* (Faber & Faber, London, 1965).

MOTA, João Leão da, and Lourival Serôa da MOTA: 'A epidemia de sarampo no Xingu', in Mário F. Simões, ed., *S.P.I.—1954* (Serviço de Proteção aos Índios, Rio de Janeiro, 1955), 131–44.

MÜLLER, Cristina, Luiz Otávio LIMA, and Moisés RABINOVICI, eds.: *O Xingu dos Villas Bôas* (Agência Estado, Metalivros, São Paulo, 2002).

NEWLANDS, Liliana, ed.: *Aritana, o homem que enxerga longe* (Universidade Católica de Goiás, Goiânia, 2007).

BIBLIOGRAPHY

NIMUENDAJÚ, Curt: 'The Cayabí, Tapanyuna, and Apiacá', in Julian Steward, ed., *Handbook of South American Indians* 3 (Smithsonian Institution, Washington DC, 1948), 307–20.

NORONHA, Ramiro: *Exploração e levantamento do rio Culuene: Principal formador do rio Xingu*, Comissão Rondon 75 (Conselho Nacional de Proteção aos Índios, Rio de Janeiro, 1952).

NUTELS, Noel: 'Medical problems of newly contacted Indian groups', in Pan-American Health Organization, *Biomedical Challenges Presented by the American Indian* (Washington, DC, 1968).

OAKDALE, Suzanne: '"How I brought everyone to the Xingu": Strangers, stances, and the making of inter-ethnic alliances', paper presented to the SALSA (Society for the Anthropology of Lowland South America) conference, Belém do Pará, 2011.

OBERG, Kalervo: *Indian Tribes of Northern Mato Grosso, Brazil* (Smithsonian Institution, Washington DC, 1953).

OLIVEIRA, Adélia Engrácia de: 'Os índios Jurúna e a sua cultura nos dias atuais', *Boletim do Museu Paraense Emílio Goeldi*, n.s. *Antropologia* (Belém) 35, 1968.

'Os índios Juruna do Alto Xingu', *Dédalo* (São Paulo) 6:11–12, 1970.

OLIVEIRA, Aracy de Passos: *Roncador-Xingu: Roteiro de uma expedição* (Editora Universidade Federal de Goiás, Goiânia, 1976).

OLIVEIRA, Roberto Cardoso de: 'Relatório de uma investigação sôbre terras em Mato Grosso', in Mário F. Simões, ed., *S.P.I.—1954* (Serviço de Proteção aos Índios, Rio de Janeiro, 1955), 173–84; also in Vanessa Lea, *Parque Indígena do Xingu: Laudo antropológico* (Campinas, São Paulo, 1997), 173–83.

OLIVEIRA FILHO, João Pacheco de, ed.: *Sociedades Indígenas e Indigenismo no Brasil* (Editora Marca Zero, UFRJ, Rio de Janeiro, 1987).

PAGLIARO, Heloisa: 'A mudança dos Kaiabi para o Parque do Xingu: Uma história de sucesso demográfico', in Roberto G. Baruzzi and Carmen Junqueira, eds., *Parque Indígena do Xingu: Saúde, cultura e história* (Terra Virgem, Universidade Federal de São Paulo, 2005), 201–24.

PECCININI, Daisy, ed.: *Sacralidade da vida: Índios do Xingu e médicos da Escola Paulista de Medicina* (Instituto Victor Brecheret, São Paulo, 2012).

PETRULLO, Vincent M.: 'Primitive peoples of Mato Grosso', *Museum Journal* (University of Pennsylvania, Philadelphia) 23:2, 1932, 84–173.

PINTO, Nicanor R. S., and Roberto G. BARUZZI: 'Male pubertal seclusion and risk of death in Indians from Alto Xingu, Brazil', *Human Biology* 63:6, Dec. 1991, 821–34; trans. as 'Reclusão pubertária masculina em índios do Alto Xingu, Brasil Central', in Roberto Baruzzi and Carmen Junqueira, eds., *Parque Indígena do Xingu: Saúde, cultura e história* (Terra Virgem, Universidade Federal de São Paulo, 2005), 175–87.

PUTTKAMER, W. Jesco von: 'Brazil's Kreen-Akarores: Requiem for a Tribe?', *National Geographic* 147:2, Feb. 1975, 254–69.

'Brazil's Txukahameis: Good-bye to the Stone Age', *National Geographic* 147:2, Feb. 1975, 270–83.

BIBLIOGRAPHY

Cunhatãs e Curumins: A criança indígena brasileira (Editora Universidade Católica de Goiás, Goiânia, 1986).

QUAIN, Buell: *The Trumai Indians of Central Brazil* (ed. Robert Murphy), American Ethnological Society **24** (University of Washington, Seattle, 1955; J. J. Augustin, New York, 1955).

RABBEN, Linda: *Brazil's Indians and the Onslaught of Civilization: The Yanomami and the Kayapó* (University of Washington Press, Seattle and London, 2004).

RAMOS, Alcida: *Uma crítica da desrazão indigenista* (Editora da Universidade de Brasília, Brasilia, 1998).

RIBEIRO, Berta: *Diário do Xingu* (Paz e Terra, Rio de Janeiro, 1979).

RIBEIRO, Darcy: 'Convívio e contaminação', *Sociologia* **18**:1, 1956, 3–50.

'Culturas e línguas indígenas do Brasil', *Educação e Ciências Sociais* (Rio de Janeiro) **2**:6, 1957, 5–102; trans. Janice H. Hopper as 'Indigenous cultures and languages in Brazil', in Janice Hopper, ed., *Indians of Brazil in the Twentieth Century* (Institute of Cross-Cultural Research, Washington DC, 1967), 77–165.

A política indigenista brasileira (Ministério da Agricultura, Brasília, 1962).

Os índios e a civilização (Civilização Brasileira, Rio de Janeiro, 1970; 2nd. edn. Editôra Vozes, Petrópolis, 1977); trans. Betty J. Meggers as *The Civilizational Process*, Smithsonian Institution Publication **4749** (Smithsonian Institution, Washington DC, 1968).

Confissões (Companhia das Letras, São Paulo, 1997).

ROCHA, Leandro Mendes: 'A marcha para o oeste e os índios do Xingu,' *Índios do Brasil* **2**, June 1992.

ROHTER, Larry: 'Amazon Indians honor an intrepid spirit', *New York Times*, 26 July 2003.

RONDON, Cândido Mariano da Silva: *Índios do Brasil: Das cabeceiras do rio Xingu, rios Araguaia e Oiapoque* (CNPI, Ministério da Agricultura, Rio de Janeiro, 1953).

SANTOS, Yolanda Lhullier dos: 'A festa do Kuarup entre os índios do Alto-Xingu', *Revista de Antropologia* **4**:2, Dec. 1956, 111–116.

SCHMIDT, Max: *Indianerstudien in Zentralbrasilien: Erlebnisse und ethnologische Ergebnisse einer Reise in den Jahren 1900 bis 1901* (Dietrich Reimer, Berlin, 1905).

Unter Indianern Südamerikas: Erlebnisse in Zentralbrasilien (Berlin, 1924); trans. as *Estudos de Etnologia Brasileira*, Brasiliana (Companhia Editora Nacional, São Paulo, 1942).

'Ergebnisse meiner zweijährigen Forschungsreise in Matto Grosso, September 1926 bis August 1928', *Zeitschrift für Ethnologie* (Berlin) **9**, 1929, 85–124.

SCHULTZ, Harald: 'Informações etnográficas sôbre os índios Suyá, 1960', *Revista do Museu Paulista, Antropologia* **13**, 1961/2, 315–32.

'Hombu': Indian Life in the Brazilian Jungle (Macmillan, New York, and Colibris, Amsterdam, 1962).

'Brazil's big-lipped Indians', *National Geographic* **121**:1, Jan. 1962, 118–33.

'Lendas Waurá', *Revista do Museu Paulista*, **16**, 1965, 21–149.

'The Waurá: Brazilian Indians of the hidden Xingu', *National Geographic Magazine* **129**:1, Jan. 1966, 130–52.

BIBLIOGRAPHY

and Vilma CHIARA: 'A pá semilunar da mulher waurá', *Revista do Museu Paulista* (São Paulo) n.s. **37**:54, 1967.

SCHWARTZMAN, Stephan: 'The Panará of the Xingu National Park: The Transformation of a Society' (doctoral thesis, University of Chicago, 1987).

Os Panará do Peixoto de Azevedo e cabeceiras do Iriri: História, contato e transferência ao Parque do Xingu (Environmental Defense Fund, Washington DC, 1992).

'The Panará: indigenous territory and environmental protection in the Amazon', in Greg Dicum, ed., *Local Heritage in the Changing Tropics: Innovative Strategies for Natural Resource Management and Control* (Yale School of Forestry and Environmental Studies, New Haven, 1995).

'Panará: a saga dos índios gigantes', *Ciência Hoje* **20**:119, April 1996, 26–35.

SEEGER, Anthony: *Nature and Society in Central Brazil: The Suyá Indians of Mato Grosso* (Harvard University Press, Cambridge, MA, 1981).

Why Suyá Sing: A Musical Anthropology of an Amazon People (Cambridge University Press, Cambridge, 1987).

'Ladrões, mitos e história: Karl von den Steinen entre os suiás', in Vera Penteado Coelho, ed., *Karl von den Steinen: Um século de antropologia no Xingu* (Edusp, São Paulo, 1993), 431–44.

SCHADEN, Egon: *Aculturação indígena* (Editôra da Universidade de São Paulo, São Paulo, 1969).

SICK, Helmut: *Tukani* (Verlag Paul Parey, Hamburg and Berlin, 1957); trans. R. H. Stevens (Burke Publishing, London, 1959).

SILVA, Fernando Altenfelder: 'O mundo mágico dos bacairis', in Vera Penteado Coelho, ed., *Karl von den Steinen: Um século de antropologia no Xingu* (Edusp, São Paulo, 1993), 347–74.

SILVA, José Afonso da: 'Terras tradicionalmente ocupadas pelos índios', in Juliana Santilli, ed., *Os direitos indígenas e a constituição* (Fabris Editora, Porto Alegre, 1993), 45–50.

SIMÕES, Mário: 'Os txikão e outras tribos marginais do alto Xingu', *Revista do Museu Paulista*, n.s. **14**, 1963, 76–104.

ed.: *S.P.I.—1954* (Serviço de Proteção aos Índios, Rio de Janeiro, 1955).

SMITH, Anthony: *Mato Grosso: Last Virgin Land* (Michael Joseph, London, 1971).

STEINEN, Karl von den: *Durch Central-Brasilien: Expedition zur Erforschung des Schingú im Jahre 1884* (Leipzig, 1886); trans. Catarina Baratz Cannabrava as *O Brasil Central* (São Paulo and Rio de Janeiro, 1942).

'Über seine zweite Schingú-Expedition', *Verhandlungen der Gesellschaft für Erdkunde zu Berlin* **15**, 1888, 369–87.

Unter den Naturvölkern Zentral-Brasiliens: Reiseschilderung und Ergebnisse der zweiten Schingú-Expedition 1887–1888 (Berlin, 1894); trans. Egon Schaden as *Entre os aborígenes do Brasil Central* (São Paulo, 1940).

TASSARA, Helena, and Maureen BISILLIAT, eds.: *O índio ontem, hoje ... e amanhã?* (Memorial da América Latina/Edusp, São Paulo, 1991).

BIBLIOGRAPHY

TEVES, Angelina Cabral de: 'Notas sobre o estado atual das tribos da região dos formadores do Xingu,' *Revista Brasiliense* **31**, 1960.

VALENTE, Rubens: *Os Fuzis e as Flechas* (Companhia das Letras, São Paulo, 2017).

VANZOLIN, Marina: *A Flecha do Ciúme: O parentesco e seu avesso Segundo os Aweti do Alto Xingu* (Terceira Nome, São Paulo, 2015).

VASCONCELLOS, Vicente de Paulo Teixeira da Fonseca: *Expedição ao Rio Ronuro*, Comissão Rondon **90** (Conselho Nacional de Proteção aos Índios, Imprensa Nacional, Rio de Janeiro, 1945).

VELOSO, Nilo de Oliveira: 'Expedição Roncador-Xingu', *Revista do Clube Militar* (Rio de Janeiro) **20**:80, Jan.–Feb. 1947, 77–86.

VERSWIJVER, Gustaaf: 'Séparations et migrations des Mekrãgnoti, groupe Kayapo du Brésil Central', *Bulletin de la Société Suisse des Américanistes* (Geneva) **42**, 1978, 47–59.

'Les hommes aux bracelets noirs: une rite de passage chez les Indiens Kayapo-Mekrãgnoti du Brésil central', *Naître, Vivre et Mourir* (Musée d'Ethnographie, Neuchâtel), 1981, 95–118.

'The intertribal relations between the Juruna and the Kayapó Indians (1850–1920)', *Jahrbuch des Museums für Völkerkunde zu Leipzig* (Akademie-Verlag, Berlin) **34**, 1982, 305–15.

The Club-Fighters of the Amazon: Warfare among the Kaiapo Indians of Central Brazil (Rijksuniversiteit Gent, Ghent, 1992).

'O Parque Indígena do Xingu', in Orlando Villas Bôas Filho, *Orlando Villas Bôas e a construção do indigenismo no Brasil* (Editora da Universidade Presbiteriana Mackenzie, São Paulo, 2014), 41–9.

VIERTLER, Renate Brigitte: *Os Kamayurá e o Alto Xingu*, Instituto de Estudos Brasileiros, Publicação **10** (USP, São Paulo, 1969).

VILLAS BÔAS, André, ed.: *Almanaque socioambiental, Parque Indígena do Xingu, 50 Anos* (Instituto Socioambiental, São Paulo, 2011).

VILLAS BÔAS, Cláudio and Orlando/or Orlando and Cláudio: 'Atração dos índios Txukahamãi', in Mário F. Simões, ed., *S.P.I.—1954* (Serviço de Proteção aos Índios, Rio de Janeiro, 1955), 79–88.

'Saving Brazil's stone-age tribes from extinction', *National Geographic* **134**, Sept. 1968, 424–44.

Xingu: Os índios, seus mitos (Zahar Editores, Rio de Janeiro, 1970; Kuarup, Porto Alegre, 1990); trans. Susana Hertelendy Rudge as *Xingu: The Indians, their Myths* (ed. Kenneth S. Brecher) (Farrar, Straus & Giroux, New York, 1973; Souvenir Press, London, 1974 and reprinted 2004).

'Os Juruna no Alto-Xingu', *Revista Reflexão* (Universidade Federal de Goiás, Goiânia) **1**:1, May 1970, 61–86.

'Os Villas Boas e os índios gigantes e outras aventuras', *Veja* **218**, 8 Nov. 1972, 45–60.

'Memorias dos irmãos Villas Boas: Os 32 anos de Cláudio e Orlando com os índios brasileiros', *Visão*, 10 Feb. 1975 (Orlando interviewed by José Marquez).

'As fantásticas histórias do Xingu', a series of articles in *Revista de Atualidade Indígena* (Funai, Brasília):

BIBLIOGRAPHY

IV 'Estranhos objetos sobrevoam aldeias' 1:4, 1977, 60–1
V 'Cláudio conta ... sua grande aventura na selva' 1:5, 1977, 46–8
VI 'Fawcett: Orlando guarda ossada do explorador inglês' 1:6, 1977, 26–33
VII 'As expedições que desapareceram no roteiro de Fawcett' 2:7, 1977, 49–54
VIII 'Os acidentados vôos dos Villas Boas sobre a floresta' 2:8, 1978, 33–9
IX 'O animalzinho que tentei salvar era sobrenatural' 2:9, 1978, 12–15
X 'O inesperado encontro com os Xavante' 2:10, 1978, 51–2
'A conquista do jakuí' 2:12, 1978, 52–5
'Trumai torna realidade o isolamento voluntário' 2:11, 1978, 51–6
'Kuadê: Juruna mata o sol' 3:13, 1978, 15–16
'Diário da selva: I 'Encontro com os Juruna' 3:14, 1979, 31–40
II 'Viagem pioneira pela Maritsauá' 3:15, 1979, 17–24
'Índios ainda desconhecidos vivem isolados no Xingu' 3:15, 1979, 35–40.

Xingu: O velho Káia (conta a história do seu povo) (Editora Kuarup, Porto Alegre, 1984).

Xingu: Os contos do Tamoin (Editora Kuarup, Porto Alegre, 1986).

Xingu: Os náufragos do Rio das Mortes e outras histórias (Editora Kuarup, Porto Alegre, 1988);

Xingu: Os Kayabí do Rio São Manoel (Editora Kuarup, Porto Alegre, 1989).

Xingu: Histórias de índios e sertanejos (Editora Kuarup, Porto Alegre, 1992).

'Memórias de Orlando e Cláudio Villas Boas', *Carta* (Gabinete do Senador Darcy Ribeiro, Brasília) **9**, 1993, 187–203.

A Marcha para o Oeste: A epopéia da Expedição Roncador-Xingu (Editôra Globo, São Paulo, 1994; enlarged 2nd edition, Editora Schwarcz, São Paulo, 2012).

Almanaque do sertão: História de visitantes, sertanejos e índios (Editora Globo, São Paulo, 1997).

A arte dos pajés: Impressões sobre o universo espiritual do índio xinguano (Editora Globo, São Paulo, 2000).

'Um povo na ignorância de seu passado', in Luiz Antonio Aguiar, ed., *Para entender o Brasil* (Alegro, São Paulo, 2001), 265–73.

'Rompendo fronteiras', in Cristina Müller et al., eds., *O Xingu dos Villas Bôas* (Metalivros, São Paulo, 2002), 146–65.

História e causos: Autobiografia (ed. Orlando Villas Bôas Filho) (Editora FTD, São Paulo, 2006).

VILLAS BÔAS, Orlando, Carmen JUNQUEIRA, Clarival VALADARES, and Raphael BASTOS: *Xingu dia, Xingu noite, Xingu terra* (XIII Bienal de São Paulo, 1975).

VILLAS BÔAS Filho, Orlando, ed.: *Orlando Villas Bôas: Expedições, reflexões e registros* (Metalivros, São Paulo, 2006).

Kuarup, a última viagem de Orlando Villas Bôas (Caixa Cultural São Paulo, 2010).

'Os Villas Bôas e os índios do Xingu', in Ulisses Capozzoli, ed., 'Patrimônio cultural do Xingu: O começo do fim?', *Scientific American. Brasil*, Edição especial **44**, 2011, 28–35.

BIBLIOGRAPHY

ed.: *Orlando Villas Bôas e a construção do indigenismo no Brasil* (Editora da Universidade Presbiteriana Mackenzie, São Paulo, 2014).

'Pluralidade de olhares sobre a vida e a obra de Orlando Villas Bôas' and 'A construção do campo indigenista no Brasil', in Orlando Villas Bôas Filho, *Orlando Villas Bôas e a construção do indigenismo no Brasil* (São Paulo, 2014), 54–77, 117–82.

'A juridicização e o campo indigenista no Brasil: uma abordagem interdisciplinar', *Revista da Facultade de Direito da Universidade de São Paulo* **111**, Jan.–Dec. 2016, 1–39.

VILLELA, Murillo de Oliveira: 'Murillo Villela, uma experiência para guarder na memória', in Cristina Müller et al., eds., *O Xingu dos Villas Bôas* (Metalivros, São Paulo, 2002), 50–61.

'Primórdios da medicina de apoio aos índios no Alto Xingu', in Orlando Villas Bôas Filho, *Orlando Villas Bôas e a construção do indigenismo no Brasil* (Editora da Universidade Presbiteriana Mackenzie, São Paulo, 2014), 99–115.

VIVEIROS DE CASTRO, Eduardo Batalha: 'Indivíduo e sociedade no alto Xingu: Os Yawalapití' (thesis, Museu Nacional, Rio de Janeiro, 1977).

'Le parc des symboles: quelques paradoxes de l'identité de l'indien du Xingu', in *Regards sur les Indiens d'Amazonie* (Musée de l'Homme, Paris, 2000), 14–19.

'Dois rituais do Xingu', *Cadernos de Antropologia e Imagem* (Universidade do Rio de Janeiro) **2**, 1996, 99–104.

and Manuela CARNEIRO DA CUNHA: *Amazônia: Etnologia e história indígena* (NHII—Universidade de São Paulo, São Paulo, 1993).

WELLINGTON, Sandra: 'My tribe, my people' (interview with Aritana Yawalapiti), *Observer Magazine*, London, 18 June, 1989, 28–33.

The Art of the Brazilian Indians (Self-published, New York, 2011).

'O embaixador do Xingu', *National Geographic Brasil*, November 2011.

WEYER, Edward: *Jungle Quest* (Frederick Muller, London, 1956).

ZARUR, George: *Parentesco, ritual e economia no alto Xingu* (FUNAI, Brasilia, 1975).

'O espírito do tempo na criação da Reserva do Xingu', in Ulisses Capozzoli, ed., 'Patrimônio cultural do Xingu: O começo do fim?', *Scientific American Brasil*, edição especial **44**, 2011, 40–7.

'A revolução dos Villas-Boas: Os cinqüenta anos do Parque Indígena do Xingu', *Scientific American, Brasil*, 2011.

'Memória afetiva dos Villas Bôas e do Parque Indígena do Xingu', in Orlando Villas Bôas Filho, *Orlando Villas Bôas e a construção do indigenismo no Brasil Orlando Villas Bôas e a construção do indigenismo no Brasil* (São Paulo, 2014), 79–97.

INDEX

INDEX

INDEX

INDEX

INDEX

INDEX

INDEX

279

INDEX

INDEX

INDEX

INDEX

1963 Lopes de Lima starts work at Posto Leonardo, 100
1964 Baruzzi visits Posto Leonardo, 100; first contact with Ikpeng, 140–41
1965 Baruzzi starts work at Posto Leonardo, 100; visit to Ikpeng, 141–4
1967 Javaritu murder, 119; Tacuman–Tuvule conflict, 120; Ikpeng transferred to Xingu Park, 144–6, 182; Cachimbo airstrip incident, 161
1968 Hugh-Jones' visit, 132; Panará contact expedition, 162–5
1969 marries Marina, 103
1970 Tapayuna transferred to Xingu Park, 152, 182; birth of Orlando, 103; Transamazonica Highway announced, 154; BR-080 diverted through Xingu Park, 154–6
1971 Metuktire urged to move south, 197; conflict over death of Tuvule, 120–21
1972 University of São Paulo conference, 156; Panará contact expedition, 166–70, 174, 179, 206; Nobel Peace Prize nomination, 187; awarded Medal of Indigenist Merit, 187
1973 Panará influenza outbreak, 170; Japan visit, 187
1974 decision to transfer Panará, 175; retirement announced, 179
1975 Panará transferred to Xingu Park, 176–8, 179, 182, 206; birth of Noel, 100, 103; awarded Rio Branco Medal of Merit, 187
1976 moves to São Paulo, 180, 181; awarded Boilesen Prize, 187
1977 awarded Lions Club Humanitarian Commendation, 187

1978 Emancipation of Indians Bill, 184
1980 awarded State of São Paulo Prize, 181, 187
1984 awarded Geo Prize, 187
1988 signs manifesto addressed to constituent assembly, 189
1998 awarded Freedom of São Paulo and Medal of Human Rights, 187
2000 named National Hero, 187
2002 death, 186, 188, 210, 212–13
2003 appears on postage stamp, 188
Villas Boas Filho, Orlando, 103, 127, 181, 186, 212
Villela, Murillo, 71, 86, 100, 141–2, 161, 163, 164
vitamin deficiency, 144
Von den Steinen river, 76
Von Martius rapids, 16, 64
  BR-080 road and, 154
  Geographical Centre Expedition (1959), 69
  Juruna and, 33, 34, 59
  influenza outbreaks, 63
  Metuktire and, 60, 102, 197, 198, 200
  Xingu Park and, 76, 82
voting rights, 190

Wagley, Charles, 21, 187
Wallace, Alfred Russel, 74
'War of the Xingu' (1984), 199–200, 201
warfare, 30, 31, 61, 108, 118, 127
  Diauarum massacre (c. 1940), 31–2, 34, 58, 61, 70
  Ikpeng conflict, 137–8
  Panará–Kayapó conflict 162, 165, 167, 177, 208
  Pax Xinguana, 72, 127, 211
  settlers and, 58, 59, 60, 61, 65, 150, 197–200

INDEX